A CRIMINAL PRACTITIONER'S GUIDE TO JUDICIAL REVIEW AND CASE STATED

A CRIMINAL PRACTITIONER'S GUIDE TO JUDICIAL REVIEW AND CASE STATED

Hugh Southey
Barrister

Adrian Fulford QC
Barrister

JORDANS
1999

Published by
Jordan Publishing Limited
21 St Thomas Street
Bristol BS1 6JS

Copyright © Jordan Publishing Limited 1999

All rights reserved. No part of this publication may be reproduced, stored in a retrieval system, or transmitted in any way or by any means, including photocopying or recording, without the written permission of the copyright holder, application for which should be addressed to the publisher.

British Library Cataloguing-in-Publication Data
A catalogue record for this book is available from the British Library.

ISBN 0 85308 566 8

Typeset by Mendip Communications Ltd, Frome, Somerset
Printed by MPG Books Ltd, Bodmin, Cornwall

Foreword

A significant proportion of the Crown Office List in the Queen's Bench Division of the High Court is devoted to criminal cases. The law which is applied to them is, in many respects, common to other areas of judicial review; but in many other respects it is, both procedurally and in substance, peculiar to the criminal process. Practitioners need to make a correspondingly careful approach to criminal cases in the High Court.

Adrian Fulford's and Hugh Southey's book, based on experience as well as on learning, offers an excellent guide to this area of law and practice. It cannot answer every problem, but it sets out the existing authority and guidance and provides precedents for many of the documents that are needed.

A particularly valuable feature is the chapter anticipating the impact of the Human Rights Act 1998 when it comes into force. This is a measure which will change our legal culture. Whether it does so for the better or for the worse will be very largely in the hands of criminal practitioners. We know from experience in Canada and New Zealand, and now from Scotland, that criminal cases are likely to constitute a high proportion of the first wave of human rights appeals and reviews. If too many are mere try-ons, the last resort of a lawyer without an argument, the Act and the Convention will become devalued. If, on the other hand, practitioners sift cases knowledgeably and prepare the viable ones properly, the courts will readily engage with them.

Much, therefore, is going to depend, in the next few years, on the knowledge and skill of legal practitioners in developing existing forms of recourse in criminal cases and in exploring the new dimension afforded by the Human Rights Act 1998. They will need a book like this at their elbow if they are to avoid error and to bring the courts along with them on what is going to be a voyage of discovery for all of us.

STEPHEN SEDLEY
Royal Courts of Justice
September 1999

Preface

We wrote this book because we believe that it is important that criminal practitioners are aware of how to conduct applications for judicial review and appeals by way of case stated. In appropriate circumstances, it is undoubtedly true that the jurisdiction of the High Court can be an important way of protecting the interests of clients. In particular, it can often be the only way to correct unlawful decisions taken by magistrates' courts and the Crown Court.

The importance of judicial review and appeal by way of case stated will increase. The Human Rights Act 1998 is likely to mean that many criminal precedents will no longer be regarded as good law. As applications for judicial review and appeals by way of case stated can be used to challenge errors of law, it is likely that, in many circumstances, these forms of proceedings will be the correct way to enforce rights under the 1998 Act. We understand that the Crown Office expects that it will be faced with a substantial increase in its case-load.

Many practitioners, however, will not have conducted a large number of judicial reviews and appeals by way of case stated. As a result, we hope this book will make up for any lack of experience. This book seeks to give criminal practitioners the materials that they need to enable them to conduct competent judicial reviews and appeals by way of case stated in the circumstances that they will encounter in their practice. That is why we have also included, for example, applications for habeas corpus as there are certain limited circumstances in which it may be appropriate to apply for a writ of habeas corpus as well as applying for judicial review. We have tried to cover all issues that are likely to arise. We would, however, be keen to hear from any practitioners who have suggestions for further editions of the book.

Judicial review and appeal by case stated are undergoing significant change. The introduction of the Civil Procedure Rules 1998 is bound to have some impact on the procedure adopted during these forms of proceedings. However, whilst the terminology has changed – for example, applications for leave are now known as applications for permission – the basic procedure has only been modified. It is contained in the Rules of the Supreme Court as modified by Schedule 1 to the Civil Procedure Rules 1998. Where we make reference to the Rules of the Supreme Court it is those modified rules to which we are referring.

The Rules of the Supreme Court are, however, not exhaustive. For example, they contain no provisions governing costs. As a result, it must be assumed that the Civil Procedure Rules governing issues like costs will apply. Unfortunately, the precise impact is difficult to judge until the High Court has given further guidance.

The other change that is significant is the increasing role of human rights provisions in proceedings in the High Court. The Human Rights Act 1998 is not in force. It is, however, still essential to be aware of the provisions of this Act and other human rights provisions when bringing criminal proceedings in the High Court as this will strengthen arguments. We have considered this in detail in Chapter 13.

We should apologise that we have used male terminology throughout this book. We had hoped to produce a gender neutral book but this has proved impossible. We hope that readers will recognise that our use of male terminology is not based on any sexist assumptions.

There are a large number of people whom we need to thank for their assistance in the preparation of this book. First, we must thank Lord Justice Sedley for his kind words in the Foreword. In addition, we need to thank Jackie and Jose Luis who spent too many dinners discussing Order 53. We also need to thank Martin Sorjoo, Martin Huseyin and other members of Tooks Court Chambers for their support and suggestions. We also appreciate the understanding of our clerks, particularly Martin Parker, Michelle Houghton and Milla Cameron. Jordans have been extremely helpful and we would like to thank Stephen Honey and Mollie Dickenson. Finally, we would like to thank Rebecca, Kate and the other one.

HUGH SOUTHEY
ADRIAN FULFORD QC
Tooks Court Chambers
September 1999

Contents

	Page
Foreword	v
Preface	vii
Table of Cases	xxi
Table of Statutes	xxxvii
Table of Statutory Instruments	xli
Table of European and International Legislation	xlv
Table of Abbreviations	xlvii

Chapter 1	THE SCOPE OF THE HIGH COURT'S JURISDICTION	1
	1.1 INTRODUCTION	1
	1.2 THE INCREASING IMPORTANCE OF THESE FORMS OF PROCEEDINGS	2
	1.3 WHAT IS JUDICIAL REVIEW?	3
	1.4 WHAT IS CASE STATED?	4
	1.5 WHAT IS HABEAS CORPUS?	6
	1.6 DECISIONS OF THE CROWN COURT	6
	1.6.1 Authorities determining the scope of the High Court's jurisdiction to consider decisions of the Crown Court	7
	1.7 DECISIONS OF THE MAGISTRATES' COURT	10
	1.7.1 The effect of the right of appeal to the Crown Court on the High Court's consideration of decisions of the magistrates' court	11
	1.8 DECISIONS OF THE YOUTH COURT	13
	1.9 DECISIONS OF PUBLIC BODIES	13
	1.9.1 Private law compared with public law	14
	1.10 WHO MAY BRING AN ACTION IN THE HIGH COURT?	15
	1.11 WHICH SECTION OF THE HIGH COURT CONSIDERS CRIMINAL CASES?	17

Chapter 2	THE GROUNDS WHICH CAN BE RAISED IN AN APPLICATION FOR JUDICIAL REVIEW	19
	2.1 THE IMPORTANCE OF UNDERSTANDING THE CATEGORIES OF LEGAL CHALLENGE AVAILABLE IN THE HIGH COURT	19
	2.2 THE CATEGORIES OF ERROR SUSCEPTIBLE TO CHALLENGE IN AN APPLICATION FOR JUDICIAL REVIEW	20

		2.2.1	The importance of the decision in *Anisminic*	21
		2.2.2	Excluding the jurisdiction of courts to consider public law issues	22
		2.2.3	Factual disputes	23
	2.3	ILLEGALITY		24
	2.4	ULTRA VIRES		25
	2.5	DECISIONS IN EXCESS OF JURISDICTION		27
	2.6	BROAD STATUTORY DISCRETION AND ERRORS OF LAW		28
	2.7	PROCEDURAL IMPROPRIETY		29
	2.8	NATURAL JUSTICE AND BIAS		30
		2.8.1	Fair hearing: an introduction	32
		2.8.2	Determining whether the right to a fair hearing arises in the circumstances of the case	33
		2.8.3	Who is entitled to a fair hearing?	34
		2.8.4	The scope of the right to a fair hearing: a right to be heard	35
		2.8.5	The scope of the right to a fair hearing: a right to receive information	36
		2.8.6	The scope of the right to a fair hearing: other rights	37
	2.9	THE DELEGATION OF DECISION-MAKING POWERS		38
	2.10	IRRATIONALITY		39
	2.11	RELEVANT FACTORS AND IMPROPER MOTIVE		40
	2.12	LEGITIMATE EXPECTATION		41
	2.13	INCONSISTENCY		43
	2.14	CIRCUMSTANCES WHERE THERE IS A DUTY TO GIVE REASONS		44
		2.14.1	The importance of requesting reasons	46
		2.14.2	The scope of the duty to give reasons	46
	2.15	BAD FAITH		47
	2.16	PROPORTIONALITY		47
Chapter 3	**THE GROUNDS OF APPEAL BY WAY OF CASE STATED AND AN APPLICATION FOR HABEAS CORPUS**			**49**
	3.1	THE IMPORTANCE OF IDENTIFYING THE CATEGORY OF LEGAL ERROR WHICH HAS LED TO A DEFENDANT APPEALING BY WAY OF CASE STATED OR APPLYING FOR HABEAS CORPUS		49
	3.2	THE GROUNDS UPON WHICH A PARTY MAY APPEAL BY WAY OF CASE STATED		49

	3.3	DIFFERENCES BETWEEN THE SCOPE OF JUDICAL REVIEW AND AN APPEAL BY WAY OF CASE STATED	50
	3.4	PRACTICAL RESTRICTIONS ON THE GROUNDS WHICH CAN BE RAISED DURING AN APPEAL BY CASE STATED	51
	3.5	THE DIFFERENCE BETWEEN JUDICIAL REVIEW AND HABEAS CORPUS	52
Chapter 4		**WHEN SHOULD CRIMINAL PROCEEDINGS BE BROUGHT IN THE HIGH COURT?**	55
	4.1	INTRODUCTION	55
	4.2	POLICE INVESTIGATIONS AND OTHER OPERATIONS	55
	4.3	THE DECISION OF A PUBLIC AUTHORITY TO INSTITUTE A PROSECUTION	57
	4.4	CHALLENGES TO LEGISLATION UNDER WHICH A PROSECUTION IS BROUGHT	59
	4.5	JUDICIAL REVIEW OF DECISIONS REGARDING BAIL	60
	4.6	CHALLENGES TO DECISIONS REGARDING CUSTODY TIME-LIMITS	61
		4.6.1 Practical considerations regarding challenges to custody time-limits	63
	4.7	CHALLENGES TO COMMITTAL DECISIONS TAKEN BY MAGISTRATES	64
	4.8	JUDICIAL REVIEWS OF THE TRANSFER OF PROCEEDINGS TO THE CROWN COURT BY THE PROSECUTION	65
	4.9	APPEALS BY WAY OF CASE STATED AGAINST INTERIM DECISIONS IN CRIMINAL PROCEEDINGS	66
	4.10	JUDICIAL REVIEWS OF INTERIM DECISIONS IN CRIMINAL PROCEEDINGS	67
	4.11	SHOULD A DEFENDANT APPEAL TO THE CROWN COURT AGAINST A CONVICTION IN THE MAGISTRATES' COURT OR SHOULD HE APPEAL BY WAY OF CASE STATED?	69
	4.12	SHOULD A DEFENDANT APPEAL TO THE CROWN COURT AGAINST A CONVICTION IN THE MAGISTRATES' COURT OR SHOULD HE APPLY FOR JUDICIAL REVIEW?	70
	4.13	SHOULD A DEFENDANT APPEAL BY WAY OF CASE STATED OR JUDICIALLY REVIEW A CONVICTION FOLLOWING AN APPEAL TO THE CROWN COURT?	71

	4.14	THE SCOPE OF JUDICIAL REVIEW OR APPEAL BY WAY OF CASE STATED AS A WAY OF CHALLENGING A CONVICTION	72
	4.15	TACTICAL FACTORS INFLUENCING A DECISION TO PROCEED BY JUDICIAL REVIEW OR APPEAL BY CASE STATED	73
	4.16	CHALLENGES TO ACQUITTALS	74
	4.17	SHOULD A SENTENCE BE CHALLENGED BY JUDICIAL REVIEW OR BY APPEAL BY WAY OF CASE STATED?	75
	4.18	SHOULD A SENTENCE IMPOSED BY THE MAGISTRATES' COURT BE CHALLENGED BY JUDICIAL REVIEW OR BY AN APPEAL TO THE CROWN COURT?	76
	4.19	JUDICIAL REVIEWS OF SENTENCES IMPOSED BY THE CROWN COURT ON MATTERS NOT RELATED TO TRIAL ON INDICTMENT	77
	4.20	THE LIMITATIONS ON THE RIGHT OF APPEAL TO THE CROWN COURT FROM A FINAL DECISION OF THE MAGISTRATES' COURT	78
	4.21	JUDICIAL REVIEWS OF DECISIONS OF MAGISTRATES WHICH DO NOT ATTRACT RIGHTS OF APPEAL TO THE CROWN COURT	80
	4.22	CHALLENGING FINAL DECISIONS OF THE CROWN COURT	81
	4.23	CHALLENGES TO DECISIONS REGARDING COSTS	81
	4.24	CHALLENGES TO THE DECISIONS OF MAGISTRATES TO COMMIT FOR EXTRADITION	82
	4.25	JUDICIAL REVIEW OF DECISIONS TAKEN AFTER CONVICTION	84
Chapter 5	**CONSIDERATIONS THAT ARISE BEFORE APPLYING TO THE HIGH COURT**		**87**
	5.1	THE IMPORTANCE OF KNOWING WHETHER A MATTER IS A CRIMINAL CAUSE OR MATTER	87
		5.1.1 The decision that determines whether a matter is a criminal cause or matter	88
		5.1.2 The definition of a criminal cause or matter	88
	5.2	DETERMINING WHETHER THERE HAS BEEN DELAY IN JUDICIAL REVIEW PROCEEDINGS	90

		5.2.1	The effect of delay on an application for judicial review	92
		5.2.2	The need for disclosure of delay	94
	5.3	PREMATURE APPLICATIONS FOR JUDICIAL REVIEW		95
	5.4	ALTERNATIVE REMEDIES AND JUDICIAL REVIEW		95
	5.5	DELAY AND HABEAS CORPUS		96
	5.6	DELAY AND APPEALS BY WAY OF CASE STATED		96
	5.7	SHOULD AN ORDER BE SOUGHT LIMITING THE REPORTING OF THE MATTER?		98
	5.8	RESTRICTIONS ON REPORTING IN THE CONTEXT OF CASES INVOLVING YOUNG PEOPLE		99
	5.9	OTHER PARTICULAR CONSIDERATIONS IN CASES INVOLVING JUVENILES		100
	5.10	PARTICULAR CONSIDERATIONS IN THE CASE OF A PERSON SUFFERING FROM MENTAL HEALTH PROBLEMS		102

Chapter 6	**PROCEDURAL MATTERS COMMON TO ALL CROWN OFFICE PROCEEDINGS**			103
	6.1	PROCEDURE RULES GOVERNING PROCEEDINGS IN THE CROWN OFFICE		103
	6.2	EXPEDITION		103
	6.3	LISTING ARRANGEMENTS IN CASES WHERE EXPEDITION HAS NOT BEEN ORDERED		104
	6.4	PRACTICE GOVERNING DOCUMENTS TO BE FILED WITH THE CROWN OFFICE		105
		6.4.1	Documents to be filed with the Crown Office before the substantive hearing of matters	105
	6.5	SOLICITORS CEASING TO ACT		107
	6.6	UNCONTESTED AND WITHDRAWN PROCEEDINGS IN THE CROWN OFFICE		108
	6.7	SERVICE OF DOCUMENTS		109
	6.8	TIME-LIMITS		110
	6.9	INTERIM APPLICATIONS		110

Chapter 7	**THE PROCEDURE FOR BRINGING AN APPLICATION FOR JUDICIAL REVIEW**		113
	7.1	INTRODUCTION	114
	7.2	A LETTER BEFORE ACTION	114

	7.3	URGENT OUT-OF-HOURS APPLICATIONS FOR JUDICIAL REVIEW	115
	7.4	DOCUMENTS TO BE LODGED WITH THE CROWN OFFICE OF THE HIGH COURT	116
	7.5	ADDITIONAL MATTERS TO BE CONSIDERED WHEN THE APPLICATION FOR PERMISSION IS FILED	118
	7.6	DECIDING WHETHER THE APPLICATION FOR PERMISSION SHOULD BE LISTED FOR ORAL ARGUMENT	119
	7.7	THE DUTY OF DISCLOSURE WHICH APPLIES WHEN DRAFTING PAPERS IN SUPPORT OF THE APPLICATION	120
	7.8	THE DETERMINATION OF WHETHER AN APPLICANT SHOULD BE GRANTED PERMISSION TO APPLY FOR JUDICIAL REVIEW	121
	7.9	AMENDMENT OF THE GROUNDS AND SERVICE OF ADDITIONAL EVIDENCE	123
	7.10	FURTHER STEPS FOLLOWING A REFUSAL OF PERMISSION	124
	7.11	COMMENCING THE JUDICIAL REVIEW APPLICATION AFTER OBTAINING PERMISSION	125
	7.12	FURTHER STEPS TO BE TAKEN BY THE APPLICANT BEFORE THE SUBSTANTIVE HEARING	127
	7.13	ACTING FOR AN INTERESTED PARTY WHO HAS NOT BEEN SERVED WITH THE CLAIM FORM	128
	7.14	EVIDENCE AND ORAL SUBMISSIONS ON BEHALF OF RESPONDENTS OR OTHER INTERESTED PARTIES	129
	7.15	OTHER PROCEDURAL STEPS TO BE TAKEN ON BEHALF OF RESPONDENTS OR OTHER INTERESTED PARTIES	131
	7.16	SUBSTANTIVE HEARING	132
Chapter 8		**PROCEDURE FOR APPLYING FOR A WRIT OF HABEAS CORPUS**	133
	8.1	INTRODUCTION	133
	8.2	COMMENCING THE APPLICATION	134
	8.3	HABEAS CORPUS AS A TWO-STAGE PROCESS	136
	8.4	ADVISING A RESPONDENT	138
	8.5	THE SUBSTANTIVE HEARING	138

Chapter 9	**PROCEDURE FOR APPEALING BY WAY OF CASE STATED**	**141**
	9.1 INTRODUCTION	142
	9.2 SERVICE OF DOCUMENTS	142
	9.3 COMMENCING THE APPEAL	142
	9.4 THE OBLIGATIONS IMPOSED ON THE COURT IN RECEIPT OF THE APPLICATION	144
	9.5 CHALLENGING A DECISION TO REFUSE TO STATE A CASE	146
	9.6 OBTAINING A FIRST DRAFT OF THE CASE STATED	147
	9.7 CONTENTS OF THE CASE STATED	148
	9.8 OBTAINING AGREEMENT OF THE PARTIES TO THE CASE STATED	149
	9.9 PROCEDURE WHERE A PARTY IS UNHAPPY WITH THE FINAL CASE	150
	9.10 DELAY DURING THE PREPARATION OF THE APPLICATION TO STATE A CASE	152
	9.11 COMMENCING THE APPLICATION IN THE HIGH COURT	152
	9.12 PROCEDURE AFTER THE CASE HAS BEEN LODGED IN THE CROWN OFFICE	154
	9.13 THE SUBSTANTIVE HEARING	155
Chapter 10	**ORDERS FOR INTERIM RELIEF AVAILABLE TO THE HIGH COURT DURING PROCEEDINGS**	**157**
	10.1 INTRODUCTION	157
	10.2 MATTERS COMMON TO BAIL IN ALL PROCEEDINGS IN THE CROWN OFFICE	157
	10.2.1 Bail in judicial review proceedings	158
	10.2.2 Bail in habeas corpus proceedings	159
	10.2.3 Bail applications during appeals by way of case stated	160
	10.3 SUSPENSION OF DISQUALIFICATION FROM DRIVING	161
	10.4 STAYS OF THE ENFORCEMENT OF OTHER PENALTIES	161
	10.5 STAYS OF PROCEEDINGS PENDING A JUDICIAL REVIEW CHALLENGE	162
	10.6 OTHER FORMS OF INTERIM RELIEF AVAILABLE DURING APPLICATIONS FOR JUDICIAL REVIEW	163
	10.7 THE PROCEDURE FOR APPLYING FOR INTERIM RELIEF	164

Chapter 11	ORDERS FOR RELIEF AVAILABLE TO THE HIGH COURT AT THE END OF PROCEEDINGS	167
11.1	INTRODUCTION	167
11.2	DISCRETION AND JUDICIAL REVIEW	167
11.3	JUDICIAL REVIEW AND ACADEMIC CHALLENGES	168
11.4	DISCRETION AND HABEAS CORPUS	169
11.5	DISCRETION AND APPEAL BY WAY OF CASE STATED	170
11.6	JUDICIAL REVIEW ORDERS	170
11.7	THE HIGH COURT'S POWER TO VARY A SENTENCE FOLLOWING A JUDICIAL REVIEW	172
11.8	THE HIGH COURT'S POWER TO AWARD DAMAGES AT THE CONCLUSION OF A SUCCESSFUL APPLICATION FOR JUDICIAL REVIEW	172
11.9	THE POWERS OF THE HIGH COURT AT THE CONCLUSION OF AN APPLICATION FOR A WRIT OF HABEAS CORPUS	173
11.10	THE POWERS OF THE HIGH COURT AT THE CONCLUSION OF AN APPEAL BY WAY OF CASE STATED	174

Chapter 12	LEGAL AID AND ORDERS FOR COSTS	175
12.1	INTRODUCTION	175
12.2	THE RULES GOVERNING COSTS BETWEEN THE PARTIES	175
12.3	SPECIAL COSTS CONSIDERATIONS IN JUDICIAL REVIEW AND HABEAS CORPUS PROCEEDINGS	177
12.4	SPECIAL CONSIDERATIONS WHEN THE UNSUCCESSFUL PARTY IS IN RECEIPT OF LEGAL AID	178
12.5	SPECIAL CONSIDERATIONS WHEN MAGISTRATES ARE THE RESPONDENT	179
12.6	SPECIAL CONSIDERATIONS AS TO THE COSTS OF THIRD PARTIES AND NON-PARTIES	181
12.7	COSTS FROM CENTRAL FUNDS	182
12.8	ADVANCE ORDERS FOR COSTS	182
12.9	WASTED COSTS AGAINST LEGAL ADVISERS	183
12.10	ASSESSMENT OF COSTS	183
12.11	LEGAL AID TO COVER PARTICIPATION IN PROCEEDINGS IN THE HIGH COURT	184
12.12	EMERGENCY LEGAL AID	186

	12.13	PRACTICAL CONSIDERATIONS WHEN A CLIENT IS IN RECEIPT OF LEGAL AID	187
	12.14	THE STATUTORY CHARGE	188
	12.15	FUTURE DEVELOPMENTS REGARDING LEGAL AID	188
Chapter 13		**CRIMINAL PROCEEDINGS IN THE HIGH COURT AND HUMAN RIGHTS**	**191**
	13.1	INTRODUCTION	191
	13.2	THE CURRENT STATUS OF THE EUROPEAN CONVENTION ON HUMAN RIGHTS IN UK DOMESTIC LAW	191
	13.3	HUMAN RIGHTS OBLIGATIONS CONTAINED IN UK DOMESTIC LAW	192
	13.4	OTHER INTERNATIONAL HUMAN RIGHTS OBLIGATIONS	193
	13.5	THE KEY PROVISIONS OF THE EUROPEAN CONVENTION ON HUMAN RIGHTS	194
	13.6	THE INTERPRETATION OF THE PROVISIONS OF THE CONVENTION	197
	13.7	AN INTRODUCTION TO THE EFFECT OF THE HUMAN RIGHTS ACT 1998	198
	13.8	THE IMPACT OF THE 1998 ACT ON THE INTERPRETATION OF LEGISLATION	199
		13.8.1 The powers of the courts when it is impossible to interpret legislation in a way which is consistent with the Convention	199
	13.9	THE IMPACT OF THE 1998 ACT ON PUBLIC BODIES	201
	13.10	ENFORCING RIGHTS UNDER THE 1998 ACT	202
		13.10.1 Should judicial review proceedings be brought before or after conviction where there is said to be a breach of the Convention?	202
		13.10.2 The effect of the 1998 Act on committal proceedings	204
	13.11	REMEDIES AVAILABLE TO THE COURTS UNDER THE 1998 ACT	205
	13.12	PRACTICAL EXAMPLES OF THE APPLICATION OF THE 1998 ACT	206
	13.13	THE EFFECT OF THE CONVENTION ON THE ADMISSIBILITY OF EVIDENCE	206
		13.13.1 The Convention and evidence obtained in breach of the right to silence or the protection against self-incrimination	206

		13.13.2	The Convention and hearsay evidence	208
		13.13.3	The Convention and anonymity of witnesses	209
		13.13.4	Interference with correspondence	209
		13.13.5	The right to respect for private and family life	209
	13.14	THE EFFECT OF THE CONVENTION ON THE RIGHT TO BAIL		210
		13.14.1	The effect of the Convention on the procedure for obtaining bail	211
		13.14.2	Challenging bail decisions said to be contrary to the Convention	212
	13.15	THE EFFECT OF THE CONVENTION ON DISCLOSURE		212
	13.16	THE EFFECT OF THE CONVENTION ON THE TRIAL PROCEDURE		214
		13.16.1	The Convention and the right to be tried within a reasonable time period	215
	13.17	THE SPECIFIC RIGHTS CONTAINED IN ARTICLE 6(3) OF THE CONVENTION		216
	13.18	THE CONVENTION AND SENTENCING		216
	13.19	HUMAN RIGHTS AND THE PROSECUTION		216
	13.20	THE CONVENTION AND SPECIFIC OFFENCES		217
	13.21	THE CONVENTION AND PRISON CONDITIONS		217
	13.22	PRACTICAL CONSIDERATIONS REGARDING JUDICIAL REVIEW		218

APPENDICES 219
Appendix 1 Precedents – Judicial Review 221
    1. Letter before action 221
    2. Notice of application 222
    3. Other useful clauses 231
    4. Affidavit in support 234
    5. Exhibit to affidavit 239
    6. Witness statement in support 240
    7. Exhibit to a witness statement 241
    8. Bail application 242
    9. Claim form 244
    10. Witness statement as to service 246
    11. Affidavit in response 249
    12. Application for an interim order 253
    13. Draft interim order 254
    14. Skeleton argument 255
    15. Consent order 257
    16. Application notice for renewal in the Court of Appeal 258

Appendix 2	**Precedent – Claim Form for Writ for Habeas Corpus**		261
	1.	Form 87	261
Appendix 3	**Precedents – Case Stated**		263
	1.	Application to state a case	263
	2.	Other useful clauses	265
	3.	Case stated	267
	4.	Notice of entry of a case stated	271
Appendix 4	**Procedural Guides**		273
	1.	Deciding whether to proceed with a judicial review or an appeal by way of case stated	273
	2.	Judicial review	277
	3.	Appeal by case stated from a decision of the magistrates' court	284
	4.	Appeal by case stated from a decision of the Crown Court	291
Appendix 5	**Legislation and Forms**		299
		Civil Procedure Rules 1998, Sch 1, Rules of the Supreme Court Ords 53, 54 and 56	299
		Forms N235, N434, N244	312
		Magistrates' Courts Act 1980 (as amended), ss 111–114	317
		Magistrates' Courts Rules 1981, rr 76–81	319
		Supreme Court Act 1981 (as amended), ss 28, 28A, 29, 31, 43	322
		Crown Court Rules 1982, r 26	326
		Human Rights Act 1998, ss 1–9, Sch 1	328
Index			343

Table of Cases

References are to paragraph numbers and Appendix numbers.

AG of Gambia v Mormodu Jobe [1984] AC 689	13.8
Akbarali v Brent London Borough Council and Other Cases [1983] 2 AC 309; [1983] 1 All ER 226; [1983] 2 WLR 16	2.3
Airey v Ireland [1979] 2 EHRR 305	12.10
Amand v Home Secretary [1943] AC 147	5.1.2
Amand, Re [1941] 2 KB 239	8.3, 10.2.1, 10.2.2
American Cynamid Co v Ethicon Ltd [1975] AC 396; [1975] 1 All ER 504	10.6
Anisminic Ltd v Foreign Compensation Commission [1969] 2 AC 147; [1969] 1 All ER 208; [1969] 2 WLR 163	2.2, 2.2.1, 2.5, 3.3, 4.7
Arsenal Football Club v Ende [1979] AC 1; [1977] 2 All ER 267; [1977] 2 WLR 974	1.10
Ashton and Others, Re; R v Manchester Crown Court ex p DPP [1994] 1 AC 9; [1993] 2 All ER 263; [1993] 2 WLR 846	1.6.1, 4.22
Associated Provincial Picture Houses Ltd v Wednesbury Corporation [1948] 1 KB 223; [1947] 2 All ER 680; 177 LT 641	2.10
Atkinson v United States Government [1971] AC 197; [1969] 3 All ER 1317; [1969] 3 WLR 107	1.7
Attorney-General v Leveller Magazine [1979] AC 440; [1979] 1 All ER 745; [1979] 2 WLR 247	5.7
Aydin v Turkey (1997) 25 EHRR 251	13.19
B v Croydon Health Authority (No 2) [1996] 1 FLR 253; [1995] 1 All ER 683; [1995] 2 WLR 294; [1995] 2 WLR 294	12.6
Barker, Re (1998) *The Times*, 14 October	3.5, 8.1, 11.4
Basingstoke and Dean Borough Council v Houlton and Webb [1995] COD 86	9.9
Benham v United Kingdom (1996) 22 EHRR 293; (1996) *The Times*, 24 June; (1996) *The Independent*, 19 June	13.17
Bezicheri v Italy (1989) 12 EHRR 210	13.14.2
Blyth v Appeal Committee of Lancaster [1944] 1 All ER 587	10.2.1
Boddington v British Transport Police [1998] 2 All ER 203; [1998] 2 WLR 639; (1998) 162 JP 455	2.1, 2.2.1, 2.4, 3.5, 4.3, 4.4, 9.13, 13.8.1
Bone, Re [1995] COD 94; (1995) 159 JP 111; [1995] 159 JPN 146	3.5
Bonisch v Austria (1985) 9 EHRR 191	13.16
Borgers v Belgium (1993) 15 EHRR 92	13.16
Boujlifa v France (unreported) 21 October 1997	13.18
Bracegirdle v Oxley [1947] 1 KB 349; [1947] 1 All ER 126; 176 LT 187	3.4
Brink's Mat Ltd v Elcombe [1988] 1 WLR 1350	7.7
Brigan and Others v UK (1988) 11 EHRR 117	13.16.1
Bromley London Borough Council v Greater London Council [1983] 1 AC 768; [1982] 1 All ER 153; [1982] 2 WLR 92	2.10
Bugg v DPP [1993] QB 473; [1993] 2 All ER 815; [1993] 2 WLR 628	4.4
C and P, Re [1992] 2 AC 182; [1992] 3 All ER 277; [1992] 3 WLR 99	2.14.2

Canterbury City Council v Cook (1992) *The Times*, 23 December 12.2
Carr v Atkins [1987] QB 963; [1987] 3 All ER 684; [1987] 3 WLR 529 5.1.1, 5.1.2
Clooth v Belgium (1991) 14 EHRR 717 13.14
Colfox v Dorset County Council [1996] COD 275 9.6, 9.9, 11.10
Collet v Bromsgrove District Council [1997] Crim LR 206; (1996) 160 JP 593;
    (1996) *The Times*, 15 July 9.11
Collins v Jamaica (356/1989) 13.4
Cook v Southend Borough Council [1990] 2 QB 1; [1990] 1 All ER 243; [1990]
    2 WLR 61 1.10, 4.16
Council of Civil Service Unions v Minister for the Civil Service [1985] AC 374;
    [1984] 3 All ER 935; [1984] 1 WLR 1174 1.9, 2.1, 2.2, 2.10, 2.17, 3.3
Credit Suisse v Alderdale Borough Council [1997] QB 306; [1996] 4 All ER
    129; [1996] 3 WLR 894 1.9.1, 11.2
Cuoghi v Governor of Brixton Prison and Another [1999] 1 All ER 466; [1998]
    1 WLR 1513; (1998) 95(22) LSG 28 5.1, 5.1.2

Davy v Spelthorne Borough Council [1984] AC 262; [1983] 3 All ER 278;
    [1983] 3 WLR 742 11.8
Day v Grant [1987] QB 972; [1987] 3 All ER 678; [1987] 3 WLR 537 5.1
Dewings v Cummings [1971] RTR 295 4.7
DPP v Clarke and Others (1992) 94 Cr App R 359; [1992] Crim LR 60; (1992)
    156 JP 267 9.9
DPP v Coleman [1998] 1 All ER 912; [1998] 1 WLR 1708; [1998] 2 Cr App R 7 4.16,
    5.6
DPP v Hutchinson [1990] 2 AC 783; [1990] 3 WLR 196; (1990) 2 Admin LR
    741 2.4, 4.4
DPP v Kirk [1993] COD 99 9.7
DPP v McKeown; DPP v Jones [1997] 2 Cr App R 155 2.3
DPP v Price (1992) *The Independent*, 15 June 9.7
Dudgeon v UK (1981) 4 EHRR 149 13.20

Edwards v UK (1992) 15 EHRR 417 13.5
EF Hardwick, Re (1883) 12 QB 148 5.1.2
Ekbatani v Sweden (1998) 13 EHRR 504 13.16
Environment Agency v Singer [1998] Env LR 380 9.2, 9.8

Fairmount Investments Ltd v Secretary of State for the Environment [1976] 1
    WLR 1255 2.8.1
Ferrantelli v Italy (1996) 23 EHRR 288 13.22
Fitzgerald v Williams [1996] QB 657; [1996] 2 All ER 171; [1996] 2 WLR 447 7.7
Folkestone Magistrates' Courts, ex p Bradely [1994] COD 138 1.7.1
Fossett v East Northamptonshire District Council [1995] COD 167 11.10
Foucher v France (1997) 25 EHRR 234 13.16
Funke v France (1993) 16 EHRR 297 13.13.1

Golder v UK (1975) 1 EHRR 524 13.13.4, 13.21
Government of Denmark v Nielson (1984) 79 Cr App R 1 4.24
Greene v Secretary of State for the Home Department [1942] AC 284 11.4

Table of Cases

Griffith v Jenkins [1992] 2 AC 76; [1992] 1 All ER 65; [1992] 2 WLR 28   11.5, 11.10
Gross v Southwark Crown Court [1998] 11 CL 137   2.14

Hadjianastassiou v Greece (1992) 16 EHRR 219   13.16
Haime v Walklett [1983] RTR 512; [1983] Crim LR 556; (1983) 5 Cr App R (S) 165   4.17
Hamilton, Re; Re Forrest [1981] AC 1038; [1981] 3 WLR 79; (1981) 73 Cr App R 267   2.8.3, 2.8.4
Harley Development Inc v Commissioner of Inland Revenue [1996] 1 WLR 727; [1996] STC 440; (1996) 140 SJLB 93   5.4
Harrington v Roots [1984] AC 743; [1984] 2 All ER 474; (1984) 79 Cr App R 305   4.16
Herbage, Re (1985) *The Times*, 25 October   1.6.1, 1.7.1, 4.5, 13.14.2
Hillingdon London Borough Council v Commission for Racial Equality [1982] AC 779; [1982] 3 WLR 159; [1982] IRLR 424   2.8.3
HLR v France (1997) 26 EHRR 29   13.20
Hoffman-La Roche (F) & CO AG v Secretary of State for Trade and Industry [1975] AC 295; [1974] 2 All ER 1128; [1974] 3 WLR 104   2.8.5

Inland Revenue Commissioners ex p National Federation of Self-Employed and Small Businesses Ltd [1982] AC 617; [1981] 2 All ER 93; [1981] 2 WLR 722   7.8
Ireland v UK (1978) 2 EHRR 25   13.21

Jaramillo-Silva (Francisco Javier) v Secretary of State for the Home Department [1994] Imm AR 352   2.12
Jespers v Belgium (1981) 2 DR 61   13.5
Johnson v Leicestershire Constabulary (1998) *The Times*, 7 October   2.8, 3.4, 4.14
Kanda v Government of Malaysia [1962] AC 322; [1962] 2 WLR 1153   2.7
Kaufman v Belgium (1987) 50 DR 98   13.16
Kemper Reinsurance Co v Minister of Finance [1998] 3 WLR 630; (1998) 142 SJLB 175   7.10
Kjeldson and Others v Denmark (1976) 11 EHRR 711   13.6
Konig v FRG (1978) 2 EHRR 170   13.16.1
Kostovoski v Netherlands (1989) 12 EHRR 434   13.13.2

Laird v Simms (1988) *The Times*, 7 March   9.7
Lamy v Belgium (1989) 11 EHRR 529   13.5
Leech v Deputy Governor of Parkhurst Prison [1988] AC 533; [1998] 1 All ER 485; [1988] 2 WLR 290   5.4
Letellier v France (1991) 14 EHRR 83   13.14
Lingens v Austria (1986) 8 EHRR 406   13.13.1
Liverpool City Council v Worthington (1998) *The Times*, 16 June   5.6
Liversidge v St John Anderson [1942] AC 206   8.4
Lloyd v McMahon [1987] AC 625; [1987] 1 All ER 1118; [1987] 2 WLR 821   2.8.2
Loade v DPP [1990] 1 QB 1052; [1990] 1 All ER 36; [1989] 3 WLR 1281   4.9

M, Re [1994] 1 AC 377   10.5, 10.6, 11.6
Maile v Manchester City Council [1998] COD 19; (1997) 74 P & CR 443;
   (1997) *The Times*, 26 November   9.13
Malone v UK (1984) 7 EHRR 14   13.13.4
Manley v Law Society [1981] 1 All ER 401; [1981] 1 WLR 335; (1980) 125 SJ 81
   12.14
Mass Energy Ltd v Birmingham City Council [1994] Env LR 298   7.8
Matznetter v Austria (1969) 1 EHRR 198   13.14
McCallum v UK (1990) 13 EHRR 597   13.13.5
McKay White v DPP [1989] Crim LR 375   4.6
Mercury Energy Ltd v Electricity Corporation of New Zealand Ltd [1994] 1
   WLR 521; (1994) 138 SJLB 61   1.3, 2.2.2
Meredith, Re [1973] 2 All ER 234; [1973] 1 WLR 435; (1973) 57 Cr App R 451   1.6.1,
   4.23
Michael v Gowland [1977] 2 All ER 328; [1977] 1 WLR 296; (1976) Fam Law
   109   5.6, 12.12
Minister of Foreign Affairs, Trade and Industry v Vehicles and Supplies Ltd
   [1991] 4 All ER 65; [1991] 1 WLR 550; (1991) 135 SJLB 12   10.5
Moustaquim v Belgium (1991) 13 EHRR 802   2.16
Mulloch v Aberdeen Corporation [1971] 1 WLR 1578   2.8.1
Murray v UK (1996) 22 EHRR 29   13.13.1

Neumeister v Austria (No 1) (1968) 1 EHRR 91   13.14, 13.14.1, 13.16.1
Neville v Gardner Merchant Ltd (1985) 5 Cr App R (S) 349; [1984] 83 LGR
   577; (1984) 148 JPN 238   4.23
Newport Association Football Club Ltd v Football Association of Wales Ltd
   [1995] 2 All ER 87; (1994) 144 NLJ 1351   10.6

O'Brien v Sim-Chem Ltd [1980] 3 All ER 132; [1980] 1 WLR 1011; [1980] ICR
   573   13.8
O'Hara v Chief Constable of the Royal Constabulary [1997] AC 286; [1997] 1
   All ER 129; [1997] 2 WLR 1   2.6
Olotu v Home Office and Another [1997] 1 All ER 385; [1997] 1 WLR 831;
   (1996) *The Times*, 11 December   4.6, 11.8
O'Reilly v Mackman [1983] 2 AC 237; [1982] 3 All ER 1124; [1982] 3 WLR
   1096   1.9, 2.7

P and M Supplies (Essex) Ltd v Hackney London Borough Council (1992) 11
   Tr LR 52; (1990) 154 JP 814; [1991] Crim LR 832   2.6, 5.6
Padfield v Minister of Agriculture Fisheries & Food [1968] AC 997; [1968] 1
   All ER 694; [1968] 2 WLR 924   2.14
Parsons v FW Woolworth & Co Ltd [1980] 3 All ER 456; [1980] 1 WLR 1472;
   (1980) 124 SJ 775   9.10, 11.2. 11.5
Peacock v R (1858) 22 JP 403   5.6
Pepper (Inspector of Taxes) v Hart and Related Appeals [1993] AC 593;
   [1993] 1 All ER 42; [1992] 3 WLR 1032   6.4
Pickstone v Freemans Plc [1989] 1 AC 66; [1988] 3 CMLR 221   13.8
Pierre-Bloch v France (1998) 26 EHRR 202   13.6
Pinochet Ugarte, Re [1999] 1 All ER 577; [1999] 1 WLR 272; (1999) 11 Admin
   LR 57   2.8

Table of Cases xxv

Poh, Re [1983] 1 All ER 287; [1983] 1 WLR 2; (1983) 127 SJ 16   7.10
Practice Directions Supplementing the Civil Procedure Rules 1998, see entries after the Schedule to the Civil Procedure Rules 1998 in the Table of Statutory Instruments
Practice Direction [1997] 1 WLR 52   7.4
Practice Direction (Authorities) [1961] 1 WLR 400, [1961] 1 All ER 541   6.4.1, App 4(2), (3), (4)
Practice Direction (Cases Stated by Crown Courts) (1979) 68 Cr App R 119   9.7, App 4(4)
Practice Direction (Crown Office List) (No 2) [1991] 1 WLR 280   6.5, 7.4
Practice Direction (Crown Office List: Consent Orders) [1997] 1 WLR 825   6.6, 6.9, App 1(15), App 4(3), (4)
Practice Direction (Crown Office List: Legislation Bundle) [1997] 1 WLR 52   App 4(2)
Practice Direction (Crown Office List: Preparation for Hearings) [1994] 1 WLR 1551, [1994] 4 All ER 671   6.3, 6.4, 6.4.1, 7.4, 7.9, 9.12, App 4(2), (3), (4)
Practice Direction (Hansard Extracts) [1995] 1 WLR 192   6.4.1, App 4(2), (3), (4)
Practice Direction (Uncontested Proceedings: Crown Office List (Applications Outside London): Judicial Review) [1983] 1 WLR 925   5.2.1, 5.2.2
Practice Note [1990] 1 All ER 128   7.11
Practice Note (Case Stated) [1953] 1 WLR 334   9.9, App 4(3)
Practice Note (Judicial Review: Affidavit in Reply) [1989] 1 WLR 358, [1989] 1 All ER 1024   7.14
Practice Statement (Supreme Court Judgments) [1998] 1 WLR 825   6.4, 7.4, App 1(2)

Quinn v UK (1996) 23 EHRR 29   13.13.2

R v Acton Crown Court ex p Bewley (1988) 10 Cr App R (S) 105; (1988) 152 JP 327; (1988) 152 JPN 332   4.18
R v Arts Council of England ex p Women's Playhouse Trust [1998] COD 175   7.12
R v Bakewell Magistrates' Court and Derbyshire CPS ex p Brewer [1995] COD 98   2.8.2, 4.8
R v Barnes (1910) 102 LT 860   4.12
R v Barnsley Metropolitan Borough Council ex p Hook [1976] 3 All ER 452; [1976] 1 WLR 1052; 120 SJ 182   7.9
R v Barry (Glamorgan) Justices ex p Kashim [1953] 2 All ER 1005; [1953] 1 WLR 1320; 97 SJ 742   2.9
R v BBC ex p Lavelle [1983] 1 All ER 241; [1983] 1 WLR 23; [1983] ICR 99   1.9.1
R v Bedwelty Justices ex p Williams [1997] AC 225   2.2.1, 2.3, 3.4, 4.7, 13.10.2
R v Birmingham City Juvenile Court ex p Birmingham City Council [1988] 1 All ER 683; [1988] 1 WLR 337; [1988] 1 FLR 424   2.8.6
R v Birmingham City Juvenile Court ex p H (1992) 156 JP 445; (1992) SJLB 54; (1992) *The Times*, 4 February   4.23
R v Birmingham Crown Court ex p Rashid Ali (1999) 163 JP 145; [1999] Crim LR 504; (1999) 163 JPN 533   4.5
R v Board of Visitors of HM Prison The Maze ex p Hone [1988] AC 379   2.8.6
R v Board of Visitors of Hull Prison ex p St Germain [1979] QB 425; [1979] 2 WLR 42; (1978) 122 SJ 697   5.1, 5.1.2
R v Bournemouth Crown Court ex p Weight [1984] 2 All ER 673; [1984] 1 WLR 980; (1984) 79 Cr App R 324   1.6, 4.16
R v Bow Street Magistrates' Courts ex p DPP (1992) 95 Cr App R 9; [1990] Crim LR 318; (1990) 154 JP 237   1.7.1, 4.7

R v Brighton and Hove Magistrates' Court ex p Clarke (1997) Archbold News,
June   5.2
R v Bristol Crown Court ex p Commrs for HM Customs & Excise [1990] COD
11; (1989) *The Times*, 23 August   4.5, 4.6
R v Bristol Crown Court ex p Cooper [1990] 2 All ER 193; [1990] 1 WLR 1031;
[1990] COD 312   2.8
R v Bristol Magistrates' Court ex p Hodge [1997] QB 974; [1996] 4 All ER 924;
[1997] 2 WLR 756   12.5
R v Brixton Prison Governor ex p Schtraks [1994] AC 556   4.24
R v Bromley Licensing Justices ex p Bromley Licensed Victuallers Association
[1984] 1 All ER 794; [1984] 1 WLR 585; (1984) 148 JP 495   2.7
R v Bromley Magistrates' Court ex p Waitrose Ltd [1980] 3 All ER 464   9.2
R v Burton ex p Young [1897] 2 QB 468   2.8
R v Burton-upon-Trent Justices ex p Hussain (1997) 9 Admin LR 233; (1996)
160 JP 808; (1996) 160 JPN 1078   2.14
R v Camborne Justices ex p Pearce [1954] 2 All ER 850; [1954] 2 All ER 850;
118 JP 488   7.14
R v Cambridge Justices ex p Peacock [1993] COD 19; (1992) 156 JP 895;
(1992) 156 JPN 732   2.9
R v Camden London Borough Council ex p Martin [1997] 1 All ER 307;
[1997] 1 WLR 359; [1997] 1 FLR 950   12.3, 12.9
R v Cardiff Crown Court ex p Jones [1974] QB 113; [1973] 3 WLR 497; [1973]
Crim LR 626   1.6.1
R v Carslile Crown Court ex p Jackson, Watson and McDonagh [1991] COD
273   9.4
R v Central Criminal Court and Nadir ex p Director of the Serious Fraud
Office [1993] 2 All ER 399; [1993] 1 WLR 949; (1993) 96 Cr App R 248   1.6.1,
                                                                                2.2.1, 4.8
R v Central Criminal Court ex p Crook (1984) *The Times*, 8 September   1.6.1
R v Central Criminal Court ex p Francis & Francis [1989] AC 346; [1988] 3
WLR 989; (1989) 88 Cr App R 213   2.5
R v Central Criminal Court ex p Guney [1996] AC 616; [1996] 2 WLR 675;
[1996] 2 Cr App R 352   7.14
R v Central Criminal Court ex p Propend Finance Property Ltd [1994] COD
386; (1994) *The Times*, 5 April; (1994) *The Independent*, 29 March   2.14
R v Central Criminal Court ex p Raymond [1986] 2 All ER 379; [1986] 1 WLR
710; (1986) 83 Cr App R 94   1.6.1
R v Central Criminal Court ex p Simpkins [1999] 1 FLR 480; [1999] Crim LR
159; [1999] Fam Law 93   5.8
R v Chelmsford Crown Court ex p Chief Constable of the Essex Police [1994] 1
All ER 325; [1994] 1 WLR 359; (1994) 99 Cr App R 59   1.6
R v Chichester Crown Court ex p Abodunrin (1984) 79 Cr App R 293; [1984]
Crim LR 249; (1985) 149 JP 54   1.6.1
R v Chief Constable of Kent ex p L; R v DPP ex p B [1993] 1 All ER 756;
(1991) 93 Cr App R 416; [1991] Crim LR 841   4.3, 4.10
R v Chief Constable of North Wales ex p AB [1997] 4 All ER 691; [1997] 3
WLR 724; [1997] COD 395   4.2
R v Chief Constable of North Wales ex p Thorpe [1998] 3 WLR 57   4.2, 5.1.2
R v Chief Constable of Sussex ex p International Trader's Ferry Ltd [1998] 3
WLR 1260   4.2
R v Chief Constable of the Warwickshire Constabulary and Another ex p
Fitzpatrick and Others [1998] 1 All ER 65   1.9, 1.9.1, 4.2

Table of Cases

R v Civil Service Appeal Board ex p Cunningham [1991] 4 All ER 310; [1992]
ICR 817; [1991] IRLR 297   2.14
R v Clerkenwell Stipendiary Magistrates ex p DPP [1984] QB 221; [1984] 2 All
ER 193; [1984] 2 WLR 244   4.14
R v Commissioner of the Police for the Metropolis ex p Blackburn [1968] 2
QB 118   1.1, 1.9, 4.3
R v Comptroller of Patents [1899] 1 QB 909   1.9, 4.3
R v Cotswold DC ex p Barrington Parish Council (1998) 75 P & CR 515; [1997]
EGCS 66; [1997] NPC 70   5.2, 7.2
R v CPS ex p Hitchens (unreported) 13 June 1997   4.3
R v CPS ex p Hogg (1994) 6 Admin LR 778; (1994) *The Times*, 14 April   7.15
R v CPS ex p Treadway (1997) *The Times*, 31 October   4.3
R v CPS ex p Waterworth (unreported) 1 December 1995   4.3
R v Criminal Injuries Compensation Board ex p A [1999] 2 WLR 974; (1999)
96 (17) LSG 25; (1999) 149 NLJ 522   5.2.1, 7.15
R v Cripps ex p Muldoon [1984] 1 QB 686; [1984] 2 All ER 705; [1984] 3 WLR
53   2.5
R v Crown Court of Portsmouth ex p Thomas [1994] COD 373   9.4, 9.5
R v Croydon Crown Court ex p Commissioners of Customs & Excise (1997)
Archbold News   4.6.1
R v Croydon Crown Court ex p Miller (1987) Cr App R 152   4.18, 4.19
R v Croydon Justices ex p Lefore Holdings Ltd [1981] 1 All ER 520; [1980] 1
WLR 1465; [1980] Crim LR 722   5.6, 9.3
R v Croydon Magistrates' Court ex p Morgan (1997) 161 JP 169; [1997] COD
176; (1997) JPN 87   9.4
R v Croydon Youth Court ex p DPP [1997] 2 Cr App R 411; [1997] COD 419   2.5, 2.6
R v Customs & Excise Commissioners ex p Eurotunnel Plc [1995] COD 291;
(1995) *The Independent*, 23 February   7.15
R v Dairy Produce Quota Tribunal ex p Caswell [1990] 2 AC 738; [1990] 2 All
ER 434; [1990] 2 WLR 1320   5.2.1, 11.2, 11.3
R v Darlington Borough Council ex p Association of Darlington Taxi Owners
(No 2) [1995] COD 128; (1994) *The Times*, 19 January   12.6
R v DDP ex p Burke [1997] CL 184   4.3
R v DPP ex p Camelot Group Plc (1998) 10 Admin LR 93; [1998] COD 54;
(1998) 162 JPN 67   4.3
R v DPP ex p First Division Civil Servants (1998) *The Times*, 24 January   2.9
R v DDP ex p Kebilene and Others, R v DPP ex p Rechaci [1999] 3 WLR 175;
(1999) *The Times*, 31 March   13.2
R v DDP ex p Lee [1999] 2 All ER 737; (1999) 143 SJLB 174; (1999) *The Times*,
26 April   2.8.5
R v DDP ex p M (unreported) 13 June 1997   4.3
R v DDP ex p Panayiotu [1997] COD 83   1.1
R v Department of Health ex p Gandhi [1991] 4 All ER 547; [1991] 1 WLR
1053; [1991] ICR 805   2.8.6
R v Derwentside Magistrates' Court ex p Swift [1997] RTR 89; (1996) 160 JP
468; [1996] COD 203   1.4, 4.12, 4.15, 10.1, 10.3
R v Devon County Council ex p Baker & Johns [1995] 1 All ER 73; (1994) 6
Admin LR 113; [1993] COD 253   2.8.1, 2.12
R v Dover Magistrates' Court ex p Kidner [1983] 1 All ER 475; (1983) Fam Law
208; (1983) 147 JP 254   2.7
R v Ealing Justices ex p Scrafield [1994] RTR 195;(1993) *The Times*, 29 March   1.7.1
R v Ealing Magistrates' Court ex p Sahota (1997) 141 SJLB 251; (1997) *The
Times*, 9 December   2.11

R v Elmbridge Borough Council ex p Activeoffice Ltd (1997) *The Times*, 29 December 1.1, 1.9, 4.3
R v Essex County Council ex p C [1994] 1 FCR 773; [1993] COD 398; (1993) *The Times*, 9 December 5.2
R v Essex County Council ex p Jackson Projects Ltd [1995] COD 155 5.2.1
R v Evans and Others ex p Pinochet Ugarte (1998) *The Times*, 26 November 7.13
R v Folkestone & Hythe Juvenile Court Justices ex p R (A Juvenile) [1981] 3 All ER 840; [1981] 1 WLR 1501; (1982) 74 Cr App R 58 2.3
R v Folkestone Magistrates' Court ex p Bradley [1994] COD 138 4.6
R v Gloucestershire Crown Court ex p Chester (1998) *The Independent*, 6 July 4.14, 7.14
R v Gough [1993] AC 646; [1993] 2 All ER 724; [1993] 2 WLR 883 2.8
R v Governor of Brixton Prison ex p Kolczynski [1955] 1 QB 540 4.24
R v Governor of Brixton Prison ex p Percival [1907] 1 KB 696 4.24
R v Governor of Canterbury Prison ex p Craig [1991] 2 QB 195; [1990] 2 All ER 654; [1990] 3 WLR 127 4.6
R v Governor of Haslar Prison ex p Egbe (1991) *The Times*, 4 June 8.3, 10.2.2
R v Governor of Pentonville Prison ex p Tarling [1979] 1 All ER 981; [1979] 1 WLR 1417; (1978) 68 Cr App R 297 4.24, 10.2.2
R v Governor of Winchester Prison ex p Roddie [1991] 2 All ER 931; [1991] 1 WLR 303; (1991) 93 Cr App R 190 2.5
R v Greenwich London Borough Council ex p Governors of John Ball Primary School (1990) 154 LG Rev 678 5.2.2
R v Guildford Crown Court ex p Siderfin [1990] 2 QB 683; [1989] 3 All ER 73; [1990] 2 WLR 152 2.8.6
R v Guildford Magistrates' Court ex p Healy [1983] 1 WLR 108; [1983] Crim LR 111; (1982) 126 SJ 746 4.7
R v Haringey Justices ex p Branco (1997) *The Independent*, 1 December 2.2.2, 7.12
R v Harrow Crown Court ex p Dave [1994] 1 All ER 315; [1994] 1 WLR 98; (1994) 99 Cr App R 114 2.14, 2.14.2
R v Harrow Crown Court ex p DPP [1991] 3 All ER 315; [1991] 1 WLR 395; (1991) 93 Cr App R 114 2.8.3
R v Harrow Crown Court ex p Perkins (1998) 162 JP 527; (1998) 162 JPN 483; (1998) *The Times*, 28 April 1.6, 1.6.1, 4.23
R v Hastings Licensing Justices ex p John Lovibond & Sons Ltd [1968] 2 All ER 270; [1968] 1 WLR 735; (1968) 132 JP 332 12.6
R v Hatfield Justices ex p Castle [1980] 3 All ER 509; [1981] 1 WLR 217; (1980) 71 Cr App R 287 4.10
R v Haydon (1974) 60 Cr App R 304 4.23
R v Hendon Justices ex p DPP [1994] QB 167; [1993] 1 All ER 411; [1993] 2 WLR 862 2.10, 4.16
R v Henn & Darby [1979] ECR 379; [1980] 2 All ER 166; (1980) 71 Cr App R 44 2.4
R v Hereford Magistrates' Court ex p Macrae (1999) 163 JP 433; (1999) 96(4) LSG 39; (1999) 143 SJLB 27 2.6
R v Hereford Magistrates' Court ex p Rowlands and Ingram; R v Harrow Youth Court ex p Prussia [1998] QB 110; [1997] 2 WLR 854; [1997] 2 Cr App R 340 1.1, 1.7.1, 4.12, 5.4
R v Hertfordshire County Council ex p Cheung (1986) *The Times*, 4 April 2.13
R v Highbury Magistrate ex p Di Matteo [1991] 1 WLR 1374 2.11
R v Higher Education Funding Council ex p Institute of Dental Surgery [1994] 1 WLR 242; [1994] 1 All ER 651; [1994] COD 147 2.14

Table of Cases xxix

R v Highgate Magistrates' Court ex p Riley [1996] RTR 150; [1996] COD 12   2.8
R v Hillingdon London Borough Council ex p Puhlofer [1986] AC 484; [1986]
    1 All ER 467; [1986] 2 WLR 259   1.3
R v Honourable Society of Middle Temple ex p Bullock [1996] ELR 349;
    [1996] COD 376   12.3
R v Horseferry Road Magistrates' Courts ex p Bennett [1994] 1 AC 42; [1993]
    3 All ER 138; [1993] 3 WLR 90   1.7.1, 4.7, 4.10, 7.2, 13.1, 13.10.1
R v Horseferry Road Magistrates' Courts ex p Independent Broadcasting
    Authority [1987] QB 54   4.10
R v Horsham District Council ex p Wenman [1994] 4 All ER 681; [1995] 1
    WLR 680; (1992) 24 HLR 669   7.2
R v Hull University Visitors ex p Page [1993] AC 682; [1993] 1 All ER 97;
    [1993] 3 WLR 1112   2.3, 2.4, 3.3
R v Humphreys [1977] AC 1   4.3
R v Huntingdon Magistrates' Court ex p Percy [1994] COD 323   9.5, 12.2, 12.5
R v Immigration Appeal Tribunal ex p Begum [1985] Imm AR 385   2.13
R v Immigration Appeal Tribunal ex p Gulbamer Gulsen [1997] COD 430   12.9
R v Immigration Appeal Tribunal ex p Secretary of State for the Home
    Department (1993) *The Times*, 15 July   2.5
R v Independent Television Commission ex p Church of Scientology [1996]
    COD 443   12.2
R v Independent Television Commission ex p TV NI Ltd (1991) *The Times*, 30
    December   5.2, 12.12
R v Industrial Disputes Tribunal ex p American Express Co Inc [1954] 1 WLR
    1118   12.6
R v Inland Revenue Commissioners ex p Rossminister [1980] AC 952; [1980] 1
    All ER 80; [1980] 2 WLR 1   7.12
R v Inner London Crown Court ex p Baines & Baines [1988] 1 QB 579; [1987]
    1 All ER 1025; [1988] 2 WLR 548   2.8.5
R v Inner London Crown Court ex p Benjamin (1987) 85 Cr App R 267;
    [1987] Crim LR 417   1.6.1
R v Institute of Chartered Accountants in England and Wales ex p Andreou
    [1996] 8 Admin LR 557; [1996] COD 489   7.11
R v Isleworth Crown Court ex p Irwin [1992] RTR 281; (1992) 156 JP 453;
    (1991) *The Times*, 5 December   2.12, 4.19
R v Jockey Club ex p RAM Racecourses [1993] 2 All ER 225; [1990] COD 346;
    (1991) 5 Admin LR 265   2.12
R v Jockey Club Licensing Committee ex p Wright [1991] COD 306   7.7
R v Keepers of the Peace and Justices of the County of London (1890) 25 QB
    357   1.10
R v Kensington and Chelsea Borough Council ex p Hammell [1989] QB 518;
    [1988] 20 HLR 666   7.8, 10.5, 10.6
R v Kensington Income Tax Commissioners ex p Princess Edmond De
    Polignac [1917] 1 KB 486   8.2
R v Kirk (1983) 76 Cr App R 194; (1982) 126 SJ 769; (1983) 80 LS Gaz 35   1.6.1
R v Knightsbridge Crown Court ex p Foot [1998] COD 165; [1999] RTR 21   9.5
R v Knightsbridge Crown Court ex p International Sporting Club [1982] QB
    304; [1981] 3 All ER 417; [1981] 3 WLR 574   2.2.1, 2.14, 3.3
R v Knutsford Crown Court ex p Jones (1985) Cr App R (S) 448   4.18
R v Lambeth Borough Council ex p Wilson [1997] 3 FCR 437; (1997) 94(14)
    LSG 25; (1997) *The Times*, 25 March   12.6
R v Lancashire County Council ex p Huddleston [1986] 2 All ER 941; (1986)
    136 New LJ 562   7.14

R v Leeds Crown Court ex p Barlow [1989] RTR 246; (1989) 153 JP 113;
(1989) 153 JPN 170   4.15
R v Leeds Crown Court ex p Whitbread (1998) Archbold News, August   5.2.2
R v Legal Aid Area No 8 (Northern) Committee ex p Angell [1991] 3 Admin
LR 189   2.14.2
R v Legal Aid Board ex p Bateman [1992] 3 All ER 490; [1992] 1 WLR 711;
[1992] COD 388   1.10
R v Legal Aid Board ex p Hughes (1993) 5 Admin LR 623; (1992) 24 HLR 698;
(1992) 142 NLJ 1304   7.8, 12.11
R v Leicester Crown Court ex p S [1992] 2 All ER 659; [1993] 1 WLR 111;
(1992) 94 Cr App R 153   5.8
R v Leicester JJ ex p Barrow [1991] 2 QB 260   2.8.1, 2.8.6
R v Lewes Crown Court ex p Sinclair (1993) 5 Admin LR 1; [1992] Crim LR
868; [1993] COD 63   1.6.1
R v Lewes Justices ex p Secretary of State for the Home Department [1973] AC
388; [1972] 2 All ER 1057; [1972] 3 WLR 279   11.3
R v Lincoln Justices ex p Count (1996) 8 Admin LR 233; [1995] RVR 195;
[1995] COD 351   12.5
R v Liverpool City Council ex p Filla [1996] COD 24   7.7, 12.2
R v Liverpool City Council ex p Newman [1993] COD 65; (1993) 5 Admin LR
669; (1992) *The Times*, 3 November   12.2
R v Liverpool City Justices ex p P (1998) 162 JP 766; [1998] COD 453; (1998)
162 JPN 962   12.12
R v Liverpool Magistrates' Court ex p Ansen [1998] 1 All ER 692   2.8.3
R v London Borough of Hackney ex p Rowe [1996] COD 155   12.3
R v Lord Chancellor ex p CPAG; R v DPP ex p Bull and Another [1998] 2 All
ER 755; [1999] 1 WLR 347; [1998] COD 267   12.8
R v Lord Chancellor ex p Witham [1998] QB 575; [1997] 2 All ER 779; [1998]
2 WLR 849;   9.5, 13.3
R v Maidstone Crown Court ex p Clark [1995] 1 WLR 831; [1995] 2 Cr App R
617   1.5, 2.11, 3.5, 4.6, 4.10
R v Maidstone Crown Court ex p Gill [1987] 1 All ER 129; [1986] 1 WLR 1405;
(1987) 84 Cr App R 96   1.6.1
R v Maidstone Crown Court ex p Harrow London Borough Council (1999) *The
Times*, 14 May   1.6
R v Maidstone Crown Court ex p Shanks & McEwan (Southern) Ltd [1993]
Env LR 340   1.6.1, 1.7.1
R v Manchester City Magistrates' Court, ex p Birtles (1994) *The Times*, 25
January   2.8.1
R v Manchester City Magistrates' Court, ex p Davies [1989] QB 631   2.5, 11.8
R v Manchester Coroner ex p Tal [1985] QB 67   2.2.1, 4.7
R v Manchester Crown Court ex p DPP [1993] 1 WLR 1524; (1994) 94 Cr App
R 461; (1993) 143 NLJ 1711   1.6.1, 4.8, 5.2.1
R v Manchester Crown Court ex p McDonald and Other Cases [1999] 1 WLR
841; [1999] 1 All ER 805; [1999] 1 Cr App R 409   4.6
R v Manchester Crown Court ex p Taylor [1999] 2 All ER 769; [1988] 1 WLR
705; [1988] Crim LR 386   2.8.3
R v Manchester Crown Court ex p Wallwork (1997) COD 417   9.4
R v Manchester Stipendiary Magistrate, ex p Hill [1983] 1 AC 328; [1982] 3
WLR 331; (1982) 75 Cr App R 346   2.5, 2.9
R v Medicines Control Agency ex p Pharma Nord Ltd [1996] ECR 1-5819;
(1997) 34 BMLR 141; (1997) *The Times*, 29 July   2.2.2

Table of Cases

R v Merthyr Tydfil Crown Court ex p Chief Constable of Dyfed-Powys Police (1998) *The Times*, 17 December; (1998) 95(46) LSG 35; (1998) 142 SJLB 284   4.23

R v Merthyr Tydfil Crown Court ex p West and Others (1997) Archbold News, June   4.6

R v Metropolitan Borough of Sandwell ex p Cashmore (1993) 25 HLR 544   5.2.1, 12.12

R v Metropolitan Stipendiary Magistrate ex p Ali (1997) *The Independent*, 12 May   9.5, 10.6, 12.5

R v Metropolitan Stipendiary Magistrate ex p London Waste Regulation Authority [1993] 3 All ER 113; (1993) *The Times*, 14 January   5.4

R v Mid Glamorgan Family Health Services ex p Martin [1995] 1 All ER 356; [1995] 1 WLR 110; [1995] 1 FLR 282   13.2

R v Mid Worcestershire Justices ex p Hart [1989] COD 397   4.12

R v Mildenhall Magistrates' Court ex p Forest Heath District Council [1997] COD 352; (1997) 161 JP 401; (1997) *The Times*, 16 May   5.6, 9.4, 9.5

R v Ministry of Defence ex p Smith [1995] 4 All ER 427; (1995) 145 NLJ Rep 1689; (1995) *The Times*, 6 November   13.2

R v Morpeth Ward JJ ex p Ward (1992) 95 Cr App 215; [1992] Crim LR 497; (1992) 142 NLJ 312   4.14

R v Newcastle under Lyme ex p Massey [1995] 1 All ER 120; [1994] 1 WLR 1694; (1998) 158 JP 1037   12.5

R v Newcastle upon Tyne Justices ex p Devine (1998) 162 JP 602; [1998] RA 97; (1998) *The Times*, 7 May   2.8.4

R v Newcastle upon Tyne Justices ex p Skinner [1987] 1 All ER 349; [1987] 1 WLR 312; (1987) 84 Cr App R 311   9.4

R v Newtonabbey Magistrates' Court ex p Belfast Telegraph Newspapers Ltd (1997) *The Times*, 27 August   5.7

R v North London Metropolitan Magistrate ex p Haywood [1973] 3 All ER 50; [1973] 1 WLR 965   2.8.4

R v North Yorkshire County Council ex p M [1989] QB 411; [1989] 1 All ER 143; [1989] 1 FLR 203   11.6

R v Northampton Magistrates' Courts ex p Commissioners of Customs and Excise [1994] Crim LR 598; [1994] COD 382; (1994) 158 JPN 701   2.10, 4.10

R v Northavon District Council ex p Smith [1994] 2 AC 402; [1994] 3 All ER 313; [1994] 3 WLR 403   12.4

R v Norwich Crown Court ex p Cox (1993) 5 Admin LR 689; (1993) 97 Cr App R 145; (1993) 157 JP 593   1.6.1

R v Norwich Crown Court ex p Parker and Ward (1993) 96 Cr App R 68; [1992] Crim LR 500; (1992) 156 JP 818   4.6

R v Nottingham Justices ex p Davies [1981] QB 38; [1980] 2 All ER 775; [1980] 3 WLR 15   13.1.4.1

R v Oldham Justices and Another ex p Cawley [1997] QB 1; [1996] 1 All ER 464; [1996] 2 WLR 681   3.5, 4.21, 7.14, 8.2

R v Oldham Metropolitan Borough Council ex p Garlick [1993] AC 509; [1993] 2 All ER 65; [1993] 2 WLR 609   2.5

R v Oxford Justices ex p D [1987] QB 199; [1986] 3 All ER 129; [1986] 2 WLR 447   11.6

R v Panel on Take-Overs and Mergers ex p Datafin [1987] 1 QB 815; [1987] 1 All ER 564; [1987] 2 WLR 699   2.5

R v Panel on Take-Overs and Mergers ex p Fayed [1992] BCC 524; [1992] BCLC 938; (1992) *The Times*, 15 April   4.3

R v Panel on Take-Overs and Mergers ex p Guinness Plc [1990] 1 QB 146;
[1989] 1 All ER 509; [1989] 2 WLR 863   1.7.1, 11.2
R v Parkhurst Prison Governor ex p Philpot [1960] 1 All ER 165; [1960] 1
WLR 115; 44 Cr App R 49   1.5, 3.5
R v Parole Board ex p Lodomez [1994] COD 525; (1994) *The Times*, 3 August   2.7
R v Pateley Bridge Magistrates' Court ex p Percy [1994] COD 453   2.8.4, 2.8.6, 9.5,
                                                                  11.7, 12.2, 12,5
R v Peterborough Magistrates' Courts ex p Dowler [1997] QB 911; [1997] 2
WLR 843; [1996] 2 Cr App R 561   1.7.1, 4.12
R v Poole Magistrates' Court ex p Benham; Benham v Poole Borough Council
[1992] RVR 217l [1992] COD 148; (1992) 4 Admin LR 161   10.2.3
R v Preston Crown Court ex p Chief Constable of Lancashire Constabulary
[1998] COD 272   9.4
R v Recorder of Liverpool ex p McCann (1994) *The Times*, 4 May   1.3, 1.6, 11.6
R v Reigate Justices ex p Curl [1991] COD 66   2.2.2
R v Rent Service ex p Muldoon [1996] 1 WLR 1103   7.11
R v Richmond upon Thames London Borough Council ex p McCarthy &
Stone (Developments) Ltd [1992] 2 AC 48; [1991] 4 All ER 897; [1991] 3
WLR 841   5.2
R v Rochdale Metropolitan Borough Council ex p Schemet [1994] ELR 89;
[1993] COD 113   5.2.1
R v Rochford Justices ex p Buck (1979) 68 Cr App R 114; [1978] Crim LR 492   1.3,
                                                                  11.2
R v Salford Magistrates' Court ex p Gallagher [1994] Crim LR 374; [1993]
COD 491   4.8
R v Secretary of State for Education and Science ex p Avon CC [1991] 1 QB
558; [1991] 1 All ER 282; [1991] 2 WLR 702   10.5
R v Secretary of State for Foreign and Commonwealth Affairs ex p World
Development Movement Ltd [1995] 1 All ER 611; [1995] 1 WLR 386;
[1995] COD 211   1.10
R v Secretary of State for Health ex p Eastside Cheese Company (1998) *The
Times*, 1 December   2.16
R v Secretary of State for Social Security ex p JCWI [1996] 4 All ER 385; [1997]
1 WLR 275; (1997) 29 HLR 129   2.4
R v Secretary of State for the Environment and Shropshire County Council ex
p Parry [1998] COD 17   7.11
R v Secretary of State for the Environment ex p Kirkstall Valley Campaign Ltd
[1996] 3 All ER 304; (1996) 160 JP Rep 699; [1996] JPL 1042   12.6
R v Secretary of State for the Environment ex p Rose Theatre Trust Company
[1990] QB 504; [1990] 1 All ER 754; [1990] 2 WLR 186   10.6
R v Secretary of State for the Environment ex p Royal Society for the
Protection of Birds (1995) 7 Admin LR 434   10.6
R v Secretary of State for the Home Department ex p Abdi [1996] 1 All ER
641; [1996] 1 WLR 298; [1996] Imm AR 288   2.8.2, 3.3
R v Secretary of State for the Home Department ex p Awais Karni Butt [1994]
Imm AR 11   2.8.4
R v Secretary of State for the Home Department ex p Begum [1995] COD 176   7.7,
                                                                  7.8, 7.14, 12.13
R v Secretary of State for the Home Department ex p Bentley [1994] QB 349;
[1993] 2 WLR 101   1.9, 1.10
R v Secretary of State for the Home Department ex p Brind [1991] 1 AC 696;
[1991] 1 All ER 720; [1991] 2 WLR 588   1.3, 1.10, 2.10, 2.11, 13.2

R v Secretary of State for the Home Department ex p Cheblak [1991] 2 All ER
319; [1991] 1 WLR 890; (1992) 4 Admin LR 353   3.5
R v Secretary of State for the Home Department ex p Dannenberg [1984] QB
766   5.1.2
R v Secretary of State for the Home Department ex p Doody [1994] 1 AC 531;
[1993] 3 All ER 92; [1993] 3 WLR 154   1.9, 2.8.5, 2.14
R v Secretary of State for the Home Department ex p Fire Brigades Union
[1995] 2 AC 513; [1995] 2 All ER 244; [1995] 2 WLR 464   2.1
R v Secretary of State for the Home Department ex p Fayed [1997] 1 All ER
228; [1998] 1 WLR 763; [1997] INLR 137   2.2.1, 2.8.2, 2.14.1, 7.14
R v Secretary of State for the Home Department ex p Francois [1999] AC 43;
[1998] 1 All ER 929; [1998] 2 WLR 530   1.1, 5.2.1
R v Secretary of State for the Home Department ex p G (1990) *The Times*, 26
June   5.7
R v Secretary of State for the Home Department ex p Garner [1990] COD 457;
(1991) 3 Admin LR 33   5.1.2
R v Secretary of State for the Home Department ex p Gashi [1999] Imm AR
231; [1999] INLR 276 (1999) *The Times*, 31 March   7.7
R v Secretary of State for the Home Department ex p Ketowoglo (1992) *The
Times*, 6 April   7.15
R v Secretary of State for the Home Department ex p Khawaja [1984] AC 74;
[1983] 1 All ER 765; [1983] 2 WLR 321   2.5, 8.3
R v Secretary of State for the Home Department ex p Leech [1994] QB 198;
[1993] 4 All ER 539; [1993] 3 WLR 1125   13.3
R v Secretary of State for the Home Department ex p Li Bin Shi [1995] COD
135   7.7
R v Secretary of State for the Home Department ex p Mehari [1994] QB 474;
[1994] 2 All ER 494; [1994] 2 WLR 349   11.3
R v Secretary of State for the Home Department ex p Mohammed Yasin [1995]
Imm AR 118   2.13
R v Secretary of State for the Home Department ex p Ogilvy [1996] COD 497   7.10
R v Secretary of State for the Home Department ex p Osman [1993] Crim LR
214   4.24
R v Secretary of State for the Home Department ex p Oyeleye [1994] Imm AR
268   5.2.1
R v Secretary of State for the Home Department ex p Panther (1996) 8 Admin
LR 154   7.10
R v Secretary of State for the Home Department ex p Pierson [1998] AC 539;
[1997] 3 All ER 577; [1997] 3 WLR 492   5.1.2
R v Secretary of State for the Home Department ex p Quinn (1999) 96(21)
LSG 40; (1999) 143 SJLB 136 (1999) *The Times*, 17 April   13.1, 13.3
R v Secretary of State for the Home Department ex p Rahman [1998] QB 136;
[1996] 4 All ER 945; [1997] 3 WLR 990   3.4, 3.5, 8.2
R v Secretary of State for the Home Department ex p Rofanthullah [1989] QB
219   1.3
R v Secretary of State for the Home Department ex p Ruddock [1987] 1 WLR
1482   5.2
R v Secretary of State for the Home Department ex p Stafford [1999] 2 AC 38;
[1998] 4 All ER 7; [1998] 3 WLR 372   1.9
R v Secretary of State for the Home Department ex p Tukoglu [1988] QB
398   10.2.1, 10.2.2
R v Secretary of State for the Home Department ex p Venables [1998] AC 407;
[1997] 3 All ER 97; [1997] 2 WLR 67   2.6

xxxiv *A Criminal Practitioner's Guide to Judicial Review and Case Stated*

R v Secretary of State for the Home Department ex p Vera Lawson [1994] Imm AR 58   2.8.6
R v Secretary of State for the Home Department ex p Wynne [1993] 1 All ER 574; [1993] 1 WLR 115; (1993) 137 SJLB 38   11.3
R v Secretary of State for Trade and Industry ex p Greenpeace Ltd [1998] Env LR 415; [1998] EU LR 48; [1998] COD 59   5.2, 11.2
R v Secretary of State for Transport ex p Factortame (No 2) [1991] 1 AC 603; [1991] 1 All ER 70; [1990] 3 WLR 818   10.6, 11.8
R v Secretary of State for Transport ex p Richmond-upon-Thames London Borough Council [1994] 1 All ER 577; [1994] 1 WLR 74; [1994] Env LR 134   2.11
R v Seisdon Justices ex p Dougan [1983] 1 All ER 6; [1982] 1 WLR 1476; (1983) 76 Cr App R 1   2.7
R v Sheffield JJ ex p Turner [1991] 2 QB 472; [1991] 1 All ER 858; [1991] 2 WLR 987   1.3, 1.7.1, 4.6
R v Smith (M) [1975] QB 531; [1974] 1 All ER 651; [1974] 1 WLR 1510   1.6.1
R v Snaresbrook Crown Court ex p Director of the Serious Fraud Office (1998) 95(44) LSG 35; (1998) 142 SJLB 263; (1998) *The Times*, 26 October   1.6.1, 4.8
R v Somerset CC and ARC Southern Ltd, ex p Dixon [1997] COD 323   1.10
R v Somerset Health Authority ex p S [1996] COD 244   5.7
R v South Worcestershire Magistrates' Court ex p Lilley [1995] 4 All ER 186; [1995] 1 WLR 1595; [1995] Crim LR 954   2.8
R v Southampton Justices ex p Green [1976] QB 11; [1975] 2 All ER 1073; [1975] 3 WLR 277   5.1
R v Southwark Crown Court ex p Bowles [1998] AC 641; [1998] 2 WLR 715; [1998] 2 All ER 193   7.13
R v Southwark Crown Court ex p Brooke [1997] COD 81   2.14.2, 4.14, 9.5
R v Southwark Crown Court ex p Collman (1998) Archbold News, August   2.8, 7.14
R v Southwark Crown Court ex p Ward [1996] Crim LR 123   1.6.1
R v Special Ajudicator ex p Kandasamy [1994] Imm AR 333; (1994) *The Times*, 11 March   2.13
R v St Albans Crown Court ex p Cimmamond [1981] QB 480; [1981] 1 All ER 802; [1981] 2 WLR 681   4.18, 4.19, 4.23
R v Stafford Crown Court ex p Reid (1995) *The Independent*, 13 March   2.14, 5.6
R v Staines Magistrates' Court ex p Utting [1994] COD 189   2.12
R v Stratford on Avon District Council ex p Jackson [1985] 3 All ER 769; [1985] 1 WLR 1319; (1985) P & CR 76   5.2.1
R v Stratford Justices ex p Imbert (1999) *The Times*, 25 February   13.16
R v Swansea Crown Court ex p Davies (1989) *The Times*, 2 May   4.18
R v Tamworth Magistrates' Court ex p Walsh [1994] COD 277; (1994) *The Times*, 3 March   2.8.4, 2.8.6
R v Taylor (G) [1995] Crim LR 253; (1994) *The Times*, 17 August   13.13.3
R v Tavistock General Commissioners ex p Worth [1985] STC 564   5.2.1
R v Teeside Crown Court ex p Bullock [1996] COD 6   2.11
R v The Crown Court of Southwark ex p Samuel [1995] COD 249   2.14.1
R v The Southend Stipendiary Magistrate ex p Rochford District Council [1995] Env LR 1   2.14, 4.11
R v Thanet Justices ex p Dass [1966] COD 77   4.21, 5.2, 10.2.1, 10.2.3
R v Tottenham Justices ex p Joshi [1982] 2 All ER 507; [1982] 1 WLR 631; [1982] Crim LR 307   2.6, 4.23
R v Tower Bridge Magistrates' Court ex p Osborne [1988] Crim LR 382; (1988) 152 JP 310; (1988) 152 JPN 286   5.7
R v Trafford Magistrates' Court ex p Riley [1995] COD 73   2.8.2

R v Tunbridge Wells Justices ex p Tunbridge Wells Borough Council (1996) JPN 514	5.2
R v University College London ex p Ursula Riniker [1995] ELR 213	5.2, 5.2.1
R v Uxbridge Justices ex p Heward-Mills [1983] 1 WLR 56	2.8.5
R v Wallace (1996) *The Times*, 31 December	2.14
R v Walton Street Justices ex p Crothers [1982] Crim LR 875; [1992] COD 473; (1992) 136 SJLB 221	2.8.3
R v Wandsworth Justices ex p Read [1942] 1 KB 281	3.4
R v Wareham Magistrates' Court ex p Seldon [1998] 1 All ER 746; [1988] 1 WLR 825; [1988] 2 FLR 269	2.8.2
R v Warrington Magistrates' Court ex p Worsley [1996] COD 346	9.6
R v Warwickshire County Council ex p Collymore [1995] ELR 217	5.2.1, 7.7
R v Wellingborough Magistrates' Court ex p Francois [1994] COD 462; [1994] 158 JP 813; (1994) 158 JPN 587	2.8.6
R v Wicks [1998] AC 92; [1997] 2 All ER 801; [1997] 2 WLR 876	2.2.1, 4.4
R v Winchester Crown Court ex p B (A Minor) [1999] 1 WLR 788; (1999) 96(5) LSG 35; (1999) 143 SJLB 31	1.6.1
R v Winchester Crown Court ex p Lewington [1982] 1 WLR 1277	1.7.1, 4.11, 9.2
R v Winchester Crown Court ex p Morris and Others [1982] 1 WLR 127; [1996] COD 104; [1982] Crim LR 664	2.14.2
R v Worcester Justices ex p Daniels (1997) 161 JP 121; (1996) *The Times*, 31 December; (1997) 161 JPN 110	2.8.4
R v York City Justices ex p Farmery (1989) 153 JP 257	12.5
R v York Justices ex p Grimes (1997) *The Times*, 27 June	4.19
Racal Communications Ltd, Re; *sub nom* Company, Re [1981] AC 374; [1980] 2 All ER 634; [1980] 3 WLR 181	2.2.1
Ramage v DPP [1995] COD 313	9.9
Reckley v Minister of Public Safety and Immigration (No 2) [1996] 1 AC 527; [1996] 1 All ER 562; [1996] 2 WLR 281	1.9
Reid v DPP [1993] COD 111	9.11
Rice v UK (1988) 10 EHRR 425	13.13.5
Ridehalgh v Horsefield [1994] Ch 205; [1994] 3 All ER 848; [1994] 3 WLR 462	12.9
Ridge v Baldwin [1964] AC 40; [1963] 2 All ER 66; [1963] 2 WLR 935	2.8.1, 2.8.2, 2.8.5
Riley v DPP (1990) 91 Cr App R 14; (1990) 154 JP 453; [1990] Crim LR 322	9.7
Robinson v Whittle [1980] 3 All ER 459; [1980] 1 WLR 1476; (1980) 124 SJ 807	9.4
Russian Commercial and Industrial Bank v British Bank for Foreign Trade Ltd [1921] 2 AC 438	11.3

S v Special Educational Needs Tribunal [1995] 1 WLR 1627	2.14.2
S (An Infant) v Recorder of Manchester [1971] AC 481	4.20
Salabiaku v France (1993) 13 EHRR 379	13.13.1
Sampson, Re [1987] 1 All ER 609; [1987] 1 WLR 196; (1987) 84 Cr App R 376	1.6.1
Saunders v UK (1996) 23 EHRR 313	13.13.1
Save Britain's Heritage v Number 1 Poultry Limited [1991] 1 WLR 153	2.14.2
S-C (Mental Patient: Habeas Corpus), Re [1996] QB 599	3.5, 13.3
Schenk v Switzerland (1988) 13 EHRR 242; (1997) 2 BHRC 358; [1997] BCC 872	13.13
Secretary of State for Education and Science v Tameside Metropolitan Borough Council [1977] AC 1014	2.10

Silver v UK (1983) 5 EHRR 347 — 13.13.5
Smalley, Re [1985] AC 622; [1985] 1 All ER 769; [1985] 3 WLR 538 — 1.6, 1.6.1
Steele Ford and Newton v Crown Prosecution Service (No 2) [1994] 1 AC 22;
 [1993] 2 All ER 769; [1993] 2 WLR 934 — 12.7
Streames v Copping [1985] QB 920; [1985] 2 All ER 122; [1985] 2 WLR 993 — 1.3, 1.4,
 1.7, 4.9, 4.10, 7.2

T v Ipswich Youth Court (1998) Archbold News, December — 9.8
Tarling, Re [1979] 1 WLR 1417 — 8.5
Tesco Stores Ltd v Seabridge (1988) *The Times*, 29 April; (1988) *Daily Telegraph*,
 6 May — 9.8
Tesco Stores Ltd v Secretary of State for the Environment [1995] 2 All ER 636;
 [1995] 1 WLR 759; (1995) 70 P & CR 184 — 2.11
Thomann v Switzerland (1996) 24 EHRR 533 — 13.22
Thurrock Borough Council ex p Tesco Stores Ltd [1993] 3 PLR 114 — 2.11
Tomasi v France (1992) 15 EHRR 1 — 13.14.1
Toth v Austria (1991) 14 EHRR 551 — 13.14.1
Trivedi v UK [1997] EHRLR 521 — 13.13.2
Turner v Kingsbury Colleries Ltd [1921] 3 KB 169 — 11.6
Turner v Plasplugs Ltd [1996] 2 All ER 939; 146 NLJ Rep 370; (1996) *The
 Times*, 1 February — 12.4
Turtington v United Co-operatives Ltd [1993] Crim LR 376 — 9.7
Tyrer v UK (1978) 2 EHRR 1 — 13.21

UDT v Bycroft [1954] 3 All ER 455 — 12.11
Unterpringer v Austria (1986) 13 EHRR 175 — 13.13.2

Van Mechelen and Others v Netherlands (1997) 25 EHRR 647 — 13.13.4
Vasquez and O'Neil v R [1994] 1 WLR 674; [1994] 1 WLR 1304; [1994] Crim
 LR 845 — 13.8
Vigon v DPP [1998] Crim LR 289; (1998) 162 JP 120; (1998) 30 HLR 853 — 2.4, 4.14
Vine v National Dock Labour Board [1957] AC 488 — 11.6

W (An Infant), Re [1971] AC 682 — 2.10
Wemhoff v Germany (1968) 1 EHRR 55 — 13.13.5
Whitehead v Haines [1965] 1 QB 200; [1964] 2 All ER 530; [1994] 3 WLR 197 — 9.2
Wilkinson v CPS (1998) 162 JP 591; [1998] Crim LR 743; [1998] COD 367 — 1.7
Wiseman v Borneman [1971] AC 297; [1969] 3 All ER 285; [1969] 3 WLR 706 — 2.8.1,
 2.8.2

X v Austria (1963) 11 CD 31 — 13.16

Z v Finland (1998) 25 EHRR 371; (1999) 45 BMLR 107 — 2.17, 13.13.5
Zimmerman v Switzerland (1983) 6 EHRR 17 — 13.16.1

Table of Statutes

References are to paragraph numbers and Appendix numbers.

Access to Justice Bill	7.16, 9.13, 12.7, 12.15	Criminal Justice Act 1948	
		s 27(1)(b)(i)	10.2.3
Administration of Justice Act 1960		s 37(1)(b)(ii)	10.2.1
		(d)	10.2.1
s 1	7.16, 8.5	Criminal Justice Act 1967	
s 14(1)	1.11, 8.3, 8.5	s 22(1)	1.7, 10.2.3
(2)	8.5	Criminal Justice Act 1987	1.6.1
s 15(1)	8.5	s 4	4.8
(2)	8.5	(3)	4.8
(3)	8.5	s 6(1)	4.8
		(5)	2.2.2, 4.8
		Criminal Justice Act 1988	
Bail Act 1976	13.14	s 23	13.13.2
s 4(2)	10.2	s 24	13.13.2
s 5(6)	10.2	s 25	13.13.2
Sch 1, Part 1	13.14	s 26	13.13.2
Bail (Amendment) Act 1993		Criminal Justice Act 1991	4.8
s 1	4.5	s 40(3A)	4.19
Betting, Gaming and Lotteries Act 1963	1.6	s 53	4.8
		(1)	4.8
		Sch 2	4.20
		Sch 6, para 5	4.8
Children and Young Persons Act 1933		Criminal Justice and Public Order Act 1994	
s 39	5.8	ss 34–37	13.13.1
Companies Act 1985		s 35	13.13.1
s 434	13.13.1	Criminal Procedure and Investigations Act 1996	13.5
s 436	13.13.1	s 1(1)	13.5
Contempt of Court 1981		(a)	13.16
s 11	5.6	(2)	13.5
s 12(5)	4.20	s 21	2.8.5
Crime and Disorder Act 1998	1.2		
Crime (Sentences) Act 1997			
Sch 1, paras 2 and 3	8.1		
Criminal Appeal Act 1968	1.6.1	Dangerous Dogs Act 1991	2.8.3
s 1	4.13		
s 2(1)	11.5		
s 10	4.19	Extradition Act 1870	
(1)	4.19	s 2	4.24
(3)(a)	4.19	Extradition Act 1989	
(b)	4.19	s 1(3)	4.24
(c)	4.19	s 9	4.24
(cc)	4.19	s 10	1.7.1, 4.24
s 11(3)	4.19	s 11(1)	4.24
Criminal Appeal Act 1995	1.9, 4.25	(2)	4.24

Extradition Act 1989 – *cont*	
s 11(3)	4.24
(4)	4.24
Part III	4.24
Sch 1, para 8(1)	4.24
Football Spectators Act 1989	4.19, 4.20
s 22(7)	4.20
Gaming Act 1968	1.6
Human Rights Act 1998	1.1, 2.17, 13.1–13.22
s 1	App 5
s 2	App 5
(1)	13.6
s 3	App 5
(1)	13.8
(2)(b)	13.8.1
(c)	13.8.1
s 4	13.8.1, App 5
s 5	App 5
s 6	App 5
(1)	13.8.1
(2)	13.8.2
(3)	13.8.1
s 7	App 5
(1)	13.10
(3)	13.10
(7)	13.10
s 8	App 5
(1)	13.11
s 9	App 5
(1)	13.10
s 10(2)	13.8.1
s 21(1)	13.8.1
Sch 1	13.5
See Table of European and International Legislation for Articles to the European Convention on Human Rights.	
Justices of the Peace Act 1997	
s 54(2)(a)	12.5
(b)	12.5
(3)	12.5
Legal Aid Act 1988	
s 14(1)	12.10

s 15(1)	12.10
(2)	12.10
(3)(a)	12.10
s 16(6)	12.14
s 17(1)	12.4
(3)	12.4
s 18(4)(a)	12.4
(b)	12.4
(c)	12.4
s 19(1)	12.11
Licensing Act 1964	1.6
Local Government (Miscellaneous Provisions) Act 1982	1.6
Magistrates' Courts Act 1980	
s 6(1)	2.3, 4.7
s 50	4.20
s 108	4.21
(1)	4.20
(3)	4.20, 4.23
s 111	1.7, 1.10, App 5
(1)	1.3, 1.7, 3.2, 3.3, 4.2
(2)	5.5
(3)	5.6
(4)	1.7.1, 4.11
(5)	2.14, 9.4
(6)	11.6
s 112	App 5
s 113	App 5
(1)	10.2.3
(2)(b)	10.2.3
s 114	9.4, App 5
s 142(2)	2.6
s 148	1.7, 1.8
s 150	4.20
Sch 6, Part 1	9.5
Magistrates' Courts (Appeals from Binding Over Orders) Act 1956	
s 1	4.20
Mental Health Act 1983	
Part VII	5.10
Police and Criminal Evidence Act 1984	2.8.3, 2.8.5
s 78	13.13
Powers of Criminal Courts Act 1973	
s 43(1A)(a)	2.11
Prevention of Terrorism (Temporary Provisions) Act 1989	13.13.1

Prosecution of Offences Act 1985		s 28(2)	1.6
s 16(5)(a)	12.7	s 28A	App 5
(b)	12.7	(2)	1.4, 2.14, 9.9, 11.9
s 17	12.7	(3)	1.4, 11.10
s 22(7)	4.6	(a)	11.10
(8)	4.6	(b)	11.10
(11A)	4.6	(4)	9.13
Protection of Animals Act 1911		s 29	1.3, 1.6, 1.7, App 5
s 2	4.6	s 29(3)	1.6, 11.6
		s 31	1.3, 1.7, App 5
Road Traffic Offenders Act 1988		(6)	5.2.1
s 39(1)	1.4, 10.3	s 43	App 5
s 40(4)	1.4, 10.3	(1)	4.17, 4.19, 11.7
(5)	4.15, 10.3	(2)	4.17
		s 48	4.11
		(1)	4.18
Sexual Offences Act 1956		s 51	12.6
s 13	13.20	(6)	12.9
Sexual Offences Act 1967		s 81(1)(d)	10.2.3
s 1	13.20	(e)	10.2.1
Supreme Court Act 1981		s 88	1.11
s 18	9.13		
(1)(a)	5.1, 7.15, 9.5	Town and Country Planning Act 1990	
s 28	1.6, 2.1, App 5		
(1)	1.4, 1.10, 3.2, 3.3, 4.1	s 179(1)	4.4

Table of Statutory Instruments

References are to paragraph numbers and Appendix numbers.

Civil Legal Aid (General) Regulations 1989, SI 1989/339		r 21.4(3)	5.9
		r 21.5(2)	5.9
		(4)(b)	5.9
reg 19(2)(a)	12.12	r 21.6	5.9
(b)	12.12	r 23.3	6.9
reg 50	7.11, 8.3	r 23.4	6.9
(1)(a)	12.13	r 23.6	6.9
(4)	12.13	r 23.7(1)(b)	9.11
reg 67	12.13	r 23.10	7.15
reg 70	12.13	r 32.15(2)	7.14
reg 82(2)	6.5	r 42.2(2)	6.5
reg 83	6.5	r 42.3	6.5
reg 107	12.13	(2)(a)	6.5
(2A)	12.13	(b)	6.5
reg 124(1)	12.4	(3)(a)	6.5
Civil Procedure Rules 1998	5.1	(b)	6.5
r 1.1(1)	12.2	r 44.2	12.1
(2)	12.2	r 44.3(2)(b)	12.8
r 1.2	12.2	(1)	12.2
r 1.3	12.2	(2)	12.2
r 2.1	5.9, 6.1	(4)	12.5
r 2.3(1)	5.9	(4)(a)	12.2
r 2.8(3)	6.8	(5)(c)	12.2
(4)	6.8	(6)(d)	12.3
r 3.1(b)	9.11	(e)	12.2
r 6.2(1)(b)	6.7	r 44.4(1)	12.10
(c)	6.7	(4)	12.10
(d)	6.7	r 44.5(1)(a)	12.10
(e)	6.7	r 48.2(1)	12.6
r 6.4(2)	6.7	Sch 1	App 5
(4)	6.7	RSC Ord 53	App 5
(5)	6.7	rr 1(1), (2)	1.3
r 6.5	6.7	(1)(a), (2)	11.6
r 6.7(1)	6.7	r 3(1), (2A)	1.3, 7.8
Part 16	11.8	(2)	2.1
r 16.4	11.8	(a)(i)	App 1(2)
(1)	11.8	(a), (b)	7.4
r 19.1(2)(a)	7.13	(3)	7.6
r 21.1(2)(a)	5.9	(4)(a)	7.10, 7.15
(b)	5.10	(5)	7.10
r 21.2(1)	5.10	(6)	7.9
(2)	5.9	(7)	1.10
(3)	5.9	(10)(a)	10.5
r 21.3(2)	5.9	(10)(b)	10.6, 10.7
(3)	5.10	r 4(1)	5.2.1

Civil Procedure Rules 1998 – *cont*
  Sch 1 – *cont*
    RSC Ord 53 – *cont*
      r 4(2)   5.2
      r 5(1)   1.11
        (3)–(6)   7.11
        (7)   7.13
      r 6(1), (5)   7.11
        (2), (3)   7.9
        (3)   5.9
        (4)   7.10, 7.14,
                                   App 1(11)
      r 7(1)   1.3
        (a), (b), (2)   11.8
      r 8   7.12
      r 9(2)   App 1(2), (4)
    RSC Ord 54   App 5
      r 1(2)   8.2, 8.3
        (3)   8.2
      r 2(1)   8.3
      r 3   8.4
      r 4(1)   8.5, 11.9
      r 7(1), (2)   8.4
    RSC Ord 56   App 5
      r 1(1)   1.11, 5.1, 9.13
        (3), (4)   9.11
      r 4   9.11
      r 5(1)   9.13
      r 6(1)(a), (b)   9.11
        (2)   9.12
      r 13(1)   9.12
    RSC Ord 59
      r 1B(1)   7.15, 7.16, 9.13
        (b)   8.5
      r 14(3)   7.10
    RSC Ord 79
      r 9(1)(a), (2)(a), (b), (3)   10.2
        (11)   10.2.3
        (12)   10.2.1
  Practice Direction (Part 4 –
    Forms)   11.8, App 1(8)
  Practice Direction (Part 5 –
    Court Documents)
      para 2.2   6.4
  Practice Direction (Part 21 –
    Children and Patients)
      paras 1.5, 2.1, 2.3.2   5.9
  Practice Direction (Part 23 –
    Applications)
      paras 2.1, 6.1, 12.1   6.9
      para 12   App 1(13)
  Practice Direction (Part 32 –
    Written Evidence)
      paras 1.22–1.4   7.4, 7.14, 8.2,
                         App 1(4), App 4(2)
      para 3.2   App 1(4)
      para 4.1   App 1(4)
      para 4.2   App 1(4), App 1(11)
      para 4.3(1)   App 1(4), App
                                   1(11)
        (2)   App 1(5)
      paras 6.1(1)–(4), (6),
        6.2   App 1(4)
      para 11.3   App 1(4)
      para 16   App 1(4), App 1(11)
      paras 18.4, 20.2   App 1(6)
  Practice Direction (Part 39 –
    Miscellaneous Provisions
    Relating to Hearings)
      para 3.5   6.4.1
  Practice Direction (Part 44 –
    General Rules about
    Costs)
      paras 4.4(1), 4.5   12.10
  Practice Direction (Part 51 –
    Transitional
    Arrangements)   6.1
      paras 14, 18   6.1
  Practice Direction (Schedule
    1, RSC Order 53 –
    Application for Judicial
    Review)
      para 4.1   7.11, 11.8
  Practice Direction (The Court
    of Appeal (Civil Division))   7.10,
                                    App 1(16)
Costs in Criminal Cases
  (General) Regulations 1986,
  SI 1986/1355   4.23
Crown Court Rules 1982, SI 1982/1109
  r 19(1)   10.2.1
    (2)   10.2.3
  r 26   App 5
    (1)   5.6, 9.3
    (2)   3.1, 9.2
    (3)   9.2, 9.7
    (5)   9.4, 9.6
    (6)   2.14, 9.4
    (7)   9.6
    (8)   9.6, 9.8
    (9)(a)   9.8
  r 26(9)(b)   9.8
    (c)   9.8
    (11)   9.4
    (12)(a)   9.8
       (b)   9.8

Crown Court Rules 1982,		r 78(1)	9.8
SI 1982/1109 – *cont*		r 78(2)	9.8
r 26(13)	3.4	(3)	9.8
(14)	5.6, 9.6, 9.8	r 79	App 5
r 28	9.2	(1)	9.6
		(2)	9.8
Magistrates' Courts (Extradition)		(3)	9.8
Rules 1989, SI 1989/1579	1.7	r 80	9.2, App 5
Magistrates' Courts Rules 1981,		r 81	App 5
SI 1981/552		(1)	2.7, 3.4, 9.7
r 76	App 5	r 81(2)	9.7
(1)	9.2	(3)	9.7
(3)	9.2	Prosecution of Offences	
r 77	App 5	(Custody Time Limits)	
(1)	9.4, 9.5, 9.8	Regulations 1987, SI 1987/	
(2)	9.8	299	
r 78	App 5	reg 5	4.6

Table of European and International Legislation

References are to paragraph numbers. Bold references are to material set out in full in Appendix 5.

Convention for the Protection of Human Rights and Fundamental Freedoms	13.1–13.22
Art 2	**App 5**
Art 3	2.17, 13.5, 13.19, 13.21, **App 5**
Art 4	**App 5**
Art 5	13.3, 13.5, **App 5**
(3)	13.16.1
Art 6	13.5, 13.6, 13.13.3, **App 5**
(1)	13.13.1, 13.15, 13.16, 13.16.1, 13.17, 13.22
(2)	13.13.1
(3)	13.15, 13.16, 13.17
(b)	13.15
(c)	13.17
(d)	13.13.2, 13.13.3
Art 7	13.5, 13.18, **App 5**
Art 8	2.17, 13.5, 13.13.5, 13.18, 13.19, **App 5**
(1)	13.13.4
(2)	2.17, 13.13.4
Art 9	**App 5**
Art 10	**App 5**
Art 11	13.5, **App 5**
Art 12	**App 5**
Art 13	13.6, 13.20, **App 5**
Art 14	13.5, **App 5**
Art 15	**App 5**
Art 16	**App 5**
Art 17	**App 5**
Art 18	**App 5**
Protocol 1	**App 5**
Protocol 6	**App 5**
International Covenant on Civil and Political Rights 1966	13.4
United Nations Convention on the Rights of the Child 1989	
Art 37(c)	13.4
Vienna Convention on the Law of Treaties 1969	
Art 31	13.6

Table of Abbreviations

the Convention or the European Convention on Human Rights	Convention for the Protection of Human Rights and Fundamental Freedoms
CCR 1982	Crown Court Rules 1982
CPR 1998	Civil Procedure Rules 1998
CPR 1998, Sch 1, RSC Ord	Civil Procedure Rules 1998, Schedule 1, Rules of the Supreme Court Orders
MCA 1980	Magistrates' Courts Act 1980
MCR 1981	Magistrates' Courts Rules 1981
SCA 1981	Supreme Court Act 1981
the 1933 Act	Children and Young Persons Act 1933
the 1981 Act	Supreme Court Act 1981
the 1989 Act	Extradition Act 1989
the 1990 Act	Town and Country Planning Act 1990
the 1996 Act	Criminal Procedure and Investigations Act 1996
the 1998 Act	Human Rights Act 1998

Chapter 1

THE SCOPE OF THE HIGH COURT'S JURISDICTION

1.1 INTRODUCTION

The High Court's jurisdiction to consider applications for judicial review, appeals by way of case stated and applications for habeas corpus is an extremely important jurisdiction for competent criminal practitioners to understand. Practitioners need to be familiar with these forms of proceedings as they will often be the only way that they can protect the interests of their client or employer and assert their rights. It is not only practitioners acting for the defence who need to be aware of these proceedings. As we set out later, it is often possible for the prosecution or somebody who is not even a party to criminal proceedings to commence an action in the High Court[1]. Unusually the prosecution can even challenge acquittals.

One particularly important aspect of the High Court's jurisdiction is that it is often the only correct way to challenge an illegal decision of a magistrates' court. Lord Bingham CJ recently recognised the importance of the High Court's jurisdiction to consider decisions of magistrates' courts when he held that the availability of a right of appeal to the Crown Court did not mean that the High Court could not consider applications for judicial review. In his judgment he stated that:

> '[T]he magistrates' courts are the work-horses of the criminal justice system in England and Wales. They handle the vast majority of criminal cases, and for most citizens they represent the face of criminal justice. Given their central role, it is of obvious importance that magistrates' courts should, so far as possible, interpret and apply the law correctly and reach sound factual decisions. It is also important that proceedings in them, as in other courts, should be regularly and fairly conducted by an independent and unbiased tribunal with appropriate regard to the requirements of natural justice.'[2]

Given the volume of work handled by magistrates' courts, there are clearly many opportunities to bring proceedings in the High Court. It is not surprising that judicial review of decisions of criminal courts consists of almost 10 per cent of the judicial reviews considered by the High Court[3]. This figure, however, probably understates both the number of judicial reviews brought by criminal

---

1 See **1.10**.
2 *R v Hereford Magistrates' Court ex p Rowlands and Ingram; R v Harrow Youth Court ex p Prussia*, [1998] QB 110 at 117H, DC.
3 The Crown Office List, Review of the Year, 1997–1998.

practitioners and the potential for judicial review and appeal by way of case stated as part of a criminal practice.

The number of judicial reviews that arise from the practice of criminal practitioners is greater than the number of criminal judicial reviews recorded by the High Court, because criminal practitioners will want and need to challenge decisions that do not fulfil the technical definition of a criminal cause or matter[1].

Matters that do not come within the technical definition of a criminal cause or matter arise from two areas of practice. First, decisions of public authorities often affect their clients and these decisions can be challenged by way of judicial review. For example, it is possible to challenge by way of judicial review a decision of the police to release details of a person's previous convictions[2]. Judicial review can also be used to challenge the decisions of the prison authorities. For example, a prisoner may challenge disciplinary decisions[3].

The second area of criminal practitioners' practice that is likely to give rise to judicial review is their role as duty solicitor. In this role, they will often be asked to advise people who are before the magistrates' court for non-payment of civil liabilities such as council tax. Again proceedings in the High Court are likely to be the correct way of challenging the decisions of the magistrates' court in these circumstances.

The potential for judicial review and other proceedings in the High Court is probably greater than the statistics for applications suggest, for two reasons. First, it is our experience that many of our fellow practitioners fail to recognise the true value of judicial review. The fact that 50 per cent of substantive applications are successful clearly shows the value of judicial review[4]. Finally, the potential for judicial review is likely to increase significantly in the near future.

1.2 THE INCREASING IMPORTANCE OF THESE FORMS OF PROCEEDINGS

The policy of the present Government is likely to increase significantly the importance of the High Court in the field of crime. The Human Rights Act 1998 is considered in detail later in this book[5]. It is sufficient to say that many of the challenges that can be made under that Act will initially be made in the magistrates' court. When a party is dissatisfied by the ruling that they receive as a result of that challenge, it is likely that proceedings in the High Court will be the correct way to challenge the ruling.

---

1 See **5.1** for the technical definition of a criminal cause.
2 Eg *R v Chief Constable of the North Wales Police and Others ex p Thorpe* [1998] 3 WLR 57, CA.
3 Eg *R v Board of Visitors of Hull Prison ex p St Germain* [1979] QB 425, CA.
4 The Crown Office List, Review of the Year, 1997–1998.
5 See **13.7** et seq.

In addition, the Government is introducing legislation that will substantially change the powers of magistrates' courts. Legislation such as the Crime and Disorder Act 1998 requires these courts to consider applications for new orders, such as the anti-social behaviour order. In many cases, it will be for the High Court to interpret the legality of the decisions made as a result of these applications.

1.3 WHAT IS JUDICIAL REVIEW?

The High Court has a statutory jurisdiction to consider applications for judicial review[1]. The statutory provisions that give rise to the jurisdiction to consider applications for judicial review do not, however, define its scope. Instead, it is case-law that has held that judicial review proceedings are public law proceedings that enable the High Court to control the decisions of public bodies and courts. It is not a jurisdiction that allows the High Court to intervene merely because it disagrees with the decision of the public body or court. Instead, it is 'a remedy invented by the judges to restrain the excess or abuse of power'[2] and 'secure that decisions are made by the executive or by a public body according to law'[3]. This means, for example, that the High Court is very reluctant to consider judicial review applications that require it to substitute its own findings of fact for those of the initial decision-maker[4].

Many decisions of magistrates' courts and youth courts and some Crown Court decisions may be challenged by way of judicial review. The type of decision that may be challenged is considered later in this chapter. It is important, however, to be aware at this stage that it is not only convictions and sentences that can be challenged. For example, judicial review can be used to challenge a court's decision to refuse legal aid[5] and a decision to refuse an extension of custody time-limits[6].

Judicial review is not limited to challenges to decisions of courts. As noted earlier, the decisions of public bodies can affect the parties to criminal proceedings and judicial review can be used to challenge many of these decisions.

When the High Court considers an application for judicial review, it has a wide range of remedies available. The most important remedies are the prerogative orders of mandamus, prohibition or certiorari[7]. The High Court may also make

---

1 Supreme Court Act 1981, ss 29 and 31.
2 Per Lord Templeman, *R v Secretary of State for the Home Department ex p Brind* [1991] 1 AC 696 at 751B, HL.
3 Per Lord Templeman, *Mercury Energy Ltd v Electricity Corporation of New Zealand Ltd* [1994] 1 WLR 521 at 526A, PC.
4 Eg per Lord Brightman, *R v Hillingdon London Borough Council ex p Puhlofer* [1986] AC 484 at 518E, HL and per Lord Templeman, *R v Secretary of State for the Home Department ex p Brind* [1991] 1 AC 696 at 751B, HL.
5 Eg *R v Recorder of Liverpool ex p McCann* (1994) *The Times*, 4 May, DC; but see **1.6** for challenges regarding legal aid on matters that relate to a trial on indictment.
6 Eg *R v Sheffield JJ ex p Turner* [1991] 2 QB 472, DC.
7 CPR 1998, Sch 1, RSC Ord 53, r 1(1).

a declaration, award damages or grant an injunction when considering an application for judicial review[1]. The meaning of these orders is considered in detail later[2]. It is sufficient to say at this stage that the remedies mean that the High Court can quash a decision, force a decision-maker to act in a particular way or prevent a decision-maker from acting. There is also a wide range of interlocutory orders that are available to the High Court while the application is outstanding[3].

Clearly, the range of remedies is both wider than and different from that available in an appeal. This means that it might well be appropriate to apply for judicial review in circumstances where one would be unable to appeal. For example, judicial review can be used to challenge an unreasonable delay in taking a decision[4]. As judicial review can be used to force a decision where no decision has been taken, it is clear that it is unnecessary to wait for a final decision before applying for judicial review. Old authorities suggesting that it was necessary to wait for a final decision before applying for judicial review are bad law[5]. Applicants will, however, normally be expected to wait for a final decision[6].

The value of judicial review is restricted by the limited grounds upon which one can seek judicial review[7] and by the discretionary nature of judicial review[8]. The discretionary nature of judicial review is particularly important to understand as it means that an applicant may not obtain relief in circumstances where the decision is flawed. These limitations are considered in detail in later chapters.

Judicial review is a two-stage process[9]. An applicant for judicial review must first obtain permission to bring an action by showing that the case is arguable[10]. The application for permission is normally made without the proposed respondent being given notice of that application[11]. Once permission has been granted, the proceedings become inter partes and there is a full consideration of the merits of the application.

1.4 WHAT IS CASE STATED?

Appeal by way of case stated is statutory jurisdiction that enables the High Court to consider whether a decision of a youth court or a magistrates' court is 'wrong in law or is in excess of jurisdiction'[12]. Decisions of the Crown Court are also

---

1 CPR 1998, Sch 1, RSC Ord 53, rr 1(2) and 7(1).
2 See **11.6**.
3 See **10.1** et seq.
4 Eg *R v Secretary of State for the Home Department ex p Rofanthullah* [1989] QB 219 at 233B, CA.
5 Eg *R v Rochford Justices ex p Buck* (1979) 68 Cr App R 114, DC.
6 *Streames v Copping* [1985] QB 920, DC; see also **5.2** et seq for a discussion of the timing of an application for judicial review.
7 See Chapter 2 for details of the grounds upon which one can apply for judicial review.
8 See **11.2**.
9 See **7.8** for fuller consideration of the procedure.
10 CPR 1998, Sch 1, RSC Ord 53, r 3(1).
11 Ibid, r 3(2A).
12 Magistrates' Courts Act 1980, s 111(1).

subject to challenge on the same grounds providing that the decision does not relate to a trial on indictment[1].

Although the terms of the statutory provisions that govern appeals by way of case stated appear wide, they do not allow for an interlocutory appeal[2]. Parties to criminal proceedings should wait for a final decision in the matter. If there is some good reason why the party cannot wait until a final decision, the matter should be challenged by way of judicial review. It also has been regarded as settled law that case stated is not available to challenge a decision of magistrates taken while they are sitting as examining justices[3].

The range of remedies available to the High Court when it determines an appeal by way of case stated is considered in greater detail later[4]. However, it is important to recognise at this stage that the range is more restricted than that available to the High Court when it determines an application for judicial review. The High Court, when it determines an appeal by way of case stated, can reverse, affirm or amend the determination in respect of which the case has been stated, or it can remit the matter to the magistrates' court with the opinion of the court[5]. Alternatively, the High Court can send the case that has been stated back to the magistrates' court for amendment[6].

The interim relief that is available to the High Court when it considers an appeal by way of case stated may be of greater value to a defendant than that available when it considers a judicial review[7]. For example, during an appeal by case stated, the court that imposed a disqualification from driving and the High Court may both suspend that disqualification[8].

In the context of crime, appeal by way of case stated is only available to challenge decisions of courts and it cannot be used to challenge decisions of public bodies such as the Crown Prosecution Service and the Home Secretary. Those decisions can only be challenged by way of judicial review.

There are also significant procedural differences between judicial review and appeal by way of case stated. These differences can help to determine whether a judicial review or an appeal by way of case stated is the appropriate form of proceedings. We consider later the circumstances where bringing an appeal by way of case stated is appropriate instead of an application for judicial review[9].

The procedure for appealing by way of case stated is essentially a two-stage process. The first stage is having the case stated by the court whose decision is subject to challenge. Once the case has been stated, the appeal is then considered by the High Court.

---

1   Supreme Court Act 1981, s 28(1).
2   *Streames v Copping* [1985] QB 920, DC.
3   See **1.7** for arguments suggesting that this is no longer good law.
4   See **11.5** et seq.
5   Supreme Court Act 1981, s 28A(3).
6   Ibid, s 28A(2).
7   *R v Derwentside Magistrates' Court ex p Swift* [1996] COD 203, DC.
8   Road Traffic Offenders Act 1988, ss 39(1) and 40(4).
9   See Chapter 4, which considers when proceedings should be brought in the High Court.

1.5 WHAT IS HABEAS CORPUS?

Habeas corpus is the High Court's jurisdiction to protect personal liberty by considering the legality of current detention. In the past, it was a very important remedy as it was often used to challenge the legality of police detention. The appropriate remedy is now a bail application under the provisions of Ord 79 of the Rules of the Supreme Court. In addition, old cases that suggested one could challenge a conviction with a habeas corpus application are now regarded as bad law[1].

Extradition is the only area of criminal law in which habeas corpus is still regularly used. In extradition, it is often used in conjunction with an application for judicial review. The judicial review application is used to challenge the extradition. The habeas corpus application is used to obtain the release of the applicant if the judicial review is successful.

It may also be useful in very limited circumstances where judicial review is not available, but the liberty of the subject is at stake. For example, in a case considering whether a Crown Court arraignment was a sham, Lord Justice Glidewell expressed doubts about the court's jurisdiction to consider an application for judicial review. He did not decide the issue, as he held that he would in any event have jurisdiction to consider a habeas corpus application, as the arraignment had effectively defeated custody time-limits and led to the detention of the applicant[2].

1.6 DECISIONS OF THE CROWN COURT

The jurisdiction of the High Court to consider applications for judicial review and appeals by way of case stated from decisions of the Crown Court is governed by s 28 and s 29 of the Supreme Court Act 1981. The High Court has rejected arguments, saying that it has an inherent jurisdiction to consider judicial reviews of decisions of the Crown Court that would otherwise be excluded from the scope of judicial review by s 29(3) of the Supreme Court Act 1981[3].

Section 29(3) of the Supreme Court Act 1981 limits the scope of judicial reviews of Crown Court decisions. It is slightly different to s 28(2), which limits the scope of appeal by way of case stated. Judicial review can be used to challenge all decisions of the Crown Court other than 'matters relating to trial on indictment'[4]. Appeal by way of case stated is not available to challenge 'a judgment or other decision of the Crown Court relating to trial on

---

1   Eg *R v Parkhurst Prison Governor ex p Philpot* [1960] 1 WLR 115, DC.
2   *R v Maidstone Crown Court ex p Clark* [1995] 1 WLR 831, DC.
3   *R v Chelmsford Crown Court ex p Chief Constable of the Essex Police* [1994] 1 WLR 359, DC, but cf *R v Maidstone Crown Court ex p Harrow London Borough Council* (1999) *The Times*, 14 May, DC holding that there might be a judicial review challenging a lack of jurisdiction in circumstances where the challenge might be said to relate to trial on indictment.
4   Supreme Court Act 1981, s 29(3).

indictment'[1]. The distinction is probably of no significance, although there are no cases deciding this point. Lord Bridge has suggested in obiter remarks that the drafting is merely intended to enable the High Court to consider judicial review applications, seeking orders of mandamus and prohibition in cases of inaction or threatened action. Clearly, appeal by way of case stated cannot be used in these circumstances. The difference between s 29(3) and s 28(2) is not intended to affect the construction of the phrase 'relating to trial on indictment'[2].

In practice, most of the decisions determining whether the High Court has jurisdiction have been decided in the context of judicial review, as there are often clear tactical and procedural advantages associated with proceeding by way of judicial review[3]. For the reasons set out above, there is no reason why these authorities should not be relied on in arguments about the scope of appeal by way of case stated.

Clearly, there are some matters that do not relate to a trial on indictment, because no indictment is involved in the proceedings. For example, judicial review and appeal by way of case stated may be used to challenge the decisions of the Crown Court while exercising its jurisdiction to consider appeals from the magistrates' court[4]. Similarly, a decision to refuse legal aid in an application to remove a disqualification from driving is also subject to challenge in the High Court[5]. There are also other matters that clearly cannot be challenged in the High Court, such as conviction and sentence on a matter committed to the Crown Court for trial on indictment. In this context, the term 'trial' includes proceedings where a defendant pleads guilty to an indictment[6]. It also covers pre-trial hearings where no jury is sworn[7].

1.6.1 Authorities determining the scope of the High Court's jurisdiction to consider decisions of the Crown Court

When the Crown Court makes a decision that is ancillary to proceedings on indictment, it can be difficult to determine whether the High Court has jurisdiction to consider the matter. For example, is it possible to challenge decisions made by the Crown Court that relate to legal aid in a case being tried on indictment?

The House of Lords has considered the scope of the High Court's jurisdiction on at least four occasions. Their Lordships have declined to define the statutory phrases used to limit the jurisdiction of the High Court[8]. It has, however, stated

---

1   Supreme Court Act, 1991, s 28(2). This section also provides that case stated is not available to challenge:
    'Any decision of [the Crown] court under the Betting, Gaming and Lotteries Act 1963, the Licensing Act 1964, the Gaming Act 1968 or the Local Government (Miscellaneous Provisions) Act 1982 which, by any provision of any of those Acts, is to be final.'
2   *Re Smalley* [1985] AC 622 at 635E, HL.
3   See Chapter 4.
4   *R v Bournemouth Crown Court ex p Weight* [1984] 1 WLR 980, HL.
5   *R v Recorder of Liverpool ex p McCann* (1994) *The Times*, 4 May, DC.
6   *Re Smalley* [1985] AC 622, HL.
7   *R v Harrow Crown Court ex p Perkins* (1998) *The Times*, 28 April, DC.
8   *Re Smalley* [1985] AC 622, HL.

that if the decision of the Crown Court was one affecting the conduct of a trial on indictment given in the course of the trial or by way of pre-trial directions, it cannot be challenged by judicial review[1]. If the decision was such a decision, an aggrieved defendant normally has the opportunity to appeal to the Court of Appeal under the Criminal Appeal Act 1968. For example, a decision to refuse to grant legal aid has been held to be a matter that relates to a trial on indictment[2]. This is not surprising, because the Court of Appeal has held that it is entitled to quash a defendant's conviction where it is rendered unsafe by a trial judge's decision regarding legal aid[3].

The absence of a right of appeal to the Court of Appeal does not necessarily mean that the High Court will accept jurisdiction. For example, the High Court has no jurisdiction to consider a challenge to a decision to refuse to order costs after acquittal[4]. This is because the statutory limit on the jurisdiction of the High Court means that matters relating to a trial on indictment include orders made at the conclusion of a trial on indictment, if these orders are an integral part of the trial process[5]. Orders are an integral part of the trial process if they are based on what is learnt during the trial process[6].

Some further assistance on the scope of the High Court's jurisdiction is provided by Lord Browne-Wilkinson, who noted that decisions held to be open to challenge in the High Court are those in which the order was made in a wholly different jurisdiction or where the order has been made against someone other than the accused[7]. The only possible exception to this is serious fraud cases, where the High Court may be able to consider decisions to dismiss a case that has been transferred to the Crown Court under the special procedure provided by the Criminal Justice Act 1987[8]. Lord Browne-Wilkinson formulated the following guidance:

> ' "Is the decision sought to be reviewed one arising in the issue between the Crown and the defendant formulated by the indictment (including the costs of such issue)?" If the answer is "Yes", then to permit the decision to be challenged by judicial review may lead to delay in the trial: the matter is therefore probably

---

1   *Re Smalley* [1985] AC 622, HL.
2   *R v Chichester Crown Court ex p Abodunrin* (1984) 79 Cr App R 293, DC.
3   *R v Kirk* (1983) 76 Cr App R 194, CA.
4   *Re Meredith* (1973) 57 Cr App R 451, DC; *R v Harrow Crown Court ex p Perkins* (1998) *The Times*, 28 April, DC.
5   Per Lord Bridge in *Re Sampson* [1987] 1 WLR 194 at 198G, HL.
6   Ibid at 197E.
7   *R v Manchester Crown Court ex p DPP* [1993] 1 WLR 1524 at 1530C, HL.
8   In *R v Manchester Crown Court ex p DPP* [1993] 1 WLR 1524 at 1530G, HL, Lord Browne-Wilkinson declined an opportunity to express a view on the correctness of *R v Central Criminal Court and Nadir ex p Director of the Serious Fraud Office* [1993] 1 WLR 949, DC. Although his Lordship noted that the decision in *Ex p Director of the Serious Fraud Office* relied on cases that he held had been wrongly decided, he went on to say that the wording of the Criminal Justice Act 1987 might give rise to special considerations. Since the decision in *ex p DPP*, the High Court has continued to consider judicial reviews of decisions to dismiss proceedings following a transfer under the provisions of the Criminal Justice Act 1987. See eg *R v Snaresbrook Crown Court ex p Director of the Serious Fraud Office* (1998) *The Times*, 26 October, DC.

excluded from review by the section. If the answer is "No", the decision of the Crown Court is truly collateral to the indictment of the defendent and judicial review of that decision will not delay his trial: therefore it may well not be excluded by the section.'[1]

The decisions of the House of Lords have not prevented a degree of uncertainty about whether a matter is something that relates to a trial on indictment. Indeed, the lack of certainty has recently prompted Lord Justice Rose to call for legislation to clarify the scope of judicial review of Crown Court decisions[2]. There are, however, a number of precedents that give examples of matters that have been held to relate to a trial on indictment or matters that do not relate to a trial on indictment. These precedents can, at first glance, appear to be slightly arbitrary. For example, although a decision to remit a legal aid contribution at the end of a trial is not subject to judicial review[3], a decision to make a contribution order is subject to review[4]. These precedents, however, are a useful guide to whether the High Court will accept that it has jurisdiction to consider a challenge to a particular decision.

Matters held to be matters relating to a trial on indictment and therefore excluded from judicial review and appeal by way of case stated include the following:

(a) an order discharging a jury[5];
(b) an order that an indictment lie on the file marked 'not to be proceeded with without leave of the court'[6];
(c) the decision of a judge to order a defence solicitor to pay the costs occasioned by the granting of a defence application for an adjournment[7];
(d) a decision as to whether the trial of one indictment should proceed before the trial of another indictment faced by the same defendant[8];
(e) a refusal to stay an indictment as an abuse of process[9];
(f) an order quashing an indictment because the Crown Court lacks jurisdiction[10];
(g) an order that matters should be stayed as an abuse of process[11];
(h) an order regarding costs after the prosecution announce their intent to offer no evidence at a pre-trial hearing[12]; and
(i) an order preventing the naming of a witness under s 11 of the Contempt of Court Act 1981[13].

---

1   *R v Manchester Crown Court ex p DPP* [1993] 1 WLR 1524 at 1530F, HL.
2   *In re H, In re D* (1999) *The Times*, 13 August, DC.
3   *R v Cardiff Crown Court ex p Jones* [1974] QB 113.
4   Per Lord Bridge, in *Re Sampson* [1987] 1 WLR 194 at 199F, HL.
5   *Ex p Marlowe* [1973] Crim LR 294, DC.
6   *R v Central Criminal Court ex p Raymond* (1986) 83 Cr App R 94, DC.
7   *R v Smith (M)*, [1975] QB 531, CA (Civ Div), but note doubts expressed by Lord Bridge in *Re Smalley* [1985] AC 622 at 644F, HL.
8   *R v Southwark Crown Court ex p Ward* [1996] Crim LR 123, DC.
9   *R v Maidstone Crown Court ex p Shanks & McEwan (Southern) Ltd* [1993] Env LR 340, DC.
10 *R v Manchester Crown Court ex p DPP* [1993] 1 WLR 1524, HL.
11 *Re Ashton and Others; R v Manchester Crown Court ex p DPP* [1994] 1 AC 9, HL.
12 *R v Harrow Crown Court ex p Perkins* (1998) *The Times*, 28 April, DC.
13 *R v Central Criminal Court ex p Crook* (1984) *The Times*, 8 November, DC.

Matters that have been held to be matters that do not relate to a trial on indictment and therefore may be challenged by judicial review or appeal by way of case stated include the following:

(a) forfeiture orders made against a person who was not a defendant in the trial[1];
(b) an order committing an acquitted defendant to prison unless he agrees to be bound over[2];
(c) a decision to extend a custody time-limit[3];
(d) an order estreating the recognizance of a surety[4]; and
(e) an order lifting restrictions on the naming of juvenile defendants made under s 39(1) of the Children and Young Persons Act 1933[5].

Ingenious arguments seeking to extend the High Court's jurisdiction to consider decisions of the Crown Court have found little favour. For example, the High Court has no jurisdiction to consider a challenge to a warrant of committal to prison, if that challenge is in reality a challenge to sentence[6].

Besides the examples above, one decision of the Crown Court that cannot be challenged by judicial review, though it might not relate to a trial on indictment, is a decision by a Crown Court judge in Chambers to refuse bail[7]. This is because there is an alternative remedy as the High Court has jurisdiction to grant bail[8].

1.7 DECISIONS OF THE MAGISTRATES' COURT

The High Court has a statutory jurisdiction to consider challenges to decisions of the magistrates' court. These challenges may be by way of judicial review[9] and by way of appeal by case stated[10]. The jurisdiction of the High Court is not limited to challenges to convictions and sentences imposed by the magistrates' court. Unlike in the Crown Court, there are no decisions of the magistrates' court that are excluded from the scope of judicial review by a statutory provision. An appeal by way of case stated allows any party to proceedings in the magistrates' court or a person aggrieved to challenge a conviction, order, determination or other proceeding[11].

There are, however, two restrictions on the decisions that can be challenged by way of appeal by case stated. First, interim decisions cannot be challenged[12].

---

1 *R v Maidstone Crown Court ex p Gill* (1987) 84 Cr App R 96, DC.
2 *R v Inner London Crown Court ex p Benjamin* (1987) 85 Cr App R 267, DC.
3 *R v Norwich Crown Court ex p Cox* (1993) 5 Admin LR 689, DC.
4 *Re Smalley* [1985] AC 622, HL.
5 *In re H, In re D* (1999) *The Times*, 13 August, DC.
6 *R v Lewes Crown Court ex p Sinclair* (1993) 5 Admin LR 1, DC.
7 *Re Herbage* (1985) *The Times*, 25 October, DC.
8 Criminal Justice Act 1967, s 22(1).
9 Supreme Court Act 1981, ss 29 and 31.
10 Magistrates' Courts Act 1980, s 111(1).
11 Ibid.
12 *Streames v Copping* [1985] QB 920, DC.

Secondly, it has been regarded as settled law that appeal by way of case stated is not available to challenge a decision of magistrates sitting as examining justices[1]. The 1999 edition of *The Supreme Court Practice* doubts whether the authorities regarding examining justices are still good law[2]. It relies on the statutory definition of 'magistrates' court' which states that the magistrates' court is 'any justice or justices of the peace acting under any enactment or by virtue of his or their commission or under the common law'[3]. It suggests that there is no reason why this definition should not apply to the statutory scope of the High Court to consider an appeal by way of case stated from any proceeding before a magistrates' court[4].

In extradition cases where the magistrates refuse to commit, the possible absence of an appeal by way of case stated from a decision has been addressed. There is now a statutory provision that allows the foreign government that requested extradition to request that the court of committal state a case if committal was to have to taken place under Part III of the Extradition Act 1989[5]. The procedure that then applies is similar to that in other appeals by way of case stated[6].

Although there are no decisions of the magistrates' court that are excluded from the High Court's jurisdiction, there are other limitations on the use of judicial review that may mean that in practice challenging a decision of the magistrates' court in the High Court might not be appropriate. These are considered in more detail in Chapter 4. It is, however, important at this stage to consider whether the availability of alternative rights of appeal mean that the High Court will refuse to allow an application for judicial review.

1.7.1 The effect of the right of appeal to the Crown Court on the High Court's consideration of decisions of the magistrates' court

The High Court will often refuse to allow judicial reviews where there is an alternative right of appeal[7]. Clearly, it is often possible to appeal to the Crown Court against a decision of the magistrates' court, but this does not necessarily mean that judicial review is not available. For example, any right of appeal to the Crown Court against a conviction in the magistrates' court does not mean that a person cannot challenge that conviction by way of judicial review[8]. This is

---

1 Eg *Atkinson v United States Government* [1971] AC 197, HL.
2 Note 56/5/3 but cf *Wilkinson v CPS* [1998] COD 367, DC.
3 Magistrates' Courts Act 1980, s 148.
4 Ibid, s 111.
5 Extradition Act 1989, s 10. There is no equivalent provision governing other extraditions that do not take place under Part III of the 1989 Act. See **4.24** for details of the distinction.
6 Magistrates' Courts (Extradition) Rules 1989, SI 1989/1579.
7 Eg *R v Panel on Take-overs and Mergers ex p Guinness Plc* [1990] 1 QB 146 at 183B, CA; see also **5.4**.
8 *R v Hereford Magistrates' Court ex p Rowlands and Ingram; R v Harrow Youth Court ex p Prussia* [1998] QB 110, DC.

because Parliament intended that a person should receive two fair trials when it provided for a retrial in the Crown Court.

A Divisional Court reached the decision that the right of appeal to the Crown Court did not prevent a challenge to the conviction by way of judicial review, without overruling an earlier decision of a Divisional Court that appeared to suggest that judicial review was not available[1]. Instead, the court decided that the earlier decision had been based on the particular facts of the case. In particular, it was noted that the court which decided the earlier case had found that the application for judicial review had been made with the ulterior motive of procuring delay in a Crown Court appeal, in an attempt to secure the dropping of charges. Judicial review is also available to challenge sentences imposed in the magistrates' court, despite the right of appeal to the Crown Court[2].

Judicial review is not normally available to challenge a decision of magistrates to refuse bail[3], because there is a right to apply to the Crown Court. In contrast, there are several authorities in which the High Court appeared to accept that it was able to consider a challenge to a decision of the magistrates' court to extend custody time-limits[4]. In one of these cases, the court appeared to fail to consider the existence of an alternative remedy when it determined this matter[5]. In the later case, the court did consider the right of appeal to the Crown Court and held that judicial review of a decision of the magistrates might be the appropriate remedy where a detained person was complaining about a breach of natural justice. Where the complaint was that there was no good and sufficient cause for the extension, the detained person should appeal to the Crown Court[6].

The High Court is able to consider judicial review challenges to decisions of the magistrates' court in matters that may well be committed to the Crown Court for trial. For example, the High Court has considered a challenge to a decision of the magistrates' court to refuse to adjourn the committal of a matter[7]. Similarly, the High Court has considered a challenge to a decision to stay a matter as an abuse of process, even though the matter would otherwise have been committed to the Crown Court[8]. This jurisdiction exists, even though a decision of the Crown Court to refuse to stay a trial on indictment as an abuse of process is regarded as a matter that relates to trial on indictment and so is not subject to challenge[9].

Although an appeal by way of case stated may be brought despite the right of appeal to the Crown Court, any appeal by way of case stated will mean that

1   *R v Peterborough Magistrates' Court ex p Dowler* [1997] QB 911, DC.
2   *R v Ealing Justices ex p Scrafield* (1993) *The Times*, 29 March, DC.
3   *Re Herbage* (1985) *The Times*, 25 October, DC.
4   *R v Sheffield JJ ex p Turner* [1991] 2 QB 472, DC; *R v Folkestone Magistrates' Court ex p Bradley* [1994] COD 138, DC.
5   *R v Sheffield JJ ex p Turner* [1991] 2 QB 472, DC.
6   *R v Folkestone Magistrates' Court ex p Bradley* [1994] COD 138, DC.
7   *R v Horseferry Road Magistrates' Court ex p Bennett* [1994] 1 AC 42, HL.
8   *R v Bow Street Magistrates' Court ex p DPP* (1992) 95 Cr App R 9, DC.
9   *R v Maidstone Crown Court ex p Shanks & McEwan (Southern) Ltd* [1993] Env LR 340, DC.

rights of appeal to the Crown Court will cease[1]. As a result, there are clearly good tactical reasons why a person may not wish to appeal by way of case stated from a decision of magistrates[2].

1.8 DECISIONS OF THE YOUTH COURT

The statutory definition of a magistrates' court clearly includes the youth court[3]. Therefore, for the purposes of appeal, the youth court is regarded as the same as an adult magistrates' court. As a result, the decisions of the youth court can be challenged in the same way as decisions of the magistrates' court. When bringing proceedings in the High Court in cases that involve minors, there are specific procedural matters that need to be considered[4].

1.9 DECISIONS OF PUBLIC BODIES

Judicial review is available to challenge the decisions of public bodies. Criminal lawyers are clearly not merely concerned with the decisions of courts. For example, decisions of prosecuting authorities affect them and their clients. These decisions may well be subject to challenge by way of judicial review, but there is no appeal by way of case stated. An appeal by way of case stated is a statutory remedy that is only available in the criminal context to challenge the decision of courts.

The High Court has accepted jurisdiction to deal with judicial review in a wide range of circumstances. We have already noted judicial reviews about decisions to prosecute[5]. There have also been judicial reviews of police actions during an investigation[6]. People who have been convicted can use judicial review to challenge decisions about their treatment following conviction. This is not limited to decisions about prison conditions. Judicial review has been used to challenge the decisions of the Home Secretary regarding the tariff to be served by a prisoner[7]. Judicial review has also been used to challenge the decisions of the Secretary of State regarding the release of life prisoners[8].

---

1 Magistrates' Courts Act 1980, s 111(4). Note, however, that an appeal by way of case stated against conviction does not prevent an appeal to the Crown Court against sentence (*R v Winchester Crown Court ex p Lewington* [1982] 1 WLR 1277, DC).
2 See **4.11** for details.
3 Magistrates' Courts Act 1980, s 148.
4 See **5.8** and **5.9**.
5 Eg *R v Commr of the Police for the Metropolis ex p Blackburn* [1968] 2 QB 118, CA; *R v DPP ex p Panayiotu* [1997] COD 83, DC; *R v Elmbridge Borough Council ex p Activeoffice Ltd* (1997) *The Times*, 29 December.
6 Eg *R v Chief Constable of the Warwickshire Constabulary and Another ex p Fitzpatrick and Others* [1998] 1 All ER 65, DC, in which a Divisional Court considered a judicial review of a search warrant, but noted that, as challenges to search warrants normally involved a fact finding exercise, judicial review would rarely be an appropriate cause of action.
7 Eg *R v Secretary of State for the Home Department ex p Doody* [1994] 1 AC 531, HL.
8 Eg *R v Secretary of State for the Home Department ex p Stafford* [1998] 3 WLR 372, HL.

One area of judicial review that will become important is decisions of the Criminal Cases Review Commission. This Commission has only been in operation since 31 March 1997 and so it has reached few decisions. The provisions of the Criminal Appeal Act 1995, which established the Commission, do not exclude judicial review[1]. As a result, it would appear that judicial review will have an important role to play in controlling the way that the Commission acts.

One significant limitation on the High Court's jurisdiction to consider judicial reviews of decisions of public bodies is that it has historically been unwilling to consider challenges to a minister's exercise of certain prerogative powers[2]. As Lord Roskill stated:

> 'Prerogative powers such as those relating to the making of treaties, the defence of the realm, the *prerogative of mercy*, the grant of honours, the dissolution of Parliament and the appointment of ministers as well as others are not, I think, susceptible to judicial review because their nature and subject matter are such as not to be amenable to the judicial process.'[3] [Emphasis added]

For example, this means that the High Court will not consider a challenge to the decision of the Attorney-General regarding the entry of a nolle prosequi[4]. This historic limitation on the jurisdiction of the High Court may be becoming less significant. The High Court has considered a challenge to the exercise of the prerogative of mercy[5].

Another limitation on the High Court's jurisdiction to consider the decisions of public bodies arises as a result of the distinction between private law and public law.

1.9.1 Private law compared with public law

When considering whether a judicial review can be brought to challenge a decision of a public body, practitioners need to be aware of the divide between public law and private law. That is because persons will normally be expected to bring claims alleging a breach of public law rights by way of judicial review[6]. In contrast, judicial review is not the correct form of proceedings where there is an alleged breach of private law rights. As a result, it may be important to understand the distinction between public law and private law, although the distinction can be difficult to define.

Merely because a decision that is to be challenged has been taken by a public body does not mean that the challenge relates to public law. For example, public bodies have employees who may wish to challenge decisions that have

---

1 See eg *R v Criminal Cases Review Commission ex p Pearson* (unreported) 18 May 1999, DC.
2 *Council of Civil Service Unions v Minister for the Civil Service* [1985] AC 374, HL.
3 Ibid at 418B.
4 *R v Comptroller of Patents* [1899] 1 QB 909, CA.
5 *R v Secretary of State for the Home Department ex p Bentley* [1994] QB 349, DC, cf *Reckely v Minister of Public Safety and Immigration (No 2)* [1996] 1 AC 527, PC in which the Privy Council held that there could be no judicial review of the prerogative of mercy in a Bahamian case.
6 *O'Reilly v Mackman* [1983] 2 AC 237, HL.

been taken regarding their employment. As these decisions raise issues of private law, they are normally challenged through employment law proceedings rather than by judicial review[1].

Lord Justice Hobhouse recently considered the distinction and held that:

> 'Where a statutory corporation purports to enter into a contract which it is not empowered by the relevant statute to enter into, the corporation lacks the capacity to make the supposed contract. This lack of capacity means that the document and the agreement it contains do not have effect as a legal contract. ... The role of public law is to answer the question: what is the capacity of the local authority to contract? The role of private law is to answer the question: when one of the parties to a supposed contract lacks contractual capacity, does the supposed contract give rise to legal obligations?'[2]

As this judgment clearly shows, public law determines the scope of a public body's decision-making powers and the procedure that should be adopted to exercise those powers. In contrast private law obligations arise from the areas of civil law, such as tort and breach of contract, that govern private individuals as well as public bodies.

In the criminal law context, the distinction between public law and private law is likely to be clear. Practitioners should be well aware of the scope private law claims for matters such as unlawful arrest. There can, however, be an overlap. For example, an unlawful arrest will usually be challenged by private law proceedings for the tort of unlawful arrest, although it might also be a breach of public law if a police officer lacks jurisdiction to make an arrest[3]. A private law claim is normally the correct form of action, as the court will be in a better position to consider disputes regarding the factual background[4]. However, where the facts are not in dispute and damages are not sought, judicial review may be the correct form of proceedings.

1.10 WHO MAY BRING AN ACTION IN THE HIGH COURT?

To bring an action for judicial review, the applicant must have 'sufficient interest in the matter to which the application relates'[5]. This has a less restrictive meaning than 'person aggrieved' which was the definition that was previously used[6]. This means that the court has taken 'an increasingly liberal approach to the standing on the part of the courts during the last 12 years'[7].

---

1 Eg per Mr Justice Woolf, *R v BBC ex p Lavelle* [1983] 1 WLR 23 at 30C.
2 *Crédit Suisse v Alderdale Borough Council* [1997] QB 306 at 350E, CA.
3 See **4.2** for further consideration of public law challenges to police actions.
4 *R v Chief Constable of the Warwickshire Constabulary and Another ex p Fitzpatrick and Others* [1998] 1 All ER 65. See also **4.2** for a consideration of judicial reviews of decisions taken by the police during an investigation.
5 CPR 1998, Sch 1, RSC Ord 53, r 3(7).
6 *Cook v Southend Borough Council* [1990] 2 QB 1 at 8B, CA.
7 Per Lord Justice Rose, *R v Secretary of State for Foreign and Commonwealth Affairs ex p World Development Movement Ltd* [1995] 1 WLR 386 at 395F.

The applicant for judicial review need not be the most obvious challenger[1]. The court, however, is concerned to prevent challenges by busybodies[2].

In practice, it is unlikely that a judicial review in crime will raise issues of standing. Clearly, defendants, prosecuting authorities and victims will all have standing to bring judicial review challenges. In addition, the family members of these people may well have sufficient standing if the person is unable to bring a challenge[3].

Possibly, the only circumstance in which standing is likely to become an issue is where an applicant wishes to challenge a policy adopted by a law enforcement agency, such as the police. The applicant may not have been affected by the policy at the time that he applied for judicial review. Instead, he may merely be concerned about the civil liberties implications of the policy. The more liberal approach to standing that the courts have adopted in recent years means that it is certainly arguable that a person in these circumstances has a sufficient interest. In particular, the liberal approach has resulted in the courts accepting that, in some circumstances, the public at large has sufficient standing. For example, Mr Justice Sedley has held that:

> '[T]here will be, in public life, a certain number of cases of apparent abuse of power in which any individual, simply as a citizen, has a sufficient interest to bring the matter before the court.'[4]

In the magistrates' court, an appeal by way of case stated may be brought by:

> 'a party to any proceedings ... or [a person] aggrieved by the conviction, order, determination or other proceeding of the court.'[5]

Although this would appear to be a wide category of people, it is clearly narrower than the category of people who may bring an application for judicial review. Although it is a narrower definition, in recent years the courts have tended to adopt a liberal approach to the phrase 'person aggrieved'. For example, Viscount Dilhorne has held that:

> 'To be "aggrieved" a person must be affected by the matter of which he complains. ... [I]t was suggested that the test to be applied was that a person was not to be regarded as aggrieved unless the error ... had some demonstrable effect on his pockets, rights or interests, particularly singled out from those of the public generally. This test was rejected, and in my view rightly rejected, by the Court of Appeal.'[6]

---

1 Eg *R v Secretary of State ex p Brind* [1991] 1 AC 696, HL.
2 Eg per Lord Justice Nolan, *R v Legal Aid Board ex p Bateman* [1992] 1 WLR 711 at 718C, DC.
3 Eg *R v Secretary of State for the Home Department ex p Bentley* [1994] QB 349, DC, where the sister of an executed defendant brought a judicial review of a failure to pardon the defendant.
4 *R v Somerset CC and ARC Southern Ltd, ex p Dixon* [1997] COD 323 at 328, in which Mr Justice Sedley held that a person who was, inter alia, a local resident, a parish councillor and a member of environmental groups, had sufficient standing to bring a judicial review of a planning decision.
5 Magistrates' Courts Act 1980, s 111.
6 *Arsenal Football Club v Ende* [1979] AC 1 at 27H, HL.

That liberal approach may, however, be modified in the context of criminal proceedings by the general presumption against appeals against acquittals. For example, Lord Justice Woolf has suggested that prosecuting authorities might be excluded from being a 'person aggrieved' by the general presumption against appeals against acquittals[1]. In these cases, it may be necessary for the person to show that they have had something done against them by the direct act of the magistrate[2].

There is a more significant limitation on appeal by way of case stated from the Crown Court. These appeals can only be brought by 'any party to the proceedings'[3]. Clearly this provision is likely to prevent challenges by victims and other interested parties, such as the police.

1.11 WHICH SECTION OF THE HIGH COURT CONSIDERS CRIMINAL CASES?

All judicial review applications, appeals by way of case stated and applications for habeas corpus are processed by the Crown Office. Judges from the Queen's Bench Division of the High Court are nominated to hear cases in the Crown Office.

Criminal matters are usually heard by a Divisional Court of the High Court. Appeals to the High Court by way of case stated in 'criminal proceedings' are heard by a Divisional Court[4]. Similarly, a judicial review in 'a criminal cause or matter' is heard by a Divisional Court after the applicant has been granted permission to apply for judicial review[5]. The meaning of 'criminal proceedings' is considered later[6]. Habeas corpus applications are heard by a Divisional Court if the court directs that this is appropriate. Although a single judge can allow an application for habeas corpus in a criminal cause or matter, the application can only be refused by a Divisional Court[7]. In practice, the court is likely to direct that a Divisional Court will hear the matter as there is likely to be a linked judicial review application[8]. A Divisional Court consists of not less than two judges and may consist of three judges if the case is exceptionally difficult[9]. It is important to note that the Access to Justice Bill and consequent amendments to court rules are likely to result in a reform of High Court procedure. This will mean that many or all criminal causes or matters are considered by a single judge of the High Court.

---

1   *Cook v Southend Borough Council* [1990] 2 QB 1 at 10G, CA; clearly, prosecuting authorities are able to appeal by way of case stated, as they come within the second limb of the statutory test for standing, as they are a party to proceedings.
2   *Cook v Southend Borough Council* [1990] 2 QB 1 at 10E, CA applying the judgment of Lord Coleridge CJ in *R v Keepers of the Peace and Justices of the County of London* (1890) 25 QB 357.
3   Supreme Court Act 1981, s 28(1).
4   CPR 1998, Sch 1, RSC Ord 56, r 1(1) and r 5(1).
5   Ibid, RSC Ord 53, r 5(1).
6   See **5.1**.
7   Administration of Justice Act 1960, s 14(1).
8   See **8.1**.
9   Supreme Court Act 1981, s 66.

Chapter 2

THE GROUNDS WHICH CAN BE RAISED IN AN APPLICATION FOR JUDICIAL REVIEW

2.1 THE IMPORTANCE OF UNDERSTANDING THE CATEGORIES OF LEGAL CHALLENGE AVAILABLE IN THE HIGH COURT

Applications for judicial review, appeals by way of case stated and applications for habeas corpus are not unlimited rights of appeal to the High Court. Instead, parties applying to the High Court by way of any of these forms of procedure are restricted to raising certain limited grounds of challenge. There is clearly an overlap between these grounds. Judicial review allows the High Court to consider challenges to decisions that are said to be illegal. Similarly, an appeal by way of case stated is available where a decision is 'wrong in law or in excess of jurisdiction'[1]. Habeas corpus is available to challenge illegal detention.

In this chapter and in Chapter 3, we have set out the categories of legal error that can be challenged in an application for judicial review, an appeal by way of case stated and an application for habeas corpus. Understanding the scope of these categories is extremely important. As Lord Irvine has said:

> 'Categorisation of types of challenge assists in an orderly exposition of the principles underlying our developing public law. But these are not watertight compartments because the various grounds for judicial review run together.'[2]

Lawyers acting for applicants for judicial review will be required by the High Court to state which of the categories of legal error apply in their case. This is because the procedural rules require the errors of law to be identified. The Rules of the Supreme Court require that an application for judicial review should set out 'the grounds upon which [relief] is sought'[3]. The same rules also state that 'no grounds shall be relied upon ... at the hearing except the grounds ... set out in the statement'[4]. In practice, the High Court does not require the pleadings in judicial review proceedings to be as specific as in some other forms of civil litigation. It is also often willing to allow amendment of the grounds set out in an application for judicial review[5]. The High Court will, however, expect to see a clear explanation of how the claim fits within the possible grounds for judicial review.

---

1   Supreme Court Act 1981, s 28(1); Magistrates' Courts Act 1980, s 111(1).
2   *Boddington v British Transport Police* [1998] 2 WLR 639 at 644E, HL.
3   CPR 1998, Sch 1, RSC Ord 53, r 3(2).
4   Ibid, r 6(1).
5   See **7.9**.

It is also important to ensure that the application identifies the grounds, as it adds credibility to applications for judicial review if they are phrased in a way that shows an understanding of the grounds recognised by the High Court. The judges sitting in the High Court are concerned about the quality of applications for judicial review, so it is important that practitioners who are presenting applications show that they are familiar with the principles of judicial review. Judges have greater confidence in arguments raised by practitioners who appear to be knowledgeable.

Lawyers for respondents will wish, if possible, to argue that the case does not fall within any of the grounds recognised by the High Court. It is likely to only be in exceptional cases that the High Court will be willing to recognise novel categories of legal error[1]. Although the role of the courts in administrative law has increased significantly in recent decades, the judges also recognise that there is a limit to that role[2]. As a result, a failure to formulate a judicial review, in terms that fall within the categories of legal error that have been previously recognised, is likely to result in the High Court dismissing the application.

2.2 THE CATEGORIES OF ERROR SUSCEPTIBLE TO CHALLENGE IN AN APPLICATION FOR JUDICIAL REVIEW

Although it is important to try to identify how an error falls within the scope of judicial review, this can be difficult to do in practice. The precise scope of judicial review is unclear and so there has been considerable academic and judicial debate about the categories of legal error that allow a decision to be challenged by way of judicial review. Lord Diplock, however, gave what is often regarded as the most important statement of the categories of error of law that allow the court to intervene by way of judicial review, when he stated:

> 'The first ground I would call "illegality", the second "irrationality" and the third "procedural impropriety". That is not to say that further development on a case by case basis may not in course of time add further grounds. I have in mind particularly the possible adoption in the future of the principle of "proportionality"[3] ...
>
> By "illegality" as a ground for judicial review I mean that the decision-maker must understand correctly the law that regulates his decision-making power and must give effect to it. Whether he has or not is par excellence a justiciable question to be decided, in the event of dispute, by those persons, the judges, by whom the judicial power of the state is exercisable.
>
> By "irrationality" I mean what can by now be succinctly referred to as "*Wednesbury* unreasonableness" ... It applies to a decision which is so outrageous in its defiance of logic or of accepted moral standards that no sensible person who had applied his

---

1 Per Lord Diplock, *Council of Civil Service Unions v Minister for the Civil Service* [1985] AC 374 at 410E, HL.
2 Eg per Lord Mustill, dissenting, *R v Secretary of State for the Home Department ex p Fire Brigades Union* [1995] 2 AC 513 at 567D onwards, HL.
3 See **2.16**.

mind to the question to be decided could have arrived at it. Whether a decision falls within this category is a question that judges by their training and experience should be well equipped to answer, or else there would be something badly wrong with our judicial system ...

I have described the third head as "procedural impropriety" rather than failure to observe basic rules of natural justice or failure to act with procedural fairness towards the person who will be affected by the decision. This is because susceptibility to judicial review under this head covers also failure by an administrative tribunal to observe procedural rules that are expressly laid down in the legislative instrument by which its jurisdiction is conferred, even where such failure does not involve any denial of natural justice.'[1]

Although Lord Diplock recognised 'illegality', 'irrationality' and 'procedural impropriety' as the three categories of legal error that allowed the courts to intervene, these encompass other categories of legal error that exist within these three main categories. Some of these categories have become so important that they are effectively recognised as separate errors of law. For example, the duty to give reasons and the concept of legitimate expectation are categories of legal error that are now recognised in their own right, although they are both essentially forms of procedural impropriety or irrationality. The meaning of the various categories is set out in more detail later at **2.3** et seq.

2.2.1   The importance of the decision in *Anisminic*

Before the decision of the House of Lords in the *Anisminic* case[2], it was thought that an error of law needed either to be jurisdictional or appear on the face of the record if the High Court was to have jurisdiction to consider an application for judicial review. It is now clear that in most circumstances, any error of law that comes within Lord Diplock's categories can lead to a decision being quashed. The error need not appear on the face of the record.

There is only one category of case in which the High Court may be limited to considering errors of law that are either jurisdictional or on the face of the record. That is when the High Court considers judicial reviews of decisions of certain courts. This is because it is said that it is presumed that Parliament intended that courts can determine issues of law and so courts are presumed not to make errors of law[3]. As a result, the High Court may only be able to intervene if it is clear that the court had no jurisdiction to determine the particular question of law, or if there is a clear error on the face of the record.

In the context of judicial reviews of criminal courts, any pre-*Anisminic* limitation on the scope of judicial review is, however, unlikely to be an issue. The High Court has a clear jurisdiction to consider any errors of law made by magistrates' courts. In addition, the definition of the 'record' in the Crown Court is so wide that the pre-*Anisminic* limitations still allow almost any decision of the Crown Court to come within the scope of judicial review.

---

1   *Council of Civil Service Unions v Minister for the Civil Service* [1985] AC 374 at 410D, HL.
2   *Anisminic Ltd v Foreign Compensation Commission* [1969] 2 AC 147, HL.
3   Per Lord Diplock, *Re Racal Communications Ltd*; sub nom *Re Company* [1981] AC 374 at 382G, HL.

In the context of a judicial review of a decision of a magistrates' court, Lord Cooke of Thorndon has stated that:

> '[T]he authorities now establish that the Queen's Bench Division of the High Court has normally in judicial review proceedings jurisdiction to quash a decision of an inferior court, tribunal or other statutory body for error of law, even though the error is neither apparent on the face of the record nor so serious as to deprive the body of jurisdiction in the original and narrow sense of power to enter on the inquiry and to make against persons subject to its jurisdiction the kind of decision in question.'[1]

There have been suggestions in some cases that different principles might apply when magistrates are committing a matter for trial. It is now clear, however, that the principle set out by Lord Cooke applies to magistrates when they are considering whether a matter should be committed for trial to the Crown Court as well as when they are trying matters[2]. The High Court may, however, take account of the situation in which the legal error occurs when it decides whether to exercise its discretion to allow the application for judicial review[3]. As a result, the High Court will consider any errors made by magistrates at committal, but may decide not to intervene and quash the committal. This might happen if the Crown Court will be able to correct any injustice suffered.

In theory, judicial reviews of decisions of the Crown Court may be limited by the pre-*Anisminic* distinction. Although it is clear that the High Court is increasingly unwilling to apply the pre-*Anisminic* distinction[4], there have been no recent cases considering whether the distinction still applies to decisions of the Crown Court. This means that it may only be possible to use judicial review to challenge errors of the Crown Court that are outside jurisdiction or that are on the face of the record. As, however, the record includes oral reasons given by a Crown Court judge[5] and as there is a duty on professional judges to give reasons[6], it is highly unlikely in practice that these pre-*Anisminic* distinctions will prevent an application for judicial review. That is possibly why there have been no recent decisions considering the pre-*Anisminic* distinction in the context of decisions of the Crown Court.

2.2.2 Excluding the jurisdiction of courts to consider public law issues

The High Court may have no jurisdiction to intervene in circumstances where there are prima facie grounds for applying for judicial review, because Parliament is entitled to pass statutory provisions ousting the jurisdiction of the courts to consider public law issues[7]. The courts are, however, reluctant to interpret a statutory provision in a way that ousts jurisdiction. As Lord Irvine has held:

---

1 *R v Bedwelty Justices ex p Williams* [1997] AC 225 at 232G, HL.
2 Ibid at 234D.
3 Ibid; see also **11.2** regarding the discretionary nature of the judicial review.
4 Eg *R v Manchester Coroner ex p Tal* [1985] QB 67, DC.
5 *R v Knightsbridge Crown Court ex p International Sporting Club Ltd* [1982] QB 304, DC.
6 Ibid at 314E.
7 Eg *R v Wicks* [1998] AC 92, HL.

'[I]n approaching the issue of statutory construction the courts proceed from a strong appreciation that ours is a country subject to the rule of law. This means that it is well recognised to be important for the maintenance of the rule of law and the preservation of liberty that individuals affected by legal measures promulgated by executive public bodies should have a fair opportunity to challenge these measures and to vindicate their rights in court proceedings. There is a strong presumption that Parliament will not legislate to prevent individuals from doing so.'[1]

For example, the Court of Appeal has accepted that this approach means that a statutory provision, providing that a decision 'shall not be subject to appeal to, or review in, any court', does not exclude the jurisdiction of the High Court to consider a judicial review of that decision[2].

In a criminal context, it is most likely to be argued that a decision cannot be challenged by judicial review where the statute that provides for the making of the decision also contains a comprehensive scheme for the review of that decision. It might be said to be an exclusive scheme for review. For example, a respondent to an application for judicial review tried unsuccessfully to argue that judicial review was excluded by the provisions of s 6(5) of the Criminal Justice Act 1987. This provision stated that 'no further proceedings may be brought on a dismissed charge except by means of the preferment of a voluntary bill of indictment' where a charge had been dismissed following a transfer to the Crown Court under that Act[3].

2.2.3 Factual disputes

As has already been noted, judicial review is a remedy that gives the High Court jurisdiction to 'secure that decisions are made by the executive or by a public body according to law'[4]. This means that the High Court will not normally consider claims that a decision-maker came to mistaken findings of fact. There are some significant exceptions to this rule. It is possible to argue that the findings of fact made by a decision-maker are irrational[5]. In addition, it is possible to argue that the facts that give rise to a decision-maker's jurisdiction do not exist[6]. These exceptions exist because the findings of fact amount to an error of law or have resulted in an error of law. However, unless it is possible to argue that findings of fact come within these exceptions, it will not be possible to challenge the findings of fact in the High Court.

A related problem arises where there is a dispute about the factual background that led to the alleged error of law. For example, where it is alleged that the procedure adopted by the decision-maker or court was a breach of natural justice, the decision-maker and the applicant for judicial review may not agree

---

1   *Boddington v British Transport Police* [1998] 2 WLR 639 at 652G, HL.
2   *R v Secretary of State for the Home Department ex p Fayed* [1997] 1 All ER 228 at 235E, CA; see also *Anisminic Ltd v Foreign Compensation Commission* [1969] 2 AC 147, HL.
3   *R v Central Criminal Court and Nadir ex p Director of the Serious Fraud Office* [1993] 1 WLR 949 at 957G, DC.
4   Per Lord Templeman, *Mercury Energy Ltd v Electricity Corporation of New Zealand Ltd* [1994] 1 WLR 521 at 526A, PC.
5   See **2.10**.
6   See **2.5**.

as to what procedure was in fact adopted. The High Court is often reluctant to consider these disputes and so often proceeds on the basis that the respondent's version of events is presumed to be correct[1]. This is particularly true when the judicial review relates to alleged criminal conduct[2]. Thus, the High Court has also held that it may be preferable to challenge the procedure adopted by magistrates on appeal to the Crown Court if it is impossible to determine by written evidence what procedure was actually adopted[3].

The High Court's reluctance to consider factual disputes does not mean that it is never right to bring a judicial review in these circumstances. For example, the High Court has accepted the version of events put forward by an applicant's solicitor, where the magistrate could not back up his memory of events with any note[4]. An applicant for judicial review should always put forward the version of events that he believes to be correct. He should, however, also be aware that it may be difficult to persuade the court to accept this version of events if it becomes clear that the respondent does not.

2.3 ILLEGALITY

In one sense, all decisions that are challenged by way of judicial review must be challenged on the basis that they are illegal. That is because judicial review aims to 'secure that decisions are made by the executive or by a public body according to the law'[5]. Clearly, however, the term 'illegality' has a more restricted meaning in the context of Lord Diplock's categories. The restrictive meaning that was given to 'illegality' by Lord Diplock is the meaning that is usually used in judicial review pleadings.

Illegality is usually used to describe circumstances where a decision-maker fails to direct themselves properly about the law. As Lord Scarman stated:

> 'It is now settled law that an administrative or executive authority entrusted with the exercise of a discretion must direct itself properly in law.'[6]

In practice, the High Court regularly hears challenges that seek to argue that inferior courts and other decision-makers have misconstrued statutes that govern aspects of their work.

For example, in a criminal context, the High Court can consider a challenge that seeks to argue that the statute that gives rise to an offence has been wrongly construed by the inferior court[7]. It can also consider a challenge relating to statutes that govern the admission of evidence[8]. It can even consider whether there was any admissible evidence put before magistrates during committal

---

1 *R v Reigate Justices ex p Curl* [1991] COD 66, DC.
2 *R v Medicines Control Agency ex p Pharma Nord Ltd* (1997) *The Times*, 29 July.
3 *R v Haringey Justices ex p Branco* (1997) *The Independent*, 1 December, DC.
4 *R v Highbury Magistrate ex p Di Matteo* [1991] 1 WLR 1374, DC.
5 Per Lord Templeman, *Mercury Energy Ltd v Electricity Corporation of New Zealand Ltd* [1994] 1 WLR 521 at 526A, PC.
6 *Akbarali v Brent London Borough Council and Other Cases* [1983] 2 AC 309 at 350D, HL.
7 Eg *Vigon v DPP* [1998] Crim LR 289, DC.
8 Eg *DPP v McKeown; DPP v Jones* [1997] 2 Cr App R 155, HL.

proceedings. This is because it is an error of law to commit a person for trial where there is no evidence, because s 6(1) of the Magistrates' Courts Act 1980 requires magistrates to be satisfied that there is sufficient evidence if they are to commit a matter[1].

A detailed consideration of criminal law statutes that can be misconstrued by courts and decision-makers during criminal proceedings is outside the scope of this work. It is sufficient to say that a misconstruction of a statute by a decision-maker or court is prima facie grounds for judicial review or an appeal by way of case stated on the basis that the decision is illegal.

It is important to note that judicial review is a discretionary remedy. We consider this later in more detail in Chapter 11[2]. This means that, in practice, the High Court will not automatically intervene where a decision-maker has at some stage during proceedings misdirected himself regarding the law. Instead, the court will want to be shown that the decision is 'a relevant error of law, ie, an error in the actual making of the decision which affected the decision itself'[3]. The High Court will not intervene if the error of law is not material to the decision. For example, a decision of magistrates that relied on a statutory provision that was not in force at the date of the decision was not quashed, because the court could have relied on an alternative provision that was almost identical and was in force[4].

Clearly, it is difficult to know whether a decision can be challenged on the grounds of illegality if no reasons are given for that decision. Practitioners who appear regularly in the magistrates' court will be aware that magistrates are often unwilling to give reasons for their decisions. As a result, it can be difficult to know whether a decision of magistrates was based on an error of law or an adverse finding of fact. We discuss later the circumstances where a duty to give reasons exists[5]. Practitioners should be aware of this duty so that they can attempt to obtain the reasons needed to see whether there has been an error of law.

2.4   ULTRA VIRES

It is also illegal for a body to act in a way that is either ultra vires or in excess of its jurisdiction. It can be extremely difficult to distinguish between a decision that is ultra vires and a decision in excess of jurisdiction. This is not surprising, as the terms are sometimes given very wide meanings. For example, it has been said that all illegal decisions are ultra vires including those that are in excess of jurisdiction[6]. The position is also confused because the term 'jurisdiction' is

---

1   *R v Bedwelty Justices ex p Williams* [1997] AC 225, HL.
2   See **11.2**.
3   Per Lord Browne-Wilkinson, *R v Hull University Visitor ex p Page* [1993] AC 682 at 702C, HL.
4   *R v Folkestone & Hythe Juvenile Court Justices ex p R (A Juvenile)* [1981] 1 WLR 1501 at 1508F, DC.
5   See **2.14**.
6   Per Lord Browne-Wilkinson, *R v Hull University Visitor ex p Page* [1993] AC 682 at 701E, HL; per Lord Irvine, *Boddington v British Transport Police* [1998] 2 WLR 639 at 646B, HL.

sometimes used by judges and practitioners when they are considering whether the High Court is entitled to consider the application for judicial review. In practice, however, the terms 'ultra vires' and 'jurisdiction' should usually be used by applicants for judicial review to complain about particular errors of law.

In particular, it is normal to use a narrow definition of ultra vires when pleading ultra vires in the High Court. A decision is said to be ultra vires where legislation has conferred powers on a decision-maker or court and the decision-maker or court ignores and exceeds the limitations on those powers imposed by the statute. The High Court will apply the normal principles of statutory construction to decide the limits on a decision-maker imposed by a statute.

An example of an ultra vires decision is secondary legislation made by a public body when the primary legislation does not allow for the making of that secondary legislation. This means that, in a criminal context, it may be possible to challenge the by-laws under which a person is being prosecuted as being ultra vires. If that challenge is successful, it means that the person must be found not guilty[1]. This challenge can be either by way of judicial review or by raising a public law defence in the magistrates' court[2].

An example of an ultra vires by-law was one that restricted access to common land. It was ultra vires because the statute that provided for the making of by-laws prevented the making of by-laws that 'prejudicially affect any right of common'. As a result, protestors at Greenham Common were able to successfully challenge their convictions under that by-law[3].

The limitation on the power to make secondary legislation need not come from the particular primary legislation that enables the making of the secondary legislation. It can come from any primary legislation. Thus, in an immigration context, a statutory right of appeal could not be limited by benefits regulations that would have made it difficult to appeal[4]. The benefits regulations were held to be ultra vires.

One increasingly important limitation on the power to make legislation is European Community law. Although in the past this has had little impact on criminal litigation, it is becoming more important. For example, there has been at least one unsuccessful attempt to prevent a pornography prosecution by arguing that the restrictions on pornography are contrary to the free trade provisions of European Community law[5]. A full discussion of European Community law is outside the scope of this book, but it is particularly important to be aware that legislation that restricts trade or movement of people within Europe may be ultra vires.

---

1 *DPP v Hutchinson* [1990] 2 AC 783, HL.
2 See **4.4**.
3 *DPP v Hutchinson* [1990] 2 AC 783, HL.
4 *R v Secretary of State for Social Security ex p JCWI* [1996] 4 All ER 385.
5 *R v Henn & Darby* [1979] ECR 3795.

2.5 DECISIONS IN EXCESS OF JURISDICTION

A decision-maker or court is usually said to have made an error of jurisdiction when they have misunderstood the scope of their powers. For example, Lord Reid held that a decision should be regarded as being in excess of a decision-maker's jurisdiction if the decision-maker was not 'entitled to enter on the inquiry in question'[1]. Decisions that are said to be outside jurisdiction may include decisions that would not normally be described as ultra vires using the narrow definition set out at **2.4**, as well as those that are ultra vires. This is because a decision-maker's powers may arise from sources other than statutes[2]. The High Court is not limited to considering judicial reviews of a decision where the power to take the decision arose from a statute. In principle, there is no reason why challenges to decisions in these circumstances could not be based on an alleged absence of jurisdiction.

An example of a decision that is both in excess of jurisdiction and ultra vires is a decision of the magistrates' court to allow a defendant to reopen his plea when the court had no power to make that decision. The High Court held that the decision was in excess of jurisdiction[3]. However, although the court did not state that the decision was ultra vires, it is implicit that the decision was also ultra vires as the court relied on a limitation on the statutory power to allow the decision to be reopened[4].

Errors of jurisdiction that could arise in a criminal context include the decision-maker lacking the status required to make a particular type of decision. For example, some criminal statutes require particular decisions to be taken by judges with a particular status[5]. It is an error of jurisdiction for a judge without that status to take the decision. It is also an error of jurisdiction for a decision to be taken when the court or decision-maker is functus officio[6]. Thus, a court that has made final orders, including costs orders, cannot then amend those costs orders[7].

A decision-maker acts without jurisdiction when he acts without a condition precedent being established that permits the exercise of that power. The High Court will allow judicial review applications in these circumstances. There are many examples of this in a criminal context. The laying of an information is a condition precedent to a magistrates' court's jurisdiction to try a matter summarily on an information[8]. A committal to prison for non-payment of rates requires a means inquiry as a condition precedent[9]. An extension of custody

---

1 *Anisminic Ltd v Foreign Compensation Commission* [1969] 2 AC 147 at 171C HL.
2 *R v Panel on Take-overs & Mergers ex p Datafin* [1987] 1 QB 815, CA.
3 *R v Croydon Youth Court ex p DPP* [1997] 2 Cr App R 411, DC.
4 Ibid.
5 *R v Central Criminal Court ex p Francis & Francis* [1989] AC 346 at 368F, HL.
6 *R v Immigration Appeal Tribunal ex p Secretary of State for the Home Department* (1993) *The Times*, 15 July, CA.
7 *R v Cripps ex p Muldoon* [1984] 1 QB 686, CA.
8 *R v Manchester Stipendiary Magistrate, ex p Hill* [1983] 1 AC 328, HL.
9 *R v Manchester City Magistrates' Court ex p Davies* [1989] QB 631, CA.

time-limits requires the court to find a good and sufficient cause as a condition precedent[1].

The absence of a condition precedent is closely linked to the High Court's jurisdiction to consider precedent facts. When a precedent fact is required before a decision is taken, the High Court may determine whether that fact exists when it considers an application for judicial review[2]. This is despite the normal reluctance of the High Court to consider findings of fact when it considers applications for judicial review. The High Court has been reluctant generally to find that decisions require a precedent fact to be established. The High Court may be most willing to find that a decision requires a precedent fact where the decision relates to individual liberty[3].

2.6 BROAD STATUTORY DISCRETION AND ERRORS OF LAW

The statutory provision that empowers a decision-maker or court often gives them a wide discretion. For example, the statutory provision may state that a decision-maker may make a decision if it considers that it is 'just'. The decision-maker is unlikely to receive any explicit statutory guidance about the circumstances where making that decision will be just. The wide provisions of a discretionary statutory power do not mean, however, that all decisions that are based on a purported exercise of that power are legal.

First, the scope of that discretion needs to be determined by applying the normal principles of statutory construction to see whether there is any implicit statutory guidance as to how the power should be exercised. Thus, the discretion under s 142(2) of the Magistrates' Courts Act 1980 to allow a case to be reheard where it is 'in the interests of justice', did not allow the court to rehear a defendant's case where the defendant had entered an unequivocal plea of guilty. A decision to allow a rehearing in these circumstances is one that the court had no jurisdiction to take as a result of the limitation on the statutory power. The implied purpose of the statutory power was to allow the magistrates' court to correct mistakes and so it can only be used in these circumstances[4].

In many criminal contexts, a statute requires a decision-maker to have a particular mental state as a condition precedent to the exercise of discretion. For example, the Police and Criminal Evidence Act 1984 requires a police officer to have reasonable grounds for suspicion before he can arrest a subject. Thus, the power to arrest only exists if the arresting officer personally has reasonable suspicion and will not arise merely because the officer was ordered to carry out the arrest[5]. A decision can be challenged if it can be shown that the

---

1   *R v Governor of Winchester Prison ex p Roddie* [1991] 1 WLR 303, DC.
2   Eg *R v Oldham Metropolitan Borough Council ex p Garlick* [1993] AC 509 at 520E, HL.
3   Eg *R v Secretary of State for the Home Department ex p Khawaja* [1984] AC 74, HL.
4   *R v Croydon Youth Court ex p DPP* [1997] 2 Cr App R 411, DC.
5   *O'Hara v Chief Constable of the Royal Ulster Constabulary* [1997] AC 286, HL(NI).

decision-maker lacked the required mental state to take that decision. If the decision-maker lacks the required mental state, he lacks jurisdiction.

The exercise of a discretionary power may also be challenged in certain circumstances if the decision-maker adopted a policy to assist him with the exercise of that power. There is nothing unlawful about the adoption of a policy, because it promotes 'consistency and certainty'[1]. That policy, however, must not be inflexible so that it prevents the decision-maker taking account of relevant factors[2]. In addition, the policy must not bind the decision-maker to acting in a certain way in the future[3]. Thus, in a criminal context, a policy of a particular magistrates' court regarding costs could not justify an award of costs that was unreasonable in the particular circumstances of that case[4].

2.7 PROCEDURAL IMPROPRIETY

The most obvious form of procedural impropriety is a failure to comply with an express procedural requirement. The express procedural requirement need not arise from primary legislation. For example, a failure to comply with procedural requirements contained in the Magistrates' Courts Rules 1981 is an error that enables the High Court to intervene[5].

Legislation may impose a wide range of procedural requirements on decision-makers and courts. A person may be given the right to be heard or consulted about a decision[6]. There may also be an express right to be given notice of proceedings[7]. At the end of proceedings, there may be an express right to reasons for a decision[8]. The express procedural rules may benefit a third party who is affected by a decision, but who is not a party to proceedings. For example, a person has the right to be heard if they object to an occasional drinks licence[9]. The failure to comply with any of these express provisions will enable the court to intervene.

Practitioners need to consider the statutory provisions that impose the procedural requirements to determine whether they actually impose a mandatory procedure or whether they merely direct the decision-maker about the procedure that should normally be adopted. If the procedure is merely directory, the decision-maker or court is entitled to fail to comply with the procedure in exceptional circumstances[10]. For example, the requirement

---

1   Per Lord Woolf, *R v Secretary of State for the Home Department ex p Venables* [1997] 2 WLR 67 at 90B, CA.
2   *R v Secretary of State for the Home Department ex p Venables* [1998] AC 407 at 497B, HL.
3   Ibid, at 496H.
4   *R v Tottenham Justices ex p Joshi* [1982] 1 WLR 631, DC. Cf *R v Hereford Magistrates' Court ex p MacRae* (1998) *The Times*, 31 December, DC for an example of a policy adopted by magistrates that was held to be lawful.
5   *R v Dover Magistrates' Court ex p Kidner* [1983] 1 All ER 475.
6   *R v Bromley Licensing Justices ex p Bromley Licensed Victuallers' Association* [1984] 1 WLR 585.
7   *R v Seisdon Justices ex p Dougan* [1982] 1 WLR 1476, DC.
8   *R v Parole Board ex p Lodomez* [1994] COD 525, DC.
9   *R v Bromley Licensing Justices ex p Bromley Licensed Victuallers' Association* [1984] 1 WLR 585.
10   *O'Reilly v Mackman* [1983] 2 AC 237 at 276A, HL.

contained in s 5(8) of the Children and Young Persons Act 1969 that a local authority should be informed of the prosecution of a young person is merely directory. A decision of a criminal court will not necessarily be quashed as a result of a failure to comply with this provision[1].

If a procedural requirement is mandatory, a party complaining about a failure to comply with this procedure is not required to show prejudice[2]. One possible exception to this rule is where the failure to comply with the procedure was induced by the applicant's conduct[3].

Clearly, if the procedural requirements are merely directory, the High Court will still be able to consider a complaint alleging a failure to comply with those procedural requirements. However, because the procedure specified in the statute is directory, it is implicit that the decision-maker has a discretion to depart from that procedure[4]. As a result, the High Court will only quash a decision if it is satisfied that the decision to depart from the directory procedural requirements was not taken in accordance with the principles of public law. For example, a decision taken when the decision-maker failed to comply with the directory procedure will be quashed if it is unreasonable or taken for an improper motive.

2.8 NATURAL JUSTICE AND BIAS

Claims in the High Court based on procedural impropriety are more commonly based on a claimed breach of natural justice, rather than a failure to comply with express procedural requirements. Natural justice imposes two requirements on a decision-maker or a court. The decision-maker or court must act without bias and must give a party a fair hearing[5]. The procedural requirements for a hearing to be regarded as fair are set out in detail in the next sections of this chapter[6].

It is easier to identify bias than it is to identify a decision taken without a fair hearing. A decision will be quashed for bias if an applicant for judicial review can show actual bias or that the decision-maker had a direct interest in the outcome or apparent bias. Actual bias is very rare and hard to prove[7], so it is rarely raised in the High Court. Similarly, a direct interest is difficult to prove as the High Court will not act if the decision-maker had only a slight pecuniary interest in the outcome. For example, a member of the Law Society can sit as a justice in a case brought by the Society, as it is highly unlikely that the justice will become personally liable for any costs resulting from the proceedings[8]. It is,

---

1 *DPP v Cottier* [1996] 1 WLR 826, DC; *R v Marsh* (1996) *The Times*, 11 April, CA.
2 *O'Reilly v Mackman* [1983] 2 AC 237 at 276A, HL.
3 *R v Secretary of State for the Home Department ex p Awais Karni Butt* [1994] Imm AR 11 at 13.
4 *O'Reilly v Mackman* [1983] 2 AC 237 at 276A, HL.
5 Eg *Kanda v Government of Malaya* [1962] AC 322 at 337, PC; *O'Reilly v Mackman* [1983] 2 AC 237 at 279G, HL.
6 See **2.8.1** to **2.8.6**.
7 *R v Gough* [1993] AC 646 at 661G, HL.
8 *R v Burton ex p Young* [1897] 2 QB 468.

however, clear that in a judicial review where an applicant is not seeking damages, a direct interest does not require a pecuniary interest in the outcome. It can arise where a judge or decision-maker has shown a direct interest in promoting the cause that is being considered in the judicial review[1].

Bias is, however, important as apparent bias is relatively easy to prove. Lord Goff set out the test to be applied when considering whether the circumstances of a case indicate apparent bias on behalf of a decision-maker or court, when he held that:

> '[H]aving ascertained the relevant circumstances, the court should ask itself whether, having regard to those circumstances, there was a real danger of bias on the part of the relevant member of the tribunal in question, in the sense that he might unfairly regard (or have unfairly regarded) with favour, or disfavour, the case of a party to the issue under consideration.'[2]

The use of the phrase 'real danger' in Lord Goff's test only requires the possibility of bias rather than the probability of bias[3]. The court considering claims of bias is also not restricted to considering whether a reasonable man sitting in court would have decided that there was a real danger of bias[4]. This is because the court may have information before it that would not have been available to an observer sitting in court.

Lord Goff's test does not require the court to investigate the decision-maker's state of mind to decide whether actual prejudice is established. This is because the decision-maker may not even be conscious of bias. Thus, in proceedings in the magistrates' court, an intervention from the chairman of the bench stating it was not the practice of the court to call police officers liars, allowed the High Court to intervene. This was because the intervention indicated a real danger of unconscious bias in favour of the evidence of police officers[5].

Apparent bias may arise from information obtained by magistrates outside the trial process. Where during pre-trial hearings in criminal proceedings magistrates have heard submissions or considered evidence without the defendant and his advisers being present, the magistrates may be obliged to order that the matter should be tried by another bench. If they do not do this, there is a danger of apparent bias[6]. However, all relevant knowledge obtained outside of court proceedings does not necessarily give rise to an inference of apparent bias. For example, it is desirable that a magistrate considering licensing applications should have prior knowledge of licensing policy. As a result, a

---

1 In *Re Pinochet Ugarte* (1999) *The Times*, 18 January, HL, in which it was held that there is no need for a pecuniary interest. The question is whether a judge is acting in his own cause. In this case, Lord Hoffmann was held to have been disqualified from considering the application to extradite General Pinochet as a result of his involvement with Amnesty International.
2 *R v Gough* [1993] AC 646 at 670F, HL; note that in *Re Pinochet Ugarte* (1999) *The Times*, 18 January, HL, the House of Lords declined to consider whether this case was rightly decided, although they did note the criticisms of it in other jurisdictions.
3 *R v Gough* [1993] AC 646 at 670E, HL.
4 Ibid at 670D, HL.
5 *R v Highgate Magistrates' Court ex p Riley* [1996] COD 12, DC.
6 *R v South Worcestershire Magistrates' Court ex p Lilley* [1995] 4 All ER 186, DC.

member of the licensing committee that refused the application for a licence could sit as a magistrate considering the same application[1].

Special considerations may apply where it is alleged that there is a real danger of bias by a magistrates' clerk, because the clerk may not have actually participated in the decision that is being challenged. Lord Goff stated that in addition to bias, it must be shown that:

> 'by reason of [the clerk's] participating in the decision-making process, there was a real likelihood that he would "impose his influence on the justices or give them wrong legal advice".'[2]

Where a judicial review application is brought complaining about bias, the High Court has stated that it is desirable that it is supplied with written evidence from the prosecutor who was in court and the decision-maker who is alleged to have shown bias. Thus, in the Crown Court, the circuit judge hearing the appeal and counsel who appeared for the Crown should swear affidavits or sign witness statements[3].

2.8.1 Fair hearing: an introduction

There are no universal standards that apply in every situation and determine whether the parties to a decision-making process have had a fair hearing. Instead, the requirements for a fair hearing depend on the circumstances of the case[4]. As a result, judges have been reluctant to lay down rigid rules defining the scope of natural justice[5]. It is clear, however, that a fair hearing does not require a decision-maker to adopt the highest possible standards of procedural fairness[6]. Instead, it requires the decision-maker to act fairly.

It is uncertain whether a person complaining about the absence of a fair hearing is required to prove prejudice. There are conflicting authorities on this point[7]. However, when considering judicial reviews of decisions of criminal courts, the High Court appears to accept that procedural irregularities in the magistrates' court may lead to no injustice. If the High Court finds that there is no injustice, it will not quash the decision of the magistrates' court. For example, a committal for trial, where magistrates admitted inadmissible evidence but stated that they would not take 'any real notice of' the evidence,

---

1 *R v Bristol Crown Court ex p Cooper* [1990] 1 WLR 1031, CA; see also *Johnson v Leicestershire Constabulary* (1998) *The Times*, 7 October, DC, in which it was held that where magistrates gained knowledge that a defendant had spent time in custody as a result of one of their number being a prison visitor, the question was whether there was any real danger of bias. Lay magistrates are trained to put irrelevant matters out of their mind.
2 *R v Gough* [1993] AC 646 at 664D, HL.
3 *R v Southwark Crown Court ex p Collman* (1998) *Archbold News*, August, DC.
4 Eg per Lord Russell, *Fairmount Investments Ltd v Secretary of State for the Environment* [1976] 1 WLR 1255 at 1265H, HL.
5 Eg per Lord Morris, *Wiseman v Borneman* [1971] AC 297 at 308H, HL.
6 Eg per Dillon LJ, *R v Devon County Council ex p Baker & Johns* [1995] 1 All ER 73 at 85C, CA.
7 *Ridge v Baldwin* [1964] AC 40 at 128, HL, in which it was held the respondent could not rely on a lack of prejudice, cf *Malloch v Aberdeen Corporation* [1971] 1 WLR 1578 at 1595B, HL (Sc).

was not quashed following an application for judicial review[1]. Similarly, where a stipendiary magistrate wrongly heard representations in Chambers without the defendants being present, the convictions were not quashed following an application for judicial review as the defendants had admitted the offences charged during cross-examination[2].

When an application for judicial review is made challenging a decision of magistrates, the burden will be on the respondent to the application to show that the procedural irregularity was not material. The High Court is likely to start by presuming that a procedural irregularity should lead to a decision being quashed. This approach was endorsed by Lord Donaldson when he held that:

> 'Any unfairness, whether apparent or actual and however inadvertent, strikes at the roots of justice. I cannot be sure that the applicants were not prejudiced and accordingly I have no doubt that the justices' order should be quashed.'[3]

Although the burden may be on the respondent to show that there is no prejudice, actual prejudice or potential prejudice should always be pleaded by an applicant for judicial review if it can be shown. Prejudice is significant, as it is a factor that tends to show that the procedure adopted was not fair in all the circumstances of the case. In the context of criminal trials, it is likely to be easy to show potential prejudice, because it will normally be possible to argue that the decision of the court might have been different if a different procedure had been adopted. For example, potential prejudice occurred when parties to proceedings were prevented from obtaining legal advice. Had the parties to the proceedings been able to obtain legal advice, they might have presented their case differently[4].

2.8.2 Determining whether the right to a fair hearing arises in the circumstances of the case

The starting point for considering whether there is a right to a fair hearing is to look at the legislation that provides for the decision to be taken. A statute may exclude the application of the rules of a natural justice with a clear and express provision[5]. The courts are, however, likely to interpret such a statutory provision very narrowly. For example, a statutory provision excluding any duty to give reasons for a final decision did not exclude a duty to disclose concerns before the final decision, so that parties can respond to them[6].

If there is no express statutory provision excluding the application of the rules of natural justice, one needs to consider whether there are express procedural requirements imposed on the decision-maker. Express procedural requirements do not mean that the High Court will not hold that the right to a fair

---

1 *R v Manchester City Magistrates' Court ex p Birtles* (1994) *The Times*, 25 January, DC.
2 *R v Nottingham Magistrates' Court ex p Furnell and Marshall* [1996] COD 205, DC.
3 *R v Leicester JJ ex p Barrow* [1991] 2 QB 260 at 290D, CA.
4 Ibid.
5 Per Lord Wilberforce, *Wiseman v Borneman* [1971] AC 297 at 318C, HL.
6 *R v Secretary of State for the Home Department ex p Fayed* [1997] 1 All ER 228, CA.

hearing imposes additional procedural requirements on the decision-maker[1]. In certain circumstances, however, a precise procedural code may exclude additional procedural requirements[2]. For example, there was no breach of natural justice where a case involving either way offences was transferred to the Crown Court under s 53 of the Criminal Justice Act 1991 before the magistrates had been able to hold a hearing to determine the mode of trial. This was because there was no reason why the terms of s 53 should not be given their normal meaning and that did not require magistrates to hold a mode of trial hearing[3]. The High Court has, however, held that the Magistrates' Courts Rules 1981 do not prevent the rules of natural justice imposing additional procedural requirements on magistrates[4].

One of the key factors that needs to be considered when deciding whether the right to a fair hearing imposes additional procedural requirements is the legislative purpose of the statute[5]. Thus, in context of immigration, it has been held that there is no requirement to disclose documents that the Home Secretary relied on when making a decision that is the subject of an appeal. This was because disclosure would frustrate the legislative purpose of ensuring that appeals are considered without delay[6].

In determining whether natural justice is excluded by express procedural requirements, the High Court will also consider whether the express procedural rules provide for all parties affected by the decision to be heard. If the rules do not expressly provide for all persons to be heard when they are affected by a decision, it is likely that the High Court will imply a right. Thus, although magistrates were obliged to order the destruction of a dog under s 4 of the Dangerous Dogs Act 1991, natural justice still required that the owner of that dog should be heard[7].

The rules of natural justice will apply to a case, if they are not excluded by statutory provisions and if there are no express procedural requirements imposed by statute implicitly excluding natural justice[8]. The circumstances of the case will, however, determine the procedural requirements imposed by these rules of natural justice. For example, the rules of natural justice do not entitle everyone, including people who are not a party to the proceedings, to a fair hearing in all circumstances.

2.8.3 Who is entitled to a fair hearing?

A person is normally entitled to a fair hearing where that person will be directly affected by the decision that is to be made. Lord Fraser has stated in the context of judicial reviews of decisions of magistrates' courts that:

---

1   Eg per Lord Bridge, *Lloyd v McMahon* [1987] AC 625 at 702H, HL.
2   *R v Secretary of State for the Environment ex p Hammersmith & Fulham London Borough Council* [1991] 1 AC 521, HL.
3   *R v Bakewell Magistrates' Court and Derbyshire CPS ex p Brewer* [1995] COD 98, DC.
4   *R v Wareham Magistrates' Court ex p Seldon* [1988] 1 WLR 825.
5   Eg *Ridge v Baldwin* [1964] AC 40 at 141, HL.
6   *R v Secretary of State for the Home Department ex p Abdi* [1996] 1 WLR 298 at 315B, HL.
7   *R v Trafford Magistrates' Court ex p Riley* [1995] COD 373, DC.
8   Per Lord Wilberforce, *Wiseman v Borneman* [1971] AC 297 at 318C, HL.

'One of the principles of natural justice is that a person is entitled to adequate notice and opportunity to be heard before any judicial order is pronounced against him, so that he, or someone acting on his behalf, may make such representations, if any, as he sees fit. ... [It] applies to all judicial proceedings, unless its application to a particular class of proceedings has been excluded by Parliament expressly or by necessary implication.'[1]

The right to be heard may arise in circumstances where a person is not a party to proceedings, but is affected by the decision. Lord Diplock has stated that:

'Where an Act of Parliament confers upon an administrative body functions which involve its making decisions which affect to their detriment the rights of other persons or curtail their liberty to do as they please, there is a presumption that Parliament intended that the administrative body should act fairly towards those persons who will be affected by their decision.'[2]

Thus, in the criminal context, the owner of a dog is entitled to be heard before a destruction order is made under the Dangerous Dogs Act 1991 even if proceedings have been discontinued against the owner[3]. The terms of the Police and Criminal Evidence Act 1984 were, however, held to exclude the right of a suspect to be heard when the police applied for the disclosure of special procedure material under the provisions of that Act[4]. This was because the statutory provisions were intended to protect the person holding the documents that were the subject of the application for disclosure.

A party may even have a right to be heard where they will not be directly affected by the outcome. It is enough that a person has a sufficient interest in the outcome. Thus, the prosecution has the right to be heard regarding a warrant of commitment for the non-payment of a confiscation order, when it was the prosecution who had originally sought the confiscation order[5]. A defendant, however, cannot complain about a failure to hear the prosecution as he will not be prejudiced by that failure[6].

2.8.4 The scope of the right to a fair hearing: a right to be heard

If the circumstances of the case mean that there is a right to a fair hearing, a number of basic rights have been identified as being elements of a fair hearing. It has been held repeatedly that a right to a fair hearing gives a person a right to be heard and a right to receive sufficient information to enable him to make informed representations. In addition, there may be further rights depending on the circumstances of the case.

The right to be heard is the most fundamental right. In the context of proceedings in the magistrates' court, it has been repeatedly held that the court

---

1　*Re Hamilton; Re Forrest* [1981] AC 1038 at 1045B, HL.
2　*Hillingdon London Borough Council v Commission for Racial Equality* [1982] AC 779 at 787F, HL.
3　*R v Walton Street Justices ex p Crothers* [1992] COD 473, DC.
4　*R v Manchester Crown Court ex p Taylor* [1988] 1 WLR 705, DC.
5　*R v Harrow Justices ex p DPP* [1991] 1 WLR 395, DC.
6　*R v Liverpool Magistrates' Court ex p Ansen* [1998] 1 All ER 692, DC.

is required to provide persons affected by a decision with an opportunity to be heard. For example, it has been held that magistrates are obliged to provide a person accused of contempt of court with an opportunity to apologise[1]. Magistrates are required to ensure that a community charge defaulter has actually received notice informing him of a hearing to show why he is in default[2]. Similarly, magistrates are required to ensure that a person is given adequate notice of proceedings during which the court is considering issuing a warrant of commitment[3].

One circumstance where there is no duty to give a person an opportunity to be heard is where the court is proposing to make a bind over, because there was a disturbance in the face of the court and a breach of the peace is imminent[4]. The High Court justified this exception to the basic right to a fair hearing on the basis that it was obvious when there was a disturbance in the face of the court. The finding of the High Court may, however, also suggest that a failure to give a party a fair hearing will not result in a decision being quashed if the failure was the result of the conduct of the applicant for judicial review. This is consistent with other case-law in which it has been held that a failure to comply with an express procedural requirement cannot be challenged if the failure was induced by the conduct of the person prejudiced[5].

The entitlement to a fair hearing implies that the decision-maker or court will take account of the representations made by a party. Thus, it is an error for a magistrate to appear to be engaged in another activity instead of listening to the proceedings before him[6].

2.8.5 The scope of the right to a fair hearing: a right to receive information

The right to a fair hearing is closely linked to the right to receive sufficient information to make adequate representations. As Lord Morris stated:

> 'It is well established that the essential requirements of natural justice at least include that before someone is condemned he is to have an opportunity of defending himself, and in order that he may do so that he is to be made aware of the charges or allegations or suggestions which he has to meet. . . . My Lords, here is something which is basic to our system; the importance of upholding it far transcends the significance of any particular case.'[7]

In criminal proceedings in the magistrates' court and in the Crown Court, where the investigation of the offence began on or after 1 April 1997, the disclosure of material held by the prosecution is governed by the Criminal

---

1   *R v Pateley Bridge Magistrates' Court ex p Percy* [1994] COD 453, DC; see also *R v Tamworth Magistrates' Court ex p Walsh* [1994] COD 277, DC, where it was held that a person facing an allegation of contempt should have the opportunity to reflect on their conduct and seek advice.
2   *R v Newcastle upon Tyne Justices ex p Devine* (1998) *The Times*, 7 May.
3   *Re Hamilton; Re Forrest* [1981] AC 1038, HL.
4   *R v North London Metropolitan Magistrate ex p Haywood* [1973] 1 WLR 965, DC.
5   *R v Secretary of State for the Home Department ex p Awais Karni Butt* [1994] Imm AR 11 at 13.
6   *R v Worcester Justices ex p Daniels* (1996) *The Times*, 31 December, DC.
7   *Ridge v Baldwin* [1964] AC 40 at 113, HL.

Procedure and Investigations Act 1996 and the associated codes of conduct. The 1996 Act excludes the common law rules regarding disclosure that existed before 1 April 1997[1].

Although the previous common law rules regarding disclosure have now been abolished, the High Court has recently concluded that the provisions of the Criminal Procedure and Investigations Act 1996 do not exclude the jurisdiction of the courts to impose fresh duties of disclosure on the prosecution. In particular, it held that there can be a duty on a prosecutor to make disclosure before committal although the provisions of the 1996 Act do not apply[2].

In addition, there are still circumstances in criminal cases where a person is entitled to be informed of the case against him by a person other than the prosecution. In particular, there are occasions where the court will be obliged to inform a defendant of matters that he needs to know. For example, where a surety is unrepresented and attends a hearing to consider whether he should forfeit the recognizance, the court should assist the surety by explaining the principles involved in ordinary language[3].

The right to be informed does not only arise in the context of court hearings. For example, the courts have held that prisoners convicted of murder are entitled to be informed of a judge's reasons for making a recommendation regarding tariff, so that they can then make representations to the Secretary of State before he sets the tariff[4].

There is a limit to the extent of disclosure that is required by the right to a fair trial. In a court of law, there is no need for a decision-maker to inform the parties what he is minded to decide if the parties have been given a fair hearing at which they could present their rival cases[5]. Disclosure may also be unnecessary if it would frustrate the purpose of the criminal proceedings. For example, there is no absolute obligation on the police to disclose in advance the evidence that they seek to rely on when making an application for disclosure of special procedure material under the Police and Criminal Evidence Act 1984. Disclosure in these circumstances might frustrate the purpose of the application[6].

2.8.6 The scope of the right to a fair hearing: other rights

Depending on the circumstances of the case, the right to a fair hearing can also entitle parties to sufficient time to prepare[7], the right to representation[8], the

---

1 Criminal Procedure and Investigations Act 1996, s 21.
2 *R v DPP ex p Lee* (1999) *The Times*, 26 April, DC.
3 *R v Uxbridge Justices ex p Heward-Mills* [1983] 1 WLR 56.
4 *R v Secretary of State for the Home Department ex p Doody* [1994] 1 AC 531, HL.
5 See *Hoffman-La Roche (f) & Co AG v Secretary of State for Trade and Industry* [1975] AC 295 at 369D, HL.
6 *R v Inner London Crown Court ex p Baines & Baines* [1988] 1 QB 579, DC.
7 *R v Tamworth Magistrates' Court ex p Walsh* [1994] COD 277, DC.
8 *R v Board of Visitors of HM Prison The Maze ex p Hone* [1988] AC 379 at 392D, HL (NI); see also *R v Leicester JJ ex p Barrow* [1991] 2 QB 260, CA suggesting that in certain circumstances, the right to a fair hearing extends to other forms of legal assistance such as a McKenzie friend.

right to an oral hearing[1], and the right to cross-examine a witness[2]. For example, it is the right to a fair hearing that normally requires magistrates to offer legal representation to a person accused of contempt of court[3].

If a decision-maker is not obliged to ensure that certain standards of procedural fairness are adopted, the decision-maker may have a discretion to adopt those standards. If a decision-maker has that discretion, he must consider exercising it. For example, an immigration officer conducting an interview with a person seeking admission has no obligation to allow legal representatives to attend. He, however, has to consider whether allowing legal representation in the circumstances of the case is appropriate[4]. A failure to consider allowing legal representation when a request is made, could give rise to grounds for applying for judicial review.

2.9 THE DELEGATION OF DECISION-MAKING POWERS

The power that enables a decision-maker or court to make a decision may not allow for the delegation of that power to a third party. This is particularly important in the context of the magistrates' court, where magistrates have to be careful to ensure that it does not appear that they have passed certain decision-making powers to other persons working in the magistrates' court. For example, it is for magistrates to make findings of fact in criminal trials, so the clerk should not retire with the magistrates when the only question before the magistrates is one of fact[5]. Magistrates should not delegate their power to decide whether a bail applicant should appear in handcuffs to police officers[6].

Where it is claimed that a power has been wrongly delegated, the High Court starts by presuming that a power should not be delegated unless there is an express provision allowing for delegation. For example, the High Court has held that the statute allowing the Crown Prosecution Service to review criminal prosecutions did not allow for that review to be delegated to people who were not lawyers[7]. It is particularly likely that the High Court will find that the presumption against the delegation of a power prevents delegation where the power is a judicial power[8].

---

1   *R v Department of Health ex p Gandhi* [1991] 1 WLR 1053 at 1063F, DC.
2   *R v Wellingborough Magistrates' Court ex p Francois* [1994] COD 462, DC; *R v Birmingham City Juvenile Court ex p Birmingham City Council* [1988] 1 WLR 337, CA.
3   *R v Pateley Bridge Justices ex p Percy* [1994] COD 453, DC.
4   *R v Secretary of State for the Home Department ex p Vera Lawson* [1994] Imm AR 58; see also *R v Guildford Crown Court ex p Siderfin* [1990] 2 QB 683, DC, in which it was held that although a person was not entitled to legal representation on an appeal against a refusal to excuse a person from jury service for reasons of conscience, it would be rare that a request for an adjournment to allow legal representation should be refused.
5   *R v Barry (Glamorgan) Justices ex p Kashim* [1953] 2 All ER 1005, DC.
6   *R v Cambridge Justices ex p Peacock* [1993] COD 19, DC.
7   *R v DPP ex p First Division Civil Servants* (1988) *The Times*, 24 May.
8   Eg per Lord Roskill, *R v Manchester Stipendiary Magistrate ex p Hill* [1983] 1 AC 328 at 343D, HL.

The High Court will also consider the nature of the power when it decides whether it can properly be delegated. In particular, it will consider the impact of the exercise of the power on others. As a result, it is not surprising that only the magistrates or their clerks may issue summonses, although magistrates may delegate the receipt of informations to administrative staff[1]. Clearly, the consequence of an error in the receipt of an information is likely to be less serious than an error in the issue of a summons.

2.10 IRRATIONALITY

Irrationality that amounts to error of law is often described as *Wednesbury* unreasonableness. This comes from the statement of Lord Greene in the *Wednesbury* case that:

> '[I]f a decision on a competent matter is so unreasonable that no reasonable authority could ever have come to it, then the courts can interfere.'[2]

Clearly, it is not every mistaken exercise of judgment that can be properly categorised as unreasonable[3]. If the High Court was to intervene by way of judicial review and quash every mistaken exercise of judgment, there would be no distinction between judicial review and appellate jurisdictions[4]. As Lord Hailsham LC has stated:

> 'Two reasonable [persons] can perfectly reasonably come to opposite conclusions on the same set of facts without forfeiting their title to be regarded as reasonable... Not every reasonable exercise of judgment is right, and not every mistaken exercise of judgment is unreasonable.'[5]

The High Court imposes a heavy burden on persons claiming that a decision is irrational. It has been said that a decision is unreasonable if it is 'devoid of any plausible justification'[6], or so 'outrageous in its defiance of logic or of accepted moral standards that no sensible person who had applied his mind to the question to be decided could have arrived at it'[7]. The proof required to show unreasonableness is said to need to be 'overwhelming'[8]. In practice, the high burden on applicants for judicial review who seek to claim irrationality means that relying on irrationality as the only ground for challenge is rare. Instead, it is normally pleaded with other linked complaints such as a failure to take account of relevant factors[9].

---

1   *R v Manchester Stipendiary Magistrate ex p Hill* [1983] 1 AC 328 at 342G.
2   *Associated Provincial Picture Houses Ltd v Wednesbury Corporation* [1948] 1 KB 223 at 230, CA.
3   *Secretary of State for Education and Science v Tameside Metropolitan Borough Council* [1977] AC 1014 at 1070H, HL.
4   Per Lord Ackner, *R v Secretary of State for the Home Department ex p Brind* [1991] 1 AC 696 at 757F, HL.
5   In *Re W (An Infant)* [1971] AC 682 at 700D, HL.
6   Per Lord Diplock, *Bromley London Borough Council v Greater London Council* [1983] 1 AC 768 at 821B, HL.
7   Per Lord Diplock, *Council for Civil Service Unions v Minister for the Civil Service* [1985] AC 374 at 410G, HL.
8   *Associated Provincial Picture Houses Ltd v Wednesbury Corporation* [1948] 1 KB 223 at 230, CA.
9   See **2.11**.

In the context of criminal proceedings, the High Court has quashed the decision of a magistrates' court to accept jurisdiction as being irrational, because the case-law showed that the sentence for the offence was frequently greater than that which the magistrates could impose[1]. The High Court has also quashed a decision to dismiss informations where the prosecution had failed to attend. This was because the failure to attend was the result of misinformation supplied by the court and the prosecutor was attempting to attend court[2].

2.11   RELEVANT FACTORS AND IMPROPER MOTIVE

A failure to take account of relevant factors or taking account of irrelevant factors is a ground of challenge that is closely linked to irrationality. Clearly, a decision that ignores a relevant factor might be said to lack logic. As Lord Templeman has held:

> 'The English courts must, in conformity with the *Wednesbury* principles ... consider whether the Home Secretary has taken into account all relevant matters and has ignored irrelevant matters ... If these conditions are satisfied, then it is said that on *Wednesbury* principles the court can only interfere by way of judicial review if the decision of the Home Secretary is "irrational" or "perverse".'[3]

When deciding what factors are relevant to a decision, and what factors are irrelevant to a decision, the High Court will look at the terms of the legislation that provides for the decision-making power. The High Court will seek to determine whether the statute provides any indication of the relevant factors to be taken into account by the decision-maker[4]. For example, when magistrates are asked to consider making an order depriving an offender of property, they are required to consider the value of the property[5]. Thus, a failure to take account of the value of a car to be forfeited led to that order being quashed[6].

By applying normal principles of statutory construction, the High Court may hold that it is implied that a range of factors is to be taken into account by a decision-maker. For example, when magistrates are asked to consider whether they will rehear a case, they are not restricted to merely considering whether the delay in applying for a rehearing means that the case should not be reheard. This is because Parliament had repealed a previous statutory provision imposing a strict time-limit on the time for applications for rehearing. That implied that the delay was not the only factor that could be taken into account by magistrates when deciding whether to allow a rehearing[7].

If a decision is to be quashed as a result of a failure to approach the issue of relevant and irrelevant factors correctly, it must be shown that the mistake was

---

1   *R v Northampton Magistrates' Court ex p Commissioners of Customs and Excise* [1994] COD 382, DC.
2   *R v Hendon Justices ex p DPP* [1994] QB 167, DC.
3   *R v Secretary of State for the Home Department ex p Brind* [1991] 1 AC 696 at 751D, HL.
4   Per Lord Scarman, *Re Findlay* [1985] AC 318 at 333H, HL.
5   Powers of Criminal Courts Act 1973, s 43(1A)(a).
6   *R v Highbury Magistrate ex p Di Matteo* [1991] 1 WLR 1374, DC.
7   *R v Ealing Magistrates' Court ex p Sahota* (1997) *The Times*, 9 December, DC.

material. This means that the court must be persuaded that the decision might have been different if the irrelevant factor had been ignored or the relevant factor had been taken into account[1]. Thus, a decision of the Crown Court regarding the destruction of a dog should not be quashed as a result of a failure to take account of the dog's disposition. That factor would have made no difference to the final decision of the Crown Court[2].

If the statute does not require particular factors to be taken into account, a decision about the matters to be taken into account in the circumstances of a particular case can only be impugned on limited grounds. The High Court will need to be persuaded that the decision that a particular factor should or should not be taken into account is irrational or otherwise contrary to the principles of public law[3].

The decision about the factors that are to be taken into account is to be distinguished from the decision about the weight to give the various factors. A decision-maker is entitled to give the relevant factors whatever weight he regards as appropriate in all the circumstances of the case. The court will only intervene if the decision regarding the weight that is to be given to the relevant factors is irrational[4].

Closely linked to the concept of relevant and irrelevant factors is the concept of improper motive. A decision can be quashed if it can be shown that the decision-maker was motivated by an improper motive. For example, a decision to arraign a defendant in the Crown Court can be quashed if it was motivated by a desire to avoid the defendant being bailed, as a result of the operation of custody time-limits. This is because the purpose of arraignment is trial management and so a decision to arraign should not be motivated by other concerns[5].

2.12 LEGITIMATE EXPECTATION

An application for judicial review can be based on a claim that a decision-maker has failed to fulfil a legitimate expectation. Applicants for judicial review sometimes claim that they have a legitimate expectation without identifying clearly how their case falls within the categories of circumstances which, it has been held, give rise to a legitimate expectation. A legitimate expectation, however, only arises in certain very limited circumstances and so practitioners acting for applicants should specify precisely how the legitimate expectation arises. Lord Justice Simon Brown has identified three sets of circumstances when a legitimate expectation arises[6]:

---

1   Eg *R v Thurrock Borough Council ex p Tesco Stores Ltd* [1993] 3 PLR 114 at 124D.
2   *R v Teeside Crown Court ex p Bullock* [1996] COD 6, DC.
3   Per Laws J, *R v Secretary of State for Transport ex p Richmond-upon-Thames London Borough Council* [1994] 1 WLR 74 at 95C.
4   Per Lord Keith, *Tesco Stores Ltd v Secretary of State for the Environment* [1995] 1 WLR 759 at 764G, HL.
5   *R v Maidstone Crown Court ex p Clark* [1995] 1 WLR 831, DC.
6   *R v Devon County Council ex p Baker* [1995] 1 All ER 73, CA.

(1) Where the decision-maker has made a clear and unambiguous representation regarding a substantive right which it was reasonable for the applicant to rely on, the applicant may be entitled to that benefit. This, however, cannot give rise to a legitimate expectation if the granting of the substantive right is inconsistent with the decision-maker's statutory duty[1];

(2) Where the applicant has an interest in some ultimate benefit that he hopes to retain (or possibly attain), fairness may require the applicant to be given an opportunity to make representations about the withdrawal of that benefit[2]; and

(3) Where the decision-maker has promised that he will adopt some form of procedure that he would not otherwise be required to adopt, the applicant may be entitled to require the decision-maker to adopt that procedure[3].

Lord Justice Simon Brown also recognised that the term legitimate expectation is sometimes said to encompass the right to a fair procedure generally, but he described this use of the concept as 'superfluous and unhelpful'[4]. The right to a fair hearing is really a separate category of legal error considered earlier in this chapter[5].

Lord Justice Stuart-Smith has analysed the elements of a claim based on legitimate expectation[6]. He held that the applicant must prove:

'(1) A clear and unambiguous representation ...

(2) That since the applicant was not a person to whom any representation was directly made it was within the class of persons who are entitled to rely upon it; or at any rate that it was reasonable for the applicant to rely upon it without more...

(3) That it did so rely upon it.

(4) That it did so to its detriment. While in some cases it is not altogether clear that this is a necessary ingredient, since a public body is entitled to change its policy if it is acting in good faith, it is a necessary ingredient where, as here, an applicant is saying, "You cannot alter your policy now in my case; it is too late".

(5) That there is no overriding interest arising from [the respondent's] duties and responsibilities ... which entitled [them] to change their policy to the detriment of the applicant.

The burden of proving the first four points is, in my judgement, upon the applicant ... As to the fifth requirement, it seems to me that that is a matter for the [respondent] to establish.'[7]

It is important to recognise it is not always necessary for the applicant to show that they relied on the legitimate expectation to their detriment[8].

---

1 *R v Devon County Council ex p Baker* [1995] 1 All ER 73 at 88E.
2 Ibid at 88J.
3 Ibid at 89E.
4 Ibid at 89B.
5 See **2.8**.
6 *R v Jockey Club ex p RAM Racecourses* [1993] 2 All ER 225, CA.
7 Ibid at 236H.
8 Per Stuart-Smith LJ, *Francisco Javier Jaramillo-Silva v Secretary of State for the Home Department* [1994] Imm AR 352 at 357, CA.

In the context of criminal proceedings, the concept of legitimate expectation has been applied so that a decision by one bench of magistrates that a matter would be dealt with summarily gave rise to a legitimate expectation that a second bench would deal with the case in the same way in the absence of new information[1]. It is important to note that the conduct of the magistrates' court can give rise to a legitimate expectation that binds the Crown Court. Thus, a legitimate expectation arising in the magistrates' court that favourable reports will mean that a defendant will not be sentenced to imprisonment binds the Crown Court[2].

2.13 INCONSISTENCY

Inconsistency has long been recognised as an error that allows the court to intervene. That is because good public administration requires consistent decision-making[3]. It is also linked to the concept of irrationality, as an inconsistent decision may be said to lack logic. As Lord Russell CJ held:

> 'I do not mean to say that there may not be cases in which it would be the duty of the Court to condemn by-laws, made under such authority as these were made, as invalid because unreasonable. But unreasonable in what sense? If, for instance, they were found to be partial and unequal in their operation as between different classes; if they were manifestly unjust; if they disclosed bad faith; if they involved such oppressive or gratuitous interference with the rights of those subject to them as could find no justification in the minds of reasonable men, the Court might well say, "Parliament never intended to give authority to make such rules; they are unreasonable and ultra vires".'[4]

This principle has been applied in the context of immigration to allow the courts to quash an immigration rule made pursuant to primary legislation, because the rule discriminated between two classes of apparently similar people[5]. In crime, this principle could be used to challenge the by-laws under which a criminal prosecution was being brought if the by-laws discriminate.

Although it is clear that consistency is a matter that can be raised in an application for judicial review, the High Court will be reluctant to find that a decision of a criminal court should be quashed because it is inconsistent with a decision of the court in an apparently similar case[6]. The High Court is aware that two cases will never be precisely the same[7]. This means that in practice, it is difficult to argue that a conviction should be quashed because it is inconsistent with another decision of the convicting court.

---

1   *R v Staines Magistrates' Court ex p Utting* [1994] COD 189, DC.
2   *R v Isleworth Crown Court ex p Irwin* (1991) *The Times*, 5 December, DC.
3   *R v Hertfordshire County Council ex p Cheung* (1986) *The Times*, 4 April, CA.
4   *Kruse v Johnson* [1898] 2 QBD 91 at 99, CA.
5   *R v Immigration Appeal Tribunal ex p Begum* [1986] Imm AR 385 at 394.
6   *R v Special Adjudicator ex p Kandasamy* [1994] Imm AR 333.
7   *R v Secretary of State for the Home Department ex p Mohammed Yasin* [1995] Imm AR 118, CA.

2.14 CIRCUMSTANCES WHERE THERE IS A DUTY TO GIVE REASONS

As has already been noted, there is often a need for a decision-maker or court to give reasons if errors of law are to be identified. In judicial review proceedings, it may be possible to argue that a decision-maker or court erred by failing to give reasons if the applicant for judicial review can show that the decision-maker has a duty to give reasons. In some circumstances, the legislation governing the decision will require the decision-maker to give reasons. Clearly, where a defendant is appealing by way of case stated, the court will be required to state a case. He can only refuse to state a case if he views the appeal as frivolous[1]. If the reasons are inadequate, the High Court can send the case that has been stated back to the magistrates' court for amendment[2].

If there is no legislative requirement to give reasons, there is no general duty implied by the common law requiring reasons for all administrative and court decisions[3]. In particular, the magistrates' court has no general duty to give reasons for its decisions[4], because a defendant may appeal to the Crown Court or alternatively obtain reasons by appealing by way of case stated[5]. Similarly, there is no general duty imposed on courts that requires reasons for procedural rulings during criminal trials[6]. There is, however, a duty on professional judges to give reasons for their decisions[7].

Whether there is a duty to give reasons depends on the circumstances of the case[8]. It has been suggested that the court must consider whether fairness demands reasons when it decides whether there is a duty to give reasons in a particular case[9]. There have been few judicial attempts to define the circumstances in which fairness means that there is a common law duty to give reasons. However, Mr Justice Sedley has stated that:

> '(1) [T]here is no general duty to give reasons for a decision, but there are classes of case where there is such a duty. (2) One such class is where the subject matter is an interest so highly regarded by the law (for example, personal liberty), that fairness requires that reasons, at least for particular decisions, be given as of right.

---

1 Crown Court Rules 1982, SI 1982/1109, r 26(6); Magistrates' Courts Act 1980, s 111(5).
2 Supreme Court Act 1981, s 28A(2).
3 Per Lord Mustill, *R v Secretary of State for the Home Department ex p Doody* [1994] 1 AC 531 at 564E, HL.
4 *R v The Southend Stipendiary Magistrate ex p Rochford District Council* [1995] Env LR 1 at 6, but see *R v Burton-upon-Trent Justices ex p Hussain* (1997) 9 Admin LR 233, in which a duty was said to arise when magistrates were acting as an appellate authority.
5 Per Lord Donaldson MR, *R v Civil Service Appeal Board ex p Cunningham* [1991] 4 All ER 310 at 318A, CA.
6 *R v Wallace* (1996) *The Times*, 31 December, PC.
7 *R v Knightsbridge Crown Court ex p International Sporting Club Ltd* [1982] QB 304 at 314H, DC.
8 Per Lord Mustill, *R v Secretary of State for the Home Department ex p Doody* [1994] 1 AC 531 at 564E, HL.
9 Per Lord Donaldson MR, *R v Civil Service Appeal Board ex p Cunningham* [1991] 4 All ER 310 at 319B, CA and De Smith, Woolf and Jowell, *Judicial Review of Administrative Action*, (Sweet & Maxwell, 1995), 5th edn, para 9–047.

(3)(a) Another such class is where the decision appears aberrant. Here fairness may require reasons so that the recipient may know whether the aberration is in the legal sense real (and so challengeable) or apparent; (b) it follows that this class does not include decisions which are themselves challengeable by reference only to the reasons for them. A pure exercise of academic judgement is such a decision. And (c) Procedurally, the grant of leave in such cases will depend upon prima facie evidence that something has gone wrong.'[1]

In practice, the High Court will look at a number of factors when it decides whether fairness implies a duty to give reasons. As has already been noted, the existence of a right of appeal may mean that there is no duty to give reasons[2]. The difficulties faced by the court when it seeks to identify whether grounds for judicial review exist when there are no reasons is also a factor that is taken into account when deciding whether there is a need to give reasons[3]. Those difficulties may explain why there is a clear trend towards requiring greater openness from decision-makers[4]. The greater openness means that reasons are required in an increasing variety of circumstances.

The High Court's willingness to consider a failure to give reasons in a case where the decision appears to be 'aberrant' is important. Where the circumstances of the case suggest that a particular decision should have been taken if the decision was to accord with the legislative purpose of the decision-maker's power but another decision was taken, the absence of reasons may lead the court to draw inferences that the decision-maker had no good reasons for the decision[5]. Lord Reid stated that:

> 'If it is the Minister's duty not to act so as to frustrate the policy and objects of the Act, and if it were to appear from all the circumstances of the case that that has been the effect of the Minister's refusal, then it appears to me that the court must be entitled to act.'[6]

The court will, however, be reluctant to draw such an inference, as that would be contrary to the absence of a general duty to give reasons.

One other guide to circumstances that give rise to a duty to supply reasons is the precedents showing circumstances, where a duty to give reasons has been found and where it has been found that there is no duty to give reasons. We have already set out some of these precedents. In addition, in criminal law a duty to give reasons has been held to arise where the Crown Court is acting in an appellate capacity[7] and when a judge issues a warrant for search and seizure

---

1   *R v Higher Education Funding Council ex p Institute of Dental Surgery* [1994] 1 WLR 242 at 263A, DC.
2   Per Lord Donaldson MR, *R v Civil Service Appeal Board ex p Cunningham* [1991] 4 All ER 310 at 318A, CA. See also *R v Burton-upon-Trent Justices ex p Hussain* (1997) 9 Admin LR 233, in which a duty was said to arise when magistrates were acting as an appellate authority.
3   Per Lord Mustill, *R v Secretary of the State for the Home Department ex p Doody* [1994] 1 AC 531 at 565F, HL.
4   *R v Secretary of the State for the Home Department ex p Doody* [1994] 1 AC 531 at 561E, HL.
5   *Padfield v Minister of Agriculture Fisheries & Food* [1968] AC 997 at 1032G, HL.
6   Ibid.
7   *R v Harrow Crown Court ex p Dave* (1994) 99 Cr App R 114, DC.

of documents[1]. Although the Crown Court has a duty to give reasons when it acts in its appellate function, it has been held that there is no duty to give reasons where a Crown Court judge refuses to extend the time for appealing against a conviction in the magistrates' court. This is because the decision is procedural, not judicial[2].

2.14.1 The importance of requesting reasons

Asking for reasons is always important, because it is likely to be impossible to challenge a failure to give reasons if there has been no application for reasons[3]. In addition, if there is no duty to give reasons, the decision-maker will still have a discretion to give reasons[4]. The exercise of that discretion is governed by the same principles as the exercise of any other discretion. This means that a failure to give reasons could be challenged if it were shown that the exercise of the discretion was unlawful. For example, a failure to give reasons where there is a discretion to give reasons could be challenged if it could be shown that the failure to give reasons is irrational.

2.14.2 The scope of the duty to give reasons

Where there is a duty to give reasons, the reasons required need not be very extensive. A sentence or two giving some indication of the court's reasoning may be all that is required[5]. Where the Crown Court is acting in an appellate capacity, the presiding judge must merely demonstrate that the court has identified the main contentious issues in the case and explain how it has resolved them[6].

Although the reasons given need not be extensive, Lord Bridge has stated that reasons have to be 'proper, intelligible and adequate'[7]. He continued as follows:

> 'If the reasons given are improper they will reveal some flaw in the decision-making process which will be open to challenge on some ground other than the failure to give reasons. If the reasons given are unintelligible, this will be equivalent to giving no reasons at all. The difficulty arises in determining whether the reasons given are adequate, whether... they deal with the substantial points that have been raised or ... enable the reader to know what conclusion the decision-maker has reached on the principal controversial issues. What degree of particularity is required? ... I do not think one can safely say more in general terms than that the degree of particularity required will depend entirely on the nature of the issues falling for decision.'[8]

---

1   *R v Central Criminal Court ex p Propend Finance Property Ltd* [1994] COD 386, DC; *Gross v Southwark Crown Court* [1998] 11 CL 137, DC.
2   *R v Stafford Crown Court ex p Reid* (1995) *The Independent*, 13 March, DC.
3   *R v The Crown Court of Southwark ex p Samuel* [1995] COD 249, DC.
4   *R v Secretary of State for the Home Department ex p Fayed* [1997] 1 All ER 228, CA.
5   *R v Southwark Crown Court ex p Brooke* [1997] COD 81, DC.
6   *R v Harrow Crown Court ex p Dave* (1994) 99 Cr App R 114, DC.
7   *Save Britain's Heritage v Number 1 Poultry Limited* [1991] 1 WLR 153 at 166H, HL.
8   Ibid.

Even where a duty to give reasons arises, the absence of reasons will not necessarily result in the High Court quashing the decision. The High Court will not act if there is obviously no injustice in the failure to give reasons[1]. If the High Court does act, it may not quash the decision that is the subject of the judicial review. Instead, it may merely act to require the decision-maker to provide adequate reasons. Thus, reasons given during the course of a judicial review may result in the court refusing to grant relief[2]. However, the court will be concerned to ensure that the reasons given are not ex post facto reasons that were not the real reasons relied on at the time of the decision[3]. There are also certain circumstances where there are limitations on a decision-maker's ability to give additional reasons during the course of judicial review proceedings. Where the Crown Court is acting in its appellate capacity reasons should be given contemporaneously[4]. In addition, where the additional reasons contradict the original reasons the High Court will not take account of the additional reasons[5].

2.15 BAD FAITH

Bad faith is a self-standing ground of judicial review. In practice, however, it is extremely unusual for an application for judicial review to be based on bad faith and so it is difficult to be clear about the scope of bad faith. This is partly because it is likely to be easier to prove bias or one of the other grounds of challenge[6]. Practitioners should also be aware of the requirements of the Bar Code of Conduct that barristers should not plead fraud unless there is 'reasonably credible material' that establishes a prima facie case[7].

2.16 PROPORTIONALITY

Proportionality allows a court to quash a decision if the interference with an individual's interests is out of proportion to the interests of the State that led to the decision. At the time of writing, the High Court will not quash a decision because it is said to be out of proportion when it considers applications for judicial review[8]. Judges considering judicial review applications have, however,

---

1   *R v Winchester Crown Court ex p Morris and Others* [1996] COD 104, DC.
2   *R v Legal Aid Area No 8 (Northern) Committee ex p Angell* (1991) 3 Admin LR 189 at 207D.
3   *S v Special Educational Needs Tribunal* [1995] 1 WLR 1627 at 1637B.
4   *R v Snaresbrook Crown Court ex p Input Management Ltd* (1999) *The Independent*, 15 March, DC.
5   *Re C and P* [1992] COD 29 at 30.
6   See **2.8**.
7   See para 606(c) of the Code of Conduct of the Bar of England and Wales.
8   Although the English courts will not apply proportionality to hold that a decision should be quashed because the interference with a person's interests is out of proportion to the aim of the decision-maker, Mr Justice Moses recently applied the principle to interpret the meaning of a statutory provision in *R v Secretary of State for Health ex p Eastside Cheese Company* (1998) *The Times*, 1 December.

anticipated for some time that the concept of proportionality might become part of English law[1].

For some years, the European Court of Human Rights has applied the concept of proportionality. For example, in cases involving alleged interferences with the right to private life and family life under Article 8, the court will determine whether the interference was proportionate to the legitimate aim pursued[2]. Thus, a decision to deport a person as a result of their criminal offending will be a breach of Article 8 of the Convention for the Protection of Human Rights and Fundamental Freedoms if the interference with their private and family life is not proportionate to the aim of maintaining public order[3].

It is important to be aware that proportionality is only relevant in relation to particular Articles of the Convention. These Articles all state that breaches of the rights that they protect can be justified on the grounds set out in the Article. For example, Article 8 allows for interferences with rights to private and family life as Article 8(2) provides specific grounds for justifying such interferences[4]. In contrast, Article 3 provides no grounds for justifying inhuman and degrading treatment[5].

We consider the European Convention on Human Rights later in this book, but it is important to note that the enactment of the Human Rights Act 1998 will lead to the High Court determining issues of proportionality in the context of claims that Convention rights have been breached. This may lead to proportionality being adopted as a ground for judicial review in circumstances where it is not said that the Convention has been breached.

If proportionality does become generally recognised as a ground for judicial review, it will significantly change the nature of judicial review. As we noted earlier, at present the High Court will normally not quash a decision because it is wrong[6]. Instead the court will need to be satisfied that the decision is irrational. Proportionality would clearly allow judicial review applicants to challenge the merits of decisions in a wider range of circumstances as it is arguable that a rational decision may breach the requirements of proportionality.

---

1 Eg per Lord Diplock in *Council of Civil Service Unions v Minister for the Civil Service* [1985] AC 374 at 410E, HL.
2 *Z v Finland* (1997) 25 EHRR 371 at para 96.
3 *Moustaquim v Belgium* (1991) 13 EHRR 802.
4 See **13.5**.
5 See **13.5**.
6 See **2.10**.

Chapter 3

THE GROUNDS OF APPEAL BY WAY OF CASE STATED AND AN APPLICATION FOR HABEAS CORPUS

3.1 THE IMPORTANCE OF IDENTIFYING THE CATEGORY OF LEGAL ERROR WHICH HAS LED TO A DEFENDANT APPEALING BY WAY OF CASE STATED OR APPLYING FOR HABEAS CORPUS

For reasons set out below, the grounds that give rise to an appeal by way of case stated and an application for habeas corpus will be similar to those that give rise to an application for judicial review. During an appeal by way of case stated or an application for habeas corpus, it is likely that practitioners will be required to identify the category of legal error claimed to have occurred. For example, the Crown Court Rules require a person seeking to appeal by way of case stated shall 'state the ground on which the decision of the Crown Court is questioned'[1].

Identifying the category of legal error said to have occurred is also important as this adds credibility to the appeal or application. It gives the appearance to a judge that the legal advisers acting for an appellant or an applicant understand the nature of the proceedings. Advisers acting for respondents in appeals by way of case stated or applications for habeas corpus will want to understand the categories of legal error that can be raised, so that they can argue that the High Court has no jurisdiction to consider the matter.

3.2 THE GROUNDS UPON WHICH A PARTY MAY APPEAL BY WAY OF CASE STATED

The scope of the grounds that can be raised on an appeal by way of case stated is defined by statutory provisions. These statutory provisions provide that a person is able to appeal where a decision is wrong in law or in excess of jurisdiction[2].

---

1 Crown Court Rules 1982, SI 1982/1109, r 26(2).
2 Supreme Court Act 1981, s 28(1); Magistrates' Courts Act 1980, s 111(1).

3.3 DIFFERENCES BETWEEN THE SCOPE OF JUDICIAL REVIEW AND AN APPEAL BY WAY OF CASE STATED

Although the procedure and the remedies available to the High Court when it considers an appeal by way of case stated are significantly different to those in judicial review, the type of legal error that can be challenged by way of an appeal by way of case stated is probably not in principle significantly different. The terms that have been used to define the scope of judicial review and appeals by way of case stated may appear to be different, but the distinction is unlikely to be of any real significance.

The statutory scope of an appeal by way of case stated allows the High Court to consider errors of law and jurisdictional errors[1]. At first glance this appears to contrast with the grounds for judicial review, which were held by Lord Diplock to be 'illegality', 'irrationality' and 'procedural impropriety'[2]. A closer examination of the scope of these two jurisdictions suggests that the scope is very similar.

First, although Lord Diplock did not explicitly state that decisions that were in excess of jurisdiction could be challenged by way of judicial review, it is clear that decisions that are in excess of jurisdiction may be challenged by way of judicial review[3]. The High Court recognises that a decision that is taken outside the decision-maker's jurisdiction is an illegal decision[4]. As a result, the express statutory provision allowing an appeal by way of case stated, where a decision is 'in excess of jurisdiction', does not mean that an appeal by way of case stated has a wider scope than judicial review.

Decisions that are 'wrong in law' are also likely to be open to challenge by judicial review. That is because the High Court is usually able to consider judicial review applications relating to errors of law within jurisdiction, as well as those in excess of jurisdiction[5]. The only circumstances in a criminal context, where the High Court may not be able to consider judicial review applications relating to errors of law that are within jurisdiction, arise where it considers decisions of the Crown Court. There is some authority to suggest that in these circumstances, the High Court can only consider errors of law that are apparent on the face of the record[6]. In these circumstances, an appeal by way of

---

1   Supreme Court Act 1981, s 28(1); Magistrates' Courts Act 1980, s 111(1).
2   *Council of Civil Service Unions v Minister for the Civil Service* [1985] AC 374 at 410D, HL; see **2.2** for the full quote.
3   See **2.5** for a consideration of jurisdiction as a ground for judicial review.
4   Eg per Lord Browne-Wilkinson, *R v Hull University Visitor ex p Page* [1993] AC 682 at 701E, HL.
5   *Anisminic Ltd v Foreign Compensation Commission* [1969] 2 AC 147, HL; see **2.2.1** considering the application of the decision in *Anisminic* to criminal cases.
6   *R v Knightsbridge Crown Court ex p International Sporting Club Ltd* [1982] QB 304, DC; see also the discussion at **2.2.1**.

case stated may have a wider scope as it may be possible to challenge an error of law that is not apparent on the face of the record[1].

The scope of judicial review is also unlikely to be wider than the scope of an appeal by case stated. Although Lord Diplock's statement of the errors that can lead to a judicial review appeared to distinguish between 'illegality' and other grounds for judicial review, the other grounds are in reality other species of errors of law. As Lord Browne-Wilkinson has said:

> 'If the decision maker exercises his powers outside the jurisdiction conferred, in a manner which is procedurally irregular or is *Wednesbury* unreasonable, he is acting ultra vires his powers and therefore unlawfully.'[2]

Similarly, the Court of Appeal has recently held that a decision is not 'in accordance with the law' if it is contrary to the 'established principles of administrative or common law'[3]. As a decision that can be challenged on grounds of 'irrationality' or 'procedural impropriety' is clearly contrary to established principles of administrative law, the decision of the Court of Appeal would imply it is also illegal. This all suggests that a decision that is either flawed for 'irrationality' or 'procedural impropriety' is in fact 'wrong in law'. As a result, the scope of judicial review is no wider than an appeal by way of case stated.

3.4 PRACTICAL RESTRICTIONS ON THE GROUNDS WHICH CAN BE RAISED DURING AN APPEAL BY CASE STATED

In the light of the above, it is likely that in theory a person who wishes to challenge a decision of the Crown Court or the magistrates' court can raise the same grounds in a judicial review as they can in an appeal by way of case stated and vice versa. The decision about whether to proceed by way of judicial review or by way of appeal by case stated is normally therefore based on the different procedures and remedies rather than on the grounds that can be raised[4].

The most significant procedural limitation on an appeal by way of case stated is the format in which a case is stated for the consideration of the High Court. When appealing against a decision of the magistrates' court, the case stated

---

1   As set out at **2.2.1**, the limitation on the scope of judicial review of decisions of the Crown Court is unlikely to cause problems in practice. As a result, the wider scope of an appeal by case stated may well only be of theoretical interest.
2   *R v Hull University Visitor ex p Page* [1993] AC 682 at 701D, HL.
3   Per Peter Gibson LJ, *Secretary of State for the Home Department v Dhudi Saleban Abdi* [1996] Imm AR 148 at 157, CA.
4   See Chapter 4 for a discussion of the relative merits of applications for judicial review and appeals by way of case stated. In particular, see: **4.9** where the authority for the proposition that there can be no appeal by way of case stated from an interim decision of the courts is set out; **4.14** et seq for a discussion of the relative merits of appeal by way of case stated and judicial review following a conviction or acquittal; and **4.17** et seq for a discussion of the relative merits of an appeal by way of case stated and judicial review following a sentence.

should include the facts found and the questions of law or jurisdiction on which an opinion is requested[1]. When appealing against a decision of the Crown Court, the case stated should include the facts found by the Crown Court, the submissions of the parties, the decision complained of and the question on which the opinion of the High Court is sought[2]. Affidavit evidence explaining what happened during the court proceedings is not normally admitted, because the case stated should be the focus of the legal argument.

Certain grounds of legal error are only likely to be made out with affidavit evidence proving facts relied on. In particular, where the legal error alleged relates to the procedure adopted in the court, the court is only likely to be able to consider the procedure adopted if it has affidavit evidence setting out the procedure adopted. Thus, challenging by way of appeal by way of case stated, a decision taken in breach of natural justice is not appropriate[3]. It would also be unlikely that one could raise a claim relating to bias during an appeal by way of case stated[4]. In practice, the only errors that are normally raised on an appeal by way of case stated are those categorised in Chapter 2 as falling within the headings of illegality[5] and a failure to take account of relevant factors or taking account of irrelevant factors or acting with an improper motive[6]. A finding of fact that is said to be irrational or perverse could also be challenged by an appeal by way of case stated[7]. This is, however, rarely done in practice as there are normally procedural advantages associated with an appeal to the Crown Court against a conviction by magistrates which is said to be unreasonable[8].

3.5 THE DIFFERENCE BETWEEN JUDICIAL REVIEW AND HABEAS CORPUS

The distinction between habeas corpus and judicial review does not primarily relate to the grounds of challenge[9]. Instead it relates to the subject matter of the challenge. Like judicial review, habeas corpus is concerned with the legality of executive action. Habeas corpus is, however, only the correct form of proceedings where there is a direct challenge to the jurisdiction to detain a

---

1 Magistrates' Courts Rules 1981, SI 1981/552, r 81(1).
2 Crown Court Rules 1982, SI 1982/1109, r 26(13).
3 *R v Wandsworth Justices ex p Read* [1942] 1 KB 281.
4 In *Johnson v Leicestershire Constabulary* (1998) *The Times*, 7 October, DC, an appeal by way of case stated did raise an allegation of bias. In this case, there was no dispute about the facts so there was no need to rely on affidavit evidence.
5 See **2.3** to **2.5**. A finding of fact that was made where there was no evidence to support that finding is regarded as illegal. See, eg *R v Bedwelty Justices ex p Williams* [1997] AC 225, HL.
6 See **2.11**.
7 *Bracegirdle v Oxley* [1947] 1 KB 349, DC.
8 In particular, the case stated will rarely include details of the evidence presented. See **9.7**.
9 *R v Secretary of State for the Home Department ex p Rahman* [1996] 4 All ER 945 at 953J, CA.

person[1]. Even then, it should normally only be used where there is no other appropriate form of proceedings that can be used to challenge the detention[2]. It is not appropriate to challenge the legality of a decision that has resulted in detention. This is why habeas corpus is no longer used to challenge the legality of convictions[3].

It is also important to recognise that even where the detention is being directly challenged, habeas corpus may not be the appropriate form of proceedings. Lord Donaldson considered the scope of the two proceedings and stated:

> '*A writ of habeas corpus* will issue where someone is detained without any authority or the purported authority is beyond the powers of the person authorising the detention and so is unlawful. *The remedy of judicial review* is available where the decision sought to be impugned is within the powers of the person taking it but, due to procedural error, a misappreciation of the law, a failure to take account of relevant matters, a taking account of irrelevant matters or the fundamental unreasonableness of the decision or action, it should never have been taken. In such a case the decision or action is lawful, unless and until it is set aside by a court of competent jurisdiction.'[4] [Lord Donaldson's emphasis]

Although recent cases call into question Lord Donaldson's suggestion that decisions that are within the powers of a decision-maker are lawful until they are set aside[5], the courts have shown no enthusiasm for extending the scope of habeas corpus. Instead, they suggest that habeas corpus can only be used to challenge a very limited range of decisions where there is no other effective remedy or where it has become the accepted form of proceedings[6]. In a criminal context, habeas corpus is often used in extradition proceedings in conjunction with judicial review. It may also be the appropriate remedy to challenge decisions in the Crown Court that have directly resulted in a defendant's detention, if those decisions are outside the statutory scope of judicial review. Thus, it was used to challenge a sham arraignment intended to defeat custody time-limits[7].

---

1   In *Re S-C (Mental patient: Habeas Corpus)* [1996] QB 599 at 611B, CA; see also *Re Bone* [1995] COD 94, DC in which the High Court allowed an application for habeas corpus challenging detention when a remand in custody exceeded the statutory limits on a period in remand.
2   In *Re Barker* (1998) *The Times*, 14 October, CA; although practitioners occasionally apply for habeas corpus as applications appear to be listed before applications for judicial review.
3   *R v Parkhurst Prison Governor ex p Philpot* [1960] 1 WLR 115, DC.
4   *R v Secretary of State for the Home Department ex p Cheblak* [1991] 2 All ER 319 at 322J, CA, cited with approval by Simon Brown LJ in *R v Oldham Justices and Another ex p Cawley* [1996] 1 All ER 464 at 477J, DC.
5   Eg per Lord Irvine, *Boddington v British Transport Police* [1998] 2 WLR 639 at 646H, HL.
6   Per Simon Brown LJ, *R v Oldham Justices and Another ex p Cawley* [1996] 1 All ER 464 at 477F, DC.
7   *R v Maidstone Crown Court ex p Clark* [1995] 1 WLR 831, DC; see also Simon Brown LJ in *R v Oldham Justices and Another ex p Cawley* [1996] 1 All ER 464 at 477F, DC.

Chapter 4

WHEN SHOULD CRIMINAL PROCEEDINGS BE BROUGHT IN THE HIGH COURT?

4.1 INTRODUCTION

The statutory provisions that give rise to the High Court's jurisdiction to consider appeals by way of case stated limits the scope of that jurisdiction. In particular, in the context of criminal proceedings, an appeal by way of case stated is only available to challenge final decisions of the Crown Court and the magistrate's court[1]. In the remainder of this chapter, we consider the circumstances when it is possible to bring an application for judicial review, an appeal by way of case stated and an application for habeas corpus. If we do not refer to a particular jurisdiction of the High Court, such as appeal by way of case stated or an application for habeas corpus, it is because the particular jurisdiction clearly cannot arise in the circumstances that we are considering.

4.2 POLICE INVESTIGATIONS AND OTHER OPERATIONS

Police officers are often required to make decisions during criminal investigations. For example, they have to decide whether to apply for search warrants, arrest suspects and charge a person with a criminal charge. In principle, there is no reason why a judicial review should not be brought to challenge any of these decisions, because it is clear that police officers are public officials charged with powers and duties. Thus, bringing a judicial review application arguing that a police officer misunderstood the scope of the statutory provisions that govern the exercise of police powers should be possible.

In practice, judicial review is unlikely to be the correct procedure to challenge police operations, because there are normally factual disputes in cases that involve alleged illegal police activities. For example, the police are unlikely to accept that they lacked the reasonable suspicion needed to arrest a suspect. We have already noted that the High Court is reluctant to consider factual disputes during judicial review proceedings[2]. As a result, unless there is no factual dispute, the High Court will be reluctant to consider judicial reviews of alleged cases of police misconduct.

---

1   Supreme Court Act 1981, s 28(1); Magistrates' Courts Act 1980 s 111(1); see also **4.9** for further details of the limitations on the scope of appeal by way of case stated.
2   See **2.2.3** for a consideration of the High Court's reluctance to consider judicial reviews raising factual disputes.

For example, although the High Court recently considered a judicial review of a search warrant, it did note in passing judgment that judicial review would only be an appropriate cause of action in the 'clearest of cases'[1]. That is because challenges to search warrants normally involve a fact-finding exercise. Normally, the cause of action that should be used to challenge an alleged illegal search warrant is a private law action. The court noted that in a private law action against an illegal search warrant, it would still be possible to obtain speedy interim relief[2].

One exception to this rule is where it is alleged that the police have adopted an alleged unlawful policy to govern their activities. In these circumstances, it is unlikely that there will be a factual dispute about the terms of that policy, as the policy will be in the public domain. In addition, showing that there is any cause of action in tort may be difficult, as a person may not have suffered any obvious loss. As a result, a judicial review application claiming that the policy is illegal may well be the correct form of proceedings.

For example, the High Court and the Court of Appeal recently considered a judicial review claiming that the policy of a police force regarding the disclosure of the identities of sex offenders was illegal[3]. The High Court held that, as a matter of public law, there was a presumption that details of police investigations should not be disclosed. This presumption was independent of any cause of action in tort for breach of confidence. As a result, the High Court could quash a police policy that was contrary to this principle of public law, although on the particular facts the judicial review was not successful[4]. The appeal to the Court of Appeal did not result in that ruling being quashed[5].

In bringing a judicial review of a police power, the applicants will need to be aware that Chief Constables have a wide discretion to deploy their resources as they feel fit taking account of the overall resources available. For example, there is no obligation on a Chief Constable to take all steps possible to enable the lawful shipment of animals to continue[6].

When practitioners are considering whether a person can bring a judicial review of a police policy, they will need to be satisfied that the person who is seeking to apply for judicial review has sufficient interest to bring the application[7]. As a result, it may well be important although not essential for an applicant for judicial review to show how they have been affected by the police policy.

---

1   Per Mr Justice Jowitt, *R v Chief Constable of the Warwickshire Constabulary and Another ex p Fitzpatrick and Others* [1998] 1 All ER 65 at 80C, DC.
2   Ibid at 80E.
3   *R v Chief Constable of the North Wales Police and Others ex p Thorpe* [1998] 3 WLR 57, CA; *R v Chief Constable of North Wales ex p AB* [1997] 4 All ER 691, DC.
4   *R v Chief Constable of North Wales ex p AB* [1997] 4 All ER 691, DC.
5   *R v Chief Constable of the North Wales Police and Others ex p Thorpe* [1998] 3 WLR 57, CA.
6   *R v Chief Constable of Sussex ex p International Trader's Ferry Ltd* [1998] 3 WLR 1260, HL.
7   See **1.10** for a more detailed consideration of the requirements of standing to bring an application for judicial review.

4.3 THE DECISION OF A PUBLIC AUTHORITY TO INSTITUTE A PROSECUTION

The decision of a public authority about whether to prosecute a person is subject to judicial review[1]. Similarly, it is possible to bring a judicial review of a decision to reinstate proceedings[2]. In practice, however, it will rarely be in a defendant's interest to seek to judicially review the decision of a prosecuting authority to prosecute him. This is partly because the High Court is unlikely to exercise its discretion to quash a decision to prosecute. For example, the High Court has held that it will only quash a decision to prosecute in the most extreme circumstances, such as where the decision to prosecute was the result of fraud, corruption or mala fides[3]. The only exception to this general reluctance to quash decisions to prosecute may arise when the High Court considers prosecutions brought against juveniles. The High Court has held that it would be willing to quash a decision to prosecute a juvenile if that decision was clearly contrary to the policy of the prosecuting authority that was designed to protect the public interest[4].

It is not only as a result of the High Court's reluctance to quash a decision to prosecute that a defendant is unlikely to seek a judicial review of a decision to prosecute. A defendant is also unlikely to seek judicial review, as he will almost certainly be able to challenge the decision to prosecute during the criminal proceedings. First, the defendant will be able to argue that the prosecution should be stayed as an abuse of process. Criminal proceedings that are 'oppressive and vexatious' should be stayed as an abuse of process[5]. As a result, it is very difficult to conceive of circumstances where the High Court could quash a decision to prosecute during judicial review proceedings, but the criminal courts could not stay proceedings as an abuse of process. If such circumstances did arise, it is now clear that criminal courts have jurisdiction to consider public law defences. In particular it is able to consider arguments about the 'invalidity of subordinate legislation *or an administrative act under it*'[6] (emphasis added) unless the statute excludes this jurisdiction. The use of the phrase 'administrative act' clearly implies that a public law challenge to the decision to prosecute might be raised as a defence.

The availability of public law defences in the criminal courts is a matter that the High Court is likely to take account of when it considers whether to exercise its discretion to quash a decision to prosecute. As a result, practitioners representing prosecuting authorities should normally raise the availability of

---

1　Eg *R v Elmbridge Borough Council ex p Activeoffice Ltd* (1997) *The Times*, 29 December, in which the applicant unsuccessfully tried to challenge a decision of a local authority to prosecute in a planning matter.
2　Eg *R v DPP ex p Burke* [1997] 2 CL 184, DC holding that there was no need for special circumstances before the CPS decided to reinstate proceedings. It was enough that the decision to discontinue was clearly wrong.
3　Per Steyn LJ, *R v Panel on Take-overs and Mergers ex p Fayed* (1992) *The Times*, 15 April, CA.
4　*R v Chief Constable of Kent ex p L; R v DPP ex p B* (1991) 93 Cr App R 416, DC.
5　Per Lord Salmon, *R v Humphrys* [1977] AC 1 at 46D, HL.
6　Per Lord Irvine, *Boddington v British Transport Police* [1998] 2 WLR 639 at 651G, HL.

an alternative remedy in opposition to a defendant's application for judicial review of a decision to prosecute[1].

The High Court may be slightly more willing to entertain judicial review applications challenging a failure to prosecute[2]. As a result, there have been a number of recent judicial reviews of decisions of the Crown Prosecution Service not to prosecute[3]. For example, the High Court has recently quashed a decision not to prosecute. In this case, the Crown Prosecution Service had failed to take account of a reasoned judgment of a civil court that suggested that the evidence that would have been relied on during any criminal prosecution had merit[4]. The High Court quashed the decision not to prosecute because it was irrational in all the circumstances. In reaching its decision, the High Court took account of the Code for Crown Prosecutors. The High Court did, however, indicate that usually it would be reluctant to intervene to quash a decision not to prosecute. In part, that reluctance is because there is a presumption that civil courts should not determine whether behaviour is criminal[5].

When the High Court considers a judicial review of a decision to refuse to prosecute, it will take account of the availability of an alternative remedy when it decides whether to exercise its discretion to allow the judicial review. In particular, the possibility of a private prosecution will be considered in cases where it is as effective a remedy as judicial review. In determining the effectiveness, the High Court will take account of the resources of the applicant[6].

Historically, it has been held that the High Court will not consider judicial reviews of decisions of the Attorney-General regarding the entry of a nolle prosequi[7]. This is because the High Court has been reluctant to consider judicial reviews of the exercise of prerogative powers. There is, however, some indication that the High Court is showing a greater willingness to consider judicial reviews of the prerogative powers[8].

---

1 See **5.4** for a discussion of alternative remedies.
2 Eg *R v Commr of Police for the Metropolis ex p Blackburn* [1968] 2 QB 118, CA, in which the applicant successfully challenged a police policy against prosecuting certain illegal gambling.
3 Eg *R v CPS ex p Waterworth* (unreported) 1 December 1995, DC; *R v DPP ex p Panayiotu* [1997] COD 83, DC; *R v DPP ex p M* and *R v CPS ex p Hitchins* (unreported) 13 June 1997, DC.
4 *R v DPP ex p Treadaway* (1997) *The Times*, 31 October, DC; see the transcript for full details.
5 *R v DPP ex p Camelot Group Plc* (1998) 10 Admin LR 93 at 104D, DC.
6 Ibid at 105B.
7 *R v Comptroller of Patents* [1899] 1 QB 909, CA.
8 See **1.9**.

4.4 CHALLENGES TO LEGISLATION UNDER WHICH A PROSECUTION IS BROUGHT

In many criminal cases, the court will be considering proceedings brought under secondary legislation. Although the making of the secondary legislation might be challenged by judicial review, it is likely that any challenge to the making of the legislation will be out of time[1]. There are also practical problems associated with an application for judicial review. For example, judicial review can also be an expensive and a slow form of proceedings.

It has long been recognised that it is possible to bring certain forms of public law challenges which question the legality of by-laws under which a prosecution is being brought during the criminal proceedings. For example, protestors at Greenham Common were able to challenge their convictions on the basis that the by-laws under which they were prosecuted were ultra vires[2]. However, until recently the courts had held that the defendant in the magistrates' court could not raise a defence by arguing that secondary legislation was invalid because of some form of a procedural defect in the way that the legislation came to be made. A defendant could only argue that the legislation was on its face invalid or patently unreasonable[3].

That approach was held to have been wrongly decided in the recent decision of the House of Lords in the *Boddington* case[4]. In *Boddington*, the House of Lords held that magistrates' courts normally have jurisdiction to consider public law defences in criminal proceedings. Lord Irvine held that:

> '[T]he legislation or act which is impugned is presumed to be good until pronounced to be unlawful, but is then recognised as never having had any legal effect at all. The burden in such a case is on the defendant to establish on a balance of probabilities that the subordinate legislation or the administrative act is invalid.'[5]

The jurisdiction of the magistrates' court to consider public law defences can be excluded by a specific statutory provision. For example, the House of Lords has held that the criminal courts are unable to consider challenges to the legality of a notice when it considers a prosecution under s 179(1) of the Town and Country Planning Act 1990[6]. This is because the elaborate appeals process under the 1990 Act, that provides for challenges to enforcement notices, excludes the jurisdiction of the criminal courts.

Following *Boddington*, most defendants should be advised to raise the vires of secondary legislation and other public law defences during their criminal trial. If the magistrates' court refuses to consider the defence or wrongly rules that the secondary legislation is lawful, it is then possible to proceed to the High

---

1   See **5.2** for consideration of the time-limits associated with an application for judicial review.
2   *DPP v Hutchinson* [1990] 2 AC 783, HL.
3   *Bugg v DPP* [1993] QB 473, DC.
4   *Boddington v British Transport Police* [1998] 2 WLR 639, HL.
5   Ibid at 647A.
6   *R v Wicks* [1998] AC 92, HL.

Court by way of judicial review or appeal by way of case stated. If the Crown Court refuses to consider the defence or wrongly rules that the secondary legislation is lawful during a trial on indictment, it is then possible to appeal to the Court of Appeal.

Although it most likely that a defendant will wish to consider challenging legislation when a prosecution is being brought under by-laws, it is also possible to challenge primary legislation if that legislation is ultra vires as a result of European legislation. Clearly, the same tactical considerations arise, so it is almost certainly in the interests of a defendant that the vires, of the primary legislation is raised first during the criminal proceedings.

Finally, the judgment in *Boddington* does suggest that it is possible to raise other public law defences during criminal proceedings. Thus, challenging the legality of the decision to prosecute may be possible.

4.5 JUDICIAL REVIEW OF DECISIONS REGARDING BAIL

Judicial review is not normally available to challenge a decision of magistrates or a decision of a Crown Court judge to refuse bail[1], because the defendant is entitled to apply for bail to a High Court judge[2]. Similarly, judicial review is unlikely to be available to challenge the decisions of magistrates to grant bail as the prosecution has a right of appeal to the Crown Court against that decision[3].

In principle, there would appear to be no reason why the prosecution cannot bring a judicial review of the decision of a Crown Court judge to grant a defendant bail[4]. In practice, this never appears to happen. This is probably because there is no jurisdiction to hold a defendant in custody after he has been granted bail by a Crown Court judge. In addition, the High Court has no power to grant interim relief preventing the release of a defendant until a decision has been taken[5]. Thus, the prosecution could not seek an order from the High Court preventing the release of a defendant until the Crown Court judge had decided to grant bail. As a result it would be difficult for a prosecutor to justify a judicial review as being in the public interest if the defendant is bailed.

The limitations on judicial reviews of decisions to grant and refuse bail does not mean that judicial review is irrelevant to decisions relating to bail. Judicial review is available to challenge decisions regarding the forfeit of recognizances. For example, the High Court will quash a decision to enforce the forfeiture of a

---

1   *Re Herbage* (1985) *The Times*, 25 October, DC.
2   CPR 1998, Sch 1, RSC Ord 79, r 9.
3   Bail (Amendment) Act 1993, s 1.
4   In *R v Bristol Crown Court ex p Commrs for HM Customs & Excise* [1990] COD 11, DC, the High Court considered a judicial review brought by the prosecution of a decision of a Crown Court judge to grant bail as a result of the operation of custody time-limits. Although the decision primarily concerned the operation of custody time-limits, it does imply that the prosecution can bring a judicial review of a decision to grant bail.
5   *Ex p Amnesty International* (1998) *The Times*, 11 December, DC.

recognizance where there has been no proper enquiry into the means of the surety[1].

4.6 CHALLENGES TO DECISIONS REGARDING CUSTODY TIME-LIMITS

There is at least one authority in which a defendant appealed by way of case stated against a decision to extend custody time-limits[2]. The High Court appears to have failed to have considered whether this was an interim decision, which could not be challenged by appeal by way of case stated[3]. In practice, it is difficult to see why any person in custody would seek to challenge an extension of custody time-limits by way of appeal by case stated. The delay associated with requesting a court to state the case will almost inevitably result in significant delay. It is far better to apply to seek a judicial review of the decision, as the High Court will be able to consider the matter as soon as the application is lodged.

Where magistrates decide on an application to extend custody time-limits, both the defendant and the prosecution have the right to appeal against that decision to the Crown Court[4]. Despite this right of appeal, there are several authorities in which the High Court appeared to accept that it was able to consider a challenge to a decision of the magistrates' court to extend custody time-limits[5]. In the first of these cases, the court appeared to fail to consider the existence of an alternative remedy when it determined the matter[6]. In the later case, the court did consider the right of appeal to the Crown Court. It held that judicial review of a decision of the magistrates might be the appropriate remedy where a detained person was complaining about a breach of natural justice. Where the complaint was that there was no good and sufficient cause for the extension the detained person should appeal to the Crown Court[7]. In any event, there are clear tactical advantages associated with appealing to the Crown Court. In particular, an appeal to the Crown Court is likely to be quicker and more cost effective.

The High Court has considered numerous judicial reviews brought by defendants challenging decisions of the Crown Court to extend custody time-limits[8]. There do, however, appear to be far fewer challenges by the prosecution to decisions of the Crown Court to refuse an extension of a custody

---

1 *R v Birmingham Crown Court ex p Rashid Ali* (1998) *The Times,* 16 October, DC.
2 *McKay White v DPP* [1989] Crim LR 375, DC.
3 See **4.9**.
4 Prosecution of Offences Act 1985, s 22(7) and (8).
5 *R v Sheffield JJ ex p Turner* [1991] 2 QB 472, DC; *R v Folkestone Magistrates' Court ex p Bradley* [1994] COD 138.
6 *R v Sheffield JJ ex p Turner* [1991] 2 QB 472, DC.
7 *R v Folkestone Magistrates' Court ex p Bradley* [1994] COD 138.
8 Eg *R v Manchester Crown Court ex p McDonald and Other Cases* (1998) *The Times,* 19 November; *R v Crown Court at Norwich ex p Parker and Ward* (1993) 96 Cr App R 68, DC.

time-limit, although there has been at least one challenge[1]. This may well be because it is difficult to argue that it is in the public interest to bring an application for judicial review when a person has been released. As, however, it is not automatic that a person will be released as soon as an extension of custody time-limits is refused[2]; there may be circumstances where it is appropriate for the prosecution to apply for judicial review. The prosecution will need to be aware of the provisions regarding expedition[3].

It did become established practice that habeas corpus proceedings would be brought as well as judicial review proceedings in order to challenge certain decisions relating to custody time-limits. That is, however, unlikely to be necessary now given changes in the scope of custody time-limits. Custody time-limits in the Crown Court now only cease to apply at the 'start of the trial'[4]. The start of a trial is normally either when the jury is sworn or a guilty plea is accepted[5]. As a result, a custody time-limit can no longer be defeated by an arraignment when there is no prospect of the trial starting. Thus, questions that have been raised about whether a judicial review can be brought of an arraignment that defeats custody limits are largely academic[6]. It was these questions that led practitioners to bring habeas corpus proceedings in cases involving custody time-limits as well as judicial review proceedings. As a result, it is unlikely that there will be any need to bring habeas corpus proceedings to challenge decisions relating to custody time-limits.

Once a custody time-limit has expired and there has been no application for an extension, the defendant must be released on bail. An application for bail should be made to the court before which the substantive criminal proceedings are in progress. If that application is unsuccessful or if the court refuses to consider it, an application for judicial review of that decision can be brought in the High Court[7].

Where a judicial review application is brought challenging the decision to extend custody time-limits relating to proceedings in the magistrates' court, there should be no stay of committal proceedings in the magistrates' court pending the resolution of the judicial review proceedings[8]. As a result, the judicial review should be expedited.

---

1 R v Bristol Crown Court ex p Commrs for HM Customs & Excise [1990] COD 11, DC. In this case, a Crown Court judge ruled that he was required to grant bail as custody time-limits had expired. That order was subsequently set aside and the High Court considered an application for judicial review.
2 R v Governor of Canterbury Prison ex p Craig [1991] 2 QB 195, DC holding that custody time-limits only expire at midnight on the relevant date provided for by the regulations.
3 See **6.2**. See also R v Croydon Crown Court ex p Commissioners of Customs & Excise (1997) Archbold News, October, DC, in which the High Court held they could not make an effective order once the time-limit expired.
4 Prosecution of Offences (Custody Time Limits) Regulations 1987, SI 1987/299, reg 5.
5 Prosecution of Offences Act 1985, s 22(11A).
6 See R v Maidstone Crown Court ex p Clark [1995] 1 WLR 831, DC, in which Glidewell LJ held that it was unnecessary for him to decide whether there could be a judicial review of an arraignment as decision could be challenged by habeas corpus in any event.
7 Olotu v Home Office and Another [1997] 1 WLR 328, CA.
8 R v Merthyr Tydfil Crown Court ex p West and Others (1997) Archbold News, June, DC.

4.6.1 Practical considerations regarding challenges to custody time-limits

There are practical considerations that arise when considering a possible judicial review of a decision to extend custody time-limits. Practitioners will be aware that Crown Court judges usually give reasons for their decisions regarding custody time-limits. That is because they are obliged to give reasons as both a defendant and the prosecution are entitled to know why the judge took the decision that he did[1]. Practitioners should always ensure that the judge gives reasons for any decision and that they make a careful note of these reasons.

Reasons are needed because an applicant is likely to argue that those reasons show that the judge misdirected himself about the provisions governing custody time-limits[2]. For example, in deciding whether to allow a judicial review of a decision regarding custody time-limits, the High Court will be concerned to ensure that the purpose of custody time-limits was given due weight by the Crown Court[3]. The High Court will be concerned to ensure that the lack of availability of a court or of a judge is not too readily accepted as a good and sufficient reason for extension. A transcript is unlikely to be available when practitioners first consider applying for judicial review, so an applicant will need to rely on the notes of reasons made by persons present in court. A transcript should, however, be sought as soon as possible.

In addition, any judicial review of a decision regarding custody time-limits must clearly be pursued as a matter of urgency so that it is heard before the defendant is either committed from the magistrates' court or the trial has begun in the Crown Court[4]. If it is heard after this time, the only remedy available will be a declaration that a period of custody was unlawful. The court will not be able to order the release of a person after their detention has become lawful, even if it was previously unlawful.

It may well be that if a person cannot be released, the High Court will not consider a judicial review of the extension of custody time-limits[5]. This is because it will not consider judicial review challenges that merely raise academic issues[6]. Damages are not available from a prison governor or from the Crown Prosecution Service if it is shown that a person was held illegally in

---

1 *R v Manchester Crown Court ex p McDonald and Other Cases* (1998) *The Times*, 19 November, DC.
2 Eg *R v Luton Crown Court ex p Neaves* [1992] Crim LR 721, DC.
3 *R v Manchester Crown Court ex p McDonald and Other Cases* (1998) *The Times*, 19 November, DC.
4 See **6.2** for a consideration of expedition.
5 In *R v Leeds Crown Court ex p Whitbread* (1998) *Archbold News*, August, DC, a Divisional Court held that it would only rarely be appropriate to grant permission to apply for judicial review where a defendant in the magistrates' court had been committed for trial so that a new custody time-limit applied.
6 See **11.3** for a consideration of the High Court's reluctance to consider judicial reviews raising academic issues.

excess of the custody time-limits[1]. As a result, it is difficult to see the value of a declaration that a period of detention was unlawful[2].

4.7 CHALLENGES TO COMMITTAL DECISIONS TAKEN BY MAGISTRATES

It has been regarded as settled law that an appeal by way of case stated is not available to challenge a decision of magistrates taken while they are sitting as examining justices. This means that there is no appeal by way of case stated from a decision to commit[3]. In contrast, it is now well established that defendants may bring a judicial review of a decision to commit a defendant for trial. For example, the High Court can consider whether there was any admissible evidence put before magistrates during committal proceedings. That is because it is an error of law to commit a person for trial where there is no evidence, as s 6(1) of the Magistrates' Courts Act 1980 requires magistrates to be satisfied that there is sufficient evidence if they are to commit a matter[4]. As a result, committal decisions should be challenged by way of judicial review if they are to be challenged.

It is not only defendants who can bring judicial review proceedings to challenge a decision to commit. The prosecution can also bring judicial review proceedings to challenge a decision to refuse to commit[5].

It is clear that the principles that the High Court applies when considering judicial reviews of decisions of magistrates at committal are the same as they apply when considering judicial reviews of other decisions[6]. In particular, they are not limited to considering errors that are jurisdictional or are apparent on the face of the record[7]. This is despite some suggestions in old cases that the grounds that can be raised in a judicial review of decision of magistrates at committal are limited[8]. The High Court may, however, take account of the fact that the decision is not final when it decides whether to exercise its discretion to quash a decision to commit[9].

---

1   *Olotu v Home Office and Another* [1997] 1 WLR 328, CA.
2   In *R v Folkestone Magistrates' Court ex p Bradley* [1994] COD 138, DC the High Court did consider an application for judicial review that merely sought a declaration that the detention was unlawful. The report appears to suggest that the High Court may have been concerned that the challenge may have been academic. It may be that the court will not allow judicial reviews in these circumstances again.
3   See **1.7** for arguments suggesting that this is no longer good law. See *Dewing v Cummings* [1971] RTR 295, DC, in which the principle that there can be no appeal by way of case stated against a decision of examining justices was applied to hold that there could be no appeal by way of case stated against a decision to commit.
4   *R v Bedwellty Justices ex p Williams* [1997] AC 225, HL.
5   *R v Bow Street Magistrates' Court ex p DPP* (1992) 95 Cr App R 9, DC.
6   *R v Bedwellty Justices ex p Williams* [1997] AC 225 at 234E, HL.
7   See **2.2.1** for a discussion of the restrictions that were thought to limit the scope of judicial review before the decision of the House of Lords in *Anisminic Ltd v Foreign Compensation Commission* [1969] 2 AC 147, HL.
8   Eg *R v Manchester Coroner ex p Tal* [1985] QB 67 at 82H, DC.
9   See **11.2** for a discussion of the discretionary nature of judicial review proceedings.

Where a defendant has sought unsuccessfully to challenge the prosecution case at committal and wishes to bring a judicial review of that decision, the defendant should apply for an adjournment of the committal proceedings, so that they can bring the judicial review proceedings seeking an order of prohibition[1]. The decision to refuse the adjournment request in these circumstances may also be challenged by judicial review as well as the substantive decision to commit[2].

The High Court has a limited jurisdiction to consider decisions that relate to committal in circumstances where the magistrates have not heard argument about the merits of committal. Although magistrates may hear arguments about abuse of process, they are limited to considering arguments that relate directly to the fairness of the trial of the particular defendant or an alleged abuse of the procedures of the court. Where abuse of process arguments concern other matters, the magistrates should be asked to stay proceedings so that the High Court can consider a judicial review application, because the High Court has a wider responsibility to uphold the rule of law[3].

4.8 JUDICIAL REVIEWS OF THE TRANSFER OF PROCEEDINGS TO THE CROWN COURT BY THE PROSECUTION

In serious fraud cases, the prosecution may apply to transfer the case to the Crown Court without holding committal proceedings[4]. After this has happened, a defendant may apply to the Crown Court for the dismissal of a charge or any of the charges[5]. Where a charge is dismissed, s 6(5) of the Criminal Justice Act 1987 provides that 'no further proceedings may be brought on a dismissed charge except by means of the preferment of a voluntary bill of indictment'. In at least one case, respondents to an application for judicial review sought to argue that these words excluded judicial review[6]. However, despite the clear words of the statute, the High Court has recently held that the prosecution should normally bring a judicial review of a decision to dismiss charges if they want to challenge that decision. Judicial review was preferable to a voluntary bill as the defendant has a right to be heard and there is a possibility of an appeal against the decision[7].

It is important to note in this context that the House of Lords has specifically declined to consider whether the High Court lacks jurisdiction to consider

---

1   Eg *R v Guildford Magistrates' Court ex p Healy* [1983] 1 WLR 108, DC.
2   *R v Horseferry Road Magistrates' Court ex p Bennett* [1994] 1 AC 42, HL.
3   Per Lord Griffiths, *R v Horseferry Road Magistrates' Court ex p Bennett* [1994] 1 AC 42 at 64B, HL.
4   Criminal Justice Act 1987, s 4.
5   Ibid, s 6(1).
6   *R v Central Criminal Court ex p Director of the Serious Fraud Office* [1993] 1 WLR 949 at 957G, DC.
7   *R v Snaresbrook Crown Court ex p Director of Serious Fraud Office* (1998) *The Times*, 26 October, DC.

judicial reviews of decisions of Crown Court judges to dismiss cases following transfer[1]. The statutory limitation on judicial reviews of decisions of the Crown Court might prevent judicial reviews of the decision of a Crown Court judge to dismiss cases following transfer[2]. It is, however, clear that at present, the High Court accepts that it has jurisdiction to consider judicial reviews in these circumstances[3].

The High Court has also held that defendants are entitled to apply for a judicial review of a transfer[4]. The opportunity to apply for judicial review is not apparently excluded by the terms of s 4(3) of the 1987 Act which provides that 'a designated authority's decision to give notice of transfer shall not be subject to appeal or liable to be questioned in any court'. It is also not excluded by the opportunity to apply to a Crown Court judge for the dismissal of any charges.

The Criminal Justice Act 1991 provides for the transfer of cases to the Crown Court in certain cases involving children[5]. The conditions precedent for a transfer[6], and the provisions allowing for the dismissal of charges transferred by a Crown Court judge[7] are very similar to those that govern transfers in serious fraud cases. In particular, the provision preventing further proceedings following dismissal except by way of voluntary bill is identical[8]. As a result, it is likely that the same principles will apply to a judicial review of a decision to transfer in a case involving children as apply in a case involving serious fraud[9]. The only difference is likely to be that the court is likely to require greater expedition in cases involving children[10].

4.9 APPEALS BY WAY OF CASE STATED AGAINST INTERIM DECISIONS IN CRIMINAL PROCEEDINGS

Although the terms of the statutory provisions that govern appeals by way of case stated appear wide, they do not allow for an interlocutory appeal in criminal proceedings[11]. As a result, any challenge to an interim decision taken

---

1   Per Lord Browne-Wilkinson, *R v Manchester Crown Court ex p DPP* [1993] 1 WLR 1524 at 1530G, HL.
2   See **1.6**.
3   Eg *R v Snaresbrook Crown Court ex p Director of Serious Fraud Office* (1998) *The Times*, 26 October, DC.
4   *R v Salford Magistrates' Court ex p Gallagher* [1994] Crim LR 374, DC.
5   Criminal Justice Act 1991, s 53.
6   Ibid, s 53(1).
7   Ibid, Sch 6, para 5.
8   Ibid, para 5(7), cf Criminal Justice Act 1987, s 6(5).
9   In *R v Bakewell Magistrates' Court and Derbyshire CPS ex p Brewer* [1995] COD 98, DC, the High Court appeared to accept that it had jurisdiction to consider judicial reviews of transfers in cases involving children.
10 See **6.2** for a discussion of expedition.
11 *Streames v Copping* [1985] QB 920, DC, holding that there is no jurisdiction to hear an appeal by case stated against an interim decision in criminal proceedings in the magistrates' court; *Loade v DPP* [1990] 1 QB 1052, DC, holding that there is no jurisdiction to hear an appeal by case stated against an interim decision in criminal proceedings in the Crown Court.

during criminal proceedings must be brought by way of judicial review. In particular, the High Court held that decisions regarding jurisdiction and rulings 'on a point of law in the course of a hearing' should not be challenged by way of an appeal by case stated until there is a 'determination of the matter before [the court]'[1]. For example, a decision of magistrates about the exclusion of evidence can only be challenged if there has been no final conviction by judicial review.

4.10 JUDICIAL REVIEWS OF INTERIM DECISIONS IN CRIMINAL PROCEEDINGS

In many criminal proceedings, there will be interim decisions that practitioners might wish to challenge. For example, practitioners might wish to challenge decisions regarding the disclosure of evidence. There are, however, tactical reasons why it might not be in a defendant's interests to bring a judicial review application before there has been a final decision in the criminal proceedings. An application for judicial review is likely to add to the cost of proceedings. It is also likely to delay the final determination of the matter. In most cases, a successful judicial review of a decision about a matter, such as the exclusion of evidence, will not result in the prosecution discontinuing the proceedings. If no judicial review application is brought at the time of the interim decision and the defendant is convicted, there is nothing to prevent a challenge being brought to that conviction.

In addition to the tactical concerns, practitioners need to be aware that the High Court will be more reluctant to allow judicial reviews of decisions of criminal courts where there has been no final decision in the proceedings. Judicial review is a discretionary remedy[2]. That means that the High Court will not necessarily intervene to quash every decision where there are grounds for intervening. When deciding whether to quash a decision taken by a court during criminal proceedings, the High Court will take account of the stage that those proceedings have reached. Applicants for judicial review will normally be expected to wait for a final decision before bringing an application for judicial review. Lord Justice May has held that because nothing will be lost in most cases if parties wait until the final determination of the matter, challenges to interim decisions regarding jurisdiction should usually be left until the final determination. Other interim rulings should only be challenged before a final determination '[i]n a very special instance'[3].

There are, however, some circumstances where it will be appropriate to challenge an interim decision. It is probably not possible to identify all the circumstances in which it will be appropriate to bring a judicial review of an interim decision in criminal proceedings. There are, however, some principles

---

1   Per May LJ, *Streames v Copping* [1985] QB 920 at 929C, DC.
2   See **11.2**.
3   *Streames v Copping* [1985] QB 920 at 929, DC; see also **5.2** et seq for a discussion of the timing of an application for judicial review.

that can be seen in the decided cases. In particular, the precedents set out below show that the High Court is likely to be concerned about the reason why the applicant cannot wait for a final determination of the criminal proceedings. It is less concerned about the type of decision being challenged. As a result, applicants for judicial review should always explain in their pleadings why they have not waited for a final decision of the court before bringing a judicial review application.

The High Court has held that a decision taken during criminal proceedings that has resulted in a person being unlawfully detained may be challenged by judicial review even where there is no final conviction[1]. In addition, the High Court is more likely to exercise its discretion to quash an interim decision, where quashing that decision is likely to result in the final determination of the matter[2]. This is particularly likely to be true in the context of proceedings against juveniles, because the courts wish to avoid putting juveniles through criminal trials if there is no need for that trial[3]. The same considerations may also apply in cases where there are juvenile witnesses where there will be a desire to avoid these witnesses giving evidence unnecessarily.

It does appear to be accepted that a decision may be brought before a final conviction where mode of trial has been determined wrongly. Thus, a decision to decline jurisdiction where the matter could only be tried summarily could be challenged by judicial review before there had been a final conclusion of the matter[4]. Similarly, an unreasonable decision to accept jurisdiction could be challenged by judicial review before there had been a final conviction[5]. This is presumably because it is not in the interests of justice for a court to waste court time on a matter that it should not be considering.

---

1   Eg *R v Maidstone Crown Court ex p Clark* [1995] 1 WLR 831, DC allowing a challenge to an arraignment to defeat custody time-limits.
2   Eg *R v Horseferry Road Magistrates' Court ex p Bennett* [1994] 1 AC 42, HL in which the House of Lords held that in certain circumstances judicial review proceedings should be brought in the High Court, where it was said that a matter should be stayed as an abuse of process. See **4.7** for further details of *ex p Bennett*, above. See also *R v Horseferry Road Justices ex p Independent Broadcasting Authority* [1987] QB 54, DC, in which the High Court held that it should decide whether a criminal offence existed of the type alleged in proceedings in the magistrates' court.
3   *R v Chief Constable of Kent ex p L*; *R v DPP ex p B* (1991) 93 Cr App R 416, DC. In this case, the High Court considered an application for judicial review of a decision to prosecute juveniles. The court held that it would be more willing to quash a decision to prosecute in a case involving juveniles than it would be in a case involving adults. The same principles are likely to apply to judicial reviews of interim decisions taken during criminal proceedings.
4   *R v Hatfield Justices ex p Castle* [1981] 1 WLR 217, DC.
5   *R v Northampton Magistrates' Court ex p Commissioners for Customs & Excise* [1994] COD 382, DC.

4.11 SHOULD A DEFENDANT APPEAL TO THE CROWN COURT AGAINST A CONVICTION IN THE MAGISTRATES' COURT OR SHOULD HE APPEAL BY WAY OF CASE STATED?

When a person is convicted in the magistrates' court, he may appeal by way of case stated to the High Court. Any appeal by way of case stated will mean that rights of appeal to the Crown Court against the same decision will cease[1]. For this reason, an appeal by way of case stated from a decision of the magistrates' court is rarely the correct procedure, because it is normally difficult to be certain why a magistrates' court convicted a defendant until the application has been made to state a case. Magistrates are under no obligation to give reasons in all circumstances[2]. In practice, it is rare for magistrates to give reasons at the end of a summary trial. As a result, a defendant will often only receive reasons explaining why he was convicted after the application is made to state a case. The reasons given by the magistrates when they state a case may show that the decision-making process cannot be challenged as it contained no errors of law that were material to the conviction. Instead, the real complaint is that magistrates erred in the findings of fact that they made. It will then be too late to appeal to the Crown Court, as rights of appeal to the Crown Court cease as soon as a proper application is made to state a case[3].

In a case where the findings of fact are said to be so irrational that they can be challenged by way of an appeal by case stated[4], it is still likely to be in the interests of the defendant that the conviction is challenged by appealing to the Crown Court. This is because an appeal to the Crown Court involves a rehearing of the matter and the burden is on the prosecution to show that the defendant is guilty beyond all reasonable doubt. This contrasts with the position faced by an appellant by way of case stated who must show that the decision of the magistrates is irrational.

If the decision of the magistrates was clearly based on some other error of law, this error may be challenged on appeal to the Crown Court. The Crown Court may 'correct any error or mistake in the order or judgment incorporating the decision which is the subject of the appeal'[5], so an error of law can clearly be challenged on an appeal to the Crown Court. If the appeal is unsuccessful, it may then be possible to appeal by way of case stated against the decision of the Crown Court.

There are practical reasons why an appeal by way of case stated may not be the correct form of proceedings. An appeal to the Crown Court may well be cheaper and simpler than an appeal by way of case stated. Any form of

---

1 Magistrates' Courts Act 1980, s 111(4). Note, however, that an appeal by way of case stated against conviction does not prevent an appeal to the Crown Court against sentence (*R v Winchester Crown Court ex p Lewington* [1982] 1 WLR 1277, DC).
2 *R v The Southend Stipendiary Magistrate ex p Rochford District Council* [1995] Env LR 1 at 6.
3 Magistrates' Courts Act 1980, s 111(4).
4 *Bracegirdle v Oxley* [1947] 1 KB 349, DC.
5 Supreme Court Act 1981, s 48.

proceedings in the High Court is likely to involve the instruction of specialist counsel. It may also be that there is delay associated with an appeal by way of case stated as the Divisional Court is busy. This is particularly significant as the only interim relief available is a stay of disqualification and bail[1]. An appeal to Crown Court allows the appellant to raise matters that have emerged after conviction, such as new evidence. Often a person who is seeking to appeal a conviction in the magistrates' court will seek to rely on witnesses who were not called at the trial. That cannot be done during an appeal by way of case stated.

The only circumstance where an appeal by way of case stated is likely to be the correct remedy is where the magistrates clearly made a fundamental error of law that was material to the conviction, but where it is also very likely that the Crown Court will uphold a conviction on appeal as the evidence is strong. For example, it may be clear that there is an error of law as a result of an unsuccessful interim application. In these circumstances, it may be in the interests of a defendant to apply to the High Court to have the conviction quashed.

4.12 SHOULD A DEFENDANT APPEAL TO THE CROWN COURT AGAINST A CONVICTION IN THE MAGISTRATES' COURT OR SHOULD HE APPLY FOR JUDICIAL REVIEW?

Although there are tactical advantages associated with an application for judicial review, as opposed to an appeal by way of case stated, an application for judicial review is not always an appropriate form of proceedings. The circumstances in which the High Court will expect a conviction to be challenged by an appeal by way of case stated are set out below[2].

If, however, applying for judicial review is appropriate, an application for judicial review of a conviction in the magistrates' court does not prevent an appeal to the Crown Court. The High Court must, however, be informed of the appeal that is pending in the Crown Court[3]. As judicial review is a discretionary remedy, the possibility of an appeal to the Crown Court and the status of the appeal in the Crown Court is a matter that can be taken into account when the High Court considers whether it should intervene to quash a conviction. Thus, a judicial review that was intended to procure delay of an appeal in the Crown Court in an attempt to secure the dropping of charges was rejected[4]. The High

---

1   See Chapter 10 for details of interim relief that is available.
2   See **4.14**.
3   *R v Mid Worcestershire Justices ex p Hart* [1989] COD 397, DC. In this case the High Court endorsed the comments of Alverstone LCJ in *R v Barnes* (1910) 102 LT 860, stating that the court considering a judicial review should be told of any pending appeal. The same comments suggested that in many cases the High Court will not wish to determine a judicial review until the appeal has been concluded. However, in *ex p Hart*, Parker LJ stated that in his opinion a pending appeal was no bar to judicial review.
4   *R v Hereford Magistrates' Court ex p Rowlands and Ingram; R v Harrow Youth Court ex p Prussia* [1998] QB 110, DC considering *R v Peterborough Magistrates' Court ex p Dowler* [1997] QB 911, DC.

Court will also wish to ensure at the permission stage in an application for judicial review that there are good grounds for bringing an application for judicial review[1].

Although judicial review does not prevent an appeal to the Crown Court, there are clearly other matters that need to be taken into account when deciding whether to challenge a conviction by an application for judicial review. Judicial review is likely to be an expensive form of proceedings. It can also be a slow form of proceedings. The two-stage procedure means that it can be many months before the High Court considers an application for judicial review, although it is possible to apply for expedition[2]. This is particularly significant as there are significant restrictions on the powers of the courts to stay sentences during judicial review proceedings[3]. The High Court does, however, have jurisdiction to grant bail to an applicant for judicial review.

4.13 SHOULD A DEFENDANT APPEAL BY WAY OF CASE STATED OR JUDICIALLY REVIEW A CONVICTION FOLLOWING AN APPEAL TO THE CROWN COURT?

If a person is convicted following an appeal to the Crown Court, a judicial review or an appeal by way of case stated is the only way to challenge that conviction. The Court of Appeal is only able to consider appeals against conviction from the Crown Court when a person has been convicted on indictment[4]. As a result, there is no overlap between the jurisdiction of the High Court to consider convictions following appeals in the Crown Court and the jurisdiction of the Court of Appeal to consider convictions in the Crown Court. That is because the High Court can only consider judicial reviews and appeals by case stated from the Crown Court where the matter does not relate to a trial on indictment[5].

Although proceedings in the High Court are the only methods for challenging a conviction following an appeal to the Crown Court, careful consideration has to be given to the merits of the application. Practitioners need to be aware of the risks that an order for costs may be made if an unmeritorious challenge is brought against the conviction[6].

When considering a possible judicial review of conviction by the Crown Court, practitioners should also be aware of one possible limitation on the grounds

---

1   Per Lord Bingham CJ, *R v Hereford Magistrates' Court ex p Rowlands and Ingram; R v Harrow Youth Court ex p Prussia* [1998] QB 110 at 125E, DC.
2   See **6.2**.
3   See Chapter 10 for details of interim relief. See *R v Derwentside Magistrates' Court ex p Swift* [1996] COD 203, DC, for an example of a case where the restrictions on the court's power to stay sentences was said to be a reason for using other remedies in preference to judicial review.
4   Criminal Appeal Act 1968, s 1.
5   See **1.6**.
6   See Chapter 12.

that may be raised. As we have noted earlier, it may be that judicial review of decisions of the Crown Court is limited to challenges relating to jurisdiction or errors on the face of the record[1]. Although this is unlikely to cause significant problems to applicants, being aware of this possible limitation is still important.

4.14 THE SCOPE OF JUDICIAL REVIEW OR APPEAL BY WAY OF CASE STATED AS A WAY OF CHALLENGING A CONVICTION

The courts have held that judicial review is the only appropriate method for applying to quash a conviction imposed by the magistrates' court or the Crown Court where an appeal by case stated was inapposite or inappropriate. For example, Mr Justice Brooke criticised applicants for judicial review of a conviction in the magistrates' court when he stated:

> 'Our task in this case was made unnecessarily difficult because the applicants did not adopt the procedure prescribed by Parliament for referring a point of law which has arisen in a magistrates' court to the High Court for decision. If the justices had stated a case for our opinion, we would have known what their findings of fact had been and their reasons for the decisions they took and they would have identified the relevant points of law for our decision in the familiar way.'[2]

This approach has recently been endorsed in a judicial review of a conviction that was upheld by the Crown Court following an appeal[3]. The court did, however, go on to say that where a judicial review was brought, the court that had made the original decision that was subject to challenge should at least write a letter stating whether they intended to resist the challenge.

As a result, any challenge to a conviction should be by way of case stated, where the High Court needs a full record of the findings of fact and law made by the magistrates' court or the Crown Court. For example, this means that it is normal to challenge a conviction based on a misconstruction of the statute that gives rise to the offence by an appeal by way of case stated[4].

An appeal by way of case stated is also normally the correct remedy where a person seeks to challenge an acquittal, as there are limits to the scope of judicial reviews of acquittals[5].

In practice, the availability of an appeal by way of case stated does not prevent a significant number of judicial reviews of convictions in the magistrates' courts or the Crown Court, because the High Court often does not need a record of the findings of fact and law when it considers a challenge to the conviction.

---

1 See **2.2.1** for a fuller consideration of whether judicial review is limited in this way when the High Court is considering challenges to decisions of the Crown Court.
2 *R v Morpeth Ward JJ ex p Ward* (1992) 95 Cr App R 215 at 221, DC. It is significant to note, however, that despite these comments the High Court did consider the substantive merits of the judicial review application.
3 *R v Gloucester Crown Court ex p Chester* (1998) *The Independent*, 6 July, DC.
4 Eg *Vigon v DPP* [1998] Crim LR 289, DC.
5 See **4.16**.

Instead, it needs evidence about things that happened during the trial of the matter and this evidence cannot normally be presented during an appeal by way of case stated. The procedure that the court adopts when considering applications for judicial review is usually the only appropriate way of presenting the High Court with the evidence that it needs in these circumstances.

For example, complaints about matters such as bias, a failure to adopt a procedure that satisfies the requirements of natural justice or a decision that is contrary to the applicant's legitimate expectation do not require a record of the court's findings of fact or law. Instead, they require written evidence from persons present in court explaining the procedure adopted by the court. Judicial review is the procedure that allows a party to present this evidence[1].

In addition to cases where the procedure in judicial review is preferable to that in appeal by way of case stated, there is one circumstance where a judicial review is the appropriate method of challenging a conviction. The magistrates or the Crown Court have a discretion to refuse to state a case. In these circumstances, it is possible to bring a judicial review of the failure to state a case[2]. Where it is necessary to apply for a judicial review of the failure to state a case, the judicial review may also challenge the conviction. That enables the High Court to consider whether it is in a position to consider quashing the conviction on the basis of the information available to it[3]. The High Court will wish to avoid the unnecessary waste of time associated with ordering the magistrates or the Crown Court judge to state a case before being able to consider the merits of the conviction.

If a person wrongly applies for judicial review when they should have appealed by way of case stated or vice versa, the High Court may act to avoid that person being prejudiced. For example, in one case where a party wrongly proceeded by way of judicial review, the High Court extended the time allowed for lodging an appeal by way of case stated. That then enabled the High Court to consider the case as if it was an appeal by case stated[4].

4.15 TACTICAL FACTORS INFLUENCING A DECISION TO PROCEED BY JUDICIAL REVIEW OR APPEAL BY CASE STATED

Clearly, in many cases the procedural differences will dictate whether a conviction should be challenged by judicial review or by way of an appeal by way of case stated. There will, however, be a limited number of cases where there is a choice to be made between the two forms of proceedings.

---

1   Although judicial review is normally the correct form of proceedings, it may be possible to bring an appeal by way of case stated if the magistrates were asked to rule on an issue such as bias. See *Johnson v Leicestershire Constabulary* (1998) *The Times,* 7 October, DC.
2   See **9.5**.
3   *R v Southwark Crown Court ex p Brooke* [1997] COD 81, DC.
4   *R v Clerkenwell Stipendiary Magistrate ex p DPP* [1984] QB 821 at 836D, DC. Note, however, the strict time-limits associated with an appeal by way of case stated. See **5.6**.

One factor that needs to be considered when deciding whether to apply for judicial review or appeal by way of case stated is the interim relief that is available. When applying for judicial review, it is possible to apply for bail and other forms of interim relief that are set out later[1]. There are, however, restrictions on powers of courts to order stays of sentences. In particular, both the magistrates' court and the Crown Court are unable to stay a disqualification from driving pending a judicial review[2]. In contrast, the magistrates' court and the Crown Court may both stay a disqualification from driving while an appeal by way of case stated is pending. If the application to the court that ordered disqualification is unsuccessful, an application can be made to the High Court for a stay. As a result, an appeal by way of case stated is likely to be better when a sentence of disqualification from driving has been imposed following conviction and a stay of enforcement is required[3].

In cases where a conviction has been upheld following an appeal to the Crown Court, an appeal by way of case stated may be preferable. This is because the High Court may not remit the matter to the Crown Court following a successful judicial review of a decision of the Crown Court to dismiss an appeal from a conviction in the magistrates' court[4]. In those circumstances, the successful applicant for judicial review will be required to apply to have his appeal reinstated in the Crown Court if he wishes to attempt to have the conviction in the magistrates' court quashed.

As set out above, judicial review of a conviction in the magistrates' court does have the procedural advantage of not acting as a bar to an appeal to the Crown Court. In contrast, an appeal by way of case stated does prevent an appeal to the Crown Court[5]. This is an important incentive to apply for judicial review in a case where a defendant also wants to challenge findings of fact made by magistrates.

Finally, judicial review proceedings do not have to be commenced as soon after conviction as an appeal by way of case stated[6]. Often this is not a relevant consideration as the defendant will wish to commence the challenge to a conviction as soon as possible. However, it can have the advantage of allowing a greater time to obtain legal aid.

4.16 CHALLENGES TO ACQUITTALS

There is normally a presumption that the prosecution should not be able to appeal from an acquittal[7]. However, the wide terms of the provisions of the

---

1 See Chapter 10.
2 The High Court, however, has a power to stay disqualification pending a judicial review. Road Traffic Offenders Act 1988, s 40(5).
3 *R v Derwentside Magistrates' Court ex p Swift* [1996] COD 203, DC.
4 *R v Leeds Crown Court ex p Barlow* [1989] RTR 246, DC.
5 See **4.11**.
6 See **5.2** et seq.
7 *Cook v Southend Borough Council* [1990] 2 QB 1 at 10G, CA.

statutory provisions governing appeals by way of case stated mean that the prosecution is entitled to challenge an acquittal by an appeal by way of case stated[1].

The scope for an application for judicial review of an acquittal is far more limited. In general, judicial review is not available to contest an acquittal unless the court acted outside its jurisdiction[2]. This limitation on judicial review is based on the principle of 'autrefois acquit', so if there is no acquittal, then there can be a judicial review. For example, there can be a judicial review of a decision dismissing charges[3]. Although an appeal to the Crown Court involves a rehearing, an acquittal following an appeal is not regarded in the same way as an acquittal following a trial. As a result, it is possible to challenge by way of judicial review an acquittal following an appeal to the Crown Court[4].

4.17 SHOULD A SENTENCE BE CHALLENGED BY JUDICIAL REVIEW OR BY APPEAL BY WAY OF CASE STATED?

An appeal by way of case stated is almost never the appropriate remedy to quash a sentencing decision of the Crown Court or the magistrates' court. This is because the remedies available to the High Court when it considers an appeal by way of case stated do not allow it to substitute a new sentence for the decision that is being challenged. In contrast, the High Court has a statutory power to order a variation of a person's sentence where a person applies for an order of certiorari. The High Court may impose any sentence that was open to the magistrates' court or, where a case was committed to the Crown Court following conviction, any that was open to the Crown Court[5]. The sentence runs from the date that it would have run from if the sentence had been imposed in the proceedings in the magistrates' court or the Crown Court, although any time spent on bail is discounted from the calculation[6].

One exception to this general rule arises when the sentencing decision involved arguments regarding 'special reasons' in a driving case. In this type of case, appeals by way of case stated have been brought to challenge the decision regarding special reasons[7]. That is primarily because the decision regarding 'special reasons' is a mixed question of fact and law that is similar to that involved in convicting a defendant. As a result, it is often important to have a statement of the facts found by the court so that the High Court can consider whether the law was correctly applied to those facts.

---

1 Eg *DPP v Coleman* [1998] 1 WLR 1708, DC.
2 *Harrington v Roots* [1984] AC 743, HL.
3 *R v Hendon Justices ex p DPP* [1994] QB 167, DC.
4 *R v Bournemouth Crown Court ex p Weight* [1984] 1 WLR 980, HL.
5 Supreme Court Act 1981, s 43(1).
6 Ibid, s 43(2).
7 Eg *Haime v Walklett* [1983] RTR 512, DC.

4.18 SHOULD A SENTENCE IMPOSED BY THE MAGISTRATES' COURT BE CHALLENGED BY JUDICIAL REVIEW OR BY AN APPEAL TO THE CROWN COURT?

The Crown Court's jurisdiction to consider appeals against a sentence allows it to 'correct any error or mistake in the order or judgment incorporating the decision which is the subject of the appeal'[1]. As a result, it can consider errors of law relating to the sentence imposed in the magistrates' court.

The High Court will only act to quash a sentence following an application for judicial review if the sentence is wrong in law or in excess of jurisdiction[2]. This has been held to mean that the sentence must be shown to be harsh and oppressive and far outside the normal range of sentences imposed for the offence. In these circumstances, the High Court can conclude that its imposition must have involved an error of law[3]. Alternatively, it has been held to mean that the High Court will intervene if a sentence is 'irrational or truly astonishing'[4]. Despite these very restrictive tests, the High Court has, however, quashed sentences[5].

In contrast, the Crown Court should consider an appeal against a sentence by allowing a rehearing of the issues. It should then determine the correct sentence and when doing this it should not take account of the sentence imposed by the magistrates' court. It should then determine whether the sentence that it would impose is significantly different to that imposed in the magistrates' court. If the difference is significant, the Crown Court should impose a fresh sentence[6].

Clearly, the Crown Court is far more likely than the High Court to quash a sentence imposed by the magistrates' court. As a result, the reluctance of the High Court to consider judicial reviews of sentences means that sentences imposed in the magistrates' court should never be challenged in the High Court. Instead, a defendant should appeal to the Crown Court. If the sentence is then upheld by the Crown Court, consideration should be given to challenging that sentence in the High Court.

There are other reasons why an appeal to the Crown Court will be the correct way of challenging a sentence imposed in the magistrates' court. There is only limited interim relief available during a judicial review of a sentence[7]. As a result, the sentence is likely to be punishing the defendant while the judicial

---

1 Supreme Court Act 1981, s 48(1).
2 *R v Croydon Crown Court ex p Miller* (1987) 85 Cr App R 152, DC.
3 *R v Croydon Crown Court ex p Miller* (1987) 85 Cr App R 152, DC endorsing the judgment in *R v St Albans Crown Court ex p Cinnamond* [1981] QB 480, DC but suggesting that it should be treated with caution.
4 *R v Acton Crown Court ex p Bewley* (1988) 10 Cr App R (S) 105 at 109, DC.
5 *R v Swansea Crown Court ex p Davies* (1989) *The Times*, 2 May, in which the High Court quashed an increase in sentence following appeal to the Crown Court from a suspended sentence to an immediate sentence.
6 *R v Knutsford Crown Court ex p Jones* (1985) 7 Cr App R (S) 448, DC.
7 See Chapter 10.

review is pending. This absence of interim relief is compounded by the delay associated with a judicial review. A full hearing for judicial review will not be heard as quickly as an appeal to the Crown Court.

4.19 JUDICIAL REVIEWS OF SENTENCES IMPOSED BY THE CROWN COURT ON MATTERS NOT RELATED TO TRIAL ON INDICTMENT

A defendant may only appeal to the Court of Appeal against a sentence of imprisonment imposed by the Crown Court in a matter that has been committed from the magistrates' court for sentence, or in a case where a person has been further dealt with, having previously been sentenced to a conditional discharge, a community order or a suspended sentence in limited circumstances[1]. The circumstances where an appeal may be brought are where the court imposes a sentence of imprisonment or detention in a young offender institution that is for 6 months or more[2], or where the sentence is one that the court had no power to impose[3]. A defendant may also appeal against a recommendation for deportation, an order disqualifying a person from driving, an order regarding an existing suspended sentence, or an order under the Football Spectators Act 1989[4]. Finally, a defendant may appeal where an order is made under s 40(3A) of the Criminal Justice Act 1991[5]. When considering appeals, the Court of Appeal may quash the sentence and impose any sentence that they think is appropriate, but the appellant may not be dealt with more severely[6].

The Court of Appeal has no jurisdiction to consider appeals against sentences following an appeal to the Crown Court against a sentence in the magistrates' court[7]. As a result, the only circumstances where the Court of Appeal can consider an appeal against a sentence imposed in proceedings other than trial on indictment are those noted above.

The High Court clearly has a statutory jurisdiction to consider judicial reviews of sentences imposed by the Crown Court in matters other than trials on indictment, including matters that have been committed for sentence. In particular, it has power to substitute any sentence that the Crown Court could have imposed for one that it actually imposed[8]. In theory, this would appear to mean that the sentence could be increased. However, as the High Court will only allow a judicial review of a sentence where the sentence is so harsh and oppressive or otherwise outside the normal sentence imposed that the court

---

1 Criminal Appeal Act 1968, s 10.
2 Ibid, s 10(3)(a).
3 Ibid, s 10(3)(b).
4 Ibid, s 10(3)(c).
5 Ibid, s 10(3)(cc).
6 Ibid, s 11(3).
7 Ibid, s 10(1).
8 Supreme Court Act 1981, s 43(1).

concludes that it is an error of law[1], it is difficult to imagine circumstances where a person would be advised to apply for judicial review and the High Court would increase their sentence. However, given the apparent possibility of an increase in the sentence and given the wider discretion that the Court of Appeal has to quash a sentence, one should appeal to the Court of Appeal if that right of appeal is available.

If no appeal is available to the Court of Appeal, it is still unlikely that a judicial review of a decision imposed will succeed as a result of the High Court's reluctance to allow judicial reviews of sentences[2]. Given that reluctance, potential applicants should be aware of the limited interim relief available[3]. They should also be aware of the risks of an order of costs associated with an unmeritorious application for judicial review[4].

Although the High Court has generally been reluctant to allow judicial reviews of sentences, that reluctance is most apparent in cases where the applicant claims that a sentence is excessive. The High Court has shown a greater willingness to consider challenges where the challenge is not based on the sentence being excessive, but is instead based on some other public law claim. For example, the High Court has quashed sentences imposed in breach of a legitimate expectation[5] and where the sentencer has failed to take account of a relevant factor[6].

When considering a possible judicial review of a sentence imposed by the Crown Court, practitioners should be aware of one possible limitation on the grounds that may be raised. As we have noted earlier, it may be that judicial review of decisions of the Crown Court is limited to challenges relating to jurisdiction or errors on the face of the record[7]. Although this is unlikely to cause significant problems to applicants, being aware of this possible limitation is still important.

4.20 THE LIMITATIONS ON THE RIGHT OF APPEAL TO THE CROWN COURT FROM A FINAL DECISION OF THE MAGISTRATES' COURT

When deciding whether to challenge a final decision of the magistrates' court by either judicial review or appeal by way of case stated, it is important to be aware of the scope of the right of appeal to the Crown Court, because

---

1   *R v Croydon Crown Court ex p Miller* (1987) 85 Cr App R 152, DC endorsing the judgment in *R v St Albans Crown Court ex p Cinnamond* [1981] QB 480, DC but suggesting that it should be treated with caution.
2   See **4.18**.
3   See Chapter 10.
4   See Chapter 13.
5   *R v Isleworth Crown Court ex p Irwin* (1991) *The Times*, 5 December, DC.
6   *R v York Justices ex p Grimes* (1997) *The Times*, 27 June, DC.
7   See **2.2.1** for a fuller consideration of whether judicial review is limited in this way when the High Court is considering challenges to decisions of the Crown Court.

practitioners will wish to consider whether they should appeal to the Crown Court rather than bring proceedings in the High Court.

Section 108(1) of the Magistrates' Courts Act 1980 is the provision that appeals to the Crown Court are normally brought under. That provision states that:

> 'A person convicted by a magistrates' court may appeal to the Crown Court–
>
> (a) if he pleaded guilty, against his sentence;
> (b) if he did not, against the conviction or sentence.'

In addition to this provision, there are also rights of appeal to the Crown Court under other statutory provisions. For example, there is a right of appeal against a finding of contempt of court[1], an order binding the defendant over[2], a sentence imposed following a finding of a breach or revocation of a community service order[3] and a restriction order made under the Football Spectators Act 1989[4].

These statutory provisions clearly fail to provide a right of appeal to the Crown Court against all final decisions of the magistrates' court. For example, the decision to commit a person to prison for non-payment of a fine or community charge is excluded. This is because s 150 of the Magistrates' Courts Act 1980 provides that the term sentence:

> '[D]oes not include a committal in default of payment of any sum of money, or for want of sufficient distress to satisfy any sum of money, or for failure to do or abstain from doing anything required to be done or left undone.'

The scope of the phrase 'sentence' in s 108(1) of the Magistrates' Courts Act 1980 and thus the right of appeal to the Crown Court is also limited by s 108(3) of the same Act which provides that:

> '[A] "sentence" includes any order made on conviction by a magistrates' court, not being:
>
> ... [sub-section 108(3)(a) has been repealed]
>
> (b) an order for the payment of costs;
> (c) an order under section 2 of the Protection of Animals Act 1911 (which enables a court to order the destruction of an animal); or
> (d) an order made in pursuance of any enactment under which the court has no discretion as to the making of the order or its terms
>
> and also includes a declaration of relevance under the Football Spectators Act 1989.'

There is no equivalent statutory definition of the phrase 'conviction' in the Magistrates' Courts Act 1980, so it is not certain how the use of this phrase in s 108(1) of that Act restricts appeal rights to the Crown Court. This is because the phrase has been given different meanings depending on the context in

---

1 Contempt of Court Act 1981, s 12(5).
2 Magistrates' Courts (Appeals from Binding Over Orders) Act 1956, s 1.
3 Criminal Justice Act 1991, Sch 2.
4 Football Spectators Act 1989, s 22(7).

which it is used[1]. It is, however, likely that the phrase does imply the need for some finding of guilt.

4.21 JUDICIAL REVIEWS OF DECISIONS OF MAGISTRATES WHICH DO NOT ATTRACT RIGHTS OF APPEAL TO THE CROWN COURT

In principle, any final decision of the magistrates' court may be challenged by judicial review or appeal by way of case stated. The limitations on the scope of the rights of appeal under s 108(1) of the Magistrates' Courts Act 1980 mean that, in practice, there are many decisions of magistrates' courts that cannot be challenged by appealing to the Crown Court. These decisions can be very significant as that may have led to a person being imprisoned or suffering some other form of punishment. This has resulted in a considerable number of judicial reviews of decisions of the magistrates' court in circumstances where there is no appeal to the Crown Court. For example, there have been numerous judicial reviews of warrants of commitment issued by magistrates[2].

In theory, there is no reason why these final decisions cannot be challenged by an appeal by way of case stated. In practice, however, judicial review is almost inevitably the form of proceedings used to challenge these decisions. There are several reasons for this. First, the grounds of challenge are likely to mean that an appeal by way of case stated is not appropriate[3]. In addition, in many cases the applicant for judicial review will want bail as he is seeking to challenge his imprisonment. There are limitations on the right to apply for bail during civil proceedings, which means that an appeal by way of case stated may not be the correct form of proceedings[4]. In addition, if bail is available during an appeal by case stated, the application for bail will normally first be considered by the magistrates' court that is the subject of the appeal by way of case stated. Tactically, it is often seen as advantageous to have that bail application considered initially by a High Court judge who has the applicant's grounds for judicial review before him. The High Court is able to consider applications for bail in judicial review proceedings at very short notice. Other tactical considerations that govern the choice between judicial review and appeal by way of case stated in the context of challenges to a conviction are also relevant[5].

---

1   Per Lord Reid, *S (An Infant) v Recorder of Manchester* [1971] AC 481 at 489C, HL.
2   Eg *R v Oldham Justices and Another ex p Cawley* [1996] 1 All ER 464, DC; *R v York Magistrates' Court ex p Grimes* (1997) *The Times*, 27 June, DC.
3   See **3.4** for a consideration of the circumstances where the procedural differences between the two forms of proceedings mean that appeal by way of case stated is not an appropriate form of proceedings.
4   See **10.2.3**. If an appeal by way of case stated would be the correct form of proceedings save for the limitations on the right to apply for bail, it is possible to bring both forms of proceedings: *R v Thanet Justices ex p Dass* [1996] COD 77.
5   See **4.14**.

4.22 CHALLENGING FINAL DECISIONS OF THE CROWN COURT

In the Crown Court, the scope of judicial review and appeal by way of case stated is subject to statutory limitations[1]. The absence of a right of appeal from the decision of the Crown Court does not necessarily mean that a judicial review or an appeal by way of case stated may be brought. Thus, the absence of a right of appeal by the prosecution against a decision to stay proceedings as an abuse of process does not mean it is possible to bring a judicial review of that decision[2]. If, however, the statutory limitation does not prevent a judicial review or appeal by way of case stated, there is no other reason why the High Court lacks jurisdiction to consider a final decision of the Crown Court.

The other factor that needs to be addressed when considering judicial reviews of final decisions of the Crown Court is the possible limitation on the grounds that may be raised. As we have noted earlier, it may be that judicial review of decisions of the Crown Court is limited to challenges relating to jurisdiction or errors on the face of the record[3]. Although this is unlikely to cause significant problems to applicants, it is still important to be aware of this possible limitation.

If the High Court does have jurisdiction to consider a judicial review or an appeal by way of case stated from a final decision of the Crown Court, the issues to be considered when deciding whether a conviction should be challenged by way of judicial review or by way of appeal by case stated will be relevant[4].

4.23 CHALLENGES TO DECISIONS REGARDING COSTS

Only certain limited decisions regarding costs attract appeal rights. In particular, decisions regarding wasted costs made by a magistrates' court may be appealed to the Crown Court and decisions at first instance regarding wasted costs made by the Crown Court may be appealed to the Court of Appeal[5]. Where an appeal right exists, an appeal should be brought against a decision regarding wasted costs in preference to judicial review proceedings or an appeal by way of case stated. There are no significant tactical advantages associated with bringing proceedings in the High Court.

There is, however, no right of appeal against a refusal to order costs from central funds. As a result, a decision in these circumstances must be challenged by judicial review[6]. This may not be possible if the refusal to order costs follows a

---

1 See **1.6** et seq for a full consideration of the statutory limitation.
2 *Re Ashton and Others; R v Manchester Crown Court ex p DPP* [1994] 1 AC 9, HL.
3 See **2.2.1** for a fuller consideration of whether judicial review is limited in this way when the High Court is considering challenges to decisions of the Crown Court.
4 See **4.14** above.
5 Rule 3C of the Costs in Criminal Cases (General) Regulations 1986, SI 1986/1335 as amended.
6 Eg *R v Birmingham Juvenile Court ex p H* (1992) 156 JP 445, DC.

trial on indictment in the Crown Court. This is as a result of the statutory limitation on the scope of judicial review of decisions of the Crown Court[1].

There is no appeal to the Crown Court against an inter partes order for costs made by the magistrates' court since s 108(3) of the Magistrates' Courts Act 1980 means that an order for costs is not a sentence[2]. As a result, any challenge to an order for costs awarded by the magistrates' court should be brought by way of judicial review or appeal by way of case stated[3]. The High Court will consider whether the costs order is:

> 'so far outside the normal discretionary limits ... that its imposition must involve an error of law of some description, even if it may not be apparent at once what is the precise nature of that error'[4].

An order that a defendant pay all or part of the costs of the prosecution is a sentence when it is imposed by the Crown Court[5]. As a result, an appeal to the Court of Appeal exists where there is a right of appeal against a sentence. However, as the right of appeal to the Court of Appeal against a sentence is very limited where the sentence does not follow a conviction on indictment[6], it is likely that a costs order in these circumstances will have to be challenged by judicial review or appeal by case stated if it is to be challenged. In particular, there is no appeal to the Court of Appeal against a sentence imposed following an appeal to the Crown Court[7]. As a result, a judicial review or appeal by way of case stated will be the only way of challenging costs awarded in these circumstances[8].

4.24 CHALLENGES TO THE DECISIONS OF MAGISTRATES TO COMMIT FOR EXTRADITION

It is accepted that a decision to commit taken by magistrates in an extradition case may be challenged by way of judicial review. The decision to commit is normally challenged on the basis that evidence was such that no reasonable magistrate would have been entitled to commit[9]. In practice, the decision to commit is normally challenged by an application for habeas corpus as well as an

---

1 Re Meredith (1973) 57 Cr App R 451, DC; R v Harrow Crown Court ex p Perkins (1998) The Times, 28 April, DC.
2 See **4.20**.
3 See Neville v Gardner Merchant Ltd (1983) 5 Cr App R (S) 349, DC, for an example of a successful appeal by way of case stated against an order for costs.
4 Per Lord Lane CJ, R v Tottenham Justices ex p Joshi [1982] 1 WLR 631 at 635G, DC, adopting the judgment of Donaldson LJ in R v St Albans Crown Court ex p Cinnamond [1981] QB 480, DC.
5 R v Hayden (1974) 60 Cr App R 304, CA.
6 See **4.19** for details of the scope of the right of appeal against sentence where the sentence does not follow conviction on an indictment.
7 Criminal Appeal Act 1968, s 10(1).
8 See R v Merthyr Tydfil Crown Court ex p Chief Constable of Dyfed-Powys Police (1998) The Times, 17 December, for an example of a successful judicial review of a costs order made following an appeal to the Crown Court.
9 Eg per Lord Reid, R v Brixton Prison Governor ex p Schtraks [1964] AC 556 at 579, HL.

application for judicial review. Habeas corpus applications are even made where the defendant is on bail[1]. Indeed, the Extradition Act 1989 appears to recognise that habeas corpus is the correct procedure. For example, it provides that a person who has been committed under s 9 of the Act shall be informed of their 'right to make an application for habeas corpus'[2]. It also provides that a person shall not be removed from the UK for 15 days after the date of decision to enable the application for habeas corpus to be made[3].

A complete consideration of the scope of extradition is beyond the scope of this book. There are, however, several points that should be made. First, it is important to recognise that extradition procedures differ depending on whether or not a case is governed by Part III of the 1989 Act[4]. This is significant as it determines the scope of the jurisdiction of the High Court. In a case governed by Part III of the 1989 Act, the High Court may order discharge if:

'[I]t appears to the court ... that:

'(a) by reason of the trivial nature of the offence; or
(b) by reason of the passage of time since he is alleged to have committed it or to have become unlawfully at large, as the case may be; or
(c) because the accusation against him is not made in good faith in the interests of justice,

it would, having regard to all the circumstances, be unjust or oppressive to return him.'[5]

It will be exceptional, however, for the High Court to intervene under this provision if the Secretary of State had already ordered the applicant's return. The Secretary of State's decision is a factor for the court to consider[6].

In contrast, where an application for extradition is not governed by Part III, there is no equivalent provision. Indeed, the magistrate considering committal (and consequently the High Court) has no jurisdiction to consider arguments that the extradition is an abuse of process[7].

If an application for extradition is made under Part III of the 1989 Act and there is a challenge to the extradition under s 11(3), the High Court will be able to consider evidence that was not before the committing magistrate[8]. An application under s 11(3) of the Extradition Act 1989 is, however, not the only circumstance where the High Court will consider evidence that was not before

---

1 Eg *R v Governor of Pentonville Prison ex p Tarling* [1979] 1 WLR 1417, DC.
2 Extradition Act 1989, s 11(1).
3 Ibid, s 11(2) in relation to extraditions under Part III of the 1989 Act; para 8(1) of Sch 1 to the Extradition Act 1989 in relation to other extraditions.
4 Section 1(3) of the Extradition Act 1989 excludes extradition requests made by States where an Order in Council is in force under s 2 of the Extradition Act 1870 from the procedures under Part III.
5 Extradition Act 1989, s 11(3).
6 *R v Secretary of State for the Home Department ex p Osman* [1993] Crim LR 214.
7 *R v Governor of Pentonville Prison ex p Sinclair* [1991] 2 AC 64, HL. Although the Secretary of State is required to take account of these principles; see *ex p Patel* (unreported) 9 February 1994.
8 Extradition Act 1989, s 11(4). Eg *Re Murat Calis* (unreported) 19 November 1993.

the committing magistrate. Despite the normal limitations that restrict the role of the High Court to acting as a court of review, the High Court will consider fresh evidence in extradition cases in two very limited circumstances. First, where a defendant seeks to show that he should not be extradited, as the offence that is the subject matter of the extradition request is of a political nature, the defendant is entitled to adduce evidence that was not before the magistrate to show the political nature of the offence[1]. That is because the political nature of the offence relates to the jurisdiction of the magistrate. In addition, additional evidence may be admitted to cure technical defects such as the absence of proof regarding the evidence of the foreign jurisdiction[2].

The High Court may consider a judicial review of a decision to refuse to commit a defendant[3]. That, however, is an unsatisfactory procedure as there is no power to hold a defendant in custody pending the determination of that application for judicial review. As a result, s 10 of the Extradition Act 1989 provided foreign governments with a right of appeal by way of case stated in cases where the extradition takes place under Part III of that Act. Where the extradition does not take place under Part III, it is doubtful whether there is a right of appeal by way of case stated. That is because it has been regarded as settled law that appeal by way of case stated is not available to challenge a decision of magistrates sitting as examining justices[4]. The 1999 edition of *The Supreme Court Practice* doubts whether this is still good law[5].

4.25 JUDICIAL REVIEW OF DECISIONS TAKEN AFTER CONVICTION

A person who has been convicted of a crime may well be the subject of further administrative decisions in relation to that conviction after the proceedings in the criminal courts have been concluded. In most circumstances, the High Court is likely to be able to consider judicial reviews challenging those decisions. The only decisions of public officials that may not be subject to judicial review are those that are taken under the royal prerogative[6]. Thus, for example, it is likely that the High Court will consider a number of judicial review challenges of decisions of the Criminal Cases Review Commission to refuse to refer cases back to the criminal courts[7]. That, however, is not the only circumstance where judicial review is appropriate. Judicial review is also important to challenge the decisions of prison authorities and the Home

---

1 Eg per Lord Goddard CJ, *R v Governor of Brixton Prison ex p Kolczynski* [1955] 1 QB 540 at 550.
2 Eg *R v Governor of Brixton Prison ex p Percival* [1907] 1 KB 696.
3 Eg *Government of Denmark v Nielson* (1984) 79 Cr App R 1.
4 Eg *Atkinson v United States Government* [1971] AC 197, HL.
5 Note 56/5/3. See **1.7** for further details.
6 See **1.9** for details of the prerogative.
7 It is clear that the High Court does have jurisdiction to consider judicial reviews of the Commission's decisions as the Criminal Appeal Act 1995 includes no provision excluding the High Court's jurisdiction. See also *R v Criminal Cases Review Commission ex p Pearson* (unreported) 18 May 1999, DC.

Secretary[1]. When considering possible judicial reviews of decisions of public bodies, it is also important to be aware of the divide between public law and private law[2].

---

1 See **1.9** for further examples of judicial review challenges that may be brought against decision-makers in the context of crime.
2 See **1.9.1**.

Chapter 5

CONSIDERATIONS THAT ARISE BEFORE APPLYING TO THE HIGH COURT

5.1 THE IMPORTANCE OF KNOWING WHETHER A MATTER IS A CRIMINAL CAUSE OR MATTER

Although a judicial review application may arise out of a practitioner's criminal practice, that does not necessarily mean that it is regarded as a criminal cause or matter by the High Court. For example, a judicial review that relates to an alleged offence under the prison rules is not regarded as a criminal cause or matter by the High Court[1]. The distinction between a criminal cause or matter and other cases is significant, as the procedure adopted when bringing proceedings in the High Court depends on whether a matter is a criminal cause[2]. For example, there is no right of appeal to the Court of Appeal from any judgment of the High Court in any criminal cause or matter, except in very limited circumstances[3].

Although the issue of whether a matter is a criminal cause or matter normally arises in the context of judicial review proceedings, the distinction is significant in all forms of proceedings. Thus, the Court of Appeal had no jurisdiction to consider an appeal from an order made by a High Court judge relating to the obtaining of evidence, if that order was made during habeas corpus proceedings challenging an extradition[4].

The Civil Procedure Rules 1998 (CPR 1998) now include references to 'criminal proceedings'[5]. Although this is a new term, there is no reason to believe that the courts will define it differently to a criminal cause or matter.

The procedural distinctions that arise mean that practitioners will need to ensure that they know whether a case relates to a criminal cause or matter, so that they follow the correct procedure if they act for an applicant. If practitioners act for a respondent, they may wish to argue that the wrong procedure has been adopted, so that a particular court has no jurisdiction.

---

1 *R v Board of Visitors of Hull Prison ex p St Germain* [1979] QB 425, CA.
2 See Chapter 7.
3 Supreme Court Act 1981, s 18(1)(a).
4 *Cuoghi v Governor of Brixton Prison and Another* [1997] 1 WLR 1346, CA.
5 CPR 1998, Sch 1, RSC Ord 56, rr 1(1) and 5(1).

5.1.1 The decision that determines whether a matter is a criminal cause or matter

As has already been noted above, the most significant difference between a criminal cause or matter and other proceedings is that there is no right of appeal to the Court of Appeal. In determining whether there is a right of appeal to the Court of Appeal, the court will not be concerned with the nature of the order made by the High Court. Indeed, the orders that might be sought, when applying for a judicial review in a criminal cause or matter, are the same as those that are sought in other matters. Instead, the court will consider whether the decision that was being challenged in the High Court was a criminal cause or matter[1].

5.1.2 The definition of a criminal cause or matter

The Court of Appeal has given a wide definition to the phrase 'criminal cause or matter'. For example, Lord Esher has held that the phrase:

> '[A]pplies to a decision by way of judicial determination of any question raised in or with regard to proceedings, the subject-matter of which is criminal, at whatever stage of the proceedings the question arises.'[2]

Similarly, Lord Wright held that:

> '[I]f the cause or matter is one which, if carried to its conclusion, might result in the conviction of the person charged and in a sentence of some punishment, such as imprisonment or fine, it is a 'criminal cause or matter'.... Every order made in such a cause or matter by an English court, is an order in a criminal cause or matter, even though the order, taken by itself, is neutral in character and might equally have been made in a cause or matter which is not criminal. The order may not involve punishment by the law of this country, but if the effect of the order is to subject by means of the operation of English law the persons charged to the criminal jurisdiction of a foreign country, the order is, in the eyes of English law for the purposes being considered, an order in a criminal cause or matter.'[3]

Although these judgments appear to suggest that the phrase 'criminal cause or matter' relates to a decision of a court, other authorities show that there is no need for the decision-maker to be a court. A decision to refer or to refuse to refer a matter to the criminal courts can be a criminal cause or matter. For example, under the legislative scheme that existed before the establishment of the Criminal Cases Review Commission, a refusal by the Secretary of State to refer a matter to the Court of Appeal was a criminal matter[4]. Presumably, a decision of the Criminal Cases Review Commission will also be a criminal matter.

---

1 *Carr v Atkins* [1987] QB 963 at 967B, CA. Although this case only considered the approach in judicial review, there is no reason why the same approach should not apply to other review proceedings in the High Court. This is clearly consistent with the decision in *Cuoghi v Governor of Brixton Prison and Another* [1997] 1 WLR 1346, CA.
2 *Ex p Alice Woodhall* (1888) 20 QBD 832 at 836, CA.
3 *Amand v Home Secretary* [1943] AC 147 at 162, HL.
4 *R v Secretary of State ex p Garner* [1990] COD 457, CA.

The decision also need not be a final decision of a criminal court for it to be a criminal cause or matter. For example, a decision relating to evidence that may be used in criminal proceedings is a criminal cause or matter even if the proceedings have not commenced. Thus, an order of a Crown Court judge in relation to the production of special procedure material under Sch 1 to the Police and Criminal Evidence Act 1984 is a criminal cause or matter, even if proceedings have not commenced[1].

Once the criminal courts have imposed a sentence, a decision about the effect of the penalty imposed by the criminal court has also been treated as a criminal cause or matter. Thus, a recent case considering the calculation of the number of days to be served as a result of the imposition of a sentence of imprisonment was treated as a criminal cause or matter[2]. There are, however, circumstances where the effect of the sentence that has been imposed is determined by the exercise of a discretionary power by the Home Secretary. A challenge to the exercise of that executive discretion is not treated as a criminal cause or matter. Thus, a challenge to the tariff to be served by a mandatory life prisoner is not a criminal cause or matter[3]. Similarly, a deportation order made following a recommendation by a criminal court is not a criminal cause or matter, although the actual recommendation is a criminal cause or matter[4].

Although the decision that is being challenged need not be a decision of a criminal court if the case is to be a criminal cause or matter, it must however relate in some way to a possible trial by a criminal court[5]. Thus, a general challenge to a police policy is clearly not a criminal cause or matter[6]. In addition, the proceedings must relate in some way to the 'enforcement and preservation of public law and order' rather than being merely domestic disciplinary proceedings[7]. Thus, proceedings relating to an alleged breach of prison rules are not a criminal cause or matter[8]. Similarly, disciplinary proceedings against a solicitor are not a criminal cause or matter[9].

Not every decision by a criminal court in relation to criminal proceedings is a criminal cause or matter. This is because some decisions of the criminal courts are so collateral to the criminal proceedings that gave rise to the decision that the decision cannot be regarded as a criminal cause or matter[10]. The Court of Appeal has held that a decision to estreat a recognizance is not a criminal cause or matter as '[a] recognizance is in the nature of a bond. A failure to fulfil it

---

1 *Carr v Atkins* [1987] QB 963, CA.
2 *R v Secretary of State for the Home Department ex p Francois* [1999] 1 AC 43, HL.
3 *R v Secretary of State for the Home Department ex p Pierson* [1998] AC 539, HL.
4 *R v Secretary of State for the Home Department ex p Dannenberg* [1984] QB 766, CA.
5 Per Lord Justice Shaw, *R v Board of Visitors of Hull Prison ex p St Germain* [1979] QB 425 at 453C, CA.
6 Eg *R v Chief Constable of North Wales and Others ex p Thorpe* [1998] 3 WLR 57, CA.
7 Per Lord Justice Shaw, *R v Board of Visitors of Hull Prison ex p St Germain* [1979] QB 425 at 452B, CA.
8 *R v Board of Visitors of Hull Prison ex p St Germain* [1979] QB 425, CA.
9 In *Re EF Hardwick* (1883) 12 QB 148.
10 Per Sir John Donaldson MR, *Carr v Atkins* [1987] 1 QB 963 at 970F, CA.

gives rise to a civil debt'[1]. The issue of a witness summons is, however, not so collateral that it is not a criminal cause or matter[2].

Challenges to the decisions of criminal courts may also not be a criminal cause or matter if the decision challenged relates to civil proceedings. For example, there are forms of civil proceedings that are brought in the magistrates' court. Thus, a decision to commit a person to jail for non-payment of non-domestic rates is not a criminal cause or matter[3].

5.2 DETERMINING WHETHER THERE HAS BEEN DELAY IN JUDICIAL REVIEW PROCEEDINGS

The timing of an application for judicial review can be crucial. The court can reject an application if it is premature and if it is late. The key provision determining whether an application is late is CPR 1998, Sch 1, RSC Ord 53, r 4(1). This provides that:

> 'An application for permission to apply for judicial review shall be made promptly and in any event within three months from the date when grounds for the application first arose unless the Court considers that there is good reason for extending the period within which the application shall be made.'

There are a number of important points that need to be made in relation to this provision. First, it is important to be aware that an application will not necessarily be regarded as being in time, merely because it is made within a 3-month period. Practitioners often wrongly assume that an application will be regarded as being in time merely because it is made within 3 months of the date on which the grounds arose. The key requirement is that the application is made promptly. As a result, an application for judicial review may be refused if there has been delay within the 3-month period[4].

The determination of whether an application has been brought promptly does not merely involve a consideration of whether an applicant acted promptly[5]. Thus, a lack of knowledge that grounds for judicial review exist does not mean that time does not start to run. It may, however, be a good reason for extending time[6].

---

1 Per Lord Denning MR, *R v Southampton Justices ex p Green* [1976] QB 11 at 15H, CA. Care must be taken when considering this case as it is clear that the full scope of the judgment of the Court of Appeal is regarded as unreliable. See, eg Sir John Donaldson MR, *Carr v Atkins* [1987] 1 QB 963 at 969E onwards, CA.
2 *Day v Grant* [1987] QB 972, CA.
3 *R v Thanet Justices ex p Dass* [1996] COD 77.
4 *R v Independent Television Commission ex p TV NI Ltd* (1991) *The Times*, 30 December, CA; *R v Brighton and Hove Magistrates' Court ex p Clarke* (1997) *Archbold News*, June, DC; cf *R v Tunbridge Wells Justices ex p Tunbridge Wells Borough Council* (1996) JPN 514, DC where delay within the 3-month period was not fatal. There was no hardship caused by the delay as the need for the prosecution to bring proceedings only arose as a result of the defendant's ill-founded submission of no case to answer.
5 *R v Cotswold DC ex p Barrington Parish Council* (1998) 75 P& CR 515.
6 Per Mr Justice Taylor, *R v Secretary of State for the Home Department ex p Ruddock* [1987] 1 WLR 1482 at 1485F. See also **5.2.1** for details of the court's approach to extending time.

In the case of an application for certiorari[1] in respect of a judgment, order, conviction or proceeding, the grounds for the application will be taken to have arisen on the 'date of [the] judgment, order, conviction or proceeding'[2]. Although there are no provisions determining when time begins in other judicial review applications, it is likely the time will be taken as beginning on the same date when the judicial review relates to the decision of a court.

In cases challenging executive decisions, it may be more difficult to determine when time commences[3]. For example, in certain circumstances, it may be possible to argue that there is a continuing breach of a decision-maker's public duty. The effect of this may be that it is possible to argue that time for bringing an application for judicial review has never started to run. However, the fact that there is a continuing breach does not necessarily mean that it is irrelevant to consider the date at which the breach began[4]. The court will be anxious to see that there is a prompt application for judicial review.

Occasionally, applicants have requested a decision-maker to review a decision that has already been taken. If the decision-maker agrees to this request, it can then be argued that the result of that review is a fresh decision that attracts its own time-limits[5]. Where an applicant is seeking to raise these arguments, it may also be possible to argue that in any event, the time for bringing an application for judicial review should be extended. This is because the application for a review of the decision is a reasonable attempt to resolve the matter without bringing an application for judicial review[6].

Clearly, the concepts of continuing breach and fresh decisions are unlikely to be relevant in the context of judicial reviews of final decisions of courts. This is because the court will probably be functus officio after it has taken a decision and so unable to review that earlier decision.

As we have already noted, the High Court is reluctant to allow judicial reviews of interim decisions taken during the course of criminal proceedings[7]. A decision to wait until a final determination of the criminal proceedings will not, however, lead to the court regarding a judicial review application as being delayed, because it will be a challenge to the final decision of the criminal court. It will be said that the final decision is flawed as a result of the interim decision. Time will, as a result, only run from the date of the final decision.

---

1 See Chapter 11 for a description of the orders that can be sought during an application for judicial review.
2 CPR 1998, Sch 1, RSC Ord 53, r 4(2).
3 This is considered in more detail at **5.3** when premature applications are considered.
4 Eg per Jowitt J, *R v Essex County Council ex p C* [1993] COD 398.
5 See, eg *R v Richmond upon Thames London Borough Council ex p McCarthy & Stone (Developments) Ltd* [1992] 2 AC 48, HL, where the challenge was to a decision to refuse to revoke a policy that had been affecting the applicant for several years, cf *R v Secretary of State for Trade and Industry ex p Greenpeace Ltd* [1998] COD 59 rejecting arguments that a particular decision could be challenged where the real focus was an earlier decision.
6 Eg *R v University College London ex p Ursula Riniker* [1995] ELR 213 at 215B, in which it was held that attempts to obtain relief without bringing judicial review proceedings were a good reason for extending time.
7 See **4.10**.

Clearly, the time-limit contained in CPR 1998, Sch 1, RSC Ord 53, r 4 refers to the lodging of the application for permission rather than the decision on the application for permission or the substantive application[1]. Any other interpretation would mean that an application might be ruled out of time as a result of delay on the part of the High Court. As a result, for time to cease to run, it is crucial that the application is lodged in the correct form with the Crown Office[2].

Although time ceases to run when the application for permission is lodged, it is also important to put a potential respondent on notice of a potential judicial review as soon as possible and to supply him with all the information that he reasonably requests about the application. This is because the High Court may take account of this when it decides what action should be taken as a result of any delay[3].

5.2.1 The effect of delay on an application for judicial review

Before seeking to justify the delay in an application for judicial review, applicants may wish to consider whether they can obtain the consent of the respondent to proceedings being brought out of time. There is no express provision providing that the consent of the respondent will always enable proceedings to be brought out of time. The High Court does, however, appear to consider that the consent of the respondent is relevant to the issue of delay, by enabling confirmation of the consent to be submitted with the application[4].

Where there has been delay, the High Court is entitled to extend time for the making of the application if it is satisfied that there is a good reason for extending the time period[5]. The decision as to whether time should be extended should be made at the hearing of the application for permission to apply for judicial review[6]. It is for the applicant for judicial review to show that there is a good reason for extending time[7]. The good reason for extending time can be an explanation for the delay in applying for judicial review, such as problems obtaining legal aid[8]. Similarly, mistakes made by legal advisers[9] and

---

1   *R v Stratford on Avon District Council ex p Jackson* [1985] 3 All ER 769, CA.
2   See Chapter 7 for details of the procedural requirements that must be complied with if an application for judicial review is to be properly lodged.
3   *R v Cotswold DC ex p Barrington Parish Council* (1998) 75 P & CR 515. See also **7.2** for a consideration of the need for a letter before action.
4   *Practice Direction (Uncontested Proceedings: Crown Office List (Applications Outside London): Judicial Review)* [1983] 1 WLR 925.
5   CPR 1998, Sch 1, RSC Ord 53, r 4(1).
6   *R v Criminal Injuries Compensation Board ex p A* [1999] 2 WLR 974, HL.
7   Per Judge J, *R v Warwickshire County Council ex p Collymore* [1995] ELR 217 at 228F.
8   *R v Stratford on Avon District Council ex p Jackson* [1985] 3 All ER 769, CA; but see *R v Metropolitan Borough of Sandwell ex p Cashmore* (1993) 25 HLR 544, in which it was held that it is not automatic that time will be extended as a result of problems obtaining legal aid.
9   *R v Secretary of State for the Home Department ex p Oyeleye* [1994] Imm AR 268; but see *R v Tavistock General Commissioners ex p Worth* [1985] STC 564, in which it was held that reliance on an adviser who was not legally qualified was no good reason for delay.

an attempt by the applicant to seek other legitimate remedies[1] may be good reason for extending the time for bringing a judicial review.

The good reason for extending time is not restricted, however, to matters that are an explanation for delay. In particular, the importance of the issues raised may be a good reason for the extension of time. For example, Mr Justice Taylor held that:

> 'I have concluded that since the matters raised are of general importance, it would be a wrong exercise of my discretion to reject the application on grounds of delay, thereby leaving the substantive issues unresolved. I therefore extend time to allow the applicant to proceed.'[2]

In determining whether to extend time for the bringing of an application for judicial review, the High Court will be concerned about the strength of the application for judicial review[3]. If the grounds for judicial review are particularly strong, the court will be reluctant to hold that delay is sufficient reason for refusing to consider the application[4]. The court is also likely to be concerned about the nature of the decision that is being challenged. For example, the High Court will be reluctant to extend the time for bringing an application for judicial review to challenge an interim decision taken in criminal proceedings, as that will result in the substantive criminal proceedings being delayed[5].

If the court finds that there is good reason why time should be extended despite delay in the case, that does not mean that delay becomes irrelevant. The court can still refuse relief at the substantive hearing[6]. If this is to happen, the High Court will need to be satisfied that the provisions of s 31(6) of the Supreme Court Act 1981 mean that the relief sought by the applicants for judicial review should not be granted[7]. Section 31(6) of the 1981 Act provides that:

> 'Where the High Court considers that there has been undue delay in making an application for judicial review, the Court may refuse to grant – (a) leave for the making of the application, or (b) any relief sought on the application, if it considers that the granting of the relief sought would be likely to cause substantial

---

1 Eg *R v University College London ex p Ursula Riniker* [1995] ELR 213 at 215. It is important to note that pursuit of alternative remedies will not automatically be a good reason for the extension of time. For example, in *R v Essex County Council ex p Jackson Projects Ltd* [1995] COD 155, delay caused by a decision to pursue a compensation claim resulted in the rejection of an application for judicial review.
2 *R v Secretary of State for the Home Department ex p Ruddock* [1987] 1 WLR 1482 at 1485G.
3 Per Judge J, *R v Warwickshire County Council ex p Collymore* [1995] ELR 217 at 228G.
4 The court may still take account of the delay when it decides what form of relief to order. Eg per Roch J, *R v Rochdale Metropolitan Borough Council ex p Schemet* [1994] ELR 89.
5 Per Lord Browne-Wilkinson, *R v Manchester Crown Court ex p DPP* [1993] 1 WLR 1524 at 1529F, HL, holding that delay was one reason why judicial review was not available to challenge decisions taken by a Crown Court in relation to matters being tried on indictment.
6 Although the terms of s 31(6) of the 1981 Act suggest that permission may be refused. In *R v Criminal Injuries Compensation Board ex p A* [1999] 2 WLR 974 at 979A, HL, Lord Slynn held, obiter, that once permission had been granted, it could not be refused at the substantive hearing unless there is an application to set it aside.
7 *R v Stratford on Avon District Council ex p Jackson* [1985] 3 All ER 769, CA.

hardship to, or substantially prejudice the rights of, any person or would be detrimental to good administration.'

The consideration of the issues relevant to s 31(6) of the 1981 Act should generally take place at the substantive hearing rather than the permission hearing, because the High Court is unlikely to have the information that it requires to determine this issue at the permission stage[1]. Although the High Court should not review the decision to extend time at the substantive hearing, that does not mean that the factors taken into account when deciding to extend time are irrelevant. The reasons for the delay, as well as any failure to make full disclosure, are considered when the High Court decides whether to exercise its discretion to refuse relief under s 31(6) of the 1981 Act[2].

5.2.2 The need for disclosure of delay

One of the basic principles that governs judicial review is that applicants are subject to a duty of candour. They are obliged to disclose many matters that are averse to their interests. A failure to disclose such matters can result in permission to bring an application being set aside or it can affect orders made for costs[3]. Delay is one of the matters that applicants for judicial review are required to disclose. A Practice Direction requires that:

> 'Where an application for leave to apply for judicial review under RSC Order 53 is not made promptly and in any event within 3 months from the date when grounds for the application first arose as required by RSC Order 53 rule 4 the application should set out the reasons for the delay.'[4]

It is clear from this Practice Direction that there is a need to disclose the reasons for delay in cases where the application is made within 3 months[5]. This may be particularly relevant in a criminal context where detention is being challenged. For example, the High Court will clearly expect challenges to decisions to extend custody time-limits to be brought as a matter of urgency[6]. Clearly, if there is some good reason why this has not happened, the pleadings should specify this reason.

---

1 Per Lord Goff, *R v Dairy Produce Quota Tribunal ex p Caswell* [1990] 2 AC 738 at 747D, HL.
2 *R v Criminal Injuries Compensation Board ex p A* [1997] 3 WLR 776, CA. The application of s 31(6) of the 1981 Act was not considered by the House of Lords. See [1999] 2 WLR 974, HL.
3 See **7.7**.
4 *Practice Direction (Uncontested Proceedings: Crown Office List (Applications Outside London): Judicial Review)* [1983] 1 WLR 925.
5 See also *R v Greenwich London Borough Council ex p Governors of John Ball Primary School* [1990] COD 103, in which Mr Justice Pill held that there are cases where there is a need to disclose reasons for a delay of less than 3 months in the application for permission to apply for judicial review.
6 See, eg *R v Leeds Crown Court ex p Whitbread* (1998) *Archbold News*, August, DC, in which the High Court held that an applicant would rarely be granted permission to apply for judicial review when the custody time-limit related to proceedings in the magistrates' court and the applicant had been committed to the Crown Court for trial so that a new custody time-limit applied.

5.3 PREMATURE APPLICATIONS FOR JUDICIAL REVIEW

Although applicants for judicial review need to be aware that the High Court will expect them to act speedily, they will have to guard against the High Court dismissing the application as being premature. There are a number of matters that need to be considered by potential applicants. First, the High Court will be reluctant to consider applications for judicial review that challenge interim decisions of criminal courts[1]. Similarly, the High Court will be reluctant to consider judicial reviews of decisions taken by members of the executive who have not been given an opportunity to consider the grounds that are said to give rise to the judicial review. As a result, applicants will normally be expected to write a letter before action[2]. The concept of a premature judicial review is also linked to the High Court's discretion to refuse an application for judicial review where there is an appropriate alternative remedy.

5.4 ALTERNATIVE REMEDIES AND JUDICIAL REVIEW

The existence of an alternative statutory remedy could theoretically be held to exclude the High Court's jurisdiction to consider applications for judicial review if it appears to be comprehensive. However, as we have already noted, the High Court is extremely reluctant to hold that a statutory provision excludes its jurisdiction to consider an application for judicial review. As a result, in practice it is unlikely that the existence of an alternative remedy will be held to exclude judicial review.

If the existence of an alternative remedy is not an automatic bar to judicial review proceedings, that does not mean that the existence of an alternative remedy is irrelevant. That is because the High Court will take account of the alternative remedy when it decides whether to exercise its discretion to grant the remedies sought. For example, Lord Justice Watkins held that:

> '[J]udicial review is a remedy of last resort in the sense that where an applicant invokes this jurisdiction without having sought to deploy another remedy which is available to him, he is likely to find that, in the exercise of the court's discretion, he will be refused relief here. ... But, as has often been acknowledged, it is a matter of discretion; and it follows that the court is entitled to take into account the convenience of the other remedy and the common sense of the situation.'[3]

It has sometimes been said that judicial review applications should only be brought in exceptional circumstances if there is an alternative statutory remedy available[4]. In practice, however, the High Court will often allow judicial reviews

---

1 See **4.10**.
2 See **7.2**.
3 *R v Metropolitan Stipendiary Magistrate ex p London Waste Regulation Authority* [1993] 3 All ER 113 at 120B, DC, rejecting the right to apply for a voluntary bill as an alternative remedy.
4 Eg per Lord Jauncey, *Harley Development Inc v Commissioner of Inland Revenue* [1996] 1 WLR 727 at 736C, PC.

despite the existence of an alternative remedy in circumstances that are not exceptional. The court will consider whether the alternative remedy is 'adequate'[1]. Thus, in a criminal context, the right to appeal against a conviction to the Crown Court does not mean that the High Court will not consider an application for judicial review[2]. This is because Parliament clearly intended that defendants in the magistrates' court are entitled to two fair trials, as it provided a right to a rehearing in the Crown Court. The right of appeal to the Crown Court is not an adequate remedy, as it may result in only one fair trial.

In Chapter 4, we considered the variety of circumstances that might arise in a criminal context where an application for judicial review might be brought. In that chapter, we considered whether there is an alternative remedy and whether that alternative remedy is likely to result in the High Court exercising its discretion to refuse an application for judicial review. The existence of an alternative remedy is a matter that must be disclosed by the applicant for judicial review, as a result of the duty of candour on applicants for judicial review[3].

5.5 DELAY AND HABEAS CORPUS

There are no time-limits requiring an application for a writ of habeas corpus to be brought within a particular period of time, because an application for a writ must be brought to challenge present detention rather than historic detention. Clearly, it would be unjust to allow unlawful detention to continue merely because it had not been challenged within any particular period of time. Practitioners should, however, be aware that this concern about the continuation of unlawful detention means that in practice, the High Court will expect applications for habeas corpus to be regarded as urgent matters.

5.6 DELAY AND APPEALS BY WAY OF CASE STATED

The time-limit for bringing appeals by way of case stated both against decisions of the magistrates' court and against decisions of the Crown Court is 21 days[4]. In the magistrates' court, time runs from the date of sentence if a defendant is convicted and the case is then adjourned for sentence[5]. In the Crown Court, time runs from the date of the decision that the appeal relates to[6]. If the time

---

1 Per Lord Bridge, *Leech v Deputy Governor of Parkhurst Prison* [1988] AC 533 at 566H, HL.
2 *R v Hereford Magistrates' Court ex p Rowlands and Ingram; R v Harrow Youth Court ex p Prussia* [1998] QB 110, DC.
3 See **7.7**.
4 Magistrates' Courts Act 1980, s 111(2) governing the time-limit in the magistrates' court; and Crown Court Rules 1982, SI 1982/1109, r 26(1).
5 Magistrates' Courts Act 1980, s 111(3). See *Liverpool City Council v Worthington* (1998) *The Times*, 16 June, DC, holding that where a decision on costs is the final decision, time runs from the date of that decision.
6 Crown Court Rules 1982, SI 1982/1109, r 26(1).

period ends on a date when the court is closed, that does not mean that time is extended to the next working day[1].

When an appeal is to be brought against a decision in the magistrates' court, the magistrates' court and the High Court have absolutely no discretion to extend this time period[2]. When an appeal is brought against a decision of the Crown Court, however, a judge is entitled to extend time even where the application to extend time is made out of time[3]. In practice, however, both time-limits should be regarded as rigid time-limits that should always be complied with. Although in principle, there is likely to be no reason why a judicial review should not be brought challenging a decision to refuse to extend time, in practice, this may well be difficult. A Crown Court judge is unlikely to be obliged to give reasons for refusing to extend the time period for appealing by way of case stated[4]. Clearly, without reasons, it is likely to be impossible to know whether a Crown Court judge erred in his approach to the application to extend time.

Where a Crown Court judge does decide that time should be extended to enable an appellant to state a case, there is no obligation on that judge to obtain the consent of the magistrates who sat with him[5]. If, however, it is the prosecution that is appealing out of time, the acquitted defendant should be consulted by the Crown Court judge before the decision is taken to extend time[6].

If magistrates seek to argue that they have no jurisdiction to respond to an application to state a case as the application was out of time, there may be further steps that can be taken on behalf of an applicant. It is important to consider the precise reasons given by the magistrates for finding that the application was made out of time. The High Court has shown that it is willing to interpret the rule against out-of-time applications flexibly. For example, the High Court has held that, where an application is posted so that it would have been received in time in the normal course of events, it is a timely application[7].

An application that fails to comply with the procedural rules regarding the content of the application may be treated as being in time, providing that the defect is remedied and there was substantial compliance with the rules[8]. Thus, an application to state a case that failed to identify a question of law was regarded as a proper application, because the magistrates must have been

---

1   *Peacock v R* (1858) 22 JP 403.
2   *Michael v Gowland* [1977] 1 WLR 296, DC, applying the Magistrates' Courts Act 1952 which contained an almost identical provision to the Magistrates' Courts Act 1980, s 111.
3   Crown Court Rules 1982, SI 1982/1109, r 26(14).
4   In *R v Stafford Crown Court ex p Reid* (1995) *The Independent*, 13 March, DC, it was held that Crown Court judges are not obliged to give reasons for a decision to refuse to extend time for an appeal to the Crown Court as the decision is procedural not judicial. Similar principles are likely to apply to an appeal by way of case stated. Cf *R v Mildenhall Magistrates' Court ex p Forest Heath District Council* (1997) *The Times*, 16 May, CA.
5   *DPP v Coleman* [1998] 1 WLR 1708, DC.
6   Ibid.
7   *P and M Supplies (Essex) Ltd v Hackney London Borough Council* (1990) 154 JP 814, DC.
8   *R v Croydon Justices ex p Lefore Holdings Ltd* [1980] 1 WLR 1465, CA.

aware of the issue in the case and the question that was put before them. It did not matter that the question was put after the expiry of the time for applying to state a case[1]. If the magistrates wrongly hold that an application to state a case was made out of time, a judicial review may be brought of that decision.

Where an application for a case to be stated is made to the magistrates out of time, that out-of-time application does not prevent an appeal to the Crown Court[2].

5.7 SHOULD AN ORDER BE SOUGHT LIMITING THE REPORTING OF THE MATTER?

There is no inherent power to restrict reporting of court proceedings[3]. Section 11 of the Contempt of Court Act 1981, however, gives the High Court and any other court the power to make:

> 'such directions prohibiting the publication of [a] name or matter in connection with the proceedings as appear to the court to be necessary for the purpose for which it was so withheld [in the proceedings before the court].'

This provision is the one that would be relied on whenever an adult who is a party to proceedings seeks to limit or prevent reporting of the matter[4]. Thus, for example, it is the provision used where the court wished to avoid news reporting of a person who had provided assistance to the police[5].

In general, it is a rule of the English legal system that the administration of justice should be done in public. This means that in general nothing should prevent the 'publication to a wider public of fair and accurate reports of proceedings'[6]. As a result, the High Court will base the consideration of any application for an order restricting reporting of proceedings on a presumption that no order should be made. The general rule will only be departed from:

> '[W]here the nature or circumstances of the particular proceeding are such that the application of the general rule in its entirety would frustrate or render impracticable the administration of justice or would damage some other public interest for whose protection Parliament has made some statutory derogation from the rule.'[7]

An example of circumstances where an order under s 11 of the Contempt of Court Act 1981 should be made arises when there is a real risk that a person 'will suffer real significant physical or mental harm' as a result of publication[8]. It

---

1   *R v Croydon Justices ex p Lefore Holdings Ltd* [1980] 1 WLR 1465, CA.
2   *P and M Supplies (Essex) Ltd v Hackney London Borough Council* (1990) 154 JP 814, DC.
3   *R v Newtonabbey Magistrates' Court ex p Belfast Telegraph Newspapers Ltd* (1997) *The Times*, 27 August, QBD (NI).
4   See **5.8** for special provisions regarding young people.
5   See, eg *R v Secretary of State ex p G* (1990) *The Times*, 26 June, CA, for an example of a case where such an order was made.
6   Per Lord Diplock, *Attorney-General v Leveller Magazine* [1979] AC 440 at 450B, HL.
7   Ibid, at 450C.
8   Per Mr Justice Dyson, *Re D* (unreported) 17 November 1997, CO/3369/97.

is unnecessary in these circumstances for the court to consider whether an applicant for judicial review would withdraw proceedings if there was no order preventing publication.

Mr Justice Brooke has recently considered the procedure that should be adopted when applying for an order under s 11 of the Contempt of Court Act 1981 in proceedings in the Crown Office. First, the applicant should contact the Crown Office before lodging papers if there is any concern that the papers lodged may reveal details that will give rise to adverse publicity. That will enable the applicant to ensure that the application can be considered immediately. In any event, it may be appropriate to hold the hearing to determine whether the order should be made in camera. Alternatively, it may be appropriate to make an interim order pending a full consideration of the merits of the application. Such an order might be made if it would enable the applicant to obtain further evidence to show that a final order would be justified[1].

Linked to the provision allowing the reporting of proceedings to be restricted is the inherent power of the High Court to hold the hearing of a matter in camera. As noted above, this may well be appropriate where there is an application for an order under s 11 of the Contempt of Court Act 1981, during which the applicant will seek to rely on sensitive material. The application should be heard in camera if the disclosure of the material relied on in support of the application for an order will frustrate the purpose of the order[2].

5.8 RESTRICTIONS ON REPORTING IN THE CONTEXT OF CASES INVOLVING YOUNG PEOPLE

Special considerations arise in relation to reporting restrictions in cases regarding young people. The reporting of cases in these circumstances is governed by s 39 of the Children and Young Persons Act 1933 which provides that the court may direct that:

> 'no newspaper report of the proceedings shall reveal the name, address, or school, or include any particulars calculated to lead to the identification of any child or young person concerned in the proceedings.'

The Court of Appeal has held that, although the public normally have a legitimate interest in receiving reports of criminal proceedings, the mere fact that a person appearing before the courts is a child or young person can be sufficient to justify the making of an order under s 39 of the 1933 Act[3]. In deciding whether to make an order under s 39 of the 1933 Act, the court will take account of the nature of that provision, as it is clearly a child welfare

---

1   *R v Somerset Health Authority ex p S* [1996] COD 244.
2   *R v Tower Bridge Magistrates' Court ex p Osbourne* [1988] Crim LR 382, DC.
3   Per Watkins LJ, *R v Leicester Crown Court ex p S* [1993] 1 WLR 111 at 114D, DC. Note, however, that it is now clear that it is not only 'rare and exceptional cases' where an order should not be made. See *R v Central Criminal Court ex p Simpkins* (1998) *The Times*, 26 October, DC; *Anthony Lee* (1993) 96 Cr App R 188, CA.

provision, and the stage that any substantive criminal proceedings have reached.[1]

5.9 OTHER PARTICULAR CONSIDERATIONS IN CASES INVOLVING JUVENILES

The CPR 1998 provide that a 'child must have a litigation friend to conduct proceedings on his behalf'[2]. The court may, however, make an order allowing proceedings to be conducted without a litigation friend[3]. The rule applies to juveniles as a child is defined as being a person under 18[4]. The terms of this rule appear wide and would appear to include criminal proceedings in the High Court[5]. In practice, it appears that criminal cases are often brought in the High Court without the intervention of a litigation friend[6]. That, however, cannot be regarded as good practice. A litigation friend should be appointed to act at the commencement of litigation in the High Court, unless an order is sought dispensing with the need for a litigation friend[7].

The role of a litigation friend is set out in a Practice Direction. This states that:

> 'It is the duty of a litigation friend fairly and competently to conduct proceedings on behalf of a child or patient. He must have no interest in the proceedings adverse to that of the child or patient and all steps and decisions he takes in the proceedings must be taken for the benefit of the child or patient.'[8]

In practice, a parent is usually appointed to act as litigation friend, as they are most likely to be able to take on the obligations set out above.

The court may make orders appointing a person to act as litigation friend[9]. If a person is to act as litigation friend for a juvenile and no court order has been obtained appointing that person, a certificate of suitability signed by that person should be lodged with the Crown Office[10]. The rules provide a standard form certificate that is set out in Appendix 5. That certificate must state that the

---

1 *In re H, In re D* (1999) *The Times*, 13 August 1999, DC.
2 CPR 1998, r 21.2(2).
3 Ibid, r 21.2(3).
4 Ibid, r 21.1(2)(a).
5 Indeed, CPR 1998, r 2.1 states that the CPR 1998 apply to all proceedings in the High Court save for certain exceptions. These exceptions do not include judicial review, appeals by way of case stated and applications for a writ of habeas corpus.
6 The CPR 1998 have only recently come into force. The litigation that we considered to determine current practice was not governed by these rules. The authors, however, expect that parties will still continue to fail to recognise the obligation to have a litigation friend appointed.
7 There is no reason why an application to state a case should be made through a next friend. However, when the appeal is lodged in the High Court and so proceedings start in the High Court, it is good practice that the action is brought through a next friend.
8 *Practice Direction (CPR 1998, Part 21 – Children and Patients)*, para 2.1.
9 CPR 1998, r 21.6.
10 Ibid, r 21.5(4)(b).

litigation friend consents to act and that he believes the party is a child[1]. It must also state that the person:

'(a) can fairly and competently conduct proceedings on behalf of the child or patient;
'(b) has no interest adverse to that of the child or patient; and
'(c) where the child or patient is a claimant[2], undertakes to pay any costs which the child or patient may be ordered to pay in relation to the proceedings, subject to any right he may have to be repaid from the assets of the child or patient.'[3]

The title of the case in any pleadings where there is a litigation friend should state the juvenile's name in the form set out below:

'John Smith, (a child, by James Smith, his litigation friend).'[4]

Alternatively, if there is no litigation friend, the pleadings should state the juvenile's name in the following form.

'John Smith, (a child).'[5]

Clearly, the rules regarding litigation friends do not merely govern cases brought by juveniles. Where the defendant in an appeal by way of case stated by the prosecution is a juvenile, or where a juvenile is appearing as the interested party in a judicial review brought by the prosecution, a litigation friend should be appointed to act on their behalf unless an order is obtained dispensing with the need for a litigation friend. Practitioners acting for parties other than juveniles in cases involving juveniles should be aware that they need the permission of the court to take any steps in proceedings save for serving a claim form or making an application for the appointment of a litigation friend unless the juvenile has a litigation friend[6]. It might well be cumbersome to seek the permission of court for bringing each stage. As a result, it is sensible to seek an order either appointing a litigation friend or dispensing with the need for a litigation friend.

Any order sought in relation to litigation friends should be handled in the same way as other interim orders in proceedings in the Crown Office[7].

---

1 *Practice Direction (CPR 1998, Part 21 – Children and Patients)*, para 2.3.2.
2 A claimant is defined as a person who makes a claim (CPR 1998, r 2.3(1)). This would not appear to include an applicant for judicial review as they are described in the rules as applicants (eg CPR 1998, Sch 1, RSC Ord 53, r 6(3)).
3 CPR 1998, r 21.4(3).
4 *Practice Direction (CPR 1998, Part 21 – Children and Patients)*, para 1.5.
5 Ibid.
6 CPR 1998, r 21.3(2).
7 See **6.9** for details.

5.10 PARTICULAR CONSIDERATIONS IN THE CASE OF A PERSON SUFFERING FROM MENTAL HEALTH PROBLEMS

The need for a litigation friend arises not only in the case of juveniles. It also arises where a person is a 'patient'[1]. A patient is defined as 'a person who by reason of mental disorder within the meaning of the Mental Health Act 1983 is incapable of managing and administering his own affairs'[2]. The court has no power to make an order dispensing with the need for a litigation friend where a party is a patient[3].

Part VII of the Mental Health Act 1983 provides for the appointment of a person to conduct litigation on behalf of a patient. If such a person has been appointed, an official copy of the order appointing the person under Part VII of the 1983 Act should be lodged with the court[4]. If no person has been appointed under Part VII of the 1983 Act, a next friend may be appointed in the same way as in the case of a juvenile. Other procedures relating to a litigation friend for a patient are also the same as the procedures for a juvenile.

Clearly, it is possible that a person may become a patient after an action has been commenced. If that happens, no steps may be taken in the proceedings without the permission of the court until the patient has a litigation friend to act on their behalf[5].

---

1   CPR 1998, r 21.2(1).
2   Ibid, r 21.1(2)(b).
3   Ibid, r 21.2(1).
4   Ibid, r 21.5(2).
5   Ibid, r 21.3(3).

Chapter 6

PROCEDURAL MATTERS COMMON TO ALL CROWN OFFICE PROCEEDINGS

6.1 PROCEDURE RULES GOVERNING PROCEEDINGS IN THE CROWN OFFICE

All proceedings in the High Court including proceedings in the Crown Office are governed by the CPR 1998[1]. We have included the most significant rules in Appendix 5[2].

These new rules apply to proceedings issued on or after 26 April 1999. Proceedings that were issued before that date are governed by a mixture of the previous rules and the new rules[3]. As the new rules are generally the same as the old rules in the fields of judicial review, habeas corpus and appeal by way of case stated, the transitional arrangements are unlikely to cause any real problems. There are two matters of significance. First, all interim applications must be made in accordance with the new rules if they are made on or after 26 April 1999[4]. Second, costs will be determined in accordance with the new rules if the assessment takes place on or after 26 April 1999. There is, however, a presumption that no costs for work done before 26 April 1999 will be disallowed if they would have been allowed under the old rules[5].

6.2 EXPEDITION

If the High Court decides that expedition should be ordered during a judicial review application, the order for expedition is normally made by the judge who grants permission to apply for judicial review. The notice of application should state that an order for expedition is part of the relief sought[6]. Similarly, when the court considers an application for habeas corpus, any order for expedition will normally be made by the judge who considers the application without notice[7]. The need for expedition can be raised at court without there being any need for a formal notice of application. If expedition is not ordered at these stages, an interim application can be made to the Master of the Crown Office. If

---

1 CPR 1998, r 2.1.
2 See *Civil Court Service* (Jordans) and at www.civilcourtservice.co.uk.
3 CPR 1998, Part 51 and *Practice Direction (CPR 1998, Part 51 – Transitional Arrangements)*.
4 *Practice Direction (CPR 1998, Part 51 – Transitional Arrangements)*, para 14.
5 Ibid, para 18.
6 See Appendix 1 for a precedent.
7 It is very likely that expedition will be ordered during proceedings for a writ of habeas corpus as the legality of detention of a person is being questioned.

that application is unsuccessful, a renewed application can be made to a judge or a Divisional Court[1].

The procedure is clearly different when the High Court is considering an appeal by way of case stated, as there is no stage that is equivalent to the application for permission. As a result, any application for expedition should initially be made to the Master of the Crown Office[2]. If that application is unsuccessful, a renewed application can be made to a judge or to a Divisional Court[3].

Where an interim application needs to be made to a Master or to the court for orders relating to matters such as expedition, the procedure for obtaining orders is the same as that adopted when applying for other interim orders[4].

In cases where an order for expedition is sought, orders might also be sought abridging the time for service of the respondent's evidence in a judicial review or application for habeas corpus and abridging the notice that must be given to the respondent before the matter can be heard.

When expedition has been ordered, the clerk to counsel instructed by an applicant must supply the Crown Office with a time estimate for the substantive hearing and details of counsel instructed. Cases where expedition has been ordered are placed in Part D of the list[5]. This means that they will be listed as soon as practicable.

6.3 LISTING ARRANGEMENTS IN CASES WHERE EXPEDITION HAS NOT BEEN ORDERED

In a case where expedition is not ordered, the case will progress through up to four parts of the Crown Office list[6]. The first part, Part A, is for cases that are not ready to be heard, because the time for the respondent to serve written evidence or take other steps, such as the return of a writ of habeas corpus, has not expired. Appeals by way of case stated and applications for a writ of habeas corpus where the writ has not been issued will not normally enter Part A as there will be no steps for the respondent to take.

When time-limits for action by the respondent have expired, the case moves into Part B. This happens whether or not there has been compliance with time-limits imposed on the respondent. At this stage, the Crown Office will write to the applicant's solicitor. That solicitor should forward that letter to the clerk to counsel instructed by the applicant and to parties served with the claim form. On receipt, the clerk to the applicant's counsel is obliged to provide the

---

1 *Practice Direction (Crown Office List)* [1987] 1 WLR 232, [1987] 1 All ER 368.
2 Ibid. See also Rules of the Supreme Court, Ord 56, r 13(1) which provide that interlocutory applications in an appeal by way of case stated can be made to any judge or a Master of the Queen's Bench Division.
3 *Practice Direction (Crown Office List)* [1987] 1 WLR 232, [1987] 1 All ER 368.
4 See **6.9** for details.
5 *Practice Direction (Crown Office List)* [1987] 1 WLR 232, [1987] 1 All ER 368.
6 Ibid.

Crown Office with a time estimate in writing[1]. When the case enters the Part B list or at any later stage, the parties may apply to the Master of the Crown Office to have the case stood out into Part C. Part C is the part of the list reserved for cases that are not ready. Cases are often placed in Part C when there is a prospect of the case being settled. If the Master refuses to agree that the case should be stood out, an application may be made to a judge or a Divisional Court. The final part of the list is Part E, which contains cases listed for hearing. Applications for orders regarding listing are made in the same way as applications for other interim orders[2].

As far as possible, cases are taken from the top of the Part B list for listing in the order that they entered[3]. The applicant's solicitors will be informed by letter when the case reaches the top of the Part B list[4]. They will also be informed that the case may be listed at short notice after a particular date ('the warned date') or alternatively, the case will be listed for a fixed date. Again, the applicant's solicitors will be responsible for informing all relevant parties of the warned date or fixed date[5].

Crown Office listing can be contacted on 0171 936 6013 if parties have any queries regarding a listing matter.

6.4 PRACTICE GOVERNING DOCUMENTS TO BE FILED WITH THE CROWN OFFICE

Where the documents in support of any application or an appeal consist of 10 or more pages, they should be filed in an indexed and paginated bundle[6]. The documents in the bundle must be clearly legible[7]. The pages of the bundle should be numbered consecutively[8]. The normal practice is to use black numbers at the centre of the bottom of the page. In addition, every document should, where possible, be typed single-sided on A4 paper with a 3.5 cm margin[9].

6.4.1 Documents to be filed with the Crown Office before the substantive hearing of matters

As we have set out below, applicants and respondent must file documents with the Crown Office before the substantive hearing of a matter. If the case is to be heard by a Divisional Court, two copies of these documents should be lodged

---

1 *Practice Direction (Crown Office List)* [1987] 1 WLR 232, [1987] 1 All ER 368.
2 See **6.9**.
3 *Practice Direction (Crown Office List)* [1987] 1 WLR 232, [1987] 1 All ER 368.
4 *Practice Direction (Crown Office List: Preparation for Hearings)* [1994] 1 WLR 1551, [1994] 4 All ER 671.
5 Ibid.
6 Ibid.
7 *Practice Direction (CPR 1998, Part 5 – Court Documents)*, para 2.2.
8 Ibid.
9 *Practice Direction (CPR 1998, Part 5 – Court Documents)*, para 2.2.

with the court, otherwise only one copy should be lodged[1]. A failure to comply with these requirements may result in the adjournment of the case and orders for costs[2].

Solicitors acting for an applicant or appellant must lodge a paginated, indexed bundle with the court at least 5 clear working days before the fixed or warned date for a substantive hearing[3]. This bundle must be lodged, even where a bundle has already been lodged, to obtain permission to apply for judicial review. This bundle should include all documentation that the court will need to rely on when determining the application. In particular, it should include any decisions of the High Court regarding interlocutory matters. The bundles must be secured together, arranged in chronological order beginning with the earliest documents first[4], indexed and paginated consecutively with the numbers at centre bottom[5]. If the bundle contains more than 100 pages, numbered dividers should be placed at intervals between groups of documents[6]. The bundle should usually be in a lever arch file. The documents contained in the bundles must be legible.

The applicant or appellant's counsel is also required to lodge a skeleton argument at least 5 clear working days before the fixed or warned date[7]. It must also be served on other parties. The skeleton argument must state the Crown Office reference and the fixed or warned list date. It must also state:

(a) the time estimate (even though this should have been given earlier);
(b) a list of issues;
(c) a list of propositions of law (together with authorities relied on and page references to passages relied on)[8];
(d) a chronology of events (with page references to the applicant's bundle);
(e) a list of essential reading (with page references to the applicant's bundle); and

---

1 *Practice Direction (Crown Office List: Preparation for Hearings)* [1994] 1 WLR 1551, [1994] 4 All ER 671. It is the practice in an appeal by way of case stated to supply 3 copies of all documents.
2 *Practice Direction (Crown Office List: Preparation for Hearings)* [1994] 1 WLR 1551, [1994] 4 All ER 671.
3 Ibid.
4 In practice, documents of the same type are usually grouped together so that the application or appeal is normally placed at the front of the bundle, orders made by the High Court follow and the evidence is then included in chronological order.
5 *Practice Direction (CPR 1998, Part 39 – Miscellaneous Provisions Relating to Hearings)*, para 3.5.
6 Ibid.
7 Although the skeleton argument can be lodged up to 5 days before the date of the hearing, it is preferable that it is lodged earlier.
8 Where the authorities relied on are not reported in the major law reports, it is good practice to supply copies of the authorities with the skeleton argument. See, however, *Practice Statement (Supreme Court: Judgments)* [1998] 1 WLR 825 which limits the use of transcripts to circumstances where there is no official report and counsel can assure the court that the judgment contains a relevant legal principle not found in reported cases. It also requires the use of the official transcript.

(f) a list of dramatis personae where there are a large number of people who feature in the documents[1].

Although the skeleton argument must be supplied 5 clear working days before the hearing, it may be supplemented up to 1 working day before the hearing[2]. A precedent skeleton argument is included in Appendix 1.

Similarly, counsel acting for respondents or other parties seeking to appear at the oral hearing must file skeleton arguments and serve them on other parties. The contents should be the same as those in a skeleton argument filed for an applicant. This skeleton argument must be filed at least 3 clear working days before the date of hearing, although it can be updated up to 1 working day before the hearing.

It is now clear that the High Court can consider extracts from *Hansard* when it determines questions of law[3]. If *Hansard* is to be cited, a copy of the citation together with a summary of the argument relating to the parliamentary material must be served on all parties and two copies must be lodged with the Head of the Crown Office. This must happen at least 5 days before the date of the hearing[4].

By 9.30 am on the morning of the hearing, counsel for the applicant and respondent must supply the usher with a list of authorities to be relied on[5].

6.5 SOLICITORS CEASING TO ACT

Where a solicitor is acting for a party under the terms of a legal aid certificate and that certificate is revoked or discharged, the solicitor should send the notice revoking or discharging legal aid to the court so that he ceases to be the solicitor on the record[6]. He must give notice to the other parties and to counsel[7]. If the party wishes to continue the action he must serve notice of change of representation on all the parties.

---

1   *Practice Direction (Crown Office List: Preparation for Hearings)* [1994] 1 WLR 1551, [1994] 4 All ER 671.
2   Ibid.
3   *Pepper (Inspector of Taxes) v Hart and Related Appeals* [1993] 1 All ER 42, HL, in which the House of Lords held that extracts from *Hansard* may be relied on when a statute is ambiguous and the statements to be relied on are clear and were made by the bill's promoter. This may not be the only circumstance in which *Hansard* is referred to. Lord Browne-Wilkinson stated at 68D that:
    '[T]he Attorney General's contentions are inconsistent with the practice which has now continued over a number of years in cases of judicial review. In such cases, *Hansard* has frequently been referred to with a view to ascertaining whether a statutory power has been improperly exercised for an alien purpose or in a wholly unreasonable manner.'
4   *Practice Direction (Hansard Extracts)* [1995] 1 WLR 192.
5   *Practice Direction (Authorities)* [1961] 1 WLR 400, [1961] 1 All ER 541.
6   Civil Legal Aid (General) Regulations 1989, SI 1989/339, reg 83.
7   Ibid, reg 82(2).

Otherwise, where a solicitor ceases to act in proceedings in the Crown Office, the party is obliged to give notice of that change of representation[1]. The Civil Procedure Rules provide a standard notice which is included in Appendix 5. If the party fails to give notice of the change of representation, the former solicitor may apply to the Master of the Crown Office for an order that they have ceased to act[2]. Without an order, the Crown Office will continue to regard the previous solicitor as acting. As a result, the previous solicitor will be responsible for notification of the warned or fixed date and compliance with other Practice Directions. They will also be responsible for briefing counsel[3].

Notice of the application for an order must be given to the party for whom the solicitor formerly acted[4]. It must also be supported by evidence explaining the basis of the application[5]. A precedent of an application is included in Appendix 1. If an order is obtained, it must be served on all parties to the proceedings[6]. Once the order is served, a certificate of service must be filed with the court[7].

6.6 UNCONTESTED AND WITHDRAWN PROCEEDINGS IN THE CROWN OFFICE

There is provision for the High Court to adopt a simplified procedure when it determines uncontested proceedings. Applications can be heard in open court without the attendance of the parties so that the court can consider the terms of a proposed order[8]. The court will want a document signed on behalf of the parties setting out the terms of the proposed order, together with two copies of that document[9]. The court will also want a short statement that sets out the matters justifying the making of the proposed order, together with the authorities and statutory materials relied on[10]. A precedent is set out in Appendix 1.

It should not be assumed that an order will be made by the High Court merely because all parties consent to the terms of the order. The judge may request more information from the parties[11]. Alternatively, the judge may order that the matter is listed in court in the normal way[12]. As a result, the reasons should be as clear as possible.

---

1 CPR 1998, r 42.2(2) requires the notice to be filed and served on all parties.
2 CPR 1998, r 42.3; *Practice Direction (Crown Office List) (No 2)* [1991] 1 WLR 280.
3 *Practice Direction (Crown Office List) (No 2)* [1991] 1 WLR 280.
4 CPR 1998, r 42.3(2)(a). Proof of service will be required if the party does not attend a hearing regarding this matter.
5 Ibid, r 42.3(2)(b).
6 Ibid, r 42.3(3)(a).
7 Ibid, r 42.3(3)(b).
8 *Practice Direction (Crown Office List: Consent Orders)* [1997] 1 WLR 825.
9 Ibid.
10 Ibid.
11 Ibid.
12 Ibid.

When an applicant or appellant does not require the leave of the court to withdraw the proceedings, a notice of withdrawal should be lodged with the Crown Office and a copy should be served on all other parties[1]. If leave is required and all parties have consented to this procedure, a consent order should be lodged with the Crown Office in the same way as when the parties consent to some other disposal of proceedings[2].

6.7 SERVICE OF DOCUMENTS

The CPR 1998 govern the service of all documents once proceedings have begun in the High Court. In an appeal by way of case stated, the procedure rules governing the magistrates' court and the Crown Court will govern the service of documents until a final case has been signed by the magistrates or the Crown Court judge[3]. At this stage, proceedings will begin in the High Court so the CPR 1998 apply.

The CPR 1998 provide that documents may be served by:

(a) personal service[4];
(b) first-class post[5];
(c) leaving the document at an address for service[6];
(d) a document exchange in accordance with the relevant Practice Direction[7]; or
(e) fax or other means of electronic communication in accordance with the relevant Practice Direction[8].

The place for service is also defined by the rules[9]. Individuals may be served at their usual or last known residence. Businesses that are not incorporated may be served at their principal or last place of business. A company can be served at the principal office or any place of business that has a real connection with the proceedings.

The rules provide for the deemed day of service[10]. Documents served by first-class post and document exchange are deemed served on the second day

---

1 *Practice Direction (Crown Office List: Consent Orders)* [1997] 1 WLR 825.
2 Ibid.
3 See **9.2** for details.
4 If a party has been notified that a solicitor is authorised to be served with documents, a document may not be served personally. The solicitor must be served (CPR 1998, r 6.4(2)). Where a company is to be served, the service may be on a person holding a senior position (CPR 1998, r 6.4(4)). Where a partnership is to be served, the service may be on a partner or a person with control of the business (CPR 1998, r 6.4(5)).
5 CPR 1998, r 6.2(1)(b).
6 Ibid, r 6.2(1)(c).
7 Ibid, r 6.2(1)(d).
8 Ibid, r 6.2(1)(e).
9 Ibid, r 6.5.
10 Ibid, r 6.7(1).

after posting. Documents served by fax are deemed served on the day of service if that day is a business day and they are served by 4pm. Otherwise they are deemed served on the next business day.

6.8 TIME-LIMITS

The time-limits for stages in proceedings are considered later in this book when we consider the procedure. When proceedings are pending in the High Court, time-limits are determined by reference to the CPR 1998[1]. These provide that the day on which a time period starts is not included in that period[2]. In addition, where a period is 5 days or less, Saturdays, Sundays, bank holidays, Good Friday and Christmas Day do not count[3].

6.9 INTERIM APPLICATIONS

Interim applications are usually made by filing an application notice with the Crown Office[4]. There is also a fee which is presently £50. In general, the application notice must be served on other parties unless the rules or a court order provide that this is unnecessary[5]. The application notice must state the order that is being sought and why it is being sought[6]. It must also state the title of the case, the reference number of the claim, the full name of the applicant, the address for service if the applicant for the order is not a party to the proceedings, and a request for a hearing or a request that the matter is considered without a hearing[7]. If there is a request that the matter is considered without a hearing, the court may still order that a hearing must take place[8]. The CPR 1998 provide that Form N244 may be used. This is included in Appendix 5. A precedent of the contents of an application notice in a case where a solicitor is applying for an order that they cease to act is included in Appendix 1.

When a party seeks an interim order, they should normally seek the consent of the other parties. If all parties consent, the parties should sign the draft order which should also include a statement of the reasons why the order should be made[9]. That order should then be filed with the Crown Office so that a judge can consider whether the order should be made[10]. A consent order for the settlement of proceedings is included in Appendix 1.

---

1   When application is made to state a case, the CPR 1998 only apply after the case has been commenced in the High Court.
2   CPR 1998, r 2.8(3).
3   Ibid, r 2.8(4).
4   Ibid, r 23.3.
5   Ibid, r 23.4.
6   Ibid, r 23.6.
7   *Practice Direction (CPR 1998, Part 23 – Applications)*, para 2.1.
8   Ibid, para 2.5.
9   *Practice Direction (Crown Office List: Consent Orders)* [1997] 1 WLR 825.
10 Ibid.

Procedural Matters Common to all Crown Office Proceedings

Except in cases where the order sought is very simple, the applicant for an order should produce a draft of the order sought[1]. In cases where the order sought is very complex, the draft should be supplied on computer disk in WordPerfect 5.1 format[2].

Where a hearing of the interim application is necessary, that hearing may take place by telephone. This is a new procedure, so it is unclear how it will work in practice. If a hearing is to take place by telephone, no party can be acting in person and all parties must consent to the hearing taking place by telephone[3].

---

1   *Practice Direction (CPR 1998, Part 23 – Applications)*, para 12.1.
2   Ibid.
3   *Practice Direction (CPR 1998, Part 23 – Applications)*, para 6.1.

Chapter 7

THE PROCEDURE FOR BRINGING AN APPLICATION FOR JUDICIAL REVIEW

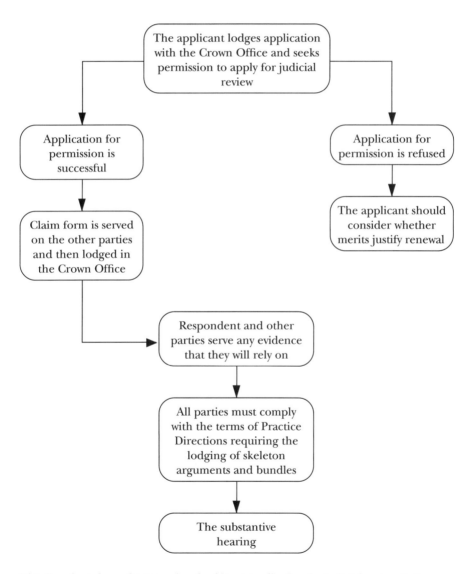

This flowchart shows the stages involved in an application for judicial review. Reference should also be made to the Procedural Guide contained in Appendix 4.

7.1 INTRODUCTION

The introduction of the CPR 1998 from 26 April 1999 has had little effect on the procedure for bringing an application for judicial review. In particular, many of the case management provisions and the provisions for tracking cases are not being applied in the Crown Office. The terminology has, however, changed significantly. When reading law reports or older text books, it is important to be aware of the old terminology. The significant differences are set out below.

Old term	New term
Application for leave to move for judicial review	Application for permission to bring an application for judicial review
Motion	Claim form
Ex parte application	Application without notice[1]

We have already noted that there are significant procedural differences between a judicial review in a 'criminal cause or matter' and a judicial review in another type of matter. As we have also already stated, an applicant should determine whether their application relates to a 'criminal cause or matter' before they bring the application[2]. Where the procedure for bringing an application for judicial review is different depending on whether a matter is a 'criminal cause or matter', we have set out the differences in the text of this chapter. If there is no reference to any difference, it should be assumed the procedure is the same for both types of matter.

7.2 A LETTER BEFORE ACTION

In general, it is now accepted practice that most applicants for judicial review will write to the proposed respondents explaining the basis of the challenge. This letter should also give the decision-maker an opportunity to reverse their decision before proceedings start[3]. A precedent letter before action is included in Appendix 1.

One exception to the need for a letter before action arises where the decision being challenged has been taken by a court, because the decision challenged will normally be a final decision. As a result, the court will often be functus officio and so unable to reverse the decision challenged. It is still, however, good practice to inform the court that an application is being brought for judicial review.

---

1   Although ex parte applications are now known as applications without notice, cases are still called *R v The Respondent ex p The Applicant*.
2   See **5.1** for a consideration of the definition.
3   *R v Horsham District Council ex p Wenman* [1995] 1 WLR 680, in which legal advisers were fortunate to avoid a wasted costs order for failing to conduct a judicial review properly. Mr Justice Brooke held, inter alia, that applicants should write a letter before action except in exceptional circumstances as litigation should normally be regarded as a weapon of last resort (at 709F).

Where the judicial review seeks to challenge an interim decision of a criminal court that is not functus officio, the criminal court should be put on notice that a judicial review will be sought. The applicant should apply for an adjournment of the proceedings before the criminal court so that the application for judicial review may be brought[1]. If the application for an adjournment is refused, the decision may also be challenged[2]. A stay of proceedings in the criminal court may also be sought from the High Court as a form of interim relief[3].

There will also be cases where the urgency of the application means that it is not practical for a detailed letter before action to be written. The urgency may also mean that it is impossible to give the decision-maker an opportunity to reverse their decision. It is still regarded as good practice to inform the respondent that an application is being brought for judicial review[4].

If a letter before action has been written to the decision-maker, it should be exhibited to the applicant's written evidence in support of the application. If there is no letter before action, the written evidence should include an explanation for the failure to write a letter before action, unless the decision-maker is a court. If the decision-maker is a court, the written evidence should state whether the proceedings are still pending and whether an application has been made for an adjournment.

7.3 URGENT OUT-OF-HOURS APPLICATIONS FOR JUDICIAL REVIEW

Normally, an application for judicial review is commenced by lodging an application in the form set out below. There are, however, cases where the delay associated with lodging papers in the case will defeat the purpose of the application. For example, in a case where the judicial review application relates to a decision of magistrates to lift reporting restrictions preventing the naming of a juvenile, there may be no benefit to be gained from an application if the juvenile has already been named in press reports. Although the magistrates should be asked for a stay of the lifting of the order pending the judicial review, they may refuse to make this order. The High Court has procedures that enable it to make rapid decisions in this type of urgent situation. In particular, it is possible to apply to a duty judge at night and during the weekend.

As soon it becomes clear that there is a need to apply to the duty judge, the duty judge's clerk should be contacted on 0171 936 6000. He will then make arrangements for the duty judge to hear the application. The application will

---

1 *Streames v Copping* [1985] QB 920 at 929, DC.
2 Eg *R v Horseferry Road Magistrates' Court ex p Bennett* [1994] 1 AC 42, HL, in which an applicant successfully applied, inter alia, for a judicial review of a decision of a magistrate to refuse to adjourn a matter pending a judicial review.
3 See **10.5**.
4 See *R v Cotswold DC ex p Barrington Parish Council* (1998) 75 P & CR 515, for an example of the importance attached to informing parties who may be affected by a judicial review that an application has been made.

be heard either by telephone or in person, depending on the location of the duty judge and the urgency of the application. Although the application is likely to focus on whether the interim relief sought should be ordered, there is no reason in principle why the duty judge should not grant permission to apply for judicial review.

The duty judge will be aware that he lacks the depth of information he normally has when he considers an application for permission to apply for judicial review. As a result, he will want to know why the application cannot wait until the next day when the court sits, and why it could not have been brought on the last date when the court sat. For example, in a case where the urgency results from the applicant being in custody, it is unlikely that the court will be satisfied that this is a good reason for the matter to be considered out of hours. This is because it is unlikely that an inmate will be released until the start of the next working day, as the prison will require official notification from the court of any order releasing the applicant.

We comment later on the duty of disclosure that arises when a person applies for judicial review[1]. When an application is made to the duty judge, it is particularly important to ensure that the judge is aware of all material facts and law. The duty judge may well not be as experienced in Crown Office matters as the judges who normally sit in the Crown Office. They are also unlikely to be assisted by representations on behalf of the respondent. In these circumstances, a failure to make proper disclosure is likely to be regarded as a serious matter by the High Court.

Where an application is made to the duty judge out of hours, he is likely to require the applicants to lodge the papers required to commence an application with the Crown Office at the start of business on the next working day. As a result, it is important that the applicant's solicitor works on those papers while counsel is making the application. It is also important that the applicant's solicitor keeps in contact with counsel, as the solicitor is likely to be required to inform parties affected of the terms of any orders for interim relief.

7.4 DOCUMENTS TO BE LODGED WITH THE CROWN OFFICE OF THE HIGH COURT

It is crucial that applications for judicial review are properly lodged with the Crown Office. A failure to comply with the procedural requirements may result in the papers being returned. That return may result in delay with consequent problems for the applicant. In particular, it might result in an application being brought outside the 3-month time-limit if the defective papers were only lodged shortly before the expiry of the 3-month time-limit[2].

Other than in urgent cases, judicial review applications are commenced by lodging an application notice in Form 86A and written evidence verifying the

---

1 See **7.7**.
2 See **5.2** for details of delay in judicial review.

facts relied on with the Crown Office of the High Court[1]. A copy of these documents must be lodged with the Crown Office as well as the originals, unless the matter is to be considered by a Divisional Court when two copies will be required. If the applicant is in receipt of legal aid, a copy of the legal aid certificate must also be lodged with the Crown Office.

Form 86A must include the name and description of the applicant, the relief sought and the grounds upon which it is sought, the name and address of the applicant's solicitors (if any), and the applicant's address for service[2]. A precedent for Form 86A is set out in Appendix 1.

The written evidence must verify 'the facts relied on'[3]. Until the introduction of the CPR 1998, the written evidence had to be in the form of an affidavit. The rules make it clear that a witness statement will suffice, but an applicant may swear an affidavit[4]. It is very unlikely that judges will give greater weight to affidavits as the rules make no distinction[5]. This is important as in some circumstances it will be considerably easier to obtain a witness statement. For example, clearly it will be considerably easier to have a witness statement signed where the applicant is in custody.

The person who swears the affidavit or makes the witness statement need not be the applicant. Applications are often submitted with affidavits sworn by the applicant's solicitor, because it may well cause unnecessary delay if the written evidence is obtained from the applicant, particularly if the applicant is in custody. Precedents for the written evidence are set out in Appendix 1.

A fee must also be paid before the papers in support of the application can be lodged with the Crown Office. The fee is at present £30, but this should be checked against an up-to-date list of court fees. Alternatively, the Crown Office can be contacted on 0171 936 6205. That is also the number that should be used for any other general enquiries regarding lodging applications for judicial review.

In practice, the filing requirements are more complex than they might at first appear. This is because there are a number of Practice Directions and procedure rules that determine how the documents should be filed in all proceedings in the Crown Office[6]. There are also specific Practice Directions governing applications for judicial review. In particular, applications should be accompanied by copies of any primary or secondary legislation relied on[7]. This

---

1   CPR 1998, Sch 1, RSC Ord 53, r 3(2).
2   Ibid, r 3(2)(a).
3   Ibid, r 3(2)(b).
4   *Practice Direction (CPR 1998, Part 32 – Written Evidence)*, paras 1.2 – 1.4.
5   This is particularly true as para 1.2 of *Practice Direction (CPR 1998, Part 32 – Written Evidence)* makes it clear that evidence 'should normally' be given by witness statement at proceedings other than trial. See also *Practice Direction (CPR 1998, Schedule 1, RSC Order 53 – Application for Judicial Review)* which suggests that written evidence may either be by affidavit or witness statement and CPR 1998, r 32.15(2) which provides that the extra cost of swearing an affidavit will not be recovered without a court order.
6   See **6.4**.
7   *Practice Direction* [1997] 1 WLR 52.

bundle of legislation should not be paginated as part of the main bundle in support of the application, but is normally supplied in a second paginated and indexed bundle. In practice, the Crown Office also requires this bundle to include copies of any reports or transcripts of judgments relied on that have not been published in law reports that are readily available[1].

A list of the pages of essential reading for the judge should also be provided with the bundles. This list may be provided as a separate document or by annotating the index to the bundle. If only part of the page is essential reading, this should be shown by sidelines or in some other way, but not by highlighting[2].

The Crown Office may not accept applications that fail to comply with requirements of Practice Directions and procedure rules, even where an undertaking is offered to correct errors, except in exceptional circumstances such as urgency. The Crown Office has stated that an application will not be regarded as urgent except where a decision is required from the High Court within 14 days of lodging the application[3].

7.5 ADDITIONAL MATTERS TO BE CONSIDERED WHEN THE APPLICATION FOR PERMISSION IS FILED

In a case where bail is sought, a bail application should be lodged with the Crown Office at the same time as the other documents supporting the application. A precedent is set out in Appendix 1[4]. Form 86A should also include bail as a form of relief sought. The Crown Office should be informed if the matter needs to be listed as a matter of urgency because of the need to apply for bail or for another reason. That should enable the Crown Office to list the matter as soon as possible. Normally, the Crown Office will list the matter at extremely short notice where a very urgent hearing is sought, so it is important that counsel is available on standby. Details of that counsel should be supplied to the Crown Office so that they can be contacted when the hearing has been arranged.

The Crown Office should also be informed of any other special features of the application besides urgency. For example, if an applicant seeks an order restricting the reporting of the matter, the Crown Office should be informed of this at the outset of the application[5]. As noted earlier, they can be contacted by telephone on 0171 936 6205 to discuss such matters.

---

1 When relying on transcripts, practitioners should be aware of *Practice Statement (Supreme Court: Judgments)* [1998] 1 WLR 825 which limits the use of transcripts to circumstances in which there is no official report and counsel can assure the court that the judgment contains a relevant legal principle not found in reported cases. It also requires the use of the official transcript.
2 *Practice Direction (Crown Office List: Preparation for Hearings)* [1994] 1 WLR 1551, [1994] 4 All ER 671.
3 *Note to All Users* Crown Office, 9 January 1997.
4 See also **10.2** for the procedure for applying for bail.
5 See **5.7**.

The Crown Office will also expect applicants to supply a written time estimate when papers are lodged, if the application for permission will take longer than normal. A normal application is one where the applicant's submissions at the hearing will take no longer than 20 minutes and the submissions by any person who attends to respond will take no longer than 10 minutes[1]. In practice, it is expected that most applications for permission can be presented within 20 minutes.

7.6 DECIDING WHETHER THE APPLICATION FOR PERMISSION SHOULD BE LISTED FOR ORAL ARGUMENT

The Crown Office will need to be informed when the papers are lodged whether an oral hearing is required to determine the application for permission to bring the judicial review. If this is not specified, it will normally be assumed that an oral application is not required. As a result, the applicant will need to consider whether the application for permission should be listed for oral hearing or whether it can be considered on the papers. An application considered on the papers is described as a table application. If an oral application is required, Form 86A should state this[2].

Where the matter is very urgent and there is a request for interim relief, an oral application should normally be requested. This is primarily because oral argument gives counsel an opportunity to address any concerns that the judge may have and that are not covered adequately in the paperwork in support of the application. In addition, where the matter is urgent and so not subject to normal listing practice, having the matter listed for oral hearing is often quicker than having it determined on the papers.

If the matter is not urgent, it will normally be better to have the matter considered on the papers. That will be cheaper as it will not require the instruction of counsel for oral argument. For this reason, applicants who are in receipt of legal aid will normally be expected to have the matter considered on the papers, unless there are good reasons why this should not happen. It is also likely to be quicker to have the matter considered on the papers. It generally takes longer for an oral application for permission to be heard than it does for a table application to be considered when there is no urgency. A table application also allows the matter to be renewed for oral argument if the table application is refused and the applicant's advisers believe that there is still merit in the light of the reasons given by the judge[3]. If the applicant requests a table determination of the application for permission, the judge still has discretion to require an oral hearing of that application if he feels that an oral hearing is necessary[4]. The judge will normally do this when he is uncertain whether permission should be granted.

---

1 *Practice Direction (Crown Office List) (No 2)* [1991] 1 WLR 280.
2 CPR 1998, Sch 1, RSC Ord 53, r 3(3).
3 See **7.10** for details of renewing applications for judicial review.
4 CPR 1998, Sch 1, RSC Ord 53, r 3(3).

7.7 THE DUTY OF DISCLOSURE WHICH APPLIES WHEN DRAFTING PAPERS IN SUPPORT OF THE APPLICATION

The grounds set out in the notice of application and the written evidence in support must comply with the duty of disclosure imposed on applicants. As applications for permission to bring judicial review proceedings are often considered without notice being served on other parties, the High Court expects applicants to disclose all material facts in the notice of application and the written evidence. A fact is material if it 'might affect the judge's decision whether to grant relief or what relief to grant'[1]. It is for the court and not for an applicant to decide whether a fact is material[2]. The duty of disclosure relates to facts[3] and law[4]. Disclosure is particularly relevant when there has been delay[5] or where there is an alternative remedy available to the applicant[6].

Although the duty of disclosure arises in part from the difficulties that arise when a judge is required to consider an application without the respondent being represented, there is still a duty of disclosure that arises when the respondent is represented[7].

The duty is not limited to matters known to the applicant and his advisers. It has been held that applicants are under a duty to carry out proper enquiries, so that they are obliged to disclose facts that they could have discovered if they had carried out proper enquiries[8]. This is consistent with a judgment of Sir Thomas Bingham MR who held that it is no answer to say that any failure to disclose material facts was made in good faith[9]. However, if a failure to disclose was made in good faith, that is a relevant factor for the court to consider when it determines what action to take as a result of a failure to make full disclosure[10]. The High Court has a discretion about whether to take any action as a result of

---

1 Per Sir Thomas Bingham MR, *Fitzgerald v Williams* [1996] QB 657 at 667H, CA.
2 *Brink's Mat Ltd v Elcombe* [1988] 1 WLR 1350 at 1356H, CA, applied in the context of judicial review in *R v Jockey Club Licensing Committee ex p Wright* [1991] COD 306.
3 Eg *R v Secretary of State for the Home Office ex p Begum* [1995] COD 176, in which a wasted costs order was made against the applicant's legal advisers for failing to put a letter from the respondents before the court despite a request to do so.
4 Eg *R v Secretary of State for the Home Department ex p Li Bin Shi* [1995] COD 135, in which permission was set aside as a result of a failure to disclose a number of relevant legal authorities. See also para 610(c) of the Bar Code of Conduct which provides that a barrister when conducting proceedings at court:
  'must ensure that the Court is informed of all relevant decisions and legislative provisions of which he is aware whether the effect is favourable or unfavourable towards the contention for which he argues and must bring any procedural irregularity to the attention of the Court during the hearing and not reserve such matter to be raised on appeal.'
5 See **5.2** for a consideration of delay.
6 See **5.4** for a consideration of alternative remedies.
7 See, eg *R v Secretary of State for the Home Department ex p Gashi* (1999) *The Times*, 31 March, CA.
8 *Brink's Mat Ltd v Elcombe* [1988] 1 WLR 1350 at 1356H, CA, applied in the context of judicial review in *R v Jockey Club Licensing Committee ex p Wright* [1991] COD 306.
9 *Fitzgerald v Williams* [1996] QB 657 at 668A, CA.
10 *Brink's Mat Ltd v Elcombe* [1988] 1 WLR 1350 at 1357D, CA, applied in the context of judicial review in *R v Jockey Club Licensing Committee ex p Wright* [1991] COD 306.

non-disclosure[1]. In particular, the High Court has a discretion whether to refuse the relief sought[2]. Alternatively, the High Court has a discretion to take account of a failure to make disclosure when it makes orders for costs[3]. When it exercises that discretion, the High Court will seek to ensure that an applicant is deprived of any advantage that they may have gained through a failure to make full disclosure[4].

Although an adverse matter must be disclosed, it does not necessarily need to be highlighted. It is enough that it is not hidden[5]. Tactically, however, it may be better to highlight the problem in the grounds and then explain the applicant's answer to the problem. If the applicant's advisers do not do that, they run the risk that the judge will identify the problem and dismiss the application as a result.

7.8 THE DETERMINATION OF WHETHER AN APPLICANT SHOULD BE GRANTED PERMISSION TO APPLY FOR JUDICIAL REVIEW

Judicial review is a two-stage process, as no application for judicial review may be brought without the permission of the High Court[6]. As a result, the High Court will first determine whether permission should be granted. Until the introduction of the CPR 1998, applying for permission was known as applying for leave. When reading old judgments, it is important to be aware of this.

In determining whether to grant permission, the court takes account of the purpose of the requirement that applicants obtain permission. Lord Diplock has held that the permission stage is intended to:

> '[P]revent the time of the court being wasted by busybodies with misguided or trivial complaints of administrative error, and to remove the uncertainty in which public officers and authorities might be left as to whether they could safely proceed with administrative action while proceedings for judicial review of it were actually pending even though misconceived.'[7]

---

1   In *Fitzgerald v Williams* [1996] QB 657 at 668B, CA, Sir Thomas Bingham MR emphasised that non-disclosure will not always result in permission being set aside.
2   Eg *R v Jockey Club Licensing Committee ex p Wright* [1991] COD 306, for an example of a case where permission was set aside as a result of material non-disclosure.
3   The discretion with respect to costs is not limited to wasted costs being ordered against lawyers acting for applicants. In *R v Liverpool City Council ex p Filla* [1996] COD 24, applicants were refused inter-partes costs as a result of material non-disclosure. See also CPR 1998, r 44.3(4)(a), that provides when considering costs orders, the High Court will take account of the conduct of the parties.
4   *Brink's Mat Ltd v Elcombe* [1988] 1 WLR 1350 at 1357C, CA, applied in the context of judicial review in *R v Jockey Club Licensing Committee ex p Wright* [1991] COD 306.
5   *R v Warwickshire County Council ex p Collymore* [1995] ELR 217 at 229F, relying on the fact that adverse material was expressly referred to in the grounds of application.
6   CPR 1998, Sch 1, RSC Ord 53, r 3(1).
7   *R v Inland Revenue Commissioners ex p National Federation of Self-Employed and Small Businesses Ltd* [1982] AC 617 at 643A, HL.

Thus, the Court of Appeal has held that the judge considering an application for permission should consider whether the case is suitable for full investigation at a hearing of which all parties have been given notice[1]. That approach has led the courts to hold on numerous occasions that permission should not be granted if the application for judicial review is unarguable[2].

The High Court is not merely restricted to considering whether a case is arguable when it decides whether to grant permission. It will also consider delay[3] and the availability of an alternative remedy[4]. The availability of an alternative remedy is particularly important in the context of crime, as it may require the High Court to be satisfied that there are good reasons why permission should be granted. For example, the High Court will want to know why an applicant should not seek to cure any harm caused by an interim decision in criminal proceedings by obtaining the result he seeks at the conclusion of those proceedings[5].

Lord Diplock has stated that the permission stage should only involve a 'quick perusal of the material then available'[6]. That statement, however, does not accurately reflect the current practice of the High Court[7]. Many applications for permission involve a far more detailed consideration of the case than a quick perusal and judges often seem to want to be satisfied that there is clear merit. There have even been cases where the court has received a considerable volume of material and heard extensive argument from both the applicant and the respondent[8].

It is also possible to see how the High Court gives greater scrutiny to applications for permission in the approach that it takes to the role of the respondent at the hearing to determine whether permission should be granted. The applicant for judicial review is permitted to make an application for permission without the Form 86A and other documents being served on any other party[9]. That does not mean, however, that applications for permission are always heard without parties other than the applicant attending. Increasingly, it is common for the respondent or another interested party to be represented at a hearing to determine whether permission should be granted. Indeed there

---

1 *R v Secretary of State for the Home Department ex p Begum* [1990] COD 107, CA.
2 See, eg *R v Secretary of State for the Home Department ex p Begum* [1990] COD 107, CA, in which permission was refused as the case was unarguable; *R v Legal Aid Board ex p Hughes* (1993) 5 Admin LR 623 at 628D, CA, in which Lord Donaldson MR held that permission should be granted if an application is prima facie arguable.
3 See **5.2**.
4 See **5.4**.
5 See **4.10**.
6 *R v Inland Revenue Commissioners ex p National Federation of Self-Employed and Small Businesses Ltd* [1982] AC 617 at 644A, HL.
7 In *R v Legal Aid Board ex p Hughes* (1993) 5 Admin LR 623, CA, Lord Donaldson MR held that things had moved on from Lord Diplock's dicta.
8 Eg *Mass Energy Ltd v Birmingham City Council* [1994] Env LR 298, CA. In this case, all relevant material was placed before the court and the court heard very extensive argument. As a result, the Court of Appeal held that they were only willing to grant permission if the case was 'likely to succeed'.
9 CPR 1998, Sch 1, RSC Ord 53, r 3(2A).

appears to be no case where a respondent has been prevented from appearing at a hearing to determine whether permission should be granted. In many cases, High Court judges will specifically request that a respondent or another interested party attends the hearing to determine whether permission should be granted, so that they can make representations.

When the court decides whether to grant permission, it will normally also decide whether interim relief should be ordered[1]. If interim relief is sought, this should be specified on the Form 86A. Where interim relief is sought, the respondent should, wherever possible, be put on notice[2]. Respondents who are considering whether to attend should consider the costs implications[3].

7.9 AMENDMENT OF THE GROUNDS AND SERVICE OF ADDITIONAL EVIDENCE

The grounds lodged with the Crown Office may be amended with the permission of the court that is considering the application for permission to apply for judicial review if the court thinks fit[4]. Although there appears to be no case-law considering how this discretion should be exercised, the practice of the High Court is that it generally is willing to allow amendments of the grounds at the permission stage. A copy of the proposed amended grounds should be supplied to the court as soon as possible. This should, if possible, be before the hearing of the application for permission.

The High Court also has a discretion to allow the amendment of grounds and the submission of additional evidence on behalf of the applicant after it has granted permission to apply for judicial review[5]. However, all parties must be given notice and served with copies of the proposed amendments or additional written evidence[6]. The notice should be given at least 5 clear working days before the fixed date or warned list date. If notice is not given at least 5 days before the fixed date or warned list date, the High Court will be reluctant to allow amendment or the use of additional written evidence save in exceptional circumstances[7]. Otherwise, the High Court is likely to be willing to allow amendment, particularly as it will be aware that grounds often change as a result of evidence served by the respondent after the grant of permission[8].

---

1   See Chapter 10 for details of interim relief that is available.
2   Per Parker LJ, *R v Kensington and Chelsea Borough Council ex p Hammell* [1989] QB 518 at 539B, CA.
3   See **12.3**.
4   CPR 1998, Sch 1, RSC Ord 53, r 3(6).
5   Ibid, r 6(2).
6   Ibid, r 6(3).
7   *Practice Direction (Crown Office List: Preparation for Hearings)* [1994] 1 WLR 1551, [1994] 4 All ER 671.
8   Eg per Lord Denning, *R v Barnsley Metropolitan Borough Council ex p Hook* [1976] 1 WLR 1052 at 1058C, CA, noting that grounds 'should not be treated as rigidly as a pleading in an ordinary civil action'.

The respondent may also apply for permission to rely on additional written evidence after the time for service of evidence has expired[1]. The High Court may be more reluctant to grant permission as the time-limit was extended to 56 days to enable respondents to have a realistic time to file evidence. In any event, this additional evidence should be served at least 5 days before the warned or fixed date[2].

7.10 FURTHER STEPS FOLLOWING A REFUSAL OF PERMISSION

When a table application for permission to apply for judicial review is refused, the application can always be renewed. In a criminal cause or matter, the renewed application is made to a Divisional Court[3]. In any other case, the renewed application is made to a single judge sitting in open court, unless the court directs that the application should be considered by a Divisional Court[4]. The applicant will, however, be supplied with the written reasons of the judge who refuses permission and these should be considered carefully when deciding whether the application should be renewed.

When the application for permission is refused following an oral hearing of the application before a single judge in open court, it is also always possible to renew the application. In a criminal cause or matter, the renewed application is again made to a Divisional Court[5]. In any other case, the renewed application is made to the Court of Appeal[6]. Again, however, the judgment of the single judge should be considered when deciding whether to renew. This is particularly true when deciding whether to renew an application in the Court of Appeal, as that court will be particularly alert to renewed applications that lack merit[7].

An application for permission to apply for judicial review cannot be considered by the House of Lords[8]. In addition, an application for permission in a criminal cause or matter cannot be renewed in the Court of Appeal[9].

An application for judicial review should never be renewed without a careful review of the merits. If the decision is taken to renew the application in the High Court, it is done by lodging a Form 86B with the Crown Office within 10

---

1   CPR 1998, Sch 1, RSC Ord 53, r 6(4).
2   *Practice Direction (Crown Office List: Preparation for Hearings)* [1994] 1 WLR 1551, [1994] 4 All ER 671.
3   CPR 1998, Sch 1, RSC Ord 53, r 3(4)(a).
4   Ibid, r 3(4)(b).
5   Ibid, r 3(4)(a).
6   CPR 1998, Sch 1, RSC Ord 59, r 14(3).
7   *R v Secretary of State for the Home Department ex p Panther* (1996) 8 Admin LR 154 at 162F, CA, in which Lord Justice Butler-Sloss held that the taxing master should consider the fact that an application to the Court of Appeal lacked merit when legal aid costs were determined.
8   *Re Poh* [1983] 1 WLR 2, HL; see, however, *Kemper Reinsurance Co v Minister of Finance* [1998] 3 WLR 630, PC which suggests that the decision in *Re Poh* is open to challenge.
9   *R v Secretary of State for the Home Department ex p Ogilvy* [1996] COD 497, CA.

days of service of the judge's decision[1]. Form 86B is normally supplied by the Crown Office when they serve the judge's decision. There is no fee for renewing an application for judicial review in the High Court.

In the Court of Appeal, the application must be renewed within 7 days of the refusal[2]. The application is made by filing in duplicate an application notice and a copy of the High Court's order refusing permission[3]. The application notice should be in the form set out in Appendix 1. A fee of £100 must also be paid. The procedure in the Court of Appeal is governed by the Rules of the Supreme Court and by a new Practice Direction that sets out the procedure in full[4]. In particular, the Practice Direction sets out the strict requirements for the submission of bundles and skeleton arguments soon after the application notice has been lodged. Solicitors need to be aware that core bundles will be required shortly after the filing of the application notice. Advocates need to be aware that skeleton arguments will be required shortly after the filing of the application notice. The Civil Appeals Office should write shortly after the application notice has been lodged specifying the requirements of the court regarding bundles and skeleton arguments.

7.11 COMMENCING THE JUDICIAL REVIEW APPLICATION AFTER OBTAINING PERMISSION

Technically, judicial review proceedings only begin once permission has been obtained to bring those proceedings. Proceedings are normally commenced in the Crown Office. Occasionally, where permission to bring proceedings is granted by the Court of Appeal, the Court of Appeal will order that it will hear the substantive application. This, however, is rare and normally only happens when the High Court will be bound by precedent that the Court of Appeal wishes to review[5]. Proceedings are commenced after the grant of permission by entering the application for hearing within 14 days of the grant of permission[6].

Before the application can be entered for hearing, a claim form in Form 86 must be served on 'all persons directly affected'[7]. Clearly, it must be served within 14 days after the grant of permission, as the application for hearing must be entered within this time period. A precedent of a claim form is included in Appendix 1. There is very little case-law on the meaning of the phrase, 'all persons directly affected'. The only thing that is clear is that a person will only be directly affected if they will be affected without the intervention of another

---

1 CPR 1998, Sch 1, RSC Ord 53, r 3(5).
2 Ibid, RSC Ord 59, r 14(3).
3 *Practice Direction (CPR 1998 – The Court of Appeal (Civil Division))*.
4 CPR 1998, Sch 1, RSC Ord 59 and *Practice Direction (CPR 1998 – The Court of Appeal (Civil Division))*.
5 *Practice Note* [1990] 1 All ER 128.
6 CPR 1998, Sch 1, RSC Ord 53, r 5(5).
7 Ibid, rr 5(3) and 5(6).

agency[1]. In a criminal context, any prosecuting authority must clearly be served as well as any respondent court. Where the respondent is a court, the rules specify that the claim form must be served on the clerk or registrar of the court[2]. In addition, if the application complains about the conduct of a judge, the claim form must be served on the judge[3]. Although the rules do not state that magistrates should be served, if there is a complaint about their conduct, it is advisable that they are served.

Form 86A and grounds must accompany the claim form when it is served[4]. It is also regarded as good practice to serve a copy of the written evidence with the claim form, as any party can request a copy of any written evidence on payment of proper charges[5]. If the applicant is in receipt of legal aid, the other parties must also be served with notice of issue of legal aid[6]. The format of this notice is specified by the Legal Aid Board[7].

Service of the claim form on affected parties must take place at least 10 days before the hearing of the substantive application, unless the court that grants permission directs otherwise[8]. In most cases, this is unlikely to cause a problem as the hearing will take place months after the grant of permission and the claim form must be served on affected parties before it is filed at the Crown Office. However, in a case that is very urgent, the applicant should apply for an order shortening this period of time. This application should normally be made when permission to bring the application is sought.

Assuming that the substantive application is not to be heard by the Court of Appeal, the claim form is filed at the Crown Office after it has been served on the other parties. It must be filed within 14 days of the grant of permission[9]. The fee for filing a full application is at present £120. The 14 day time-limit is regarded as a very strict time-limit that is rarely extended[10]. As a result, an applicant should never fail to comply with this time-limit. If an applicant does fail to comply with this time-limit, they should attempt to obtain the consent of the respondent to late filing. A respondent may be willing to consent, if they believe that there is an important issue raised by the case that it is in the public interest to resolve.

---

1   *R v Rent Service ex p Muldoon* [1996] 1 WLR 1103, HL. In this case, the Department of Social Security was not directly affected by a judicial review of local authority's housing benefits, payments even though it was responsible for meeting a significant proportion of the costs of those benefit payments.
2   CPR 1998, Sch 1, RSC Ord 53, r 5(3).
3   Ibid.
4   Ibid, r 6(1), *Practice Direction (CPR 1998, Schedule 1, RSC Order 53 – Application for Judicial Review)*, para 4.1.
5   Ibid, r 6(5).
6   Civil Legal Aid (General) Regulations 1989, SI 1989/339, reg 50.
7   See the *Legal Aid Handbook 1998/1999* (Sweet & Maxwell) for a precedent.
8   CPR 1998, Sch 1, RSC Ord 53, r 5(4).
9   Ibid, r 5(5).
10 Eg *R v Institute of Chartered Accountants in England and Wales ex p Andreou* (1996) 8 Admin LR 557, CA, cf *R v Secretary of State for the Environment and Shropshire County Council ex p Parry* [1998] COD 17, in which the court extended time as the applicant should not be prejudiced by a misjudgement by their solicitor.

The applicant is required to file at the court written evidence stating the names and addresses, and places and dates of service, of the persons served with the claim form at the time that he files the claim form[1]. If there is a party who should have been served but who has not been served, the written evidence should state this and explain why they have not been served. A precedent for the written evidence of service is included in Appendix 1.

Once the claim form has been filed, the case enters the Crown Office list. The operation of the Crown Office list was considered earlier[2].

7.12 FURTHER STEPS TO BE TAKEN BY THE APPLICANT BEFORE THE SUBSTANTIVE HEARING

Once permission has been granted, the applicant should consider whether there is a need for any specific orders governing the conduct of the matter. In particular, there is provision for obtaining orders requiring the supply of further evidence, disclosure of documents, cross-examination and other interlocutory applications[3]. However, the reluctance of the High Court to consider factual disputes during an application for judicial review means that these orders are rarely made during judicial review proceedings[4]. For example, the High Court will be reluctant to consider a dispute about the facts that are said to give rise to an allegation of bias on the part of magistrates[5]. As a result, the High Court is extremely unlikely to hear oral evidence and cross-examination of witnesses to determine whether there was bias.

The High Court will also be reluctant to make interlocutory orders for matters such as the supply of further information or the disclosure of documents, as it will expect the respondent to provide it with all the information that it requires[6]. In practice, the High Court will want to be satisfied that there is a particularly good reason why an order for the supply of further information or the disclosure of documents should be made.

When the respondent and any other parties have served all the written evidence that they will rely on, the applicant should always review the merits of the application. Clearly, counsel is prevented from arguing 'any contention which he does not consider to be properly arguable'[7]. The respondent's evidence may well mean that a matter that was properly arguable at the permission stage

---

1   CPR 1998, Sch 1, RSC Ord 53, r 5(6).
2   See **6.2** and **6.3**.
3   CPR 1998, Sch 1, RSC Ord 53, r 8.
4   Eg *R v Inland Revenue Commissioners ex p Rossminster* [1980] AC 952, HL at 1027B, in which Lord Scarman stated that these powers should be used 'sparingly'.
5   In *R v Harringey Justices ex p Branco* (1997) *The Independent*, 1 December, DC, it was held that a defendant should normally appeal to the Crown Court in these circumstances.
6   See **7.14** for details of the duty of candour imposed on respondents. In *R v Arts Council of England ex p Women's Playhouse Trust* [1998] COD 175, it was held that interlocutory orders for discovery would not be made unless there was something to suggest that prima facie an affidavit was inaccurate, incomplete or misleading.
7   Paragraph 606(b) of the Bar Code of Conduct.

becomes unarguable. In addition, in a case in which the application is legally aided, it is likely that the legal aid certificate will require counsel to advise on the merits after the service of the respondent's evidence. Without that advice, legal aid will not be extended to cover the substantive hearing[1]. If it is decided that the application should be withdrawn, a consent order should be obtained dealing with issues such as costs[2].

If it is decided that the merits of the application are still sufficient to justify proceeding to the substantive hearing, the applicant should consider whether they wish to lodge any additional written evidence in response to any evidence served by the respondent[3]. Whether or not a decision is taken to lodge additional evidence, there are further documents that must be lodged with the court by the applicant. In particular, bundles and skeleton arguments must be lodged with the Crown Office in accordance with Practice Directions[4].

The bundle in an application for judicial review should include any evidence served by the respondents. It should also include the bundle of statutory materials. If an application is to be made for an amendment of the grounds or for the admission of additional evidence, the original grounds and evidence should be included in the bundle as well as the amended grounds and additional evidence. This is because the court may refuse permission to allow amendment and so will need to be able to consider the original papers.

7.13 ACTING FOR AN INTERESTED PARTY WHO HAS NOT BEEN SERVED WITH THE CLAIM FORM

If a party is aware of judicial review proceedings but has not been served with the claim form, an application can be made to the court that he should be heard. That is because the court has a discretion to order that the claim form should be served on any party who ought to have been served[5]. The High Court is not restricted to considering submissions made by parties who should be served with the claim form. The court may hear any person who is a 'proper person'[6]. Again, if a party believes that he is a proper person, he should apply to the High Court for permission to be heard.

In practice, the High Court is sometimes willing to allow interested parties to appear. For example, the courts considering judicial review applications regularly hear amicus curiae instructed by the Treasury Solicitor when the court feels it will be assisted by submissions[7]. Indeed, if a judicial review raises

---

1 See **12.12**.
2 See **6.6** for details of consent orders.
3 See **7.9** for details of how to lodge additional evidence.
4 See **6.4.1** for details.
5 CPR 1998, Sch 1, RSC Ord 53, r 5(7).
6 Ibid, r 9(1).
7 Eg *R v Southwark Crown Court ex p Bowles* (1998) *The Times*, 7 April, HL. See also *R v Evans and Others ex p Pinochet Ugarte* (1998) *The Times*, 26 November, HL, in which the court considered submissions from a number of human rights organisations and other interested parties.

important issues that will affect many cases, it is worth applicants considering whether the Treasury Solicitors should be approached to see whether they wish to instruct an amicus curiae.

The CPR 1998 may mean that it becomes more common for an amicus curiae to appear before the court, as the rules provide that the court may order a person to be added as a party if it is desirable 'so that the court can resolve all the matters in dispute'[1].

7.14 EVIDENCE AND ORAL SUBMISSIONS ON BEHALF OF RESPONDENTS OR OTHER INTERESTED PARTIES

If a party has been served with the claim form or has obtained permission to be heard, the first thing that he should do is consider whether he opposes the application. If a party does not oppose the application, he should attempt to obtain the agreement of all the parties about the terms of a consent order[2]. It is always important to obtain the consent of all parties. In particular, in a judicial review of a decision of another court taken during criminal proceedings, the High Court is unlikely to agree to a consent order unless the consent of the prosecution is obtained even though the prosecution will not formally be the respondent[3].

If a party has been served or obtained permission to attend and does not wish to consent to the order sought, he should consider whether he wishes to serve written evidence that should be considered by the court. A party may do this even if he does not wish to be represented at the hearing. For example, magistrates will often not be represented at a judicial review hearing. Indeed, it has been held that magistrates should not be represented by counsel unless there is some special factor such as an allegation of misconduct on the part of the magistrates[4]. However, the High Court will wish to have the views of the respondent when it determines the application[5]. As a result, in most cases respondents should serve written evidence commenting on the application. In particular, the written evidence should highlight any factual matters in the applicant's written evidence and grounds that are not agreed or any other

---

1   CPR 1998, r 19.1(2)(a).
2   See **6.6** for details of the procedure for obtaining a consent order.
3   Eg *R v Central Criminal Court ex p Guney* [1996] AC 616, HL, is an example of a case where the court accepted that the prosecution was the effective respondent.
4   *R v Camborne Justices ex p Pearce* [1954] 2 All ER 850 at 856A, DC. But note the remarks of Lord Justice Simon Brown asking Treasury Solicitors to instruct counsel to review the merits of a large number of judicial reviews of warrants of commitment in the light of his judgment in *R v Oldham Justices ex p Cawley* [1996] 1 All ER 464 at 481G, DC, which suggests that the court increasingly finds that it is assisted by respondents being represented.
5   Eg, in *R v Gloucester Crown Court ex p Chester* (1998) *The Independent*, 6 July, DC, it was held that even where an applicant erred by bringing judicial review proceedings instead of an appeal by case stated, the respondent should at least write a letter stating whether they opposed the application.

matters that the court will find relevant. This is particularly true where there is an allegation of bias on behalf of a justice or a circuit judge[1].

When drafting written evidence for a party other than an applicant, it is important to remember that the High Court will expect respondents to provide it with all relevant information. For example, Lord Woolf MR held that:

> 'it is the obligation of the respondent public body in its evidence to make frank disclosure to the court of the decision making process.'[2]

That is because the respondent to a judicial review is expected to assist the court. For example, Sir John Donaldson has held that the relationship between the courts and respondents should be one of 'partnership'[3]. The duty of disclosure applies not only to all relevant facts. All relevant documents should be exhibited. It is not acceptable to fail to disclose evidence merely because it may give rise to other grounds for judicial review.

If written evidence is to be relied on, it must be filed at the Crown Office as soon as practicable and in any event within the time specified for lodging. This is normally 56 days from the date when the applicant serves the claim form, unless the time has been abridged[4]. If written evidence is to be filed after the expiry of the time-limit for filing, permission must be sought before filing from the Master of the Crown Office[5]. The application should be made in the same way as other interim applications[6]. If the Master refuses permission, it is possible to apply to a judge hearing Crown Office cases. Time is, however, unlikely to be extended. The time-limit for service of written evidence was extended from 21 days to 56 days specifically to give respondents a realistic opportunity to file evidence[7]. As a result, it is unlikely that it will be accepted that any respondent has not had sufficient time to file written evidence.

Until the introduction of the CPR 1998, the written evidence had to be in the form of an affidavit. The rules make it clear that a witness statement will suffice, but respondents may swear an affidavit[8]. It is unlikely that judges will give greater weight to affidavits as the rules make no distinction[9]. Precedents for written evidence are set out in Appendix 1.

---

1   *R v Southwark Crown Court ex p Collman* (1998) *Archbold News*, August, DC.
2   *R v Secretary of State for the Home Department ex p Fayed* [1997] 1 All ER 228 at 239D, CA.
3   *R v Lancashire County Council ex p Huddleston* [1986] 2 All ER 941 at 945C, CA.
4   CPR 1998, Sch 1, RSC Ord 53, r 6(4).
5   *Practice Note (Judicial Review: Affidavit in Reply)* [1989] 1 WLR 358, [1989] 1 All ER 1024.
6   See **6.9**.
7   *Practice Note (Judicial Review: Affidavit in Reply)* [1989] 1 WLR 358, [1989] 1 All ER 1024.
8   *Practice Direction (CPR 1998, Part 32 – Written Evidence)*, paras 1.2–1.4.
9   This is particularly true as para 1.2 of *Practice Direction (CPR 1998, Part 32 – Written Evidence)* makes it clear that evidence 'should normally' be given by witness statement at a hearing other than trial. See also *Practice Direction (CPR 1998, Schedule 1, RSC Order 53 – Application for Judicial Review)* which suggests that written evidence may either be by affidavit or witness statement and CPR 1998, r 32.15(2) which provides that the extra cost of swearing an affidavit will not be recovered without an order.

7.15 OTHER PROCEDURAL STEPS TO BE TAKEN ON BEHALF OF RESPONDENTS OR OTHER INTERESTED PARTIES

The respondent should consider whether he wishes to make any interlocutory applications. The court is no more likely to grant applications made by respondents for matters such as disclosure of documents than it is to grant applications made by applicants[1]. One interlocutory order that is only available to parties other than applicants is an order setting aside the grant of permission[2]. Given that the parties seeking to set aside the grant of permission will also be able to make representations at the substantive hearing, it is only rarely that an order setting aside should be sought.

One situation where it may be appropriate to seek an order setting aside the grant of permission, is where a party has good reason to believe that an applicant has failed to make disclosure[3]. This is particularly true where the failure to make disclosure relates to delay. That is because the High Court applies a different approach to delay at the hearing to decide whether to grant permission to that which it applies at the substantive hearing[4].

If the High Court does set aside the grant of permission, it is possible to challenge the decision in the Court of Appeal in a matter that is not a criminal cause or matter[5]. However, it is not clear whether this is by way of renewed application for permission or an appeal against the order setting aside permission[6]. In a criminal cause or matter, the Court of Appeal cannot consider an appeal from the High Court[7]. As a result, it is clear that the Court of Appeal cannot consider the order of the High Court setting aside the grant of permission. There is no case-law deciding what procedure should be used by an applicant in these circumstances. Presumably, an applicant should seek to renew the matter in a Divisional Court if the order was not made by a Divisional Court, because an applicant has a right to renew an application for permission in a Divisional Court[8].

---

1 See **7.12** for details of the court's treatment of applications for matters such as requests for further information, disclosure of documents and cross-examination.
2 CPR 1998, r 23.10. See also *R v Customs & Excise Commissioners ex p Eurotunnel Plc* [1995] COD 291, DC, in which it was held that the High Court has an inherent power to regulate its own procedures that allows it to consider applications from third parties that permission should be set aside. In this case, ferry companies who were not parties successfully contested a decision to grant permission to Eurotunnel to contest duty free regulations.
3 Eg *R v Secretary of State for the Home Department ex p Ketowoglo* (1992) *The Times*, 6 April, CA.
4 *R v Criminal Injuries Compensation Board ex p A* [1999] 2 WLR 974, HL. See also **5.2.1** for details of delay.
5 Eg *R v Secretary of State for the Home Department ex p Begum* [1990] COD 107, CA.
6 Ibid. See *R v Crown Prosecution Service ex p Hogg* (1994) *The Times*, 14 April, CA, for an example of a case where an applicant both renewed the application and appealed against the decision to set aside the grant of permission. Note, if the correct procedure is an appeal, permission will be required to appeal (see CPR 1998, Sch 1, RSC Ord 59, r 1B(1)).
7 Supreme Court Act 1981, s 18(1)(a).
8 CPR 1998, Sch 1, RSC Ord 53, r 3(4)(a).

Practitioners acting for parties other than the applicant also need to be aware of the requirement that they supply skeleton arguments and lists of authorities in advance of the substantive hearing[1].

7.16 SUBSTANTIVE HEARING

At present, substantive hearings in judicial review matters are heard by a Divisional Court when they relate to a criminal cause or matter. In other cases, they are normally heard by a single judge in open court. The Government has announced plans, included in the Access to Justice Bill, for the reform of these arrangements. It is likely that in future, most or all judicial reviews will be heard by a single High Court judge.

The orders that the High Court may make are considered in more detail in later chapters[2]. There are two important matters to consider at this stage. First, it is essential that an order for legal aid taxation is sought if the applicant is in receipt of legal aid[3]. In addition, it is important to consider whether leave to appeal should be sought. In a criminal cause or matter, any appeal can only be heard by the House of Lords. This requires leave to appeal and a certificate under s 1 of the Administration of Justice Act 1960 that the case involves a point of law of general public importance. Where the matter is not a criminal cause or matter, it is possible to appeal to the Court of Appeal. Leave to appeal is still necessary[4].

---

1 See **6.4.1**.
2 See Chapter 11 for details of orders that the court may make when allowing a judicial review and Chapter 12 for details of costs orders that the court may make.
3 See **12.13** for details of legal aid.
4 CPR 1998, Sch 1, RSC Ord 59, r 1B(1).

Chapter 8

PROCEDURE FOR APPLYING FOR A WRIT OF HABEAS CORPUS

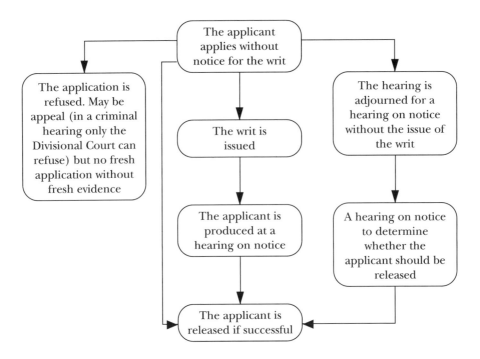

This flowchart shows the stages involved in an application for a writ of habeas corpus.

8.1 INTRODUCTION

The recent introduction of the CPR 1998 has had little effect on the procedure for bringing an application for a writ of habeas corpus. The only significant change is that the applicant can rely on a witness statement instead of an affidavit.

There are three forms of writ of habeas corpus. The procedure set out below relates to a writ of habeas corpus ad subjiciendum, which provides for a challenge to the legality of the commitment of a prisoner. This is the most common form of writ. There is, however, also provision for a writ of habeas corpus ad testificandum, which provides for a prisoner to be produced to give evidence, and a writ of habeas corpus ad respondendum, which provides for a prisoner to be produced to answer a criminal charge. In practice, these last two writs are of little importance as prisoners are normally produced by order of the Home Secretary[1]. If one of these writs is sought, the procedure is likely to be the same as that set out below[2].

The procedure for applying for a writ of habeas corpus is deliberately a very simple procedure, as it is recognised that the High Court needs to consider applications for habeas corpus as a matter of urgency. In particular, the procedure is simpler than that which governs an application for judicial review. As, however, in practice an application for habeas corpus is often made at the same time as an application for judicial review, it is often that procedure that effectively governs the linked litigation[3].

8.2 COMMENCING THE APPLICATION

An urgent application for habeas corpus may be commenced when the court is not sitting in the same way as an application for judicial review may be commenced out of hours[4]. In contrast to judicial review, the procedure rules actually make express provision for this type of urgent application[5]. The High Court, however, is unlikely in practice to show any greater willingness to hear an out-of-hours application for a writ than it is to hear an application for judicial review. It is likely to require applicants to show why the application cannot wait until the next date when the court is sitting. When considering whether to make an urgent out-of-hours application for a writ of habeas corpus, it is important to be aware that the court will be reluctant to grant bail pending the final determination of an application for a writ of habeas corpus[6].

If the application is not made out of hours, an application for a writ of habeas corpus is commenced by lodging an affidavit or witness statement in the Crown Office. If the applicant is in receipt of legal aid, a copy of the legal aid certificate should also be lodged.

Until the introduction of the CPR 1998, the written evidence had to be in the form of an affidavit. The rules make it clear that a witness statement will suffice, but an applicant may swear an affidavit[7]. It is unlikely that judges will

---

1 Crime (Sentences) Act 1997, Sch 1, paras 2 and 3
2 CPR 1998, Sch 1, RSC Ord 54, r 9 provide that an application is made by affidavit or witness statement. This is clearly similar to the procedure set out in the remainder of this chapter.
3 In *Re Barker* (1998) *The Times*, 14 October, CA, it was said that every effort should be made to harmonise proceedings when both forms of proceedings are brought at the same time.
4 See **7.3**.
5 CPR 1998, Sch 1, RSC Ord 54, r 1(1)(b).
6 See **10.2.2**.
7 *Practice Direction (CPR 1998, Part 32 – Written Evidence)*, paras 1.2–1.4.

Procedure for Applying for a Writ of Habeas Corpus

give greater weight to affidavits as the rules make no distinction[1]. In circumstances of an application for habeas corpus, it may be considerably easier to obtain a witness statement as the applicant will be in custody. As a result, a witness statement should be relied on.

The affidavit or witness statement should be sworn or signed by the applicant unless they are unable to swear or sign it[2]. If the affidavit or witness statement needs to be sworn or signed by a person other than the applicant, the person who swears the affidavit or signs the witness statement must state that it is sworn or signed on behalf of the applicant and that the applicant is unable to make the affidavit or witness statement. It must also explain why the applicant is unable to make the affidavit or witness statement[3].

The affidavit or witness statement must show 'that it is made at [the applicant's] instance and setting out the nature of the restraint'[4]. In practice, the affidavit or witness statement should be drafted so that it is effectively the facts and the grounds of the application. If possible, it should exhibit documents authorising the detention and all relevant correspondence. There will be no other documents before the court, so it is important that the affidavit or witness statement is detailed. In addition, an applicant for habeas corpus is subject to a duty of disclosure of all material facts[5]. When setting out the facts, the affidavit or witness statement can contain hearsay and double hearsay[6]. However, in general, an applicant for habeas corpus is restricted to relying on evidence that has been presented to the court or decision-maker who committed that person to prison[7]. The affidavit or witness statement must be in the format required for other documents that are lodged in the Crown Office[8]. Precedents for witness statements and affidavits in the context of judicial review are included in Appendix 1.

Once the application is lodged, the High Court will hear it as a matter of urgency as in theory applications for habeas corpus take precedence over other court business. That is, however, no reason for commencing an application for habeas corpus in preference to an application for judicial review. The High Court can consider an application for judicial review as quickly as it can hear an application for habeas corpus, although some practitioners find in practice

---

1   This is particularly true as para 1.2 of *Practice Direction (CPR 1998, Part 32 – Written Evidence)* makes it clear that evidence 'should normally' be given by witness statement at proceedings other than trial.
2   CPR 1998, Sch 1, RSC Ord 54, r 1(2) and 1(3).
3   Ibid, r 1(3).
4   Ibid, r 1(2).
5   *R v Kensington Income Tax Commissioners ex p Princess Edmond De Polignac* [1917] 1 KB 486, holding that a duty of disclosure applies whenever an applicant seeks an order without giving notice to other parties.
6   *R v Secretary of State for the Home Department ex p Rahman* [1998] QB 136, CA.
7   There are some exceptions to this rule. As an application for habeas corpus is only likely to be made in extradition, these exceptions are considered in detail at **4.24** where extradition is considered. In essence, additional evidence may be adduced where it goes to the jurisdiction of the decision-maker or the court that ordered detention.
8   See **6.4**.

that applications for habeas corpus are listed quicker than applications for judicial review[1].

If an applicant for a writ of habeas corpus has any queries about the procedure in the Crown Office, they should contact the Crown Office on 0171 936 6205.

8.3 HABEAS CORPUS AS A TWO-STAGE PROCESS

An application for habeas corpus may be made without notice being served on any other party[2]. In the case of a child, the application must be made to a judge who is not sitting in court[3]. In the case of an adult, the application is usually heard by a judge in court unless the court is not sitting or unless the court directs that it is heard by a Divisional Court[4]. In a criminal cause or matter heard by a single judge, the application will need to be adjourned to enable the case to be heard by a Divisional Court, because an application can only be refused by a Divisional Court[5]. That is likely, however, to be amended by the Access to Justice Bill so that applications for a writ of habeas corpus can be dismissed by a single judge. In cases that are not criminal causes or matters, the application is likely to be considered by a single judge.

In theory, the court can order the release of the person detained following an initial hearing of which the parties other than the applicant have not been given notice[6]. Alternatively, the court can issue a writ of habeas corpus as soon as the initial hearing has taken place[7]. In practice, the High Court is extremely unlikely to order the release of prisoner or issue the writ until it has heard from the respondent.

If the writ is issued, the writ will direct that the applicant is produced at a hearing. Other parties will have been given notice of this hearing. If the writ is not issued, the court will normally issue orders that require notice of the proceedings to be given to other parties. As a result, the application normally effectively becomes a two-stage process whether or not the writ is issued. The applicant will be required to show at the first hearing that there is sufficient merit for the case to be adjourned for notice of the proceedings to be given.

If the High Court does decide that the matter should be listed for a hearing of which other parties have been given notice, it will also make an order determining how the application should be continued. In particular, it will determine whether it will be continued by claim form to a judge or to a

---

1 *R v Oldham Justices ex p Cawley* [1996] 1 All ER 464, DC, in which it was held that the procedural differences between habeas corpus applications and applications for judicial review were no reason why challenges to warrants of commitment should not be brought by judicial review.
2 CPR 1998, Sch 1, RSC Ord 54, r 1(2).
3 Ibid, r 1(1)(c).
4 Ibid, r 1(1).
5 Administration of Justice Act 1960, s 14(1).
6 CPR 1998, Sch 1, RSC Ord 54, r 2(1).
7 Ibid, r 2(1).

Divisional Court[1]. The claim form is not the standard form used in other civil proceedings. Instead, it is a modified version of the High Court Form 87. A precedent is included in Appendix 2. If parties are served with the claim form and the applicant is in receipt of legal aid, the parties served should also be served with a notice of issue of legal aid[2]. The format of this notice is specified by the Legal Aid Board[3].

There are no express powers to make interlocutory orders during proceedings for a writ of habeas corpus. It, however, appears to be accepted that there is a power to grant bail in a criminal cause or matter[4]. It is unclear whether there is a similar power when the court hears any other form of matter. In any event, there is a clear reluctance to grant bail while the court determines the merits of an application for habeas corpus[5]. It does also appear that theoretically the High Court may order cross-examination, although the court is likely to be extremely reluctant to make such an order[6]. If an application is made for interlocutory orders, it should be done in the same way as an application for interlocutory orders during judicial review proceedings[7].

As set out below, it is likely that a respondent will serve some form of response to a prisoner's application for a writ of habeas corpus. Clearly, the applicant's advisers are obliged to review the merits of the application in the light of that response. If they determine that the application lacks merit, the application should be withdrawn[8].

The listing arrangements for an application for a writ of habeas corpus are in general the same as for other Crown Office business[9]. In addition, the Practice Directions relating to bundles and skeleton arguments apply to an application for a writ of habeas corpus[10]. In particular, prior to the substantive hearing, the applicant's solicitors should normally supply the Crown Office with sufficient copies of a bundle including all relevant documents, such as all written evidence.

---

1 CPR 1998, Sch 1, RSC Ord 54, r 2(1).
2 Civil Legal Aid (General) Regulations 1989, SI 1989/339, reg 50.
3 See the *Legal Aid Handbook 1998/1999* (Sweet & Maxwell) for precedent.
4 In *Re Amand* [1941] 2 KB 239 at 249, affirmed at [1943] AC 147, HL.
5 *R v Governor of Haslar Prison ex p Egbe* (1991) *The Times*, 4 June, CA, noting that many of the factors to be considered when deciding whether to grant bail were also factors when deciding whether to order release at the substantive hearing and so were best considered at the substantive hearing.
6 Per Lord Bridge, *R v Secretary of State for the Home Department ex p Khawaja* [1984] AC 74 at 124H, HL.
7 See **6.9**.
8 See **6.6** for details of how to withdraw proceedings.
9 See **6.2** and **6.3** for details of the listing arrangements for Crown Office business.
10 See **6.4** for details.

8.4 ADVISING A RESPONDENT

Clearly, the first thing that any respondent will wish to consider is whether they wish to oppose the application. If they decide that they do not wish to oppose the application, they should immediately release the applicant from custody. That is because by determining that they do not oppose the applicant, they are accepting that detention is unlawful.

If the respondent decides that they do wish to oppose the application, they are likely to want to place material before the court justifying the detention. In rare cases where a writ is issued, the respondent will be required to make a return which is normally annexed to or endorsed on the writ. The return is required to state 'all the causes of the detainer of the person restrained'[1]. It should be filed with the Crown Office. The respondent can subsequently amend the return by permission of the judge[2].

If the writ is not issued, there is no express provision requiring the respondents to an application to file any evidence in response to the application. However, it is implicit in the rules that a respondent is entitled to rely on affidavit evidence or witness statements. This is because the rules provide that 'every party' must serve other parties with copies of the affidavit evidence or witness statements on request[3]. In general, the burden is on a person who seeks to justify detention to show that it is legal[4]. As a result, respondents should normally serve affidavit evidence or witness statements justifying the detention unless the return of a writ fully justifies the detention.

8.5 THE SUBSTANTIVE HEARING

The applicant will not normally be produced at the hearing of the substantive matter unless the judge has ordered production or the writ has been issued. At the conclusion of the substantive hearing, it is unlikely that the writ will be issued. Instead, the High Court will use its power to order the immediate release of the applicant if the application is successful[5].

At the conclusion of the hearing counsel will need to request an order for legal aid taxation if their client is in receipt of legal aid. Counsel appearing at the substantive hearing will also wish to consider whether leave to appeal should be sought. There is no appeal from the order of a single judge in a criminal cause or matter[6]. This is not as significant as it might at first appear, because, as we have already noted, an application for a writ of habeas corpus may not be dismissed by a single judge in a criminal cause or matter[7]. The proposals in the

---

1 CPR 1998, Sch 1, RSC Ord 54, r 7(1).
2 Ibid, r 7(2).
3 Ibid, r 3.
4 Per Lord Atkin, *Liversidge v St John Anderson* [1942] AC 206 at 228, HL.
5 CPR 1998, Sch 1, RSC Ord 54, r 4(1).
6 Administration of Justice Act 1960, s 15(2); Supreme Court Act 1981, s 18(1)(a).
7 Administration of Justice Act 1960, s 15(1).

Access to Justice Bill, that an application for a writ of habeas corpus in a criminal cause or matter may be heard by a single judge, also include a proposal for a right of appeal from a decision of a single judge.

In all other cases, there is a right of appeal against both an order refusing release and an order releasing a prisoner[1]. In a criminal cause or matter, the appeal is direct to the House of Lords[2]. Unusually, there is no need for a certificate that the case raises issues of general public importance[3]. There is, however, a requirement for leave to appeal. In other cases, there is a right of appeal to the Court of Appeal. There is no need to obtain leave to appeal[4].

It is possible to make a further application for a writ of habeas corpus where an application has previously been refused. No further application, however, may be made on the same grounds unless the applicant seeks to rely on fresh evidence[5]. Fresh evidence is evidence that could not have been put forward by the applicant or could not reasonably have been put forward by the applicant[6].

---

1 Administration of Justice Act 1960, s 15(1).
2 Ibid, s 1.
3 Ibid, s 15(3).
4 CPR 1998, Sch 1, RSC Ord 59, r 1B(1)(b).
5 Administration of Justice Act 1960, s 14(2).
6 Per Gibson J, *Re Tarling* [1979] 1 WLR 1417 at 1423, DC.

Chapter 9

PROCEDURE FOR APPEALING BY WAY OF CASE STATED

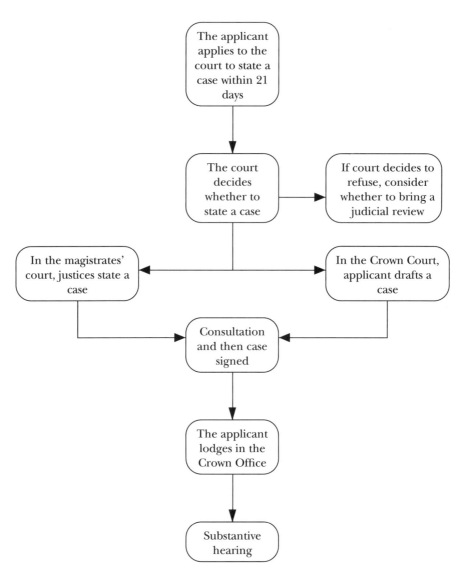

This flowchart shows the stages involved in an appeal by way of case stated. Reference should also be made to the Procedural Guides contained in Appendix 4.

9.1 INTRODUCTION

The procedure for bringing an appeal by way of case stated depends on whether the appeal is from a decision of the magistrates' court or of the Crown Court. We have highlighted the differences between the two procedures. If there is no reference to differences, the procedure is the same. The most significant difference between the two procedures is that the court clerk is responsible for drafting the case in the magistrates' court, whilst the applicant is responsible for this in the Crown Court.

When considering texts or judgments about appeals by way of case stated, it is also important to recognise that an appellant is normally described as an applicant until a final case has been stated and signed. This is because the procedure for appealing by way of case stated is essentially a two-stage process. The first stage involves obtaining a final signed case from the criminal court. This stage is governed by the procedure rules of the criminal court. Once the final signed case has been obtained, proceedings are begun in the High Court.

9.2 SERVICE OF DOCUMENTS

The procedure that is set out below requires the service of documents on the various parties to the proceedings. The service of these documents is governed by the procedure rules of the court which has conduct of the appeal at that point in time. Thus, until a final signed case has been obtained from the magistrates or the Crown Court judge, the procedure rules of the magistrates' court and the Crown Court govern service. Once proceedings are commenced in the High Court, the procedure is governed by the procedure rules of the High Court.

The rules of service that apply in the High Court are set out at **6.7**. In the magistrates' court and the Crown Court, however, the rules of service are different. Whilst the magistrates are being requested to state a case, documents must either be served by delivering them to a party or sending them by registered post or recorded delivery to the party's last known or usual place of abode[1]. Whilst a Crown Court judge is stating a case, documents may be served personally on a party or sent by post to his usual or last known residence or place of business in England and Wales[2]. There is specific provision that where a party is a company, the document may be served on the company's registered office in England and Wales[3].

9.3 COMMENCING THE APPEAL

As we noted earlier, an application should only be made to magistrates to state a case in exceptional circumstances if an appellant has the right to appeal to the

---

1 Magistrates' Courts Rules 1981, SI 1981/552, r 80.
2 Crown Court Rules 1982, SI 1982/1109, r 28.
3 Ibid.

Crown Court. The appellant must be very confident that there are good reasons for applying for the case to be stated, because an application to state a case deprives a defendant of the right to appeal to the Crown Court[1]. However, an appeal by way of case stated against conviction does not prevent an appeal to the Crown Court against sentence[2].

An appeal by way of case stated is commenced by a request to the magistrates' court or the Crown Court to state a case. That request must be made within 21 days of the decision[3]. In the magistrates' court, this request must be in writing and signed by or on behalf of the applicant[4]. The application should be sent to the clerk to the magistrates[5] and it should specify that it is being sent to the magistrates as well as the clerk.

In the Crown Court, the rules only specify that the application must be in writing[6], although it is probably good practice to ensure that the application is signed. The application must be sent to the appropriate officer of the Crown Court[7]. In addition, it must also be sent forthwith to the other parties to the proceedings in the Crown Court[8].

In the magistrates' court, the application to state a case 'shall identify the question or questions of law or jurisdiction on which the opinion of the High Court is sought'[9]. If it is said that there is no evidence to support a particular finding of fact, the finding that is questioned must be specified[10]. In the Crown Court, the decision 'shall state the ground on which the decision of the Crown Court is questioned'[11]. In practice, these provisions are likely to be interpreted in an identical way. The provisions require the applicant to state clearly their grounds of appeal. A precedent application to state a case is included in Appendix 3.

When deciding what grounds to raise, defendants are entitled to raise a defence that was not raised when they were convicted[12]. The prosecution is not, however, entitled to argue that magistrates or the Crown Court wrongly decided that there was no case to answer because it would be possible to present the prosecution case in a way that is different to the way that it was actually presented during the criminal trial[13].

As the application must be submitted rapidly, practitioners might be tempted to submit skeletal applications and update the application when there has been an opportunity to review the case. As we noted earlier, the High Court is often

---

1 See **4.11**.
2 *R v Winchester Crown Court ex p Lewington* [1982] 1 WLR 1277, DC.
3 See **5.6** for details of delay in appeals by way of case stated.
4 Magistrates' Courts Rules 1981, SI 1981/552, r 76(1).
5 Ibid, r 76(3).
6 Crown Court Rules 1982, SI 1982/1109, r 26(1).
7 Ibid.
8 Ibid, r 26(3). There is no similar obligation in the magistrates' court.
9 Magistrates' Courts Rules 1981, SI 1981/552, r 76(1).
10 Ibid, r 76(2).
11 Crown Court Rules 1982, SI 1982/1109, r 26(2).
12 *Whitehead v Haines* [1965] 1 QB 200, DC.
13 *Environment Agency v Singer* [1998] Env LR 380, DC.

willing to accept that an application to state a case was submitted in time, even though it failed to comply fully with the rules governing content[1]. It cannot, however, ever be regarded as good practice to fail to state the grounds of appeal as clearly as possible. First, a failure to provide sufficient detail may justify magistrates or a Crown Court treating the application as frivolous. An applicant should specify the grounds of appeal in sufficient detail to enable the court that is being asked to state a case to understand the grounds of appeal. In addition, although the High Court has accepted that a failure to comply with the rules may not mean that an application is invalid, there must be substantial compliance if the application is to be valid[2]. Finally, the time-limit for the amendment of errors is unclear[3].

9.4 THE OBLIGATIONS IMPOSED ON THE COURT IN RECEIPT OF THE APPLICATION

When an application is received by a court requesting the statement of a case, the first thing that the court must decide is whether it is prepared to state a case. In the magistrates' court, the magistrates must decide in sufficient time to enable the clerk to send a draft case to the appellant within 21 days of the day when the application to state a case was received[4]. In the Crown Court, the judge is required to decide whether he is willing to state a case '[o]n receipt of the application'[5].

In the magistrates' court, the magistrates are not required to state a case if they determine the application is 'frivolous' and has not been made by or under the direction of the Attorney-General[6]. If they refuse to state a case, they must issue a certificate stating that they have refused to state a case. It is also regarded as good practice for the magistrates to provide some brief reasons for their decision to treat the case as frivolous[7]. The reasons should assist an applicant to determine whether there is any merit in bringing a judicial review challenging the decision to refuse to state a case and so may save legal fees and court time.

Similarly, a Crown Court judge is not required to state a case if he determines that the application is 'frivolous'[8]. If he refuses to state a case, an applicant may require the Crown Court judge to supply a certificate supplying reasons for the decision[9]. Again, it must be good practice to supply reasons that are sufficiently

---

1 See **5.6**.
2 *R v Croydon Justices ex p Lefore Holdings Ltd* [1980] 1 WLR 1465, CA.
3 *Robinson v Whittle* [1980] 1 WLR 1476, DC, suggesting that the application might be amended at any time before the hearing of the matter; cf *R v Bromley Magistrates' Court ex p Waitrose Ltd* [1980] 3 All ER 464, DC, suggesting that the application could be amended during a 'reasonable' period after it had been lodged. Both these decisions are obiter as the application to amend was made promptly.
4 Magistrates' Courts Rules 1981, SI 1981/552, r 77(1).
5 Crown Court Rules 1982, SI 1982/1109, r 26(5).
6 Magistrates' Courts Act 1980, s 111(5).
7 *R v Mildenhall Magistrates' Court ex p Forest Heath District Council* (1997) *The Times*, 16 May, CA.
8 Crown Court Rules 1982, SI 1982/1109, r 26(6).
9 Ibid.

detailed to enable the appellant to determine whether he wishes to challenge that decision[1].

The Court of Appeal recently considered the meaning of the term 'frivolous'. Lord Bingham CJ held that:

> 'What the expression means ... is ... that the court considers the application to be futile, misconceived, hopeless or academic. That is not a conclusion to which justices to whom an application to state a case is made will often or lightly come. It is not a conclusion to which they can properly come simply because they consider their decision to be right or immune from challenge. Still less is it a conclusion to which they can properly come out of a desire to obstruct a challenge to their decision or out of misplaced amour propre.'[2]

Similarly, in the same case Lord Justice Millet held that:

> 'Where the questions which they are asked to state are academic or inappropriate or raise issues which are irrelevant to their decision, then in my view an application for a case to be stated can properly be described by the magistrates as "frivolous".'[3]

The relatively trivial nature of the criminal proceedings that are the subject of an appeal does not mean that the appeal is frivolous. For example, where a conviction has been considered on appeal and the sentence is light as it is a conditional discharge, the application to state a case following the appeal is not automatically 'frivolous'. Any person convicted of a criminal offence is entitled to have their appeal considered if they are not raising a frivolous matter[4].

Although a finding that the application is 'frivolous' is the most common reason for a refusal to state a case, there are other reasons why a Crown Court judge or magistrates may decide to refuse to state a case. Magistrates may determine that they have no jurisdiction to state a case because the application is out of time[5]. Alternatively, a Crown Court judge may refuse to extend the time in which an application may be made to extend time[6]. The magistrates or the Crown Court judge may determine that they have no jurisdiction to consider the matter. For example, this might be because the appeal is in respect of a matter that relates to a trial on indictment[7], or because the appeal relates to an interim decision[8]. It may also be that any failure to comply with the procedural

---

1 The reasoning of the judgment in *R v Mildenhall Magistrates' Court ex p Forest Heath District Council* (1997) *The Times*, 16 May, CA, must also apply to appeals from decisions of the Crown Court. This was endorsed in the context of a judicial review of a decision of the Crown Court in *R v Preston Crown Court ex p Chief Constable of Lancashire Constabulary* [1998] COD 272. Cf *R v Carlisle Crown Court ex p Jackson, Watson and McDonagh* [1991] COD 273, DC, holding that it may be sufficient for a Crown Court judge to write a letter saying that they refuse to state a case 'on the grounds that your application is frivolous in accordance with the Rules'.
2 *R v Mildenhall Magistrates' Court ex p Forest Heath District Council* (1997) *The Times*, 16 May, CA. The quote is taken from the transcript.
3 Ibid.
4 *R v Crown Court at Portsmouth ex p Thomas* [1994] COD 373, DC.
5 See **5.6**.
6 See **5.6**.
7 See **1.6**.
8 See **4.9**.

rules is so significant that they decide that the application is not an effective application[1]. There are no other reasons for refusing to state a case[2].

Before stating a case, the magistrates or the Crown Court judge may require the appellant to enter into a recognizance, with or without sureties, to prosecute the appeal without delay[3]. In the magistrates' court, the recognizance can also be required to ensure that the appellant submits to the judgment and pays the costs ordered[4].

In the Crown Court, there is an explicit obligation to consider the means of the appellant when setting the level of any recognizance[5]. Although there is no similar provision governing applications in the magistrates' court, magistrates are also required to take account of the means of an appellant when setting the level of any recognizance[6]. However, a recognizance may be required even though an applicant has no disposal assets and has received legal aid without contribution[7]. It could, however, be argued that setting a recognizance that an appellant will be unable to afford is an interference with that applicant's right of access to the courts[8]. In the magistrates' court, there is also the power to require a fee before a case is delivered in a matter that is not a criminal matter[9].

9.5 CHALLENGING A DECISION TO REFUSE TO STATE A CASE

When a court refuses to state a case, the applicant may bring judicial review proceedings to require the court to state a case. In particular, there is a specific statutory provision enabling a person to seek an order of mandamus if they have applied to magistrates for a case to be stated and that application has been refused[10]. Although there is no equivalent provision governing proceedings in the Crown Court, there is no doubt that a judicial review can be brought[11].

When bringing a judicial review of a decision to refuse to state a case, the applicant should consider whether the judicial review should challenge the substantive decision that is the subject of the proposed appeal as well as the decision to refuse to state a case. If the appellant has sufficient material to put before the court to show flaws in the substantive decision of the magistrates' court or the Crown Court, the judicial review should challenge both the refusal

---

1 See **5.6** and **9.3**.
2 *R v Manchester Crown Court ex p Wallwork* [1997] COD 417, DC.
3 Crown Court Rules 1982, SI 1982/1109, r 26(11); Magistrates' Courts Act 1980, s 114.
4 Magistrates' Courts Act 1980, s 114.
5 Crown Court Rules 1982, SI 1982/1109, r 26(11).
6 *R v Newcastle Upon Tyne Justices ex p Skinner* [1987] 1 WLR 312, DC.
7 *R v Croydon Magistrates' Court ex p Morgan* (1997) 161 JP 169, DC.
8 *R v Lord Chancellor ex p Witham* [1998] QB 575, DC, in which court fees were held to be an interference with the common law right of access to the courts.
9 Magistrates' Courts Act 1980, s 114. The present fee is £382 or £8 for a certificate where there is a refusal to state a case. See Magistrates' Courts Act 1980, Sch 6, Part 1.
10 Ibid, s 111(6).
11 *R v Crown Court at Portsmouth ex p Thomas* [1994] COD 373, DC, for an example of a judicial review of a decision of a Crown Court judge to refuse to state a case.

to state a case and the substantive decision[1]. The High Court may wish to prevent the waste of resources associated with a judicial review followed by an appeal by case stated[2]. As a result, it may quash the substantive decision if it finds that it has sufficient material to consider the merits of the substantive decision.

Where an applicant has successfully sought permission to apply for judicial review of a decision to refuse to state a case, magistrates or a Crown Court judge should be very cautious about continuing to refuse to state a case. In particular, they should carefully consider any comments made by the High Court judge when granting permission. A continuing refusal to state a case may result in the magistrates being personally liable for the costs of the application if the grant of permission is not treated with sufficient seriousness[3].

The risk of costs does not mean that a case should be stated merely because an applicant has obtained permission to apply for judicial review. If the magistrates or Crown Court judge decide to continue to refuse to state a case, they should show that they are taking the matter seriously by filing written evidence giving reasons for the decision to refuse to state a case. If the applicant successfully obtains an order of mandamus requiring the production of a case stated, the magistrates or the Crown Court judge may even wish to consider an appeal against that decision[4]. The Court of Appeal has, however, no jurisdiction to consider any appeal in a criminal cause or matter[5]. As a result, any appeal in a criminal cause or matter must be to the House of Lords.

9.6 OBTAINING A FIRST DRAFT OF THE CASE STATED

When magistrates are requested to state a case and agree that they are willing to state a case, the clerk is required to send a draft case to the applicant and the respondent within 21 days of receiving the application[6]. If the applicant is required to enter into a recognizance, the start of the 21-day period is deferred until the recognizance has been entered into[7]. When drafting the case, the clerk may well wish to consult with the magistrates and the parties. If the clerk is unable to comply with the requirement that the draft application is sent within 21 days, he should send the draft case as soon as practicable thereafter[8]. When

---

1 *R v Knightsbridge Crown Court ex p Foot* [1998] COD 165, DC, in which Lord Justice Simon Brown held that where the facts were not in dispute, a judicial review should be brought of the substantive decision as well as the refusal to state a case.
2 *R v Southwark Crown Court ex p Brooke* [1997] COD 81, DC.
3 Eg *R v Huntingdon Magistrates' Court ex p Percy* [1994] COD 323, DC; *R v Metropolitan Stipendiary Magistrate ex p Ali* (1997) *The Independent*, 12 May.
4 *R v Mildenhall Magistrates' Court ex p Forest Heath District Council* (1997) *The Times*, 16 May, CA, is an example of a case where the magistrates decided to appeal against the decision of the High Court.
5 Supreme Court Act 1981, s 18(1)(a).
6 Magistrates' Courts Rules 1981, SI 1981/552, r 77(1).
7 *R v Warrington Magistrates' Court ex p Worsley* [1996] COD 346, DC, holding that there was no obligation on magistrates to state a case unless a required recognizance was entered into.
8 Magistrates' Courts Rules 1981, SI 1981/552, r 79(1).

the application is not sent within 21 days, the draft case should be accompanied by a statement of the delay and the reasons for the delay[1].

When a Crown Court judge decides to state a case, the applicant is normally given notice in writing of this decision by the appropriate officer of the Crown Court[2]. The applicant then has 21 days to draft a case[3]. This is perhaps the most significant difference between an appeal by way of case stated from a decision of magistrates and one from a decision of the Crown Court. The applicant can apply to the Crown Court for an extension of this time period[4]. Once the applicant has drafted that case, he is required to send it to the appropriate officer of the Crown Court and to the other parties to proceedings[5]. There is provision for the judge to dispense with this procedure and personally state a case, but this rarely happens[6].

9.7 CONTENTS OF THE CASE STATED

In the magistrates' court, the case stated:

> 'shall state the facts found by the court and the question or questions of law or jurisdiction on which the opinion of the High Court is sought'.[7]

Normally, the case stated should not include a statement of the evidence unless the sufficiency of evidence is questioned[8]. In a case where the sufficiency of evidence is questioned, the particular finding of fact which it is claimed cannot be supported by evidence must be specified in the case[9]. The case must also be stated in a format that complies with the requirements of Form 155 of the Magistrates' Courts (Forms) Rules 1981, SI 1981/553. A precedent is set out in Appendix 3.

In the Crown Court, the case stated shall state the facts found by the Crown Court, the submissions of the parties (including any authorities relied on by the parties), the decision of the Crown Court in respect of which the opinion is sought and the question on which the opinion of the High Court is sought[10]. The format must be the same as in the magistrates' court[11].

Clearly, the provisions governing a case stated by the magistrates' court and one by the Crown Court are almost identical. Case-law also suggests that the High Court will expect a case stated by magistrates to have the same content as that stated by a Crown Court judge and vice versa. For example, although the

---

1 Magistrates' Courts Rules 1981, SI 1981/552, r 79(1). The reasons are important as they may be used when the High Court determines responsibility for delay. See **9.10**.
2 Crown Court Rules 1982, SI 1982/1109, r 26(5).
3 Ibid, r 26(8).
4 Ibid, r 26(14).
5 Ibid, r 26(8).
6 Ibid, r 26(7). See *Colfox v Dorset County Council* [1996] COD 275, DC, in which a case stated by a recorder without consultation was remitted because it was defective.
7 Magistrates' Courts Rules 1981, SI 1981/552, r 81(1).
8 Ibid, r 81(3).
9 Ibid, r 81(2).
10 Crown Court Rules 1982, SI 1982/1109, r 26(13).
11 *Practice Direction (Cases Stated by Crown Courts)* (1979) 68 Cr App R 119.

procedure rules do not require magistrates to state any legal argument that they have heard, it has been held that they should[1]. As a result, although much of the case-law that has decided how a case should be stated has been decided in the context of appeals from decisions of the magistrates, it is reasonable to assume that the same principles apply to appeals from decisions of the Crown Court.

The case stated should be as brief as possible. For example, a Divisional Court has held that:

> 'Justices must endeavour to ensure in stating a case that (1) the whole of their findings of fact are contained in one and of course an early paragraph of the case; (2) their reasons for rejecting a submission of no case to answer are shortly and succinctly stated; and (3) they are not drawn ... to amending a draft case so as to burden it with an over-elaborate discussion upon the law.'[2]

As a result, it should not state the evidence presented to the court unless the sufficiency of the evidence that resulted in a particular finding is challenged[3]. Instead, the facts found should be stated clearly and the questions stated should be directly relevant to the facts and the conclusions drawn[4].

9.8 OBTAINING AGREEMENT OF THE PARTIES TO THE CASE STATED

The case stated is supposed to be the document upon which the decision of the High Court is to be obtained. As a result, the court will refuse to compare the final case stated with earlier drafts[5]. Similarly, the High Court will not consider an appeal by way of case stated against a decision to find that there was no case to answer based on a claim that the prosecution could have successfully presented the case in a different way to that actually presented as disclosed by the case stated[6]. As the High Court will base its decision on the case as stated, the court whose decision is being challenged and the parties to the proceedings should attempt to agree the case stated. If that is impossible, practitioners acting for parties should ensure that the case stated will as far as possible support their arguments[7].

The procedure rules do provide for consultation with the parties before the case stated is signed. In the magistrates' court, the draft case must be sent to the

---

1 *DPP v Kirk* [1993] COD 99, DC.
2 Per Lord Justice Watkins, *Riley v DPP* (1990) 91 Cr App R 14 at 23, DC.
3 *Laird v Simms* (1988) *The Times*, 7 March, DC; *Turtington v United Co-operatives Ltd* [1993] Crim LR 376, DC, holding that no exhibits should be attached to a case stated if the findings of fact are not in question; See also Magistrates' Courts Rules 1981, SI 1981/552, r 81(3) and 81(2).
4 *DPP v Price* (1992) *The Independent*, 15 June, DC.
5 *Tesco Stores Ltd v Seabridge* (1988) *The Times*, 29 April, DC.
6 *Environment Agency v Singer* [1998] Env LR 380, DC.
7 For example, in *T v Ipswich Youth Court* (1998) *Archbold News*, December, DC, the High Court held that it would usually be unwilling to consider documents that were not properly exhibited to the case stated. As a result, if those documents are important to the argument they should be properly exhibited.

applicant and the respondent or their solicitors[1]. After receipt of the draft case, each party may make representations regarding the draft case within 21 days. The representations must be in writing and signed by or on behalf of the party[2]. The magistrates then have 21 days to adjust the case and then state and sign the case[3]. The case may be signed by any two or more magistrates whose decision is in question.[4] The case is then sent forthwith to the applicant or his solicitor[5].

The time-limits on the various stages of consultation in the magistrates' court may be extended. Where a party requires additional time to respond to the draft case, they should apply in writing to the clerk to the magistrates. If an extension is granted, the clerk will attach a statement of the extension and the reasons for the extension to the final case[6]. Where further time is required for the magistrates to sign the final case, they shall attach a statement of the delay and the reasons for the delay to the final case[7].

In the Crown Court, the applicant is required to send the draft case to the court and to the parties to proceedings[8]. The parties then have 21 days to serve a draft of an alternative case with the applicant's case on the appropriate officer of the Crown Court[9]. If a party served with a draft case does not seek an amendment of the draft case, they should do one of two things. Either they should give notice in writing to the appropriate officer of the Crown Court and to the applicant stating that they do not intend to take part in proceedings. Alternatively, they should indicate in writing on a copy of the draft case that they agree with the draft case and send that to the appropriate officer of the Crown Office[10]. The Crown Court judge is required to consider the documents received and then sign a case within 14 days of receipt of the response from the parties[11]. If a party does not respond as required to the draft case, the Crown Court judge will sign a case within 14 days of the expiry of the time for the parties' responses to the draft case[12]. The Crown Court judge may extend any of these time periods[13].

9.9 PROCEDURE WHERE A PARTY IS UNHAPPY WITH THE FINAL CASE

Clearly, despite the provisions in the procedure rules for consultation, it is possible that a party to the proceedings will review the final case stated and decide that they are dissatisfied. If this is so, it is still essential that the case is

---

1   Magistrates' Courts Rules 1981, SI 1981/552, r 77(1).
2   Ibid, r 77(2).
3   Ibid, r 78(1).
4   Ibid, r 78(2).
5   Ibid, r 78(3).
6   Ibid, r 79(2).
7   Ibid, r 79(3).
8   Crown Court Rules 1982, SI 1982/1109, r 26(8).
9   Ibid, rule 26(9)(c).
10 Ibid, r 26(9)(a) and (b).
11 Ibid, r 26(12)(a).
12 Ibid, r 26(12)(b).
13 Ibid, r 26(14).

lodged with the Crown Office within the required time period[1]. An application can then be made to the High Court for the case to be remitted for amendment.

Where the appeal relates to a decision of the magistrates' court, the High Court has a statutory power to remit the case to the magistrates for amendment[2]. It also is clear, however, despite the absence of a statutory provision that the High Court has jurisdiction to remit a case stated by a Crown Court judge for amendment[3]. The case-law deciding the approach of the High Court to applications for a final case stated to be remitted for amendment has generally been decided in the context of appeals from decisions of magistrates. There is no reason, however, why the same approach should not apply in the context of decisions of the Crown Court.

In principle, if all the parties consent to an amendment, the High Court could amend the case. However, the High Court is likely to be unwilling to amend a case stated even where there is agreement that the case stated should be amended[4]. Instead it will remit the case. That is no reason, however, why consent to the amendment should not be sought. All parties are required to co-operate with attempts to obtain an agreement to suggested amendments to a case stated[5]. If there is agreement, a letter from the magistrates or written evidence from the clerk should be obtained so that the High Court has material before it explaining the need for amendment.

Clearly, the most likely cause for dissatisfaction with the final case stated is a disagreement with the facts found by the court whose decision is the subject of an appeal. That is clearly no reason to apply for the amendment. The High Court is required to base its decision on the facts as found by the court whose decision is the subject of an appeal if those findings were findings that the court was entitled to make. As a result, the case will normally only be remitted if the court has failed to state its findings on a relevant matter[6].

If an applicant decides to apply for an order remitting the case stated back to the magistrates or to the Crown Court judge for amendment, an application should be made as soon as possible to the High Court for an order. The application should be made by application notice and should be supported by written evidence[7]. The procedure for making interim applications should be adopted[8]. A precedent application notice is set out in Appendix 5. A precedent

---

1 *Basingstoke and Dean Borough Council v Houlton and Webb* [1995] COD 96, DC.
2 Supreme Court Act 1981, s 28A(2).
3 See *Colfox v Dorset County Council* [1996] COD 275, DC, for an example of a case where the High Court required the Crown Court to amend a case that they had stated.
4 *The Supreme Court Practice*, 1999 edn, Note 56/5/11.
5 *Ramage v DPP* [1995] COD 313, DC, holding that amendment should generally be unnecessary as parties should try to agree on the terms of the case stated at the appropriate time.
6 *DPP v Clarke and Others* [1991] COD 235, DC.
7 *Practice Note (Case Stated)* [1953] 1 WLR 334.
8 See **6.9**.

of the contents of an application notice in a different context is set out at Appendix 1[1].

9.10 DELAY DURING THE PREPARATION OF THE APPLICATION TO STATE A CASE

If there is delay during the preparation of the application to state a case, this might have consequences for a party when the High Court considers the matter. In particular, the High Court has declined to adjudicate on a case where there was delay caused by an appellant. The High Court accepted that it had jurisdiction to consider appeals despite delay, as the procedure rules governing an application to state a case are merely directory and not mandatory. Despite having jurisdiction to consider the appeal, the court declined to consider the appeal, as criminal litigation must be conducted as a matter of urgency[2].

It would clearly be unjust for the High Court to decline to determine the merits of an application where a party other than an appellant has been responsible for delay. However, that delay may clearly be a matter that the court takes account of when it makes any orders for costs. As a result, all parties should regard an appeal by way of case stated as a matter that should be pursued as a matter of urgency.

9.11 COMMENCING THE APPLICATION IN THE HIGH COURT

Once a final case has been signed, all the parties should review the merits of their case. The merits of the appeal should be the subject of further review as the matter proceeds towards hearing. If the appellant is of the opinion that the appeal has no merit, it should not be pursued. An appeal by way of case stated may be withdrawn without the consent of the High Court[3]. If other parties are of the opinion that the appeal should be settled, they should seek agreement to a consent order. If all the parties agree how the appeal is to be determined, it is also possible for the parties to agree a draft order for consideration by the court without the parties attending[4].

If an appellant has decided that he will continue to pursue his appeal, the final signed case must be filed in the Crown Office by the appellant within 10 days of its receipt[5]. Three copies of the case should be provided for the court together with the relevant court fee[6]. At present that court fee is £50, but that should

---

1 The application notice is drafted for use during a judicial review application and so clearly it must be amended as appropriate.
2 *Parsons v FW Woolworth & Co Ltd* [1980] 1 WLR 1472, DC, in which the magistrates had prepared a draft case but not served it at the request of the prosecutor.
3 *Collet v Bromsgrove District Council* (1996) *The Times*, 15 July, DC.
4 See **6.6** for the consideration of the procedure for obtaining a consent order.
5 CPR 1998, Sch 1, RSC Ord 56, r 1(4) and r 6(1)(a).
6 *The Supreme Court Practice*, 1999 edn, Notes 56/1/7 and 56/6/1.

always be checked. When the appeal relates to a decision of the Crown Court, the appellant must supply three copies of the judgment, order or decision that is the subject of the appeal[1]. In addition, where the decision of the Crown Court was taken following an appeal, the appellant must supply three copies of the original judgment, order or decision that was the subject of the appeal in the Crown Court[2].

If the appellant is legally aided, a copy of the legal aid certificate should be lodged with the Crown Office when the appeal is lodged. In addition, the Crown Office should be informed of any special requirements, such as a request for an urgent hearing to consider orders restricting reporting of the matter and requiring the hearing to be expedited.

The time for the lodging of the appeal in an appeal by case stated from a decision of the Crown Court can be extended, providing that an application is made on 2 clear days' notice[3]. The time can also be extended in an appeal by case stated from a decision of the magistrates' court if the notice of the application is served as soon as practicable and at least 3 days before the hearing[4]. The application should be made by Application Notice. A precedent of an Application Notice is included in Appendices 1 and 5[5]. A fee is payable when the application to extend time is made. At present this fee is £50.

In the case of an appeal from the Crown Court, the High Court will need to be satisfied that the delay is accounted for to its satisfaction[6]. As 'pressure of work' is not a sufficient explanation, it is difficult to see what explanation will satisfy the High Court[7]. As a result, the time-limit should be regarded as very rigid. There is no guidance in the rules about the approach of the High Court in the case of an appeal from the magistrates' court. It is unlikely, however, that the High Court will show any greater enthusiasm to extend time.

Once the case has been lodged, a notice of the entry of the appeal must be served on the respondent within 4 days[8]. When the appeal is from a decision of the magistrates' court, the notice must be accompanied by a copy of the case stated[9]. It is good practice to serve the case stated on the respondent when the decision appealed against was taken by the Crown Court. A precedent of the notice is set out in Appendix 3.

If parties to an appeal by way of case stated have queries about the procedure in the Crown Office, they should contact the Crown Office on 0171 936 6205.

---

1   CPR 1998, Sch 1, RSC Ord 56, r 1(3).
2   Ibid.
3   Ibid, r 1(4).
4   CPR 1998, r 3.1(2)(a) and r 23.7(1)(b).
5   Appendix 1 contains a precedent for the contents of an application notice. Whilst it has been drafted for a judicial review, it is in essentially the same form for the present purposes. The application notice itself is set out in Appendix 5.
6   CPR 1998, Sch 1, RSC Ord 56, r 1(4).
7   *Reid v DPP* [1993] COD 111, DC.
8   CPR 1998, Sch 1, RSC Ord 56, r 4 and r 6(1)(b).
9   Ibid, r 6(1)(b).

9.12 PROCEDURE AFTER THE CASE HAS BEEN LODGED IN THE CROWN OFFICE

Once the application to state a case is lodged with the Crown Office, the case enters the Crown Office list. We considered earlier the operation of the Crown Office list[1]. There are two special features. First, the case will never enter Part A of the list as there are no steps for the respondent to take after the case has been lodged before it is ready for hearing. Instead, the court regards the case as being ready for hearing from the moment it is lodged.

In addition, where the appeal is from the decision of a magistrates' court, it cannot be heard less than 8 clear days after the service of notice that the case has been lodged with the Crown Office[2]. The court may order that this period should be reduced[3]. An order reducing this period should be sought when an order is also sought requesting the listing of the appeal as a matter of extreme urgency[4].

The Practice Directions relating to the lodging of bundles and skeleton arguments apply to an appeal by way of case stated as they apply to all proceedings in the Crown Office list[5]. The bundles should include all relevant documents. As a result, it should contain any decisions of the Crown Court or the magistrates' court in the proceedings, the signed case stated and any orders made by the High Court during the proceedings.

There is provision for interlocutory applications to be made to any judge or Master of the Queen's Bench Division during an appeal by way of case stated[6]. An interlocutory application is defined as including an 'application for an order extending the time for the entry of the appeal or for service of notice of entry of the appeal'[7]. This definition clearly does not limit the scope of interlocutory applications and, in practice, interlocutory applications could include other matters such as an application to move the case within the Crown Office list. The nature of an appeal by way of case stated is, however, likely to mean that the High Court will hold that they should not make an order for discovery or similar matters, because the case stated is the focus of the decision of the High Court[8]. That is also why it is not normal practice for a party to an appeal by way of case stated to seek to rely on written evidence.

---

1 See **6.2** and **6.3**.
2 CPR 1998, Sch 1, RSC Ord 56, r 6(2).
3 Ibid.
4 See **6.2** for details of expedition.
5 *Practice Direction (Crown Office List: Preparation for Hearings)* [1994] 1 WLR 1551, [1994] 4 All ER 671 and see also **6.4** for a consideration of the requirements of this Practice Direction.
6 CPR 1998, Sch 1, RSC Ord 56, r 13(1).
7 Ibid.
8 See **9.7** and **9.8**.

9.13 THE SUBSTANTIVE HEARING

At the time of writing, the appeal will be heard by a Divisional Court if the appeal relates to criminal proceedings[1]. It is proposed that this will change when the Access to Justice Bill becomes law so that the appeal will be heard by a single judge. In other proceedings, the case will be heard by a single judge. The hearing will consist of legal argument based on the case stated by the magistrates or the Crown Court judge.

The magistrates or the Crown Court judge should not normally appear at the hearing of the substantive appeal, because they are not parties to the proceedings. If the High Court will benefit from argument in addition to that put forward on behalf of any parties who will appear, the Treasury Solicitors can instruct counsel to appear as amicus curiae[2].

At the conclusion of the appeal, there are two matters that the parties will want to consider. First, it is essential that an order for legal aid taxation is sought if the applicant is in receipt of legal aid[3]. In addition, it is important to consider whether leave to appeal should be sought. In a criminal cause or matter any appeal can only be heard by the House of Lords. This requires leave to appeal and a certificate under s 1 of the Administration of Justice Act 1960 that the case involves a point of law of general public importance. Where the matter is not a criminal cause or matter, it is not possible to appeal from a decision of the High Court considering an appeal by case stated from a magistrates' court[4]. There appears to be no reason why it is not possible to appeal to the Court of Appeal against a decision of the High Court on appeal from the Crown Court in a matter that is not a criminal cause or matter. Leave to appeal is still necessary[5].

---

1   CPR 1998, Sch 1, RSC Ord 56, r 1(1) and r 5(1).
2   *Boddington v British Transport Police* [1998] 2 WLR 639, HL, is an example of a case where an amicus curiae was instructed.
3   See **12.13** for details of legal aid.
4   *Maile v Manchester City Council* [1998] COD 19, CA, applying ss 18 and 28A(4) of the Supreme Court Act 1981.
5   CPR 1998, Sch 1, RSC Ord 59, r 1B(1).

Chapter 10

ORDERS FOR INTERIM RELIEF AVAILABLE TO THE HIGH COURT DURING PROCEEDINGS

10.1 INTRODUCTION

The orders for interim relief that the High Court may make during proceedings depend on the form of proceedings that are being brought in the High Court. We have considered them in the same chapter, as differences in the interim relief available can assist practitioners to determine the correct form of proceedings to be brought[1]. For example, the limitation on the power to stay a disqualification from driving during a judicial review means that an appeal by way of case stated is likely to be the correct form of proceedings to challenge a decision that has resulted in disqualification[2].

10.2 MATTERS COMMON TO BAIL IN ALL PROCEEDINGS IN THE CROWN OFFICE

The right to bail under s 4 of the Bail Act 1976 does not apply to bail applications during proceedings in the High Court or during proceedings on or after conviction[3]. As a result, it clearly does not apply to any form of proceedings that is within the scope of this book. That does not, however, mean that the High Court will not grant bail. It merely means that there is no presumption that bail should be granted.

In some circumstances, it is possible to apply to the magistrates' court for bail while proceedings are pending in the High Court. When bail is refused by the magistrates' court and the defendant is unrepresented and has a right to apply for bail to the High Court, the magistrates' court must inform the defendant of that right[4]. It is probably also good practice in proceedings in the Crown Court for a Crown Court judge to inform an unrepresented defendant of any right to apply for bail in the High Court.

The procedure to be adopted when applying for bail is the same for all forms of proceedings in the High Court. There are no explicit procedural rules governing applications for bail in cases that are not a criminal cause or matter. In practice, most applications for bail adopt the procedure specified for

---

1 See Chapter 4, in particular, **4.14** as there may be no real choice about the form of proceedings in the circumstances of the case.
2 *R v Derwentside Magistrates' Court ex p Swift* [1996] COD 203 at 204, DC.
3 Bail Act 1976, s 4(2).
4 Ibid, s 5(6).

matters that are criminal causes or matters as there is no alternative procedure. Bail applications should be made by claim form in Form 97[1]. The claim form should normally be accompanied by a draft order setting out the proposed conditions for the grant of bail, as this may assist the court to obtain a rapid release of the defendant. See Appendix 1 for a precedent. There is also a £50 fee for making a bail application.

The claim form must be served on the prosecutor and on the Director of Public Prosecutions, if the prosecution is being carried on by him[2]. Service must take place at least 24 hours before the date set for the hearing[3]. The rules state that the application must be supported by a witness statement or affidavit[4]. In practice, this is usually unnecessary in an application for judicial review as the witness statement or affidavit in support of the application can normally stand as the evidence in support of the bail application. Clearly, if this is to happen, the written evidence in support must include matters relevant to the grant of bail.

Prosecutors can use the procedure of applying, using a claim form in Form 97A for an order varying the conditions imposed on bail by the High Court. At least 24 hours' notice of the application should be given to the defendant[5]. This application should be supported by an affidavit or witness statement[6].

10.2.1 Bail in judicial review proceedings

When a person has sought permission to bring judicial review proceedings for an order of certiorari challenging proceedings in the Crown Court, that person is entitled to apply to the Crown Court for bail[7]. The application to the Crown Court must be on notice. The procedure for making an application is the same as when a defendant in proceedings in the magistrates' court seeks bail in the Crown Court[8]. If the Crown Court does grant bail, and an application of judicial review is determined or withdrawn, magistrates may issue a process enforcing the decision that is the subject of the judicial review[9]. There is no equivalent power allowing the magistrates' court to grant bail[10].

Where a defendant applies for permission to seek an order of certiorari quashing a conviction or sentence in the magistrates' court or challenging proceedings in the Crown Court, there is a statutory right to apply to the High

---

1 CPR 1998, Sch 1, RSC Ord 79, r 9(1)(a).
2 Ibid, r 9(2)(a).
3 Ibid, r 9(2).
4 Ibid, r 9(3).
5 Ibid, r 9(2)(b).
6 Ibid, r 9(3).
7 Supreme Court Act 1981, s 81(1)(e).
8 Crown Court Rules 1982, SI 1982/1109, r 19(1).
9 CPR 1998, Sch 1, RSC Ord 79, r 9(11).
10 *Blyth v Appeal Committee of Lancaster* [1944] 1 All ER 587; holding that an express statutory provision is required if a person is to be bailed after conviction. This, however, contrasts with decisions of the High Court that it has an inherent power to grant bail during a judicial review.

Court for bail[1]. The High Court also has an inherent power to grant bail in applications for judicial review[2]. It has become accepted that this is true whether the case is a criminal cause or matter or some other form of proceedings[3]. As a consequence, the High Court is likely to have the power to grant bail during judicial review proceedings in all circumstances that practitioners will encounter.

The power to grant bail in judicial review proceedings that are not a criminal cause contrasts with the absence of a similar power in an appeal by way of case stated until the case has been lodged[4]. This means that judicial review proceedings should be brought, as well as an appeal by way of case stated, where it is important to obtain bail in a case that is not a criminal cause or matter[5].

In principle, there is no reason why bail should not be granted before permission to apply for judicial review has been ordered, as the inherent and statutory jurisdiction to grant bail extends to applications for permission[6]. In practice, however, the application for bail is normally considered at the same hearing as the application for permission, partly because a High Court judge is unlikely to be willing to grant bail unless they are satisfied that the application for judicial review is arguable. Clearly, when the High Court judge refuses permission to apply for judicial review, the judge is functus officio and so is unable to consider a bail application. In a matter that is not a criminal cause or matter, the applicant may, however, renew the application for permission to apply for judicial review in the Court of Appeal. If the application is renewed, the applicant may apply for bail in the Court of Appeal[7]. If the matter is a criminal cause or matter, the application for permission to apply for judicial review can only be renewed in a Divisional Court if it was refused by a single judge. Bail, however, cannot be sought in a Divisional Court when the application for permission is renewed if bail has already been refused by a single judge[8].

10.2.2 Bail in habeas corpus proceedings

In principle, the High Court is entitled to grant bail in a criminal cause or matter while an application for habeas corpus is pending[9]. It is not clear whether the High Court has a similar power when it considers an application for habeas corpus in a matter that is not a criminal cause or matter. In principle, there would appear to be no reason why the power should not extend to

---

1 Criminal Justice Act 1948, s 37(1)(b)(ii) and (d).
2 *R v Secretary of State for the Home Department ex p Tukoglu* [1988] QB 398, CA.
3 See, eg *Armand v Home Secretary* [1943] AC 147, HL for a case where in the context of a criminal habeas corpus application, it was assumed that there was an inherent power to grant bail. That inherent power may be limited following conviction: *Blyth v Appeal Committee of Lancaster* [1944] 1 All ER 587.
4 See **10.2.3**.
5 *R v Thanet Justices ex p Dass* [1996] COD 77.
6 *R v Secretary of State for the Home Department ex p Tukoglu* [1988] QB 398, CA.
7 Ibid.
8 CPR 1998, Sch 1, RSC Ord 79, r 9(12).
9 Eg *Re Amand* [1941] 2 KB 239 at 249, affirmed at [1943] AC 147, HL.

matters that are not a criminal cause or matter, as the inherent power in judicial review extends to matters that are not criminal causes[1].

The High Court has stated that it is normally unwilling to grant bail while it determines the merits of an application for habeas corpus[2]. One possible exception to this is applications for a writ of habeas corpus in extradition cases. In these cases, the High Court does occasionally grant bail[3]. This may be because applications for habeas corpus are brought in extradition cases as an alternative to judicial review proceedings, because it is the accepted form of proceedings. In essence, the focus of the habeas corpus application in these circumstances is not a challenge to detention.

10.2.3 Bail applications during appeals by way of case stated

When a person has applied to a magistrates' court or to a Crown Court judge for a case to be stated, they should apply to that court for bail. The magistrates' court has a power to grant bail if a person in custody has applied to them for a case to be stated[4]. If bail is granted, the person will be required to surrender to the magistrates' court on a date specified, which will be within 10 days after the judgment of the High Court[5]. Similarly, the Crown Court has power to grant bail if a person in custody has applied to them for a case to be stated[6]. There appear to be no rules specifying when the applicant for a case to be stated should surrender. In practice, the Crown Court is likely to require surrender shortly after the determination of the case stated. In any event, if the Crown Court does grant bail, and the appeal is determined or withdrawn, magistrates may issue a process enforcing the decision that is the subject of the judicial review[7].

Any application to the Crown Court for bail following an application to state a case must be on notice. The procedure is the same as when a defendant in proceedings in the magistrates' court seeks bail in the Crown Court[8]. There appear to be no rules specifying the procedure to be adopted when a person applying for a case to be stated by a magistrates' court seeks bail from that court. Clearly, the application should always be made on notice, as the court will be unlikely to grant bail unless it has heard from the prosecution.

In an appeal by case stated from a decision of the magistrates' court in a criminal cause or matter it is always possible to apply to the High Court for bail, if it has been refused by the magistrates' court[9]. However, until the case has been lodged, the High Court has no power to grant bail in a matter that is not a

---

1 *R v Secretary of State for the Home Department ex p Tukoglu* [1988] QB 398, CA.
2 *R v Governor of Haslar Prison ex p Egbe* (1991) *The Times*, 4 June, CA.
3 Eg *R v Governor of Pentonville Prison ex p Tarling* [1979] 1 WLR 1417, DC.
4 Magistrates' Courts Act 1980, s 113(1).
5 Ibid, s 113(2)(b).
6 Supreme Court Act 1981, s 81(1)(d).
7 CPR 1998, Sch 1, RSC Ord 79, r 9(11).
8 Crown Court Rules 1982, SI 1982/1109, r 19(1).
9 Criminal Justice Act 1967, s 22(1).

criminal cause or matter[1]. That is clearly likely to take some time. This means that the appellant should bring a judicial review as well as an appeal by way of case stated. Although the judicial review will be dismissed, it will give the High Court jurisdiction to grant bail[2]. The High Court has jurisdiction to grant bail to a person who has applied to the Crown Court for a case to be stated in civil and criminal proceedings[3].

10.3 SUSPENSION OF DISQUALIFICATION FROM DRIVING

There is a specific statutory power that enables any court that disqualifies a person from driving to suspend that disqualification pending an appeal[4]. As a result, when appealing by way of case stated from a decision of the magistrates' court or Crown Court to disqualify a person from driving, an application should always be made to the court that disqualified for a suspension of that disqualification. If that application is refused, the High Court has jurisdiction to order a suspension if the application has been made to state a case[5].

The statutory provision allowing a magistrates' court or the Crown Court to suspend disqualification does not apply to applications for judicial review. A magistrates' court or the Crown Court is unable to stay a disqualification pending a judicial review. The absence of any right to apply for a stay in a magistrates' court or the Crown Court has been held to be one reason why an appeal by way of case stated may be preferable where disqualification is challenged[6]. However, the High Court may order a stay of disqualification once an application has been made for permission to apply for judicial review[7].

If an application needs to be made to the High Court for a stay of disqualification in either judicial review proceedings or an appeal by way of case stated, it should be made in the same way as an application for any other interim order[8].

10.4 STAYS OF THE ENFORCEMENT OF OTHER PENALTIES

There are no specific statutory provisions providing for the stay of penalties other than imprisonment imposed by criminal courts while post-conviction proceedings are pending in the High Court. The only possible way of obtaining

---

1   *R v Poole Magistrates' Court ex p Benham; Benham v Poole Borough Council* [1992] COD 148, DC.
2   *R v Thanet Justices ex p Dass* [1996] COD 77.
3   Criminal Justice Act 1948, s 37(1)(b)(i).
4   Road Traffic Offenders Act 1988, s 39(1).
5   Ibid, s 40(4).
6   *R v Derwentside Magistrates' Court ex p Swift* [1996] COD 203, DC.
7   Road Traffic Offenders Act 1988, s 40(5).
8   See **6.9**.

a stay would be to apply for an injunction in judicial review proceedings in the manner set out below. There appears to be no authority considering whether the High Court can and should issue an injunction to stay the enforcement of criminal penalties. In practice, the High Court is likely to be reluctant to issue an injunction. It is likely to hold that the absence of a specific statutory provision allowing for the stay of a penalty implies that Parliament did not intend penalties to be stayed pending proceedings in the High Court.

If there is a real risk that a person who has been convicted in the Crown court or the magistrates' court will experience significant hardship as a result of the enforcement of any criminal penalty while proceedings are pending in the High Court, an application should be made for expedition[1]. The absence of any way of staying enforcement is a factor that should be raised in support of an application for an order expediting proceedings.

10.5 STAYS OF PROCEEDINGS PENDING A JUDICIAL REVIEW CHALLENGE

Challenges to interim decisions in criminal proceedings should only be brought by judicial review[2]. Normally, when a judicial review is to be sought of an interim decision, the criminal court that took that decision should be asked to stay the proceedings in that court pending the judicial review. If that is refused, a stay may be obtained as interim relief during a judicial review.

Where permission is obtained to bring an application for judicial review and an order for prohibition or certiorari is sought, the High Court can direct that the grant of permission shall operate as a stay of the proceedings that are the subject of the judicial review proceedings until the proceedings are determined or the court orders otherwise[3]. The requirement for an order for prohibition or certiorari to be sought is unlikely to cause problems. These are the orders that will be sought when an applicant for judicial review is challenging interim decisions.

A stay may be desirable where the decision being challenged was not taken by a court. An applicant in judicial review proceedings may be concerned that a stay is essential to preserve the status quo. For example, an applicant who seeks to challenge a decision to prosecute may need a stay to prevent the prosecution commencing. The Court of Appeal has held that a stay of proceedings can be issued to prevent executive decisions being taken and being acted on as well as to prevent proceedings continuing in the courts[4]. This authority may, however, not be upheld if it is ever challenged on appeal to the House of Lords as the Privy Council has doubted whether a stay can prevent executive action[5].

---

1 See **6.2**.
2 See **4.9**.
3 CPR 1998, Sch 1, RSC Ord 53, r 3(10)(a).
4 *R v Secretary of State for Education and Science ex p Avon CC* [1991] 1 QB 558, CA.
5 Per Lord Oliver, *Minister of Foreign Affairs, Trade and Industry v Vehicles and Supplies Ltd* [1991] 1 WLR 550 at 556, PC.

from the applicant for damages suffered by the respondent as a result of the injunction. In some judicial review actions, the court will be able to take a similar approach. In most actions, however, damages are not likely to be of significance. As a result, the High Court tends to be more concerned about minimising the risk of injustice when it considers an application for an injunction during judicial review proceedings[1]. However, although damages are less significant, the High Court may still be reluctant to grant an interlocutory injunction without an undertaking from the applicant for damages suffered by the respondent as a result of the injunction[2]. This may mean that an injunction is not available to an applicant in receipt of legal aid.

Although the CPR 1998 now make it clear that an interim declaration is available, the courts were previously concerned that there might not be such a power[3]. As a result, there is little case-law considering the approach of the High Court to applications for an interim declaration. The only thing that is clear is that the High Court will be keen to prevent interim declarations being made that act as an injunction, but which defeat the requirement for an undertaking regarding damages[4]. In practice, the High Court is likely to be reluctant to make an interim declaration defining the rights and obligations of parties when it has not heard the full argument. Instead, the practice of High Court judges making appropriate informal remarks on the position of the parties is likely to continue. These remarks are clearly not binding, but parties must take them seriously when they consider the merits of the case[5].

10.7 THE PROCEDURE FOR APPLYING FOR INTERIM RELIEF

Clearly, the High Court may grant interim relief at any stage[6]. In practice, however, the High Court may well be unwilling to grant interim relief until it has at least determined that an application is arguable by granting permission. In addition, the High Court will normally expect the application to be made after the other parties to the proceedings have been put on notice, unless there is a particularly good reason why this has not happened[7]. As a result, the

---

1 Per Lord Bridge, *R v Secretary of State for Transport ex p Factortame (No 2)* [1991] 1 AC 603 at 659F, HL.
2 *R v Secretary of State for the Environment ex p Rose Theatre Trust Company* [1990] COD 47.
3 Eg Lord Woolf in *Re M* [1994] 1 AC 377 at 423A, HL, who stated that he could see 'advantages' in the court having jurisdiction to make interim declarations; cf Mr Justice Jacob holding that an interim declaration would be 'juridical nonsense' in *Newport Association Football Club Ltd v Football Association of Wales Ltd* [1995] 2 All ER 87 at 92a.
4 *R v Secretary of State for the Environment ex p Royal Society for the Protection of Birds* (1995) 7 Admin LR 434 at 443, HL.
5 See, eg *R v Metropolitan Stipendiary Magistrate ex p Ali* (1997) *Independent*, 12 May.
6 CPR 1998, Sch 1, RSC Ord 53, r 3(10)(b); per Lord Woolf, in *Re M* [1994] 1 AC 377 at 422A, HL.
7 Per Lord Justice Parker, in *R v Kensington and Chelsea Borough Council ex p Hammell* [1989] QB 518 at 539B, CA.

If stays are not available in the context of executive decisions, the availability of interim injunctions means that the court clearly has jurisdiction to prevent executive action. To avoid any questions about jurisdiction to prevent the executive continuing to act, it may be preferable to apply for both an injunction and a stay. The approach of the court to the discretion to grant a stay is likely to be the same as that to the discretion to order an interim injunction.

Clearly, in most cases where a stay is sought, the judicial review proceedings will be brought as a matter of urgency. As a result, it is likely that the decision about whether to grant permission will be taken following oral argument regarding the grant of the permission[1]. The application for a stay should normally be made at this stage. If possible, it should be made after the other parties to the proceedings have been put on notice[2]. If the application is not made at the permission stage, it should be made as an interim application[3].

10.6 OTHER FORMS OF INTERIM RELIEF AVAILABLE DURING APPLICATIONS FOR JUDICIAL REVIEW

Where relief other than an order for prohibition or certiorari is sought, the High Court may grant any interim relief that is available to the court under Part 25 of the CPR 1998[4]. The requirement for the application to seek relief other than an order for prohibition or certiorari is unlikely to be a problem. The forms of interim relief that are most likely to be sought are an interim injunction or an interim declaration. If these forms of interim relief are sought, an order for an injunction or a declaration is likely to be sought as a final remedy.

Injunctions are now a very important form of interim relief in judicial review, as it is now well established that an injunction can be issued against the Crown[5]. That means that an applicant for judicial review may seek an injunction to prevent ministers acting in accordance with a decision that is being challenged by way of judicial review.

When the High Court considers an application for an interim injunction, it will consider whether the applicant or the respondent will suffer greater inconvenience as a result of the decision regarding interim relief. It will compare the position of the applicant if he is successful at the conclusion of the action, but has been refused interim relief, with the position of the respondent if interim relief is granted, but the applicant is eventually unsuccessful[6].

In private law actions, the court will take account of the adequacy of damages as a remedy for the applicant and compare this with the value of an undertaking

---

1 See **7.6**.
2 Per Lord Justice Parker, *R v Kensington and Chelsea Borough Council ex p Hammell* [1989] QB 518 at 539B, CA.
3 See **6.9** for details of the procedure for making interim applications.
4 CPR 1998, Sch 1, RSC Ord 53, r 3(10)(b).
5 In *Re M* [1994] 1 AC 377, HL.
6 *American Cynamid Co v Ethicon Ltd* [1975] AC 396, HL.

application for interim relief is usually considered at an oral application for permission. The respondent should be given notice of this hearing. Although the High Court will normally require written evidence in support of the application for interim relief, the evidence in support of the application for permission will normally suffice.

If for any reason it becomes necessary to apply for interim relief after a grant of permission, the application should be made in the same way as an application for other interim orders[1]. The only exception is that there may be no need for notice to be given if there is good reason for the application being sought as a matter of urgency. The court will normally require evidence in support of the application.

---

1   See **6.9**.

Chapter 11

ORDERS FOR RELIEF AVAILABLE TO THE HIGH COURT AT THE END OF PROCEEDINGS

11.1 INTRODUCTION

The forms of final relief that the High Court may order at the end of proceedings depend on the form of proceedings that are being brought in the High Court. There are, however, some common features. For example, discretion is an issue that arises in both judicial review and appeal by way of case stated. As a result, we have considered final relief in a single chapter so that it is possible to compare the forms of relief available when deciding what form of proceedings should be brought.

11.2 DISCRETION AND JUDICIAL REVIEW

Judicial review is a discretionary remedy[1]. Lord Justice Hobhouse has recently considered the scope of the High Court's discretion. He held that:

> 'The discretion of the court in deciding whether to grant any remedy is a wide one. It can take into account many considerations, including the needs of good administration, delay, the effect on third parties, the utility of granting the relevant remedy. The discretion can be exercised so as partially to uphold and partially quash the relevant administrative decision or act.'[2]

The High Court's discretion clearly means that a judge will not necessarily grant relief merely because an applicant for judicial review has shown that the decision that is challenged is flawed. Relief may be refused as a result of the factors identified by Lord Justice Hobhouse and other factors such as a failure by the applicant to make proper disclosure[3]. The discretionary nature of judicial review does not merely mean that all forms of relief may be refused. If all relief is not refused, the court has discretion to consider the form of relief that is ordered. Thus, the form of relief may be affected by matters such as delay[4]. This means that the High Court could determine that a decision is unlawful, but decide merely to make a declaration rather than quash the decision that is being challenged[5].

---

1 Eg per Lord Donaldson MR, *R v Panel on Take-overs and Mergers ex p Guinness Plc* [1990] 1 QB 146 at 177E, CA.
2 *Credit Suisse v Allerdale Borough Council* [1997] QB 306 at 355D, CA.
3 See **7.7**.
4 *R v Rochdale Metropolitan Borough Council ex p Schemet* [1994] ELR 89.
5 See *R v Dairy Produce Quota Tribunal ex p Caswell* [1990] 2 AC 738, HL, for an example of a case where the High Court made a declaration to govern future conduct, but refused an order giving the applicant relief in relation to previous conduct.

The High Court can consider the exercise of its discretion both when the applicant for judicial review asks for permission and when final relief is considered at the substantive hearing. We noted earlier that permission will be refused if it appears that the judicial review application is unarguable[1]. Clearly, if discretionary factors mean that the High Court will be bound to refuse relief when it considers the substantive hearing, permission will be refused.

In criminal cases there are good arguments why the High Court should not exercise its discretion to refuse the applicant relief. First, if the applicant is challenging a conviction, the High Court will be concerned that a person should not be detained or punished in some other way as a result of a decision that is unlawful. It is similar concerns that mean that habeas corpus is said not to be a discretionary remedy[2]. In addition, quashing a decision in criminal proceedings is unlikely to prejudice the interests of third parties. For example, the High Court is likely to be more reluctant to grant relief where there has been delay and a successful judicial review will affect the commercial interests of a large number of companies who are not parties[3]. This sort of concern is unlikely to arise in a criminal context.

The most significant factor that might result in the High Court refusing to exercise its discretion to grant relief in criminal judicial reviews occurs where there has been delay. The High Court has held in the context of appeals by way of case stated that criminal litigation must be conducted as a matter of urgency[4]. Where a judicial review has not been conducted as a matter of urgency, the High Court may be reluctant to grant relief particularly if the grant of relief will result in a fresh trial.

11.3 JUDICIAL REVIEW AND ACADEMIC CHALLENGES

The concept of discretion is linked to the High Court's reluctance to consider applications which raise theoretical issues. In circumstances where the applicant will not benefit from a clarification of the law, the High Court may well be reluctant to determine a question of law. For example, on a number of occasions, the courts have expressed a reluctance to consider a case as a 'test case' that will enable the courts to determine hypothetical issues[5].

Similarly, the courts have dismissed judicial review applications which rely on an error of law that has not prejudiced the applicant. For example, the High Court has shown a reluctance to quash decisions of magistrates' courts where there has been a breach of natural justice if the applicant has suffered no injustice as a result of that breach[6].

Although the High Court has shown a reluctance to consider theoretical issues that does not mean that the courts never consider such issues. The courts

---

1 See **7.8**.
2 See **11.4**.
3 Eg *R v Secretary of State for Trade and Industry ex p Greenpeace Ltd* [1998] COD 59 at 65.
4 *Parsons v FW Woolworth & Co Ltd* [1980] 1 WLR 1472 at 1475H, DC.
5 Eg *R v Secretary of State for the Home Department ex p Wynne* [1993] 1 WLR 115, HL.
6 See **2.8.1**.

increasingly recognise that there is a public interest in resolving issues that will affect the public at large. The High Court can give guidance that will assist public decision-makers to exercise their powers lawfully. Thus, in particular cases, the courts have recognised there is a role for them to give guidance in circumstances where that guidance will not determine the particular application[1]. Historically, this has often been done by making obiter remarks. The increasing use of declarations as a form of final relief may mean, however, that the High Court may be willing to make a declaration to ensure that the future conduct of a public authority is lawful[2]. In the past, it has been held that declarations can only be made in relation to real questions as opposed to hypothetical questions[3]. Recent obiter remarks have called this into question and suggested that the court may be willing to give advisory declarations[4].

In practice, lawyers acting for individual applicants will normally wish to settle an application by consent if there is no benefit for the applicant. Privately funded clients are unlikely to wish to resolve issues of law that have no relevance to their case. In addition, the duty to the Legal Aid Board will mean that it will be difficult to justify a judicial review application that has no benefit to the applicant[5]. However, lawyers acting for bodies such as the Crown Prosecution Service may well wish to settle an issue that will be relevant to other cases. They will need to be aware that they may have to show a good reason why the court should resolve the issue, if the court is not to refuse to decide the issue.

11.4 DISCRETION AND HABEAS CORPUS

The sole issue for the High Court to consider when it determines an application for habeas corpus is whether detention of the applicant is unlawful. If it is unlawful, the applicant will be released. If it is not unlawful, the applicant will not be released. As a result, there is no discretion[6]. In principle, this could mean that habeas corpus might be seen as a more attractive form of proceedings than judicial review. In practice, habeas corpus has a very restrictive scope[7]. As a result, practitioners should not normally bring habeas corpus proceedings unless the case is one where habeas corpus is the accepted form of proceedings. Instead, practitioners should compare judicial review proceedings with habeas

---

1 Eg *R v Lewes Justices ex p Secretary of State for the Home Department* [1973] AC 388 at 410H, HL, is an example of a case where the House of Lords decided to give guidance on a legal issue that was not decisive to the case in issue in response to a request by one party.
2 Eg in *R v Dairy Produce Quota Tribunal ex p Caswell* [1990] 2 AC 738, HL, the High Court made a declaration to govern future conduct, but refused an order giving the applicant relief in relation to previous conduct. Although there may well have been benefit to the applicant from this particular declaration, there would appear to be no reason why the High Court could not make a similar order in circumstances where there is no reason to believe that the applicant will benefit.
3 *Russian Commercial and Industrial Bank v British Bank for Foreign Trade Ltd* [1921] 2 AC 438 at 448, HL.
4 Eg *R v Secretary of State for the Home Department ex p Mehari* [1994] QB 474 at 491H.
5 See **12.13**.
6 *Greene v Secretary of State for the Home Department* [1942] AC 284 at 302, HL; see also transcript of *Re Barker*, (1998) *The Times*, 14 October, CA.
7 See **3.5**.

corpus proceedings to argue that the factors that mean that habeas corpus is not a discretionary remedy also mean that discretion should not be exercised against an applicant when detention is in issue[1].

11.5 DISCRETION AND APPEAL BY WAY OF CASE STATED

As we have stated above, it has been repeatedly said that judicial review is a discretionary remedy. In contrast, appeal by way of case stated is rarely said to be a discretionary remedy. That may well be because the High Court rarely seeks to exercise its discretion to refuse to determine an issue as a result of matters such as delay. As we noted in the context of judicial review, there are good reasons why the High Court may well not decide to refuse to grant relief in a criminal case[2]. Similar concerns are likely to apply in criminal appeals by way of case stated. That does not mean, however, that appeal by way of case stated is not discretionary. As we stated earlier, the High Court has refused to consider appeals by way of case stated as a result of delay[3]. That clearly shows that the High Court does have some discretion.

The courts will not merely exercise its discretion to refuse to grant relief in circumstances where there has been delay in appealing. The court can look at what fairness demands in all the circumstances of the case. Thus, the House of Lords has refused to order a rehearing following an appeal by a prosecutor in circumstances where the appeal was determined 3 years after the offences; the offences were of a trivial nature and the errors of law were not prompted by submissions from the defence[4]. This was despite the prosecutor showing that the acquitals were flawed as a matter of law.

The idea that the High Court has a discretion when it determines appeals by way of case stated is also supported by the absence of a statutory test determining the circumstances in which the appeal should be allowed. This contrasts with the Court of Appeal's obligation to allow appeals against conviction on indictment when that conviction is unsafe[5]. This clearly implies that the High Court has a wider discretion when it considers an appeal by way of case stated.

11.6 JUDICIAL REVIEW ORDERS

The High Court has jurisdiction to make orders for mandamus, prohibition or certiorari at the conclusion of an application for judicial review[6]. It may also order an injunction or make a declaration[7].

---

1 See transcript of *Re Barker*, (1998) *The Times*, 14 October, CA.
2 See **11.2**.
3 See **9.10**. See also *Parsons v FW Woolworth & Co Ltd* [1980] 1 WLR 1472 at 1475H, DC.
4 *Griffith v Jenkins* [1992] 2 AC 76 at 84E, HL.
5 Criminal Appeal Act 1968, s 2(1).
6 CPR 1998, Sch 1, RSC Ord 53, r 1(1)(a).
7 Ibid, r 1(2).

Orders for Relief available to the High Court at the End of Proceedings

An order of certiorari is the most usual order to seek in judicial review proceedings because it allows the High Court to bring up a decision and quash it. For example, this is the form of order that the High Court makes when it quashes either a conviction or a sentence. When the court makes an order for certiorari, it can also remit the decision for reconsideration.

An order for prohibition is an order preventing an inferior court or public body from acting outside its jurisdiction. As a result, it is sometimes sought in addition to an order for certiorari. If a court has already made a decision that is in excess of jurisdiction, orders for certiorari and prohibition can be sought. An order for certiorari can be sought to quash that decision and an order of prohibition can be sought to prevent the court continuing to act in excess of jurisdiction. An order of prohibition may be sought preventing a decision in excess of jurisdiction even where there is a right of appeal against that decision[1].

Mandamus is an order requiring a court or public body to carry out its duty. Mandamus is particularly significant in the context of crime, as it is the order sought when an applicant seeks to force a court to state a case[2]. Similarly, it is the order that can be sought to force a court to consider a matter when it has wrongly held that it has no jurisdiction[3].

An injunction is an order that is 'indistinguishable' in its effect from the orders for prohibition or mandamus[4], because it is an order that requires a party to either act or refrain from acting. As a result, injunctions are rarely granted as relief following the substantive hearing[5]. Instead, the High Court will normally make an order for mandamus or prohibition in preference to an injunction. Injunctions are more commonly sought as a form of interim relief[6].

Declarations enable a High Court judge to make the legal position clear by stating the position in an order[7]. As one of the roles of judicial review proceedings is to ensure that public decision-makers act according to the law, declarations are obviously important as they help decision-makers to act in accordance with the law. Thus, although the court may not be satisfied that a particular decision should be quashed, they may grant a declaration. This will benefit decision-makers with similar decisions to take. For example, although a decision to refuse legal aid might not be quashed, the High Court may make a declaration about the scope of the jurisdiction to grant legal aid[8]. In practice, the obtaining of a declaration may be almost as beneficial to an applicant as the obtaining of any other order, because public decision-makers are likely to regard themselves as being bound by the terms of the declaration.

---

1   *Turner v Kingsbury Collieries Ltd* [1921] 3 KB 169 at 174.
2   Supreme Court Act 1981, s 29(3) where the Crown Court refuses to state a case and Magistrates' Courts Act 1980, s 111(6) where the magistrates' court refuses to state a case.
3   Eg *R v Oxford Justices ex p D* [1987] QB 199.
4   Per Lord Woolf, *Re M* [1994] 1 AC 377 at 415E, HL.
5   There are, however, examples of injunctions being granted at the conclusion of judicial review proceedings, eg *R v North Yorkshire County Council ex p M* [1989] QB 411.
6   See **10.7** for details.
7   Eg per Lord Morton, *Vine v National Dock Labour Board* [1957] AC 488 at 504, HL.
8   *R v Recorder of Liverpool ex p McCann* (1994) *The Times*, 4 May, DC.

11.7 THE HIGH COURT'S POWER TO VARY A SENTENCE FOLLOWING A JUDICIAL REVIEW

Section 43(1) of the Supreme Court Act 1981 provides the High Court with a specific statutory power to vary a sentence imposed by the magistrates' court or the Crown Court following a committal for sentence or an appeal against a sentence if there has been a successful application for an order of certiorari. Before exercising the power, the High Court must be satisfied that the sentence was one that the magistrates' court or Crown Court had no power to impose. When the High Court exercises the power, it can impose any sentence that the court that passed sentence could have imposed.

Although s 43(1) requires the High Court to be satisfied that the sentence was not one that the magistrates' court or Crown Court had the power to impose, that does not mean that the power can only be exercised where the sentence imposed was in excess of the maximum prescribed by law. For example, a sentence imposed in breach of natural justice can be quashed and a fresh sentence imposed after the High Court has heard the representations that magistrates would have heard had they not acted in breach of natural justice[1].

11.8 THE HIGH COURT'S POWER TO AWARD DAMAGES AT THE CONCLUSION OF A SUCCESSFUL APPLICATION FOR JUDICIAL REVIEW

The High Court has the power to award damages at the conclusion of an application for judicial review if the notice of application for permission includes a claim for damages arising from any matter to which the application relates[2]. The application for permission to apply for judicial review must include 'a concise statement of the facts on which the claimant relies'[3]. It must also include details of any claim for interest[4] and any claim for aggravated or exemplary damages[5].

The procedure rules state that Part 16 of the CPR 1998 apply to a statement relating to a claim for damages as it applies to a statement of case. At this stage, it is a little unclear how this will operate at present as Part 16 includes provisions that were not included in the previous rules. In particular, Part 16 contains provisions regarding the contents of the claim form. For example, there needs to be a statement of the value of the claim. It would appear, however, that these provisions regarding the claim form do not apply to applications for judicial review. First, the Practice Direction provides that the claim form is not the standard claim form but, instead, is in Form 86 which does not include

---

1 *R v Pateley Bridge Justices ex p Percy* [1994] COD 453, DC.
2 CPR 1998, Sch 1, RSC Ord 53, r 7(1)(a).
3 CPR 1998, r 16.4(1).
4 Ibid, r 16.4.
5 CPR 1998, Sch 1, RSC Ord 53, r 7(2).

this information[1]. See Appendix 1 for a precedent. In addition, the requirements regarding the contents of the claim form appear to be intended to assist the court to determine whether the case has been allocated to the correct track in the correct court. There is at present no tracking in the Crown Office.

It is important to recognise that claims for damages can only be brought during proceedings for judicial review where the grounds for judicial review exist[2]. In addition, before awarding damages, the court must be satisfied that damages could have been awarded by way of a claim begun at the same time as the application for judicial review[3]. This means they can only be awarded if there is some recognised form of claim for damages. There is no general right to damages for a breach of public law[4]. As a result, damages will rarely be claimed in judicial reviews that arise from a practitioner's criminal practice unless the judicial review relates in some way to unlawful imprisonment.

When deciding whether to claim damages, it is important to consider the limitations on the scope of claims for unlawful imprisonment. A detailed consideration of the scope of unlawful imprisonment is outside the scope of this book. However, it is important to be aware that the Court of Appeal has held that the Home Office and the Crown Prosecution Service are not liable for damages for unlawful imprisonment resulting from detention in excess of custody time-limits, as only the court may order release[5]. The Court of Appeal has, however, held that magistrates are liable for damages if a decision to imprison a person is in excess of jurisdiction[6].

11.9 THE POWERS OF THE HIGH COURT AT THE CONCLUSION OF AN APPLICATION FOR A WRIT OF HABEAS CORPUS

In theory, an application for a writ of habeas corpus could merely result in the issue of a writ. That is unlikely to be of any real value to the applicant as it merely results in the applicant being produced before the High Court. In practice, the value of an application for a writ of habeas corpus is that it gives a High Court judge the power to order the release of the applicant for the writ of habeas corpus[7]. This will clearly happen if the High Court judge determines that detention of the applicant is unlawful.

---

1 *Practice Direction (CPR 1998, Schedule 1, RSC Order 53 – Application for Judicial Review)*; *Practice Direction (CPR 1998, Part 4 – Forms)*.
2 *Davy v Spelthorne Borough Council* [1984] AC 262 at 277H, HL.
3 CPR 1998, Sch 1, RSC Ord 53, r 7(1)(b).
4 Per Lord Goff, *R v Secretary of State for Transport ex p Factortame Ltd (No 2)* [1991] 1 AC 603 at 672H, HL.
5 *Olotu v Home Office* [1997] 1 WLR 328, CA.
6 *R v Manchester City Magistrates' Court ex p Davies* [1989] QB 631, CA.
7 CPR 1998, Sch 1, RSC Ord 54, r 4(1).

11.10 THE POWERS OF THE HIGH COURT AT THE CONCLUSION OF AN APPEAL BY WAY OF CASE STATED

The powers of the High Court at the conclusion of an appeal by way of case stated from a decision of magistrates are governed by s 28A of the Supreme Court Act 1981. This provides that the High Court may remit the case to the magistrates for amendment[1]. Alternatively, it may reverse, affirm or amend the determination in respect of which the case has been stated[2]. It can also remit the matter with the opinion of the court[3]. Finally, it can make any other order as it thinks fit including an order for costs[4].

Section 28A of the Supreme Court Act 1981 clearly gives the High Court a wide discretion to either determine the matter or remit it to either the same bench or a different bench[5]. If the error of law has resulted in an acquittal so that the error can only be remedied by a rehearing, remittal will normally be the correct course of action[6]. Clearly, the powers contained in s 28A are not mutually exclusive. The High Court can and does exercise more than one of these powers when it determines an appeal by way of case stated. For example, an order remitting a matter for rehearing will normally be linked to other orders, such as an order reversing the decision that is the subject of the appeal.

The terms of s 28A of the Supreme Court Act 1981 appear only to apply to decisions taken by magistrates. As a result, the scope of the powers of the High Court following an appeal by way of case stated from the Crown Court is less clear. However, the High Court appears to accept that it has inherent powers that are very similar to those under s 28A of the 1981 Act. For example, it has an inherent power to remit the case stated for amendment[7]. Similarly, it appears to accept that it has a power to allow an appeal and remit a case for rehearing[8].

---

1 Supreme Court Act 1981, s 28A(2).
2 Ibid, s 28A(3)(a).
3 Ibid, s 28A(3)(b).
4 Ibid, s 28A(3).
5 *Griffith v Jenkins* [1992] 2 AC 76, HL.
6 Ibid at 84B, HL.
7 Eg *Colfox v Dorset County Council* [1996] COD 275, DC.
8 Eg *Fossett v East Northamptonshire District Council* [1995] COD 167, DC.

Chapter 12

LEGAL AID AND ORDERS FOR COSTS

12.1 INTRODUCTION

Criminal practitioners conducting judicial review applications and appeals by way of case stated need to be very careful about the provisions regarding legal aid and orders for costs. That is because the provisions are essentially those that govern civil proceedings rather than criminal proceedings. As a result, practitioners may have little experience of those provisions and so have to be particularly careful to ensure that they understand these provisions. Clearly, practitioners owe a professional duty to their clients to ensure that they advise their clients fully about the terms of these provisions[1]. The problems experienced by criminal practitioners are likely to be increased by the introduction of the Civil Procedure Rules as these introduce significant changes.

12.2 THE RULES GOVERNING COSTS BETWEEN THE PARTIES

The CPR 1998 govern the award of costs in the High Court. In particular, Part 44 governs orders for costs against parties. Part 44 provides that the court has a very broad discretion when it considers applications for costs orders against parties to proceedings. It can determine whether costs are payable by one party to another, the level of those costs and the time for payment[2]. However, it also provides that the general rule is that the unsuccessful party will pay the costs of the successful party[3]. It is important to note that special considerations apply in certain circumstances, such as when the unsuccessful party is in receipt of legal aid[4] or the magistrates who tried the matter are a party[5]. These are considered later.

The general rule that the loser should pay the costs of the successful party is not a rigid rule. In particular, in criminal proceedings it is possible that an unsuccessful party is not responsible for the proceedings in the High Court. The High Court can take account of this when it makes orders for costs. Thus, in an appeal by way of case stated by a prosecutor, where among other things

---

1   Indeed, CPR 1998, r 44.2 imposes a duty on solicitors to inform clients of any costs orders against them within 7 days of the order. This clearly reflects a desire to ensure that clients are kept informed of their costs obligations.
2   CPR 1998, r 44.3(1).
3   Ibid, r 44.3(2).
4   See **12.4**.
5   See **12.5**.

the Crown Court had raised the point taken on appeal itself and the defendant had not been asked to consent to the appeal being allowed and had not attended the appeal, it was not appropriate for a costs order to be made against the defendant[1].

When deciding what costs orders to make, the High Court will take account of the conduct of the parties during the litigation[2]. In particular, the High Court has the power to take account of the manner in which the litigation was pursued[3]. It is clear from this that the High Court will use costs orders as a way of discouraging unreasonable litigation. To an extent, this is consistent with the practice of the High Court before the introduction of the CPR 1998[4]. However, it is likely that the introduction of the Civil Procedure Rules will mean that the High Court will be more enthusiastic to prevent unreasonable litigation with the introduction of the overriding objective.

The CPR 1998 state that the overriding objective of the High Court is to deal with cases justly[5]. This objective includes, as far as practicable, saving expense and allotting to the case an appropriate share of the court's resources, while taking into account the need to allot resources to other cases[6]. Parties have a duty to help the court further the overriding objective[7]. Clearly, unreasonable conduct by a party is likely to be in breach of this duty. The court will take account of a breach of this duty when it determines costs issues[8].

The requirement to behave reasonably means that practitioners must be particularly careful to review the merits of their case at all stages. A party to proceedings who concludes that they are very unlikely to succeed should consider settling the matter to save costs. Proceeding with a case that has little merit is likely to result in an order being made for costs including the costs of the substantive hearing. Settling the case promptly may avoid any order for costs.

The High Court will not necessarily award costs against a respondent merely because the respondent has withdrawn the decision that is being challenged or consented to a settlement that gives the other party what they have been seeking. That is because the High Court recognises that it is legitimate for a respondent to avoid the cost and uncertainty of pending proceedings by

---

1 *Canterbury City Council v Cook* (1992) *The Times*, 23 December, DC.
2 CPR 1998, r 44.3(4)(a).
3 Ibid, r 44.3(5)(c).
4 Eg *R v Liverpool City Council ex p Filla* [1996] COD 24, where costs were not awarded to a successful applicant as a result of material non-disclosure.
5 CPR 1998, r 1.1(1).
6 Ibid, r 1.1(2).
7 Ibid, r 1.3.
8 Ibid, r 1.2.

settling those proceedings[1]. In these circumstances, discontinuance is not the same as defeat. Similarly, it is legitimate for a respondent to conduct a favourable review of an initial decision while the judicial review is pending, so that the judicial review becomes academic. In these circumstances the applicant may not obtain his costs[2]. Indeed, it is clear that the High Court expects respondents to undertake such reviews. A respondent who has failed to take judicial review proceedings sufficiently seriously by reviewing the merits after a grant of permission may find that costs will be ordered against him in circumstances where no order would normally have been made[3]. A respondent may, however, have costs awarded against him if he merely acts by settling proceedings in an attempt to pre-empt almost inevitable failure in the proceedings[4].

Although the general rule is that the successful party should obtain their costs from the unsuccessful party, special considerations may arise as a result of the discretionary nature of judicial review proceedings and appeals by way of case stated. It may be proper for a party to bring proceedings to clarify the law in circumstances where they do not obtain the relief that they seek. Thus, a prosecutor may obtain costs from central funds in a case where it was proper for him to appeal although delay in determining the matter meant that the appeal should not be allowed[5].

12.3 SPECIAL COSTS CONSIDERATIONS IN JUDICIAL REVIEW AND HABEAS CORPUS PROCEEDINGS

The requirement to obtain permission to bring judicial review proceedings following an application without notice to the respondent raises special concerns regarding costs. The discretion given to the High Court regarding costs allows it to award costs in relation to particular steps in the proceedings[6] or costs incurred before proceedings have begun[7]. This includes the costs incurred by a party before the application for permission has been determined. This discretion to award costs allows the High Court to award costs to the

---

1 *R v Liverpool City Council ex p Newman* [1993] COD 65. This case was a judicial review and the judgment of Mr Justice Simon Brown makes specific reference to discontinuance in the context of judicial review. In principle, however, there is no reason why the same principles should not apply to other proceedings in the Crown Office list. For example, it may well be legitimate for a prosecutor to consent to an appeal being allowed for public interest reasons unconnected with the likely outcome. In these circumstances, it may be inappropriate to order costs against the prosecutor.
2 *R v Independent Television Commission ex p Church of Scientology* [1996] COD 443.
3 *R v Huntingdon Magistrates' Court ex p Percy* [1994] COD 323, DC, where costs were awarded against magistrates for failing to take the grant of permission sufficiently seriously in a case where the applicant was challenging a refusal to state a case.
4 *R v Independent Television Commission ex p Church of Scientology* [1996] COD 443; *R v Liverpool City Council ex p Newman* [1993] COD 65.
5 *Griffith v Jenkins* [1992] 2 AC 76 at 84G, HL.
6 CPR 1998, r 44.3(6)(e).
7 Ibid, r 44.3(6)(d).

prospective respondent, although the applications are initially made by the applicant without the respondent being a party[1]. The High Court has discretion to make such an order at the hearing when it determines whether permission should be granted[2]. In practice, however, it will be reluctant to make an order regarding costs before the decision regarding permission.

The High Court has historically been reluctant to award the applicant his costs for the period before the grant of permission unless the case is sufficiently strong and obvious[3]. This is because the High Court seeks to encourage settlement without litigation and so does not want to create a disincentive to settlement by respondents. Similarly, the respondent would normally only obtain costs if the applicant behaved unreasonably and so put the respondent to unnecessary expense[4]. It may be significant that these principles were decided before the introduction of the CPR 1998. It is unclear whether the objectives set out in the CPR 1998 will mean that the High Court will be more willing to make inter partes costs orders against an unsuccessful party at the permission stage, in an attempt to discourage unnecessary applications.

As we noted earlier, habeas corpus proceedings are usually in effect a two-stage process[5]. The limited number of applications for habeas corpus means that the authors are aware of no cases considering the approach of the High Court to costs at the first stage of the process. It is likely, however, that the same considerations apply. In considering the reasonableness of a party's behaviour when deciding whether to order costs, the High Court is likely to take account of the importance of the issue raised in habeas corpus proceedings. As a result, it may be more unwilling to hold that an applicant's behaviour is unreasonable.

12.4 SPECIAL CONSIDERATIONS WHEN THE UNSUCCESSFUL PARTY IS IN RECEIPT OF LEGAL AID

When the unsuccessful party is in receipt of legal aid, the High Court shall not order them to pay any costs that would exceed what is reasonable having regard to all the circumstances of the case including the resources of the parties and their conduct during the matter[6]. In determining the resources available to the unsuccessful party, the High Court shall discount that person's dwelling house, clothes, household furniture and the tools and implements of his trade[7]. In practice, this means that the High Court will often make an order for costs that may only be enforced with the leave of the court. This is not, however, automatic. In particular, in cases in which the unsuccessful party is required to

---

1 Eg *R v Honourable Society of the Middle Temple ex p Bullock* [1996] ELR 349 at 358H.
2 Eg *R v Camden London Borough Council ex p Martin* [1997] 1 All ER 307 at 312H.
3 *R v London Borough of Hackney ex p Rowe* [1996] COD 155.
4 *R v Honourable Society of the Middle Temple ex p Bullock* [1996] ELR 349.
5 See **8.3**.
6 Legal Aid Act 1988, s 17(1).
7 Ibid, s 17(3).

pay a contribution towards his legal aid, the High Court may be willing to require them to make payments towards their opponent's costs by instalments.

The limitation on the recovery of costs against a person in receipt of legal aid only extends to those periods of time and proceedings covered by the legal aid certificate[1]. As a result, it is potentially negligent for practitioners to fail to ensure that a legal aid certificate actually covers all steps taken on behalf of a party[2]. This is particularly important in judicial review proceedings, as the certificate issued at the start of the application is unlikely to cover all steps of the proceedings. Instead, it is likely to cover all steps up to the service of the respondent's evidence and obtaining counsel's advice on that evidence. Practitioners will need to ensure that the certificate is amended as the case proceeds to cover all steps providing the merits justify this.

After the High Court has decided the liability of the unsuccessful party for costs, it can make an order for payment of the successful party's costs by the Legal Aid Board, if an order for costs would have been made but for the provisions of the Legal Aid Act 1988[3]. The High Court must be satisfied that making an order is just and equitable[4]. In addition, in first instance proceedings the High Court must be satisfied that the proceedings were instituted by the person in receipt of legal aid and that the unassisted party will suffer severe financial hardship[5].

In general, the High Court is going to be reluctant to make a costs order against the Legal Aid Board where the unassisted party is a public body. There is generally a reluctance to transfer money from one public fund into the hands of another. The court will, however, occasionally make the order. For example, it made such an order where the public body was a small local authority and unable to afford litigation[6].

12.5 SPECIAL CONSIDERATIONS WHEN MAGISTRATES ARE THE RESPONDENT

When magistrates are involved in proceedings in the High Court as the respondent or as the decision-maker in an appeal by way of case stated, the High Court will be reluctant to order costs against the magistrates. Indeed, magistrates will not be parties to an appeal by way of case stated at which they do not attend, and so costs can only be ordered in the very limited circumstances set out later[7].

---

1   Civil Legal Aid (General) Regulations 1989, SI 339/1989, reg 124(1).
2   *Turner v Plasplugs Ltd* (1996) *The Times*, 1 February, CA.
3   Legal Aid Act 1988, s 18(4)(a).
4   Ibid, s 18(4)(c).
5   Ibid, s 18(4)(b).
6   *R v Northavon District Council ex p Smith* [1994] 2 AC 402 at 411A, HL.
7   See **12.6**.

Mr Justice Cazalet has stated that the principles that should be applied when determining whether costs should be awarded against magistrates are:

> '(i) that costs would only be awarded against justices in the rarest of circumstances when they had done something which calls for strong disapproval; and
>
> (ii) that it was a practice not to grant costs against justices merely because they have made a mistake in law, but only if they have acted perversely or with some disregard for the elementary principles which every court ought to obey, and even then only if it was a flagrant instance.'[1]

Thus, applying these principles, the High Court has awarded costs against magistrates in a case where they took a perverse decision in flagrant disregard of elementary principles[2].

In general, magistrates should not be represented in cases where their decision is being challenged[3]. If magistrates do attend at a hearing when they should not have attended, the High Court will be required to take account of the reasonableness of their conduct before ordering costs[4]. This means that if the magistrates attend and are unsuccessful, they increase the risk that costs will be awarded against them. If they are successful, the High Court will be unwilling to order costs in their favour unless they can show that there were particularly good reasons why they should attend.

The High Court will be particularly reluctant to award costs against magistrates in cases when they have not appeared[5]. That does not mean, however, that there can never be a costs order against magistrates. For example, costs have been awarded in cases where the magistrates have caused an unnecessary substantive hearing by failing to sign a consent order[6] and where they failed to take a grant of permission sufficiently seriously in a case, challenging a refusal to state a case[7].

In cases where costs are awarded against magistrates, they can obtain costs from local funds in most circumstances. In a criminal case, costs must be awarded from local funds unless it is proved that the magistrates acted in bad faith[8]. In other cases, the magistrates are required to be indemnified if they acted reasonably and in good faith in the matter that gave rise to proceedings in the

---

1 *R v Bristol Magistrates' Court ex p Hodge* [1997] QB 974 at 982C applying the test in *R v York City Justices ex p Farmery* (1989) 153 JP 257, DC.
2 Eg *R v Lincoln Justices ex p Count* (1996) 8 Admin LR 233 in which magistrates refused to adjourn a case as there was no specific statutory power enabling them to adjourn.
3 See **7.14**.
4 CPR 1998, r 44.3(4).
5 *R v Newcastle Under Lyme Justices ex p Massey* [1994] 1 WLR 1684 at 1692A, DC.
6 Ibid at 1692F.
7 *R v Huntingdon Magistrates' Court ex p Percy* [1994] COD 323, DC; see also *R v Metropolitan Stipendiary Magistrate ex p Ali* (1997) *The Independent*, 12 May, where costs were awarded against a magistrate for continuing to refuse to state a case when the judge who had granted permission had said that it would be impossible to know if the magistrate had erred if they did not state a case.
8 Justices of the Peace Act 1997, s 54(2)(a).

High Court and may be indemnified in other circumstances[1]. Decisions regarding indemnification are taken by the area committee[2].

12.6 SPECIAL CONSIDERATIONS AS TO THE COSTS OF THIRD PARTIES AND NON-PARTIES

In judicial review proceedings, it is common for third parties to be the applicant's effective opponent. For example, although magistrates may be the named respondent, it is likely to be the prosecution who actively opposes a defendant's application for judicial review. In principle, costs can be awarded against this party for maintaining the proceedings[3]. When determining whether to make an order for costs, the High Court will take account of the general rules regarding costs that are set out above[4].

Third parties who are successful may have problems obtaining their costs. In principle, there is no reason why this should not happen. However, generally the High Court will be reluctant to make more than one order of costs, unless there is some good reason why it was appropriate for more than one party to be represented[5]. In particular, the High Court will not merely award a party costs merely because it has been served with the proceedings[6].

The High Court has the power to make costs orders in favour of or against non-parties[7]. Before doing this, those persons must be added as a party and given an opportunity to be heard[8]. In practice, costs orders are rarely made against third parties. Circumstances where such orders have been made include cases where costs orders have been made against non-parties who have funded unsuccessful litigation[9] and non-parties who have caused unnecessary costs to be incurred as a result of their unreasonable conduct[10]. In general, costs orders are not made in favour of an amicus curiae[11].

---

1   Justices of the Peace Act 1997, s 54(2)(b).
2   Ibid, s 54(3).
3   Eg *R v Hastings Licensing Justices ex p John Lovibond & Sons Ltd* [1968] 1 WLR 735, DC.
4   See **12.2**.
5   Eg *R v Secretary of State for the Environment ex p Kirkstall Valley Campaign Ltd* [1996] 3 All ER 304 at 342J.
6   *R v Industrial Disputes Tribunal ex p American Express Co Inc* [1954] 1 WLR 1118.
7   Supreme Court Act 1981, s 51.
8   CPR 1998, r 48.2(1).
9   *R v Darlington Borough Council ex p Association of Darlington Taxi Owners (No 2)* [1995] COD 128.
10 *R v Lambeth Borough Council ex p Wilson* (1996) 8 Admin LR 376; although this was set aside on appeal *R v Lambeth Borough Council ex p Wilson* (1997) *The Times*, 25 March, CA.
11 See, however, *B v Croydon Health Authority (No 2)* [1996] 1 FLR 253, CA, in which an amicus curiae obtained part of their costs from the successful party as a result of the considerable assistance provided to the court.

12.7 COSTS FROM CENTRAL FUNDS

A Divisional Court has the power to award costs to a defendant from central funds in any criminal cause or matter that it determines[1]. Similarly, the House of Lords may make such an order in an appeal from a Divisional Court[2]. A similar power exists to award costs to a prosecutor who is not a 'public authority' or a person acting on their behalf or in his capacity as an official appointed by such an authority[3].

As we have noted earlier, the Access to Justice Bill is likely to mean that criminal causes are often considered by a single High Court judge rather than by a Divisional Court[4]. There appears at present to be no proposals for costs from central funds to be awarded by a single High Court judge. As a result, it is unclear whether costs from central funds will be available in the majority of cases. There is no provision for costs from central funds in civil cases or indeed in any case where there is not a statutory power to make such an order[5].

12.8 ADVANCE ORDERS FOR COSTS

It was established prior to the introduction of the CPR 1998 that the High Court had power to make a final order regarding costs before the final determination of proceedings. There appears to be no reason to believe that the CPR 1998 change this position. Indeed, although the general rule is that the successful party will obtain a costs order, the CPR 1998 explicitly provide the High Court with a discretion to make 'a different order'[6].

The power to make a final order for costs before determination of the case is important in proceedings before the High Court. This is because a party may seek to raise arguments that are of public importance, but which they will not be able to afford to proceed with if they are at risk of a costs order. In these circumstances, the High Court may make an order preventing the respondent recovering costs in any event.

Mr Justice Dyson held that the test to be applied was:

> '[T]he necessary conditions for the making of a pre-emptive costs order in public interest challenge cases are that the court is satisfied that the issues raised are truly ones of general public importance, and that it has a sufficient appreciation of the merits of the claim that it can conclude that it is in the public interest to make the order. Unless the court can be so satisfied by short argument, it is unlikely to make the order in any event. ... These necessary conditions are not, however, sufficient for the making of an order. The court must also have regard to the financial

---

1 Prosecution of Offences Act 1985, s 16(5)(a); see **5.1** for a definition of the scope of a 'criminal cause or matter'.
2 Ibid, s 16(5)(b).
3 Ibid, s 17.
4 See **1.11**.
5 *Steele Ford and Newton v Crown Prosecution Service (No 2)* [1994] 1 AC 22, HL.
6 CPR 1998, r 44.3(2)(b).

resources of the applicant and respondent, and the amount of costs likely to be in issue.'[1]

He also held that:

'The essential characteristics of a public law challenge are that it raises public law issues which are of general importance, where the applicant has no private interest in the outcome of the case.'[2]

12.9 WASTED COSTS AGAINST LEGAL ADVISERS

The High Court has a statutory power to make an order for wasted costs against a legal adviser[3]. This power does not enable a proposed respondent to obtain costs from the applicant's legal adviser at the permission stage of proceedings as the proposed respondent is not a party[4]. Before doing this, the court must be satisfied that the legal adviser has acted in an improper, unreasonable or negligent manner, that those acts have caused unnecessary costs, and that in all the circumstances it is reasonable to order payment of some or all of the costs[5]. The court must give the legal adviser an opportunity to give reasons why an order should not be made[6].

It is not certain how the introduction of the CPR 1998 will affect this area of the law. However, the principles that lay behind the introduction of the rules are likely to mean that the High Court will wish to use its powers to discourage practitioners from bringing unnecessary litigation and failing to attempt to resolve matters without litigation[7]. As a result, the High Court may be more willing to make orders for wasted costs.

12.10 ASSESSMENT OF COSTS

Where a costs order is made, the High Court can order that assessment will take place on a standard basis or an indemnity basis[8]. If the order does not state the basis of assessment, it is assumed that it is the standard basis[9]. When deciding which order to make, the court will take account of the same factors that they consider when they decide whether to make any order[10]. In either case, costs that are unreasonably incurred or unreasonable in amount will not be allowed[11].

---

1   *R v Lord Chancellor ex p CPAG; R v DPP ex p Bull and Another* [1998] 2 All ER 755 at 766H.
2   Ibid, at 762D.
3   Supreme Court Act 1981, s 51(6).
4   *R v Camden London Borough Council ex p Martin* [1997] 1 All ER 307 but see *R v Immigration Appeal Tribunal ex p Gulbamer Gulsen* [1997] COD 430 holding there was an inherent jurisdiction to order wasted costs at the permission stage.
5   *Ridehalgh v Horsefield* [1994] Ch 205, CA.
6   CPR 1998, r 48.7(2).
7   See **12.2** regarding the overriding objective.
8   CPR 1998, r 44.4(1).
9   Ibid, r 44.4(4).
10 See **12.2**.
11 CPR 1998, r 44.4(1).

In addition, if the costs are awarded on a standard basis, the court will consider whether costs were proportionately and reasonably incurred[1].

The are two methods of assessment. The court can order summary assessment and should normally do so if a hearing took less than 1 day although there is a discretion[2]. At present it is unclear whether the High Court will order summary assessment in cases in the Crown Office. In these cases, the costs claimed are often higher and the bill is more complex than those normally associated with a 1-day hearing. Until this is clear, solicitors acting for parties seeking costs at the conclusion of the substantive hearing of less than 1 day should consider filing statements of costs in accordance with the Practice Direction[3].

The rules for a detailed assessment are complex and require both the payer and payee to serve notices within time-limits. In practice, it will almost certainly be essential to rely on the advice of a costs draftsperson.

12.11 LEGAL AID TO COVER PARTICIPATION IN PROCEEDINGS IN THE HIGH COURT

The scope of criminal legal aid does not include any form of proceedings in the High Court, Court of Appeal (Civil Division) or in the House of Lords on appeal from either of these courts[4]. This clearly means that criminal legal aid is not available to cover representation in any form of proceedings considered in this book. It is, however, clear that civil legal aid is available to cover all the forms of proceedings considered in this book[5].

Civil legal aid is subject to a means test[6]. It is also subject to a merits test. Legal aid should not be granted unless a person has shown that he has reasonable grounds for taking, defending or being a party to proceedings[7]. In addition, legal aid will be refused if it is unreasonable for the person to receive legal aid[8]. In essence, this means that there is a legal merits test and a test that requires a consideration of the benefits to the person of bringing proceedings. The two tests are distinct.

When considering the legal merits test, the Legal Aid Board require practitioners to supply the best possible information about the chances of success. In general, this requires practitioners to assess whether the chances of success are: very good (over 80 per cent), good (60–80 per cent), reasonable (50–60

---

1 CPR 1998, r 44.5(1)(a).
2 *Practice Direction (CPR 1998, Part 44 – General Rules about Costs)*, para 4.4(1).
3 Ibid, para 4.5.
4 Legal Aid Act 1988, s 19(1).
5 Ibid, s 14(1) provides that civil legal aid covers any proceedings that are included in Part I of Sch 2 to that Act and that are not excluded under Part II of that schedule. Part I includes all proceedings in the High Court, Court of Appeal and House of Lords. Part II contains no relevant exclusions.
6 Legal Aid Act 1988, s 15(1).
7 Ibid, s 15(2).
8 Ibid, s 15(3)(a).

per cent), less than evens or impossible to say[1]. The fact that the prospects of success are less than evens does not necessarily mean that legal aid will be refused.

The High Court has held that the legal aid merits test is very similar to the test that it applies when it decides whether to grant permission to apply for judicial review[2]. As a result, the legal merits test should normally be satisfied if the High Court grants permission. That does not, however, mean that legal aid should only be sought after permission has been granted. Normally, legal aid should be sought before proceedings are commenced[3].

The second test requires the Legal Aid Board to consider the reasonableness of the person seeking legal aid being a party to proceedings. This is sometimes wrongly called the cost-benefit test. This is because the cost of litigation when compared with the potential benefit to the person seeking legal aid is an important factor when considering reasonableness. Cost-benefit is not, however, the only factor. The Legal Aid Board will consider other factors such as the availability of other sources of assistance, including assistance with legal expenses provided by an insurance policy.

The cost-benefit test is clearly a difficult test to apply in the context of criminal proceedings in the High Court as there will usually be no damages awarded if an application is successful. Practitioners cannot merely say that it is reasonable for proceedings to be brought because the damages that are likely to be awarded will significantly outweigh the costs of the litigation. The benefit in the criminal proceedings that are the subject of this book is more difficult to quantify. As a result, the assessment of the benefit will require a consideration of the impact on the applicant's quality of life of the decision that is being challenged. It is important to recognise that legal aid is made available for the benefit of the assisted person. As a result, it is not available to assist persons who are not parties to determine issues of public importance[4].

Clearly, in cases where detention is being challenged the benefits are likely to outweigh the costs. In contrast, the *Legal Aid Handbook* suggests that legal aid will rarely be available to fund cases where the issue at stake is a loss of stature, dignity or reputation[5]. While this statement undoubtably reflects the practice of the Legal Aid Board, it is arguable that in certain circumstances this may amount to a breach of the European Convention on Human Rights. For example, it is arguable that a loss of dignity may be all that results from some interferences with the rights of a person to a private life under Art 8. Article 13 requires a State to provide an effective national remedy. The need to provide an effective remedy may require the State to provide legal aid[6]. In general, the

---

1 *Legal Aid Handbook 1998/1999* (Sweet & Maxwell), para 7-02.5; *The General Council to the Bar's Legal Aid Guidelines.*
2 *R v Legal Aid Board ex p Hughes* (1993) 5 Admin LR 623, CA.
3 This is particularly true as proceeding without legal aid will expose the party to a risk of costs. See **12.4**.
4 *UDT v Bycroft* [1954] 3 All ER 455 at 459H, CA.
5 *Legal Aid Handbook 1998/1999* (Sweet & Maxwell) para 7-03.11.
6 *Airey v Ireland* (1979) 2 EHRR 305.

increasing importance of the European Convention on Human Rights means that the reasonableness test is more likely to be satisfied if a party can show that proceedings relate to fundamental human rights, such as those incorporated in the Convention.

12.12   EMERGENCY LEGAL AID

It is unfortunately true that the Legal Aid Board can take weeks or months to determine applications for civil legal aid. This means that it is often essential to apply for emergency legal aid. When making an application for emergency legal aid, it is necessary to satisfy the normal merits tests. In addition, the Legal Aid Board must be supplied with sufficient information to show that the applicant for Legal Aid is likely to be financially eligible[1]. Finally, the applicant will need to show that it is in the interests of justice that they receive emergency legal aid[2].

The strict approach taken to delay by the High Court may mean that the interests of justice require the grant of emergency legal aid[3]. In particular, in the context of judicial review, it is important to recognise that an application made within the 3 month time-limit will not necessarily be regarded as being in time if there is delay[4]. In addition, delay associated with obtaining legal aid will not automatically lead to an extension of the time for bringing an application for judicial review[5]. In the context of an appeal by way of case stated from a decision of the magistrates' court, there is no power to extend the time for applying for the statement of a case[6]. As a result, legal aid must be obtained urgently.

Clearly, the possibility that the application will be unsuccessful as the result of delay is not the only reason why emergency legal aid may be sought. Issues such as the need to obtain bail, or the need to prevent the application becoming academic as a result of delay, are reasons why emergency legal aid may need to be sought.

Where an emergency application must be made, it should normally be made by post or by document exchange. In cases of extreme urgency where a decision is required within that day, an application may be made by fax[7]. The application will need to justify the decision to apply by fax as well as the need to seek emergency legal aid. Telephone applications can also be made in circumstances where a decision is required before a faxed application could be considered or where the solicitor does not have access to a fax machine[8]. Even

---

1   Civil Legal Aid (General) Regulations 1989, SI 1989/339, r 19(2)(a).
2   Ibid, reg 19(2)(b).
3   See **5.2**.
4   Eg *R v Independent Television Commission ex p TV NI Ltd* (1991) *The Times*, 30 December, CA.
5   See *R v Metropolitan Borough of Sandwell ex p Cashmore* (1993) 25 HLR 544, in which it was held that delays in obtaining legal aid would not automatically result in an extension of the time for bringing an application for judicial review.
6   *Michael v Gowland* [1977] 1 WLR 296, DC. See also **5.6**.
7   *Legal Aid Handbook 1998/1999* (Sweet & Maxwell) para 6.3.2.2.1.
8   Ibid, para 6.3.3.1.1.

where emergency legal aid is granted following a telephone or faxed application, it will be a condition of the grant that full and completed application forms should be submitted within 5 working days and that the information supplied in the postal forms should be consistent with that supplied in support of the telephone or fax application[1].

The emergency legal aid certificate will have a costs limitation and will normally be limited to certain stages of proceedings. It is important to be aware of the scope of the certificate so that appropriate extensions can be sought. In the context of judicial review, the certificate is normally limited to the service of the respondent's evidence and obtaining counsel advice following receipt of that evidence. It is important to obtain that advice on the basis of the evidence obtained from the respondent[2].

12.13 PRACTICAL CONSIDERATIONS WHEN A CLIENT IS IN RECEIPT OF LEGAL AID

A solicitor who receives a legal aid certificate should send it by post to the Crown Office as soon as it is received if proceedings have begun, or it should be lodged with the Crown Office at the commencement of proceedings if proceedings have not begun[3]. In practice, solicitors are supplied with a second copy of the certificate for this purpose. In addition, a notice in a form approved by the Legal Aid Board must be served on all other parties to the proceedings[4].

At the conclusion of proceedings in the High Court, an order should be sought for legal aid taxation[5]. This means that the costs payable by the Legal Aid Board are assessed by the High Court during a taxation. A failure to seek a taxation is likely to mean that there is no basis for the payment of the costs. The only exception arises when the costs can be assessed under the legal aid regulations.

If proceedings have not been commenced, costs will be assessed by the Legal Aid Board[6]. Although persons applying for judicial review must apply for permission to bring the application, the application for permission is not normally regarded as being a step before the proceedings have commenced for legal aid purposes. As a result, the normal practice is to order legal aid taxation at the conclusion of the application for permission, although the High Court sometimes refuses to make an order if permission is granted, because legal aid taxation can be ordered later in the proceedings. Assessment may also be obtained when the costs of the applicant's solicitor and counsel will be less than £500[7].

---

1 *Legal Aid Handbook 1998/1999* (Sweet & Maxwell), para 6.4.1.
2 In *R v Liverpool City Justices ex p P* [1998] 11 CL 139, it was held that one could not rely on advice obtained at an earlier stage in proceedings when obtaining the removal of a limitation.
3 Civil Legal Aid (General) Regulations 1989, SI 1989/339, reg 50(4).
4 Ibid, reg 50(1)(a).
5 Ibid, reg 107.
6 Ibid, reg 105(2).
7 Ibid, reg 106A(4).

Practitioners involved in proceedings in which their client is in receipt of civil legal aid should be aware of the professional obligations that they owe to the legal aid fund. These obligations mean that practitioners are obliged to review the merits of their client's case and ensure that the Legal Aid Board is informed if it is no longer reasonable for their client to be in receipt of legal aid[1]. The Legal Aid Board is likely to withdraw legal aid in these circumstances.

A failure to review the merits of the application is clearly a breach of professional obligations. It may also result in problems obtaining payment. If at the conclusion of the application for permission the High Court believes that proceedings should not have been brought, it cannot refuse an order for legal aid taxation of the applicant's costs. It will, however, make the Taxing Master aware of its views on the merits of the application and this will be taken into account when the taxation takes place[2]. As a result, the applicant will have significant difficulties obtaining the payment of costs.

12.14 THE STATUTORY CHARGE

The statutory charge is unlikely to be relevant in most criminal proceedings in the High Court, because damages are not usually sought as a remedy. The statutory charge will, however, arise as an issue where any property is recovered or preserved as a consequence of the proceedings[3]. The statutory charge means that the Legal Aid Board will be able to recover costs that it has paid to assist the person in receipt of legal aid from that property save for certain exemptions[4]. The only exemption that is likely to be relevant in the context of this book is that which exempts the tools of the assisted person's trade from the effect of the statutory charge.

Legal aid forms contain warnings about the statutory charge for the benefit of the person applying for legal aid. Despite that, practitioners should ensure that persons seeking legal aid are advised of any impact that the statutory charge may have in their case. It is also important to be aware that any attempt to defeat the statutory charge when settling the case is a breach of the duty that practitioners owe to the Legal Aid Board[5].

12.15 FUTURE DEVELOPMENTS REGARDING LEGAL AID

The Access to Justice Bill includes significant reforms of the legal aid system. In particular, civil and criminal legal aid will be provided through exclusive contracts. As noted above, at present civil legal aid is used to fund criminal proceedings in the High Court. It is unclear how these proceedings will be

---

1 Civil Legal Aid (General) Regulations 1989, SI 1989/339, regs 67 and 70.
2 Eg *R v Secretary of State for the Home Department ex p Shahina Begum* [1995] COD 176.
3 Legal Aid Act 1988, s 16(6).
4 Ibid.
5 *Manley v Law Society* [1981] 1 WLR 335, CA.

funded in the future. It is possible that civil legal aid will still be required. If this happens, it is unclear how solicitors who have a contract for criminal legal aid but not for civil legal aid will obtain funding for their clients who wish to bring proceedings in the High Court.

The other development of legal aid that is likely to be particularly relevant to criminal litigation is a reform of the means test. It is clear that the merits test will be reformed, but it is unclear how this will work in practice.

Chapter 13

CRIMINAL PROCEEDINGS IN THE HIGH COURT AND HUMAN RIGHTS

13.1 INTRODUCTION

The House of Lords has held that the High Court has a particular jurisdiction to uphold the rule of law in criminal proceedings[1]. This duty may well extend to ensuring that criminal prosecutions are conducted in accordance with human rights law. For example, the High Court recently held that it had jurisdiction to consider a judicial review brought during a Crown Court criminal trial. The judicial review related to an important issue of principle regarding the fairness of the trial and the trial judge had no jurisdiction to deal with the issue that was being considered during the judicial review[2]. As a result, criminal practitioners need to be aware of human rights law as their arguments in the High Court can be strengthened by the appropriate use of human rights law.

Criminal practitioners need to be both aware of the present state of human rights law and the developments that will take place as a consequence of the Human Rights Act 1998 ('the 1998 Act') coming into force. As we set out below, the 1998 Act will, clearly, significantly increase the importance of the European Convention on Human Rights ('the Convention') in domestic law. It may also increase the importance of judicial review.

13.2 THE CURRENT STATUS OF THE EUROPEAN CONVENTION ON HUMAN RIGHTS IN UK DOMESTIC LAW

Although the 1998 Act has now been enacted, it is far from clear when it will enter into force. At the time of writing, media reports suggest that there is likely to be significant delay before it comes into force[3]. That does not, however, mean that the Convention is irrelevant. The High Court can, and does, take account of its provisions in a number of different circumstances.

First, where it is said that fundamental rights have been infringed by a decision, the High Court will subject that decision to a more rigorous review than it would otherwise. Clearly, whether fundamental rights have been infringed may be determined by reference to the Convention. For example, Lord Justice Simon Brown has held that:

---

1   *R v Horseferry Road Magistrates' Court ex p Bennet* [1994] 1 AC 42 at 64D, HL.
2   *R v Secretary of State for the Home Department ex p Quinn* (1999) *The Times*, 17 April.
3   (1999) *The Times*, 5 May.

'In short, I respectfully conclude with Neill LJ that even where fundamental human rights are being restricted, "the threshold of unreasonableness" is not lowered. On the other hand, the minister on judicial review will need to show that there is an important competing public interest which he could reasonably judge sufficient to justify the restriction and he must expect his reasons to be closely scrutinised. Even that approach, therefore, involves a more intensive review process and a greater readiness to intervene than would ordinarily characterise a judicial review challenge.'[1]

In addition, the High Court will interpret any ambiguity in a statutory provision in accordance with the UK's international treaty obligations such as the Convention[2]. That is because Parliament is presumed to act in accordance with the UK's international obligations.

The scope of the common law can also be determined by consideration of the Convention. That is because the Convention is a persuasive authority about the scope of the common law. For example, Lord Justice Evans has held that:

'The fact that the Convention does not form part of English law does not mean that its provisions cannot be referred to and relied on as persuasive authority as to what the common law is, or should be.'[3]

The enactment of the 1998 Act has already caused the courts to give greater weight to the Convention, even though it is not in force[4]. For example, the High Court has held that it can determine whether advice that a decision-maker has received about the meaning of the Convention is correct[5].

As a consequence of the above, it is already crucial to understand the scope of the provisions of the Convention that are set out below. It should be clear that, although the 1998 Act is not in force, when applying for a judicial review in the High Court or when appealing by way of case stated, arguments based on the provisions of the Convention are likely to find favour with the judges.

13.3 HUMAN RIGHTS OBLIGATIONS CONTAINED IN UK DOMESTIC LAW

Although the Convention imposes obligations on courts and decision-makers, it is not the only source of human rights law. The common law recognises that there are certain basic rights. These rights can be enforced by bringing proceedings in the High Court.

The most significant of these rights is the right of access to the courts which is now recognised as a fundamental common law right. For example, Lord Justice Steyn held that:

'It is a principle of our law that every citizen has a right of unimpeded access to a court.... Even in our unwritten constitution it must rank as a constitutional right.'[6]

---

1   R v Ministry of Defence ex p Smith [1995] 4 All ER 427 at 445F, DC.
2   R v Secretary of State for the Home Department ex p Brind [1991] 1 AC 696, HL.
3   R v Mid Glamorgan Family Health Services ex p Martin [1995] 1 WLR 110 at 118H, CA.
4   R v DPP ex p Kebilene and Others, R v DPP ex p Rechaci (1999) The Times, 31 March, DC.
5   Ibid.
6   R v Secretary of State for the Home Department ex p Leech [1994] QB 198 at 210A, CA.

This is an important right in the context of criminal law because it may be argued that the persons involved in the treatment of a defendant have infringed this right. For example, it might be argued that the actions of the Prison Service interfere with this right by interfering with a prisoner's right to correspond with his legal advisor[1]. Similarly, decisions that are said to impede a prisoner's ability to present his defence may be challenged, as the right of access to the court includes the right to a fair trial[2].

When it is claimed that there is a breach of a person's right to a fair trial, the High Court will apply the same test that it uses to determine whether there is apparent bias. This means that a person need not show that his rights have actually been interfered with. The court will hold that there has been an unlawful interference with the right to a fair trial if there is a real danger of an interference[3].

The right of access to the courts is not the only right recognised by the common law. For example, the right to only be detained according to the law is also regarded as fundamental right. For example, Sir Thomas Bingham MR has held that:

> '[N]o adult citizen of the United Kingdom is liable to be confined in any institution against his will, save by the authority of law.'[4]

The rights recognised by the Common Law are clearly closely related to the rights contained in the Convention. For example, the right to only be detained according to the law is closely related to the rights contained in Article 5 of the Convention[5]. As a result, when the 1998 Act comes into force it is likely that the Common Law will become very much less significant as a source of rights. Until that time, however, the common law rights are important because they can be directly enforced in a way that is not possible at present with the rights contained in the Convention. For example, the common law rights can be used to argue that secondary legislation is ultra vires[6].

13.4 OTHER INTERNATIONAL HUMAN RIGHTS OBLIGATIONS

Although the Convention is the UK's most important source of international human rights law, it is not the only source. Although the other obligations are not being given enhanced effect in domestic law by the introduction of domestic legislation such as the 1998 Act, they can still be relied on to interpret domestic legislation and to question the actions of decision-makers in the way

---

1 *R v Secretary of State for the Home Department ex p Leech* [1994] QB 198, CA.
2 *R v Secretary of State for the Home Department ex p Quinn* (1999) *The Times*, 17 April.
3 *R v Secretary of State for the Home Department ex p Quinn* (1999) *The Times*, 17 April, applying the test in *R v Gough* [1993] AC 646, HL, set out at **2.8**.
4 *In Re S-C (Mental Patient: Habeas Corpus)* [1996] QB 599 at 603C, CA.
5 See **13.5**.
6 *R v Lord Chancellor ex p Witham* [1998] QB 575, DC; see **13.8** for details of how it will be possible to use the 1998 Act to argue that secondary legislation is ultra vires as a result of the operation of the Convention.

that has been set out above[1]. It is also possible that they can be relied on to interpret the meaning of the Convention[2].

In general, the rights contained in these Treaties are similar to those contained in the Convention. These Treaties can, however, be more specific about the scope of the rights. For example, the UK has ratified the United Nations Convention on the Rights of the Child[3]. This has provisions that are relevant to criminal law and that can be more specific than the rights contained in the European Convention. For example, Article 37(c) provides that:

> 'Every child deprived of liberty shall be treated with humanity and respect for the inherent dignity of the human person, and in a manner which takes into account the needs of persons of his or her age. In particular, every child deprived of liberty shall be separated from adults unless it is considered in the child's best interest not to do so and shall have the right to maintain contact with his or her family through correspondence and visits, save in exceptional circumstances.'[4]

The UK has also ratified the International Covenant on Civil and Political Rights[5]. This also has provisions that are relevant to criminal proceedings. It has particular value as a result of the case-law that has been developed by the Human Rights Committee about the scope of the provisions of the Covenant. For example, there is case-law considering the extent of the right to effective assistance from counsel[6]. This case-law can be relied on in litigation about the scope of the rights protected by the Convention.

A detailed consideration of these treaties is beyond the scope of this book. Full copies of these and other treaties together with other relevant material can be found on the website of the University of Minnesota Human Rights Library at http://www1.umn.edu/humanrts/.

13.5 THE KEY PROVISIONS OF THE EUROPEAN CONVENTION ON HUMAN RIGHTS

The Convention for Protection of Human Rights and Fundamental Freedoms was agreed by the members of the Council of Europe in Rome on 4 November

---

1 See **13.2** considering the status of the Convention at present. There is no reason why the domestic courts should not consider the UK's other international human rights obligations in the same way.
2 We consider the interpretation of the Convention at **13.6**. In essence, it is our submission that the prime matter to be considered, in interpreting the Convention, is the obligation imposed by the Convention to ensure the promotion of human rights. Clearly, in considering this obligation, the courts should be able to consider the state of international human rights law as set out in other international treaties.
3 Adopted by the General Assembly on 20 November 1989, UN Doc A/44/49 (1989).
4 The UK has entered a reservation stating that:
'Where at any time there is a lack of suitable accomodation or adequate facilities for a particular individual in any institution in which young offenders are detained, or where the mixing of adults and children is deemed to be mutually beneficial, the United Kingdom reserves the right not to apply article 37(c) in so far as those provisions require children who are detained to be accommodated separately from adults.'
5 Adopted by the General Assembly on 16 December 1966, 999 UNTS 171.
6 Eg *Collins v Jamaica* (356/1989) holding that it is ineffective assistance for a counsel to withdraw an appeal without instructions.

1950. It is commonly known as the European Convention on Human Rights ('the Convention'). The key provisions of the Convention that are likely to be relevant to criminal proceedings are set out below.

'**Article 3**
Prohibition of torture

No one shall be subjected to torture or to inhuman or degrading treatment or punishment.

Article 5
Right to liberty and security

1. Everyone has the right to liberty and security of person. No one shall be deprived of his liberty save in the following cases and in accordance with a procedure prescribed by law:
   (a) the lawful detention of a person after conviction by a competent court;
   (b) the lawful arrest or detention of a person for non-compliance with the lawful order of a court or in order to secure the fulfilment of any obligation prescribed by law;
   (c) the lawful arrest or detention of a person effected for the purpose of bringing him before the competent legal authority on reasonable suspicion of having committed an offence or when it is reasonably considered necessary to prevent his committing an offence or fleeing after having done so;
   (d) the detention of a minor by lawful order for the purpose of educational supervision or his lawful detention for the purpose of bringing him before the competent legal authority;
   (e) the lawful detention of persons for the prevention of the spreading of infectious diseases, of persons of unsound mind, alcoholics or drug addicts or vagrants;
   (f) the lawful arrest or detention of a person to prevent his effecting an unauthorised entry into the country or of a person against whom action is being taken with a view to deportation or extradition.
2. Everyone who is arrested shall be informed promptly, in a language which he understands, of the reasons for his arrest and of any charge against him.
3. Everyone arrested or detained in accordance with the provisions of paragraph 1.c of this article shall be brought promptly before a judge or other officer authorised by law to exercise judicial power and shall be entitled to trial within a reasonable time or to release pending trial. Release may be conditioned by guarantees to appear for trial.
4. Everyone who is deprived of his liberty by arrest or detention shall be entitled to take proceedings by which the lawfulness of his detention shall be decided speedily by a court and his release ordered if the detention is not lawful.
5. Everyone who has been the victim of arrest or detention in contravention of the provisions of this article shall have an enforceble right to compensation.

Article 6
Right to a fair trial

1. In the determination of his civil rights and obligations or of any criminal charge against him, everyone is entitled to a fair and public hearing within a reasonable time by an independent and impartial tribunal established by law. Judgment shall be pronounced publicly but the press and public may be excluded from all or part of the trial in the interest of morals, public order or national security in a democratic society, where the interests of juveniles or the protection of the private life of the parties so require, or to the extent

strictly necessary in the opinion of the court in special circumstances where publicity would prejudice the interests of justice.
2. Everyone charged with a criminal offence shall be presumed innocent until proved guilty according to law.
3. Everyone charged with a criminal offence has the following minimum rights:
    (a) to be informed promptly, in a language which he understands and in detail, of the nature and cause of the accusation against him;
    (b) to have adequate time and facilities for the preparation of his defence;
    (c) to defend himself in person or through legal assistance of his own choosing or, if he has not sufficient means to pay for legal assistance, to be given it free when the interests of justice so require;
    (d) to examine or have examined witnesses against him and to obtain the attendance and examination of witnesses on his behalf under the same conditions as witnesses against him;
    (e) to have the free assistance of an interpreter if he cannot understand or speak the language used in court.

Article 7
No punishment without law

1. No one shall be held guilty of any criminal offence on account of any act or omission which did not constitute a criminal offence under national or international law at the time when it was committed. Nor shall a heavier penalty be imposed than the one that was applicable at the time the criminal offence was committed.
2. This article shall not prejudice the trial and punishment of any person for any act or omission which, at the time when it was committed, was criminal according to the general principles of law recognised by civilised nations.

Article 8
Right to respect for private and family life

1. Everyone has the right to respect for his private and family life, his home and his correspondence.
2. There shall be no interference by a public authority with the exercise of this right except such as in accordance with the law and is necessary in a democratic society in the interests of national security, public safety or the economic well-being of the country, for the prevention of disorder or crime, for the protection of health or morals, or for the protection of the rights and freedoms of others.

Article 11
Freedom of assembly and association

1. Everyone has the right to freedom of peaceful assembly and to freedom of association with others, including the right to form and to join trade unions for the protection of his interests.
2. No restrictions shall be placed on the exercise of these rights other than such as are prescribed by law and are necessary in a democratic society in the interests of national security or public safety, for the prevention of disorder or crime, for the protection of health or morals or for the protection of the rights and freedoms of others. This article shall not prevent the imposition of lawful restrictions on the exercise of these rights by members of the armed forces, of the police or of the administration of the State.

Article 14
Prohibition of discrimination
The enjoyment of the rights and freedoms set forth in this Convention shall be secured without discrimination on any ground such as sex, race, colour, language, religion, political or other opinion, national or social origin, association with a national minority, property, birth or other status.'

Other provisions that may be significant include Article 9, which sets out the right to freedom of thought, conscience and religion and Article 10 which sets out the right to freedom of expression.

A full copy of the Convention can be obtain from the website of the European Court of Human Rights at http://www.dhcour.coe.fr/. The case-law of the European Court can also be searched at this website. The provisions of the Convention that can be enforced under the Human Rights Act 1998 ('the 1998 Act') are set out in Schedule 1 to that Act. That includes all the provisions set out above.

13.6 THE INTERPRETATION OF THE PROVISIONS OF THE CONVENTION

It should be clear from the provisions set out above that the provisions of the Convention are not as precise as the provisions of a domestic statute. As a result, the precise effect of these provisions depends on judicial interpretation. The Convention provides for decisions to be taken on the effect of the provisions by the European Court of Human Rights, the European Commission of Human Rights and the Committee of Ministers. Its meaning cannot be properly determined without considering the decisions of these bodies. These decisions are significant as they can conflict with the provisions of national law.

An example of how the decisions of the European Court of Human Rights can conflict with national law arises in the context of Article 6 of the Convention. Article 6 distinguishes between criminal proceedings and civil proceedings. The definition of criminal proceedings in domestic law does not determine whether proceedings are criminal for the purposes of Article 6, although it is a relevant factor. The European Court of Human Rights will also take account of the nature of the offence and the nature and degree of the penalty[1].

The 1998 Act does not provide that the decisions of the European institutions bind the domestic courts of the UK. Instead it provides that:

'A court or tribunal determining a question which has arisen in connection with a Convention right must take into account any—
a) judgment, decision, declaration or advisory opinion of the European Court of Human Rights,
b) opinion of the Commission given in a report adopted under Article 31 of the Convention,
c) decision of the Commission in connection with Article 26 or 27(2) of the Convention, or
d) decision of the Committee of Ministers taken under Article 46 of the Convention,

---
1 *Pierre-Bloch v France* (1998) 26 EHRR 202.

whenever made or given, so far as, in the opinion of the court or tribunal, it is relevant to the proceedings in which that question has arisen.'[1]

Clearly, this provision allows practitioners to argue that the Convention should be interpreted in domestic law in a manner that is not consistent with the decisions of the European institutions. In particular, it may allow practitioners to argue that the rights provided for by the Convention are wider than those recognised by the European institutions.

The idea that the Convention should be given a wider interpretation than that which has so far been decided is consistent with the case-law of the European Court of Human Rights. In particular, the court has held that the Convention is 'designed to maintain and promote the ideals and values of a democratic society'[2]. Promotion of the values of a democratic society implies that the Convention should recognise the development of improved standards of human rights.

The idea that the Convention should be given a wider interpretation is also consistent with international law. The Vienna Convention on the Law of Treaties[3] governs the interpretation of Treaties. Article 31 provides that provisions of treaties should normally be given their 'ordinary meaning ... in their context and in the light of its object and purpose'. As the preamble to the European Convention on Human Rights states that an aim of the Council of Europe is 'the achievement of greater unity between its members and that one of the methods by which that aim is to be pursued is the maintenance and further realisation of human rights and fundamental freedoms', it is clearly arguable that the Convention should be interpreted in a manner that extends human rights.

13.7 AN INTRODUCTION TO THE EFFECT OF THE HUMAN RIGHTS ACT 1998

The 1998 Act does not amount to the direct incorporation of the Convention into our domestic law. The draftsmen have attempted to leave Parliamentary sovereignty intact, whilst making Convention-based human rights claims, as far as possible, justiciable in this country.

Direct incorporation would have left the domestic courts with the power to ignore, or declare as repealed or ineffective, any legislation which conflicted with Convention rights. Further, individuals would have been provided with additional grounds for suing others, based on any material infringement of their Convention rights perpetrated by another[4]. Such wide-ranging changes have been avoided by this compromise legislation.

---

1 Human Rights Act 1998, s 2(1).
2 *Kjeldson and Others v Denmark* (1976) 11 EHRR 711.
3 Signed at Vienna on 23 May 1969, 1155 UNTS 331.
4 In this context, it is significant that the 1998 Act does not provide for the enforcement of rights under Article 13 of the Convention. This is the Article that provides that States must provide effective rights for breaches of the Convention. This shows clearly that the intention of Parliament was not to provide new causes of action.

The 1998 Act has two main objectives. First, it seeks to establish consistency between domestic law and the rights enshrined in the Convention. In addition, it seeks to give individuals appropriate domestic remedies for infringement of such rights. The precise effect of the 1998 Act depends on whether the alleged infringement of Convention rights arises as a result of primary legislation, subordinate legislation or the common law.

13.8 THE IMPACT OF THE 1998 ACT ON THE INTERPRETATION OF LEGISLATION

In so far as is possible, primary and subordinate legislation must be interpreted by all courts in such ways as are compatible with Convention rights. In particular, the 1998 Act provides that:

> 'So far as it is possible to do so, primary legislation and subordinate legislation must be read and given effect in a way which is compatible with the Convention rights.'[1]

This constitutes a significant advance on the previously held rule, which merely allowed the courts to take the Convention into account if confronted with ambiguity in a statutory provision[2]. Test cases will reveal the extent to which the courts are prepared to go in order to interpret legislation in ways which are compatible with the Convention, but authorities suggest that judges will have considerable freedom in this interpretative function. It is likely that the courts will, where appropriate, read necessary safeguards into legislation[3]. Further, words not present may be implied into a section when necessary[4] or simply jettisoned from the section[5], if appropriate.

13.8.1 The powers of the courts when it is impossible to interpret legislation in a way which is consistent with the Convention

If, despite the wide powers to interpret legislation in a way that is consistent with the Convention, that proves impossible, the effect of the 1998 Act depends on whether the legislation is 'primary legislation' or 'subordinate legislation'. Primary legislation includes a public general Act of Parliament[6] and an Order in Council if it is:

> 'i) made in exercise of Her Majesty's Royal Prerogative;
> ...[7] or
> iii) amending an Act of a kind mentioned in paragraph (a), (b) or (c)[8].'[9]

---

1 Human Rights Act 1998, s 3(1).
2 See **13.2**.
3 *AG of Gambia v Momodou Jobe* [1984] AC 689 at 702G, PC.
4 *Vasquez and O'Neil v R* [1994] 1 WLR 1304 at 1314E, PC; *Pickstone v Freemans plc* [1989] 1 AC 66 at 126A, HL.
5 *O'Brien v Sim-Chem Ltd* [1980] 1 WLR 1011 at 1017G, HL.
6 Human Rights Act 1988, s 21(1).
7 Sub-paragraph (ii) is irrelevant as it only relates to Northern Ireland.
8 The Acts mentioned in paragraphs (a), (b) and (c) are public General Acts, local and personal Acts and private Acts.
9 Human Rights Act 1998, s 21(1).

In contrast, subordinate legislation includes an Order in Council other than one of the sort set out above[1] and any:

> '[O]rder, rules, regulations, scheme, warrant, byelaw or other instrument made under primary legislation (except to the extent to which it operates to bring one or more provisions of that legislation into force or amends any primary legislation)'.[2]

Where any incompatibility in primary legislation is irremovable, subsisting domestic primary legislation remains valid. The 1998 Act provides that the obligation to interpret primary legislation in accordance with the Convention 'does not affect the validity, continuing operation or enforcement of any incompatible primary legislation'[3]. In contrast, the impact on subordinate legislation depends on whether '(disregarding any possibility of revocation) primary legislation prevents removal of the incompatibility'[4]. If legislation does prevent removal of the incompatibility, the subordinate legislation continues to be valid[5]. Otherwise, the subordinate legislation can be found to be unlawful.

This definition of subordinate legislation is broad and would appear to include most forms of secondary legislation such as court procedural rules. This is important, as it may lead to secondary legislation being declared ultra vires. For example, we later consider some of the procedural requirements imposed on criminal courts by the Convention. The 1998 Act means that it is likely that the courts will be able to find that procedure rules that are inconsistent with the Convention are ultra vires. The courts are unlikely to find that the primary legislation requires the court rules to be made in a way that is inconsistent with the Convention.

The definition of subordinate legislation will also include many of the by laws under which prosecutions are brought. Defendants can raise arguments about the vires of the secondary legislation under which a prosecution is brought as a defence to a criminal charge[6]. Clearly, the 1998 Act will allow defendants to argue that they should be found not guilty as the by laws under which the prosecution is brought contravene the defendant's Convention rights.

If faced with irreconcilable provisions between the Convention and primary domestic legislation, the House of Lords, Court of Appeal or High Court can make a 'declaration of incompatibility'[7]. There is then a discretion vested in the relevant minister to react to such a declaration of incompatibility if there are compelling reasons by amending the offending legislation by remedial order (akin to a statutory instrument) so as to establish compatibility[8]. The Crown Court and the magistrates' court has no power to make a declaration. We consider later whether proceedings should be brought in the High Court before a criminal prosecution has concluded[9]. The power to make a

---

1 Human Rights Act 1998, s 21(1).
2 Ibid.
3 Ibid, s 3(2)(b).
4 Ibid, s 3(2)(c).
5 Ibid.
6 *Boddington v British Transport Police* [1998] 2 WLR 639, HL; see **4.4** for full details.
7 Human Rights Act 1998, s 4.
8 Ibid, s 10(2).
9 See **13.10.1**.

declaration of incompatibility is clearly one reason for bringing proceedings in the High Court.

13.9 THE IMPACT OF THE 1998 ACT ON PUBLIC BODIES

From the date when the 1998 Act comes into force, it will be unlawful for a 'public authority'[1] such as any court or the investigating and prosecuting authorities including the Police and HM Customs & Excise, etc, to act in ways which are incompatible with the Convention[2]. The only exception is where:

'(a) as the result of one or more provisions of primary legislation, the authority could not have acted differently; or

(b) in the case of one or more provisions of, or made under, primary legislation which cannot be read or given effect in a way which is compatible with the Convention rights, the authority was acting so as to give effect to or enforce those provisions.'[3]

Clearly, in these circumstances, if it is primary legislation that is requiring the public authority to act in a manner that it is inconsistent with the Convention, it is possible to obtain a declaration of incompatibility[4].

However viewed, this requirement to act in a way that accords with the Convention will have a profound effect on the development of the common law. The courts at all levels will be adopting a proactive role in ensuring that the law they apply accords with Convention rights. A critical question which falls to be resolved is the extent to which the Convention will take precedence over existing common law rules which are incompatible with the Convention. It is likely, however, that the courts will find that the statutory requirement of compatibility enshrined in the 1998 Act overrides the doctrine of precedence which otherwise would apply. Subject to the higher courts clarifying the full extent of the precedence over the existing common law to be accorded to the Convention and to the decisions of European institutions considering the Convention, the criminal courts at all levels will be involved in the significant undertaking of applying the provisions of the Convention.

In particular, the lower courts will now, in all likelihood, have far greater discretion in the area of the Convention. They will not be bound to follow any existing construction placed on a statute or the common law by the higher courts if they are of the view that such a construction is incompatible with the Convention. The 1998 Act obliges any court or tribunal to apply the Convention. This means that, until guidance has been given by the appellate courts in the many areas which are likely to be raised on appeal, the magistrates'

---

1 Human Rights Act 1998, s 6(3) provides that:
  '"public authority" includes—
  (a) a court or tribunal, and
  (b) any person certain of whose functions are functions of a public nature.'
2 Human Rights Act 1998, s 6(1).
3 Ibid, s 6(2).
4 See **13.8.1**.

court and the Crown Court will have significant freedom to implement the Convention in the most appropriate way.

13.10 ENFORCING RIGHTS UNDER THE 1998 ACT

Under the 1998 Act, an individual who is a 'victim' of an act that is unlawful because it is contrary to Convention can bring proceedings against the public authorities alleged to have acted in an unlawful manner[1]. The term 'victim' is limited to a person who would be a victim for the purposes of Article 34 of the Convention[2]. There is, as a result, likely to be litigation determining whether organisations such as pressure groups can be regarded as victims. It is clearly envisaged that the forms of proceedings that may be brought to challenge an unlawful act will include judicial review proceedings, as the 1998 Act provides that:

> 'If the proceedings are brought on an application for judicial review, the applicant is to be taken to have a sufficient interest in relation to the unlawful act only if he is, or would be, a victim of that act.'[3]

Alternatively, during the course of any legal proceedings, a victim, or potential victim, may rely on his Convention rights if he has been, or may be, the subject of an act by a public authority which infringes his rights under the Convention[4]. For example, this means that a defendant might seek to argue that evidence obtained in breach of the Convention should be excluded[5]. In addition, decisions of courts and tribunals can be challenged by way of judicial review or appealed if a defendant's Convention rights have been infringed by the decision of the lower court[6].

This clearly means that parties to criminal proceedings may be faced with a choice between bringing a judicial review before the criminal proceedings have been finally determined or raising Convention issues during the criminal proceedings and then appealing if dissatisfied with the ruling on those Convention issues. For example, if it is said that police officers acted in breach of the Convention when they obtained evidence, a person who is the subject of a prosecution based on that evidence may possibly assert his Convention rights by bringing a judicial review of the decision to prosecute, or bringing a judicial review of any decision to commit, or wait until the prosecution has been concluded.

13.10.1 Should judicial review proceedings be brought before or after conviction where there is said to be a breach of the Convention?

Until the courts have provided further guidance on the application of the 1998 Act, it is probably impossible to be definite about the precise circumstances of

---

1   Human Rights Act 1998, s 7(1).
2   Ibid, s 7(7).
3   Ibid, s 7(3).
4   Ibid, s 7(1).
5   See **13.3**.
6   Human Rights Act 1998, s 9(1).

when it is appropriate bring a judicial review instead of waiting until there has been a final resolution of the criminal proceedings. However, there are some factors to consider when making this decision.

The most important factor to consider is the particular role of the High Court in ensuring that the criminal proceedings are brought in accordance with the law. The House of Lords has held that the High Court has a wider jurisdiction to uphold the rule of law during criminal proceedings than that enjoyed by the magistrates' court[1]. As a result, the High Court has power to quash a decision to commit as a result of unfairness in circumstances where a magistrate would be unable to stay proceedings. In reaching this decision, Lord Griffiths stated that:

> 'If the court is to have the power to interfere with the prosecution in the present circumstances it must be because the judiciary accept a responsibility for the maintenance of the rule of law that embraces a willingness to oversee executive action and to refuse to countenance behaviour that threatens either basic human rights or the rule of law.
>
> My Lords, I have no doubt that the judiciary should accept this responsibility in the field of criminal law. The great growth of administrative law during the latter half of this century has occurred because of the recognition by the judiciary and Parliament alike that it is the function of the High Court to ensure that executive action is exercised responsibly and as Parliament intended. So also should it be in the field of criminal law and if it comes to the attention of the court that there has been a serious abuse of power it should . . . express its disapproval by refusing to act upon it.'[2]

This all suggests that, where it is said that a prosecution should not be brought as it amounts to a breach of the Convention, there are good grounds for saying that the decision to prosecute or the decision to commit should be challenged in the High Court by judicial review. It is unnecessary to wait until the criminal proceedings have been concluded as this will not be an effective remedy. A conviction in these circumstances is likely to result in the defendant being punished before any appellate court can consider the human rights issues raised.

In addition, it may be appropriate to apply to the High Court for judicial review before there has been a final conviction in the period immediately after the 1998 Act comes into force. This will provide a rapid opportunity for the higher courts to provide guidance on the workings of the 1998 Act, which will clearly benefit all the parties associated with criminal prosecutions.

Although, for the reasons set above, the High Court may have a particular role to play in interpreting the 1998 Act, recognising that there are reasons why the High Court may be reluctant to consider applications for judicial review is important. In earlier chapters, we have noted that the High Court is reluctant to consider judicial reviews that challenge interim decisions of criminal courts[3], decisions to prosecute[4] and decisions to commit[5]. This reluctance will need to

---

1   *R v Horseferry Road Magistrates' Court ex p Bennett* [1994] 1 AC 42 at 64B, HL.
2   Ibid, at 61H.
3   See **4.10**.
4   See **4.3**.
5   See **4.7**.

be overcome. In those earlier chapters, we considered some of the factors that might result in the High Court intervening, despite its normal reluctance. These included the involvement of juveniles in the case[1] and the significance of the decision being challenged[2]. If any of these factors are present, they will enhance arguments that proceedings should be brought in the High Court before the final determination of the criminal proceedings.

One other issue that will need to be considered is the reluctance of the High Court to make fresh findings of fact during judicial review proceedings. As we noted in an earlier chapter, this means that bringing challenges to the actions of police officers is quite often difficult[3]. There are, however, cases where the High Court will consider whether the factual basis for a decision-maker's jurisdiction exists[4]. It is unclear at present whether the High Court will be willing to make fresh findings of fact when it is said that a person's Convention rights have been breached. There is, however, some indication that the High Court will be willing to make fresh findings[5]. If this is wrong and the High Court will not make findings of fact, judicial review proceedings should not be brought if there is a factual dispute until the criminal courts have made relevant findings of fact that the High Court can consider.

13.10.2 The effect of the 1998 Act on committal proceedings

If, as we have suggested above, the High Court has a particular role to play in applying the 1998 Act in criminal cases, this may mean that committal proceedings increase in importance. It may well be possible to argue at committal that there is no admissible evidence as the evidence presented by the prosecution should be excluded by operation of the Convention.

We consider below some of the forms of evidence that might be excluded by operation of the Convention. Clearly, for the reasons set out above, the 1998 Act means that magistrates are obliged to consider the operation of the Convention when they decide whether to commit. If a defendant believes that the magistrates have wrongly decided to commit by misapplying the Convention and so failing to exclude evidence, a judicial review may be brought. It is well established that the High Court can intervene to quash a decision to commit where the decision was taken despite the absence of admissible evidence[6].

---

1 See **4.3**.
2 See **4.10**.
3 See **4.2**.
4 See **2.2.3** and **2.5** considering precedent fact.
5 See **13.11**.
6 *R v Bedwellty Justices ex p Williams* [1997] AC 225, HL.

13.11 REMEDIES AVAILABLE TO THE COURTS UNDER THE 1998 ACT

The 1998 Act provides that:

> 'In relation to any act (or proposed act) of a public authority which the court finds is (or would be) unlawful, it may grant such relief or remedy, or make such order, within its powers as it considers just and appropriate.'[1]

This section may come to have considerable significance in the context of criminal proceedings. In striving for compatibility between domestic law and the Convention, the criminal courts will be able to intervene at all stages of criminal proceedings to implement the Convention. The courts will be able to use their existing powers to stay proceedings, consider the legitimacy of detention and the admissibility of evidence, stop proceedings once commenced, and otherwise intervene if unlawful acts under the Convention are found. The High Court, in the exercise of its supervisory role, will be able to review decisions made in these and other areas.

The courts are likely to be enthusiastic to use the powers available to them, as set out above. Both the provisions of the 1998 Act and the debates surrounding the passage of the Bill have revealed the radically different approach, which the courts will in future adopt when making decisions. Nowhere has this been better summarised than by the Lord Chancellor, Lord Irvine, during his speech at the Tom Sergant Memorial Lecture on 16 December 1997 when he stated:

> '... The courts' decisions will be based on a more overtly principled, indeed moral, basis. The Court will look at the positive right. It will only accept an interference with that right where a justification, allowed under the Convention, is made out. The scrutiny will not be limited to seeing if the words of an exception can be satisfied. The Court will need to be satisfied that the spirit of this exception is made out. It will need to be satisfied that the interference with the protected right is justified in the public interest in a free democratic society. Moreover, the Courts will in this area have to apply the Convention principle of proportionality. This means the Court will be looking substantively at that question. It will not be limited to a secondary review of the decision making process but at the primary question of the merits of the decision itself.

> In reaching its judgment, therefore, the Court will need to expand and explain its own view of whether the conduct is legitimate. It will produce in short a decision on the morality of the conduct and not simply its compliance with the bare letter of the law.'[2]

This shows clearly that the criminal courts will be expected to take an interventionist approach to the Convention. Thus, for example, they may well act to exclude evidence obtained in breach of the Convention in circumstances

---

1   Human Rights Act 1998, s 8(1).
2   In the field of judicial review these words may have particular potential significance. If on a review by the High Court of an alleged breach of Convention rights the judges truly can impose their own decision on the merits, rather than applying the more restrictive established judicial review criteria, judicial review will become in this context a hearing de novo. Contrast this with the present role of the court as set out at **2.2.3** and **2.10**.

without finding themselves bound by the current law governing the admissibility of evidence[1].

13.12 PRACTICAL EXAMPLES OF THE APPLICATION OF THE 1998 ACT

The circumstances of potential applicability of the 1998 Act are numerous, and the criminal practitioner must constantly have the Convention in mind. Set out below are illustrations of likely areas where representations under the Convention will, on occasion, be necessary. The illustrations are not supposed to be comprehensive. The Convention calls for practitioners to be imaginative so that they identify the relevance of the Convention to the unique circumstances of their cases. Practitioners may also find it of assistance to consult a specialist text on the 1998 Act.

13.13 THE EFFECT OF THE CONVENTION ON THE ADMISSIBILITY OF EVIDENCE

One area where the 1998 Act is likely to have particular effect is on the admissibility of evidence. In particular, fresh impetus and new emphasis are likely to be given to applications to exclude evidence. The court will no longer simply focus on the concept of fairness within the proceedings[2], but will, henceforth, have to consider as well the wider concerns enshrined in the Convention. The potential implications of this are profound and wide-ranging. It is important to note, however, that Article 6 of the Convention does not include any provisions regarding the admissibility of evidence. As a result, the Convention does not mean that evidence obtained in breach of the Convention should automatically be excluded[3].

13.13.1 The Convention and evidence obtained in breach of the right to silence or the protection against self-incrimination

Article 6(2) of the Convention contains a presumption of innocence[4], and thereby raises the issue of the extent to which a defendant should be protected from self-incrimination. European decisions have, however, recognised that domestic laws can require the defendant to establish certain elements of his defence[5] and presumptions of law or fact can be in favour of the prosecution if they are within 'reasonable limits'[6].

Linked to the presumption of innocence is the right to a fair trial under Article 6(1) of the Convention. This right includes a right to silence. The consistent

---

1 See **13.13**.
2 Police and Criminal Evidence Act 1984, s 78 and common laws that survived the implementation of that section.
3 *Schenk v Switzerland* (1988) 13 EHRR 242.
4 See **13.5**.
5 *Lingens v Austria* (1986) 8 EHRR 407.
6 *Salabiaku v France* (1993) 13 EHRR 379 at para 28.

approach of the court has been that any legal compulsion to produce incriminating evidence infringes that right of silence. For example, the court has held that it was inconsistent with this recognised right to silence to compel someone to produce bank statements which were material to a customs investigation[1].

Under current domestic law, there has been both a partial loss of the right of silence and the implementation, in certain circumstances, of questioning under compulsion. Under both of these developments, the defendant is put at risk of self-incrimination and has arguably lost his right to silence.

For example, ss 434 and 436 of the Companies Act 1985 oblige company officers to answer questions posed by Board of Trade Inspectors. Similarly, when an individual is confronted by the representatives of the Serious Fraud Office acting under s 2 of the Criminal Justice Act 1987, he must supply information, produce documents and answer questions as requested.

The European Court of Human Rights has held that the right to silence and the right not to incriminate oneself were generally recognised standards which lay at the heart of the notion of a fair procedure under Article 6 of the Convention. The court held that the use of statements made under compulsion to company inspectors under s 434 of the Companies Act 1985 during a criminal trial deprived the defendant of the right to a fair hearing under Article 6(1)[2]. Interestingly, the court's view was that it was immaterial that the statements were neutral, since they could still be used as a part of the prosecution case.

Sections 34 to 37 of the Criminal Justice and Public Order Act 1994 have significantly eroded the right to silence as inferences can be drawn that are adverse to the accused. For example, under s 34 of the 1994 Act, an inference can arise from a failure to mention a relevant fact relied on as part of a defence when it might reasonably have been mentioned during questioning.

On the basis of the previous decisions of the European institutions as set out above, the domestic courts may well find that these sections are inconsistent with either Article 6(1) or Article 6(2). The presumption of innocence is founded in part on the principle that the prosecuting authorities must be able to establish guilt without compelling the accused to answer questions, thereby exposing him to the risk of self-incrimination, either through his answers or his silence. As a result, the instances of legal compulsion to speak contained in ss 34 to 37 of the Criminal Justice and Public Order Act 1994 may well be directly incompatible with this important Convention protection.

Particular considerations may apply in relation to s 35 of the Criminal Justice and Public Order Act 1994. A provision similar to s 35 of the Criminal Justice and Public Order Act 1994 has been given some anticipatory attention[3]. The defendant was detained under the Prevention of Terrorism (Temporary Provisions) Act 1989 and he consistently refused to answer police questions and declined to give or call evidence at trial. The court confined its decision to the

---

1   *Funke v France* (1993) 16 EHRR 297 at para 44.
2   *Saunders v UK* (1996) 23 EHRR 313 at paras 75 and 76.
3   *Murray v UK* (1996) 22 EHRR 29.

instant facts, and found that the drawing of inferences from silence in that case did not interfere with the right to a fair trial. However, the court expressly stated:

> '[T]here can be no doubt that the right to remain silent under police questioning and the privilege against self-incrimination are generally recognised international standards which lie at the heart of the notion of a fair procedure under Article 6. By providing the accused with protection against improper compulsion by the authorities these immunities contribute to avoiding miscarriages of justice and to securing the aim of Article 6.'[1]

Further, both the Commission and the court recognised that a jury, which does not give reasons in the way a 'Diplock Judge' must, might not so carefully consider the weight to be given to the adverse inference. Finally, in this case the independent evidence against the accused was overwhelming and there was substantial dissent on the part of Judges. It is likely, therefore, that this case will not be determinative of a challenge to the compatibility of s 35, particularly given that a further challenge to the legality of drawing such inferences in Northern Irish cases has been declared admissible by the Commission[2].

13.13.2 The Convention and hearsay evidence

Article 6(3)(d) requires that witnesses should be called to give oral evidence and be cross-examined. This general principle that hearsay evidence should not be used in criminal proceedings accords with the common law rule in England and Wales. The validity, under the Convention, of the domestic exceptions to this principle will fall for full consideration in due course. In particular, ss 23 and 24 of the Criminal Justice Act 1988 will need to be considered. These provisions provide, inter alia, exceptions to the hearsay rule in relation to witnesses who are unfit, abroad, dead, untraceable or who have been intimidated. The safeguards are set out in ss 25 and 26, depending on the nature of the statement.

A general overview of the relevant cases decided by the European Court, although not consistent, reveals a particular concern when the hearsay evidence substantially founded the conviction, or when it was the only significant item of evidence. Accordingly, when convictions are based critically on hearsay evidence, notwithstanding the safeguards of ss 25 and 26, they may be in breach of Article 6[3].

A further debate will revolve around hearsay evidence which the defence wishes to rely on. Article 6(3)(d) is aimed at evidence which the prosecution wish to use, and, under the Convention, it is arguable that the requirement of ensuring a fair trial for the defendant involves permitting greater flexibility as regards defence hearsay. Not infrequently, the defendant wishes to refer to third party confessions which are currently excluded. This prohibition is likely to be challenged under the Convention.

---

1 *Murray v UK* (1996) 22 EHRR 29 at para 45.
2 *Quinn v UK* (1996) 23 EHRR CD 41.
3 See *Trivedi v UK* [1997] EHRLR 521; *Quinn v UK* (1996) 23 EHRR CD 41; *Unterpertinger v Austria* (1986) 13 EHRR 175; *Kostovski v Netherlands* (1989) 12 EHRR 434.

13.13.3 The Convention and anonymity of witnesses

The use of anonymous witnesses may also give rise to challenges under the Convention. It is not unknown under domestic law for witnesses to give evidence when they are screened from a defendant, with their voices distorted to prevent recognition, and, in exceptional circumstances, to have their identity in all respects concealed[1]. Under Article 6(3)(d) of the Convention, the defendant has a right to examine and have examined witnesses against him.

The European Court of Human Rights has held that, although the use of evidence from anonymous witnesses is not under all circumstances inconsistent with Article 6, a conviction should not be based to a decisive extent on such material[2]. The court decided in particular that police witnesses should only remain anonymous in the last resort, when necessary to ensure their usefulness in future operations. This decision will be of great importance when it is suggested that key witnesses should be allowed to preserve their anonymity.

13.13.4 Interference with correspondence

Interference with correspondence can violate Article 8(1) and requires justification under Article 8(2)[3]. Whilst most cases touching on correspondence have arisen in respect of prisoners, the principle applies to everyone[4]. In the UK, letters from prisoners containing either supposed admissions or statements against interest have been used frequently in criminal proceedings. In the future, evidence founded on intercepted mail is likely to be subjected to far greater scrutiny. That is because cases brought under the Convention reveal that a prisoner has the right to correspond with his or her lawyer which is almost unfettered[5]. In addition, whilst the prison authorities may censor non-legal correspondence, European decisions reveal that this interference should now be scrutinised with care to ensure it is restricted to communications which might be prejudicial to security or of a criminal nature[6]. Accordingly, reading mail to try to find some incriminatory evidence to use for an existing prosecution is likely to be deemed unlawful, and it may lead to the exclusion of that evidence.

13.13.5 The right to respect for private and family life

Article 8 is also relevant to other forms of evidence. Under Article 8, there is the right to respect for private and family life. The European Court of Human Rights has relied on this Article to find that respect for confidentiality of an individual's medical records is a vital principle and that domestic law must

---

1   Eg *R v Taylor (G)* (1994) *The Times*, 17 August, CA.
2   *Van Mechelen and others v Netherlands* (1997) 25 EHRR 647 at paras 52–55.
3   Although most of the cases considering correspondence have considered letters, correspondence includes telephone calls (*Malone v UK* (1984) 7 EHRR 14). Presumably it also extends to other forms of electronic media.
4   Eg *Malone v UK* (1984) 7 EHRR 14 considering the telephone calls and letters made by the applicant while not in custody.
5   *Golder v UK* (1975) 1 EHRR 524; *McCallum v UK* (1990) 13 EHRR 597.
6   *Silver v UK* (1983) 5 EHRR 347; *Boyle and Rice v UK* (1988) 10 EHRR 425.

afford proper safeguards to prevent disclosure which is incompatible with Article 8[1]. Further, they found that these principles apply with particular force to information about HIV infection.

However, the investigation and prosecution of crime and the publicity of court proceedings can, in the public interest, outweigh the need to protect this confidentiality. It must be shown, however, that there is the most careful scrutiny applied before disclosure, and safeguards imposed afterwards to secure effective protection.

For example, the European Court of Human Rights has considered a case where the applicant's doctor had been compelled to give evidence as to the applicant's medical history on the trial of her husband on charges of manslaughter based on his infection of others with the HIV virus[2]. The medical records had become part of the investigation file. Although it was found there had been an interference with her right to respect for her private life, that did not amount to a breach of the Convention. The interference was deemed necessary in a democratic society, as the evidence was potentially decisive. The national authorities were entitled to think that weighty public interests militated in favour of the investigation and prosecution of the serious allegation that the husband was aware of his infection[3].

13.14 THE EFFECT OF THE CONVENTION ON THE RIGHT TO BAIL

To justify detention before trial, the prosecution must establish 'relevant and sufficient' circumstances for the continuing detention[4] and the suggested justification will be set against the undoubted strong presumption in favour of bail under the Convention. The provisions of the Bail Act 1976 generally, but not entirely, match the requirements of the Convention. The potential justifications for a refusal to grant bail under the Convention are as set out below.

The risk of absconding is a potential justification for deciding to refuse bail. The decided cases refer to such factors as relate to 'the character of the person involved, his morals, his home, his occupation, his assets, his family ties and all kinds of links with the country in which he is being prosecuted'[5] as being relevant to this issue. It is important to observe that, while the potential severity of sentence is something which the court can have in mind, it is not of itself an independent ground for refusing bail, and could not alone justify continued detention[6].

---

1 *Z v Finland* (1997) 25 EHRR 371.
2 Ibid.
3 It is significant that a 10-year limitation on the confidentiality of the data was not justified and so did amount to a breach of the Convention. The data was required to be kept confidential for a far longer period.
4 *Wemhoff v Germany* (1968) 1 EHRR 55 at para 12.
5 *Neumeister v Austria (No 1)* (1968) 1 EHRR 91 at para 10.
6 *Neumeister v Austria (No 1)* (1968) 1 EHRR 91; *Letellier v France* (1991) 14 EHRR 83.

A fear that a defendant will interefere with the course of public justice can justify detention. The critical issue here is that the risk must be well founded, in the sense that it is identifiable and supported by evidence[1]. The predictable areas of interference are relevant, such as interfering with witnesses, tipping off other suspects and concealing or destroying material evidence[2].

A need to prevent other offences can also justify detention. It must be established that there are good grounds for believing that the detainee, once released, is likely to commit further offences[3]. The good grounds can include the nature of previous offences and the severity of sentences imposed[4]. It is questionable whether the restriction in domestic law on a grant of bail for a fresh offence that applies where a person is on bail for another offence is consistent with the Convention. This is because this provision is distinct from the restriction on the right to bail where there is a fear of further offences and so appears to be unrelated to the fear of further offences[5].

The need to preserve the peace can also justify detention. This ground relates to the exceptional class of grave case where the potential public reaction is such that release on bail will lead to public disorder. In such circumstances, temporary detention on remand may be justified[6]. Clearly, it is questionable whether the domestic power to refuse bail for the protection of the defendant is consistent with the Convention[7].

13.14.1 The effect of the Convention on the procedure for obtaining bail

The Convention may well give rise to potential arguments about the procedure for granting bail. In this context, we consider the issue of disclosure prior to bail applications later when we consider disclosure generally. It is significant to note, however, that the prosecution may well be obliged to provide additional disclosure prior to bail applications[8].

Another example of the effect of the Convention is that conditions imposed on bail can be contrary to the Convention. The European Court of Human Rights has held that the conditions attached to any grant of bail must be carefully imposed and they must be reasonable. Personal circumstances must be assessed, and if a surety is fixed, it must be in a sensible sum[9]. This requirement is breached on occasion, when unobtainable sums are fixed by the court granting bail.

Further, courts will have to be alive to the need for giving adequate reasons for a refusal to grant bail[10]. As a result, it is questionable whether the current practice

---

1   *Clooth v Belgium* (1991) 14 EHRR 717 at para 44.
2   *Letellier v France* (1991) 14 EHRR 83.
3   *Matznetter v Austria* (1969) 1 EHRR 198; *Toth v Austria* (1991) 14 EHRR 551.
4   *Toth v Austria* (1991) 14 EHRR 551.
5   Bail Act 1976, Sch 1, Part I, paras 2 and 2A.
6   *Letellier v France* (1991) 14 EHRR 83.
7   Bail Act 1976, Sch 1, Part I, para. 3.
8   See **13.15**.
9   *Neimeister v Austria (No 1)* (1968) 1 EHRR 91.
10   *Tomasi v France* (1992) 15 EHRR 1.

of ticking boxes on a standard form, and announcing which boxes have been so marked, fulfils this requirement.

The current domestic regime which governs repeat applications for bail is founded on the principle of the need to establish a change of circumstance[1]. This may also be contrary to the Convention as the European Court of Human Rights has held that a defendant should be allowed to make renewed applications at reasonable intervals[2].

13.14.2 Challenging bail decisions said to be contrary to the Convention

As should be clear from the case-law set out above, the grounds for refusing bail and the procedure for applying for bail will provide a fertile source of debate over apparent inconsistencies between Convention and domestic law. As a result, the question arises as to how to challenge bail decisions that are said to be contrary to the Convention.

Normally, it is not possible to apply for a judicial review of a decision to refuse bail[3]. This is because one should normally appeal decisions on bail to a judge of the Crown Court or to a High Court judge in Chambers. However, where issues of principle involving the application of the Convention arise, there may be grounds for applying for judicial review. As we noted above, the High Court is likely to have an important role in interpreting the Convention and the Act[4]. As a result, it may be willing to consider judicial reviews that raise important issues of principle regarding the Convention so that it can give guidance that will have general effect. In these circumstances the judicial review will probably not be a challenge to the decision to refuse bail. It will also challenge something more fundamental such as the policy of prosecution regarding disclosure.

13.15 THE EFFECT OF THE CONVENTION ON DISCLOSURE

A likely source of dispute will be the extent of the prosecution's duty to disclose evidence prior to bail applications. The European case-law suggests that it is clear that the Convention requires far greater disclosure of evidence at the time of applying for bail than that which is currently provided by domestic law[5]. The Criminal Procedure and Investigations Act 1996 only requires disclosure for summary offences when a plea of not guilty has been entered[6], and for cases to be transferred or committed for trial when committal or transfer has occurred[7].

---

1   *R v Nottingham Justices ex p Davies* [1981] QB 38, DC.
2   *Bezicheri v Italy* (1989) 12 EHRR 210.
3   *Re Herbage* (1985) *The Times*, 25 October, DC.
4   See **13.10.1**.
5   Criminal Procedure and Investigations Act 1996, compared with *Lamy v Belgium* (1989) 11 EHRR 529.
6   Criminal Procedure and Investigations Act 1996, s 1(1).
7   Ibid, s 1(2).

The obligation to disclose material does not merely arise in the context of bail. Cases decided under the Convention impose a burden on the prosecution to disclose any material in their possession, or to which they could gain access, which may assist the accused in exonerating himself or in obtaining a reduction in sentence[1]. The extent to which there is a discretion to withhold such evidence is questionable. Indeed, the European Court has expressly left as an open question whether or not the current rules in relation to public interest immunity are adequate for the purposes of the Convention[2]. This issue was raised then in the context of non-disclosure of material relating to a witness's credibility.

As regards the general duty, in relation to disclosure the Court observed:

'[That it] considers that it is a requirement of fairness under Article 6(1), indeed one which is recognised under English law, that the prosecution authorities disclose to the defence all material evidence for or against the accused and that the failure to do so in the present case gave rise to a defect in the trial proceedings.'[3]

Similarly, the Commission has also stated that:

'... [T]he prosecution has at its disposal, to back the accusation, facilities deriving from its powers of investigation supported by judicial and police machinery with considerable technical resources and means of coercion. It is in order to establish equality, as far as possible, between the prosecution and the defence that national legislation ... if it entrusts the investigation to the Public Prosecutor's Department, instructs the latter to gather evidence in favour of the accused as well as evidence against him. ...

[E]veryone charged with a criminal offence should enjoy ... the opportunity to acquaint himself, for the purposes of preparing his defence, with the results of investigations carried out throughout the proceedings ... [A] right of access to the prosecution file ... can be inferred from Article 6, paragraph 3(b). ...

In short, Article 6, paragraph 3(b) recognises the right of the accused to have at his disposal, for the purposes of exonerating himself or of obtaining a reduction in his sentence, all relevant elements that have been or could be collected by the competent authorities.'[4]

It had been held that, where domestic law provided for proof of offences by the production of an official report, it was particularly important that a defendant should have access to the case file and have the opportunity to take copies of the documents therein. Denial of such access had made it impossible for him to prepare his defence and was inconsistent with his right to a fair trial under Articles 6(1) and 6(3)(b)[5].

While some aspects of the current procedures under the Criminal Procedure and Investigations Act 1996 will be upheld, it is submitted that the limitations

---

1 *Jespers v Belgium* (1981) 27 DR 61 at para 58.
2 *Edwards v UK* (1992) 15 EHRR 417.
3 Ibid, at para 36.
4 *Jespers v Belgium* (1981) 27 DR 61 at para 55 onwards.
5 *Foucher v France* (1997) 25 EHRR 234. See, however, *R v Stratford Justices ex p Imbert* (1999) *The Times*, 25 February, DC in which it was held that a refusal to disclose witness statements before trial was not a breach of the Convention.

on disclosure will need to be carefully reexamined after implementation. In particular, with summary offences, the duty of disclosure only exists if there is a plea of not guilty[1]. This imposes a limitation not envisaged by cases decided under the Convention. That limitation is inconsistent with the duty to disclose all relevant material so as to enable the accused to gather material which may be relevant to the level of sentence. It may also be a breach of Article 6 to impose on the defence the duty to serve a defence statement prior to secondary disclosure.

13.16 THE EFFECT OF THE CONVENTION ON THE TRIAL PROCEDURE

The Convention clearly sets minimum standards for the procedure to be adopted during a criminal trial. In particular, Article 6(1) entitles a defendant to a fair trial. The right to disclosure is just one particular aspect of the general right under the Convention to a fair trial. The right to a fair trial is clearly a broad principle that may require judges to review aspects of the trial process to determine whether they are fair. In making those determinations, judges will clearly take account of the principles that have been identified by the European Court of Human Rights as being essential elements of a fair trial.

The principle that is likely to prove most significant in practice is that which requires that parties to criminal trials be given an equality of arms. This means that a defendant must have 'a reasonable opportunity of presenting his case to the court under conditions which do not place him at a substantial disadvantage vis-à-vis his opponent'[2]. When applying this principle, the European Court has emphasised the importance of the appearance of fairness in the administration of justice[3]. This principle arises from Article 6(1) and so it has wider application than the specific rights in Article 6(3). This means that arguments about equality of arms are not restricted to arguments about obligations to provide the sort of facilities required by Article 6(3).

An example of the importance of equality of arms arises in the context of expert evidence. It is a breach of the principle if a defence expert is not accorded equal treatment to one appointed by the prosecution or court[4]. In addition the disclosure requirements set out above arise from the principle of equality of arms[5].

Another principle that may give rise to litigation is the right to a reasoned judgment. The European Court has held that national courts must indicate with 'sufficient clarity' the reasons for their decisions so that a defendant may exercise any right of appeal[6]. It has clearly been accepted that a jury trial is

---

1   Criminal Procedure and Investigations Act 1996, s 1(1)(a); see, however, *R v DPP ex p Lee* (1999) *The Times*, 26 April, DC holding that a duty to make disclosure can arise in circumstances that are not governed by the 1996 Act.
2   *Kaufman v Belgium* (1987) 50 DR 98 at 115.
3   *Borgers v Belgium* (1991) 15 EHRR 92 at para 24.
4   *Bonisch v Austria* (1985) 9 EHRR 191.
5   See **13.15**.
6   *Hadjianastassiou v Greece* (1992) 16 EHRR 219 at para 33.

consistent with the Convention, so the obligation to give reasons is unlikely to affect the Crown Court. The obligation to give reasons, however, may mean that magistrates are required to give reasons for their decisions in circumstances where they have not been previously required[1]. Reasons are necessary so that defendants can decide whether magistrates have correctly applied the law and so decide whether to appeal by case stated or apply for judicial review.

The principles set out above are not the only principles that Article 6(1) is held to impose on the conduct of criminal trials. Other principles include a right to silence[2], a right to be present at trial[3], and a right to be tried without a 'virulent press campaign against the accused'[4].

13.16.1 The Convention and the right to be tried within a reasonable time period

Two Convention obligations require criminal trials to be conducted within a reasonable time period. First, Article 5(3) governs the length of detention and so implicitly governs the length of the period until trial, by imposing time limits on the various stages of criminal proceedings. For example, this has been held to mean that detention in police custody for periods in excess of 4 days and 11 hours without charge amounted to a breach of Article 5(3) in the circumstances of the case[5]. There is then a further obligation under Article 5(3) to bring the detainee to trial within a reasonable period.

Article 6, however, imposes an additional obligation to bring proceedings to a conclusion within a reasonable period, whether or not a defendant is in custody. The reasonable time period is not necessarily the same, so that delay prior to trial can amount to a breach of Article 5(3) but not a breach of Article 6[6].

In determining whether a trial has taken place within a reasonable time period, the European Court has concluded that a number of factors are relevant. First, it is the obligation of the State to organise its legal systems so that they comply with Article 6(1)[7]. As a consequence, a lack of resources is no justification for delay. In contrast, the defendant's conduct may be an explanation, even if he has merely been exercising his lawful rights[8]. Finally, the complexity of the case is a relevant factor[9].

---

1   See **2.14.2** for a consideration of the present duty to give reasons.
2   See **13.3.1**.
3   *Ekbatani v Sweden* (1988) 13 EHRR 504. This right may be waived by the defendant; *C v Italy* (1998) 56 DR 40.
4   *X v Austria* (1963) 11 CD 31 at 43.
5   *Brogan and Others v UK* (1988) 11 EHRR 117.
6   *Neumeister v Austria (No 1)* (1968) 1 EHRR 91.
7   *Zimmerman v Switzerland* (1983) 6 EHRR 17.
8   *Konig v FRG* (1978) 2 EHRR 170.
9   *Neumeister v Austria (No 1)* (1968) 1 EHRR 91.

13.17 THE SPECIFIC RIGHTS CONTAINED IN ARTICLE 6(3) OF THE CONVENTION

The rights contained in Article 6(3) are specific rights that apply in addition to the general principles requiring a fair trial under Article 6(1). Thus, for example, there is a specific right to legal aid in certain circumstances. Thus, the fact that, increasingly, defendants are appearing in the magistrates' court unrepresented, as legal aid has been turned down by the court and possibly the Legal Aid Board, may be a breach of the Convention.

Although the rights under Article 6(3)(c) are not without limit, the core right is to free legal assistance if one is indigent and if the interests of justice so require. For example, the court has held that, where a defendant was denied legal aid for committal proceedings for poll tax default, there had been a violation of Articles 6(1) and 6(3)(c) taken together[1]. The court focused on the twin issues of the complexity of the case and the potential severity of the penalty in finding breaches of the Convention.

13.18 THE CONVENTION AND SENTENCING

The Convention contains specific restrictions regarding sentencing. For example, Article 7 of the Convention provides that there should be no punishment for an act that was not an offence at the date of commission[2]. In practice, however, it may well be that provisions of the Convention that contain specific obligations regarding sentencing are not the provisions that result in the greatest number of challenges to sentences under the 1998 Act. Instead, it may be other provisions that implicitly limit sentencing that give rise to challenges.

For example, Article 8 of the Convention is of particular relevance to sentencing, as many sentences interfere with a defendant's family life or private life. For example, if a criminal court is considering making a recommendation for deportation it might be argued that deportation is a breach of Article 8[3]. For this argument to succeed, it would be necessary to show that there was an interference with the defendant's family or private life that could not be justified as being necessary in a democratic society. Article 8 allows the court to take account of the seriousness of the offence when it considers whether any interference is justified.

13.19 HUMAN RIGHTS AND THE PROSECUTION

The European Convention is not merely a set of rules that restrict the actions of prosecutors. There is clear authority that the Convention obliges prosecutors

---

1 *Benham v United Kingdom* (1996) 22 EHRR 293.
2 See **13.5**.
3 Eg *Boujlifa v France* (unreported) 21 October 1997.

to act in certain circumstances. For example, the right to an effective remedy for alleged breaches of the Convention means that it is a breach of the Convention for a prosecutor to fail to carry out a thorough and proper investigation when it is said that a person has been the victim of ill-treatment that amounts to a breach of Article 3 of the Convention[1]. As breaches of Article 3 can arise from the actions of persons who are not agents of the State[2], it is certainly arguable that it is a breach of Article 3 for a prosecutor to fail to carry out a thorough and proper investigation into allegations of serious violent crime.

The significance of this is clear. Some of the obligations of the Convention enable the State to justify behaviour in certain limited circumstances. For example, breaches of Article 8 of the Convention can be justified in certain limited circumstances. One possible justification would be the positive obligations placed on prosecutors by the Convention.

13.20 THE CONVENTION AND SPECIFIC OFFENCES

We have concentrated on the effect of the 1998 Act on criminal procedure as this is likely to be the most common area of challenge. It is important, however, to be aware that, in principle, it could be argued that the definition of the offence being prosecuted constitutes a breach of the Convention.

For example, s 13 of the Sexual Offences Act 1956 provides that it is an offence to commit an act of gross indecency. It is likely that certain forms of consensual homosexual activity are in breach of this provision. Section 1 of the Sexual Offences Act 1967 provides that consensual homosexual acts in private are not an offence. However, it also defines private acts as acts not involving more than two people. As a result, consensual acts involving three or more people can be an offence.

It is clearly arguable that the present interpretation of s 13 of the Sexual Offences Act 1956 is a breach of the Convention. This is because the European Court of Human Rights has held that legislation that limiting homosexual activity was a restriction of the applicant's private life[3].

13.21 THE CONVENTION AND PRISON CONDITIONS

The 1998 Act will also be relevant to other situations that a criminal practitioner may be asked to advise on. In particular, it may well result in prisoners bringing actions based on Convention rights to assert their rights. The Convention has

---

1   *Aydin v Turkey* (1997) 25 EHRR 251. Note that the right to an effective remedy is provided by Article 13 of the Convention. Although rights under Article 13 are not enforceable under the 1998 Act, the previous Common Law position must mean that public officials should act in accordance with Article 13 unless than can provide a significant public interest reason for a decision to fail to act in accordance with Article 13.
2   *HLR v France* (1997) 26 EHRR 29.
3   *Dudgeon v United Kingdom* (1981) 4 EHRR 149.

historically been used by prisoners to develop rights that the prison service has refused to recognise. For example, cases have been brought regarding interference with correspondence[1].

When advising on a prisoner's rights, it is unlikely that cases will arise in which it will be possible to advise that the conditions of detention amount to a breach of Article 3. The case-law on Article 3 shows clearly that the standards of detention need to be particularly low before the European Court will find a breach of Article 3. For example, the European Court of Human Rights has held that detention conditions that resulted in extreme discomfort and which involved irksome and painful exercises were not a breach of Article 3[2].

The area where the European Court has been most willing to find breaches of Article 3 is where there has been deliberate physical assault. For example, the use of the birch as a criminal sentence on the Isle of Man was held to be a breach of Article 3[3].

13.22 PRACTICAL CONSIDERATIONS REGARDING JUDICIAL REVIEW

Under Article 6(1), a defendant is entitled to trial by an impartial tribunal. The High Court frequently remits cases back to the magistrates' court, or other tribunals, following a judicial review or an appeal by way of case stated for further hearing. The European Court has held that Article 6(1) does not require, as a general rule, that the further proceedings must be considered by a differently constituted court. The fact that a defendant who had been convicted in absentia and is subsequently retried in his presence by the same judge or judges is insufficient to cast doubt on the impartiality of the tribunal. Impartiality can be avoided if, at the second trial, the court undertakes a fresh consideration of the whole case, including new evidence[4].

The Convention case law does not mean, however, that a successful party in the High Court is prevented from arguing that the common law rules against apparent bias mean that any retrial should take place before a fresh tribunal[5]. The absence of any requirement under the Convention does not mean that the common law cannot impose such a requirement. The statutory requirement that courts should not act in a manner that is contrary to the Convention does not mean that the courts should not uphold common law rights if they do not conflict with the Convention.

---

1 Eg *Golder v UK* (1975) 1 EHRR 524. See **13.3.4**.
2 *Ireland v UK* (1978) 2 EHRR 25 at paras 179 to 181.
3 *Tyrer v UK* (1978) 2 EHRR 1.
4 *Thomann v Switzerland* (1996) 24 EHRR 533. See, however, *Ferrantelli v Italy* (1996) 23 EHRR 288 in which a defendant's right to a trial by an impartial tribunal was infringed when their case was considered at different stages by the same judge. The European Court of Human Rights based this finding on the particular facts of the case.
5 See **2.8**.

Appendices

		Page
Appendix 1: Precedents – Judicial Review		221
1.	Letter before action	221
2.	Notice of application	222
3.	Other useful clauses	231
4.	Affidavit in support	234
5.	Exhibit to affidavit	239
6.	Witness statement in support	240
7.	Exhibit to a witness statement	241
8.	Bail application	242
9.	Claim form	244
10.	Witness statement as to service	246
11.	Affidavit in response	249
12.	Application for an interim order	253
13.	Draft interim order	254
14.	Skeleton argument	255
15.	Consent order	257
16.	Application notice for renewal in the Court of Appeal	258
Appendix 2: Precedent – Claim Form for Writ for Habeas Corpus		261
1.	Form 87	261
Appendix 3: Precedents – Case Stated		263
1.	Application to state a case	263
2.	Other useful clauses	265
3.	Case stated	267
4.	Notice of entry of a case stated	271
Appendix 4: Procedural Guides		273
1.	Deciding whether to proceed with a judicial review or an appeal by way of case stated	273
2.	Judicial review	277
3.	Appeal by case stated from a decision of the magistrates' court	284
4.	Appeal by case stated from a decision of the Crown Court	291
Appendix 5: Legislation and Forms		299
	Civil Procedure Rules 1998, Sch 1, Rules of the Supreme Court Orders 53, 54 and 56	299
	Forms N235, N434, N244	312
	Magistrates' Courts Act 1980 (as amended), ss 111–114	317
	Magistrates' Courts Rules 1981, rr 76–81	319

Supreme Court Act 1981 (as amended), ss 28,
28A, 29, 31, 43   322
Crown Court Rules 1982, r 26   326
Human Rights Act 1998, ss 1–9, Sch 1, the
Articles, Parts I–III   328

Appendix 1: Precedents – Judicial Review

1. Letter before action

We act for the above named. We write to inform you that our client has instructed us in relation to your decision to refuse to prosecute James Grey for the assault of our client. We have considered your letter to our client dated 10 December 1998 in which you set out your reasons for deciding not to prosecute Mr Grey.

We note that in your letter you state that you have reviewed the evidence and have concluded that you 'cannot be certain that a prosecution will be successful'. The current code for Crown Prosecutors states that you must merely be satisfied that there is a 'realistic prospect of conviction'. As a result, you would have appeared to have erred by either failing to take account of your code for Crown Prosecutors or by treating our client in a way that is inconsistent with the way in which other victims of crime are treated[1].

We have been instructed to bring judicial review proceedings challenging your decision to refuse to prosecute Mr Grey. Given the need to act promptly when applying for judicial review, we will commence judicial review proceedings unless we receive a satisfactory response to this letter within 21 days[2].

---

1 The letter before action should set out in general terms the grounds for applying for judicial review.
2 A reasonable time-limit should be set unless there is some need for more urgent action. If there is a need for urgent action, the letter should set out the reasons why proceedings are being brought as a matter of urgency.

2. Notice of application

Set out below is a specimen application for judicial review. The application relates to a case in which the applicant is challenging the decision of a magistrates' court to commit her to prison for non-payment of a fine. Further precedents in this appendix are based on the same set of fictitious facts. At the end of this precedent, some sample clauses are included that might be appropriate in other applications.

Drafting an application for judicial review is not like drafting a pleading in other forms of civil proceedings. That is partly because the rules are less precise about what must be included in the application. It is also because the High Court has a wide discretion to allow amendments to the notice of application[1]. As a result, it is not necessarily fatal if the application fails to include a ground. The precedent is detailed because it is important to supply the judge or judges with full details of the applicant's case in the application. The application is very likely to form the basis of the judge's decision and oral argument is likely to be of only limited value.

Form 86A

IN THE HIGH COURT OF JUSTICE

Applicant's Ref No.   Crown Office Reference No.

NOTICE OF APPLICATION

for Permission to Apply for

JUDICIAL REVIEW

(Order 53, r.3)

To the Master of the Crown Office, Royal Courts of Justice, Strand, London, WC2 2LL.

Applicant's Name and Address: Doris Smith
                                  1 Chancery Lane, EC4

and the description of the Applicant: A person committed to prison as a result of the decision in respect of which relief is sought[2].

Decision in respect of which relief is sought:

---

1 See **7.9** for details of the power of the High Court to allow amendments applications for judicial review.
2 Rule 3(2)(a)(i) of CPR 1998, Sch 1, RSC Ord 53 states that the application must include a 'description' of the applicant. Unfortunately the rules do not specify what is meant by the phrase 'description'. In most cases, the description is unlikely to be of any significance. However, in cases where it might be suggested that the applicant lacks standing to bring the application for judicial review it is important to include a brief statement explaining how the applicant has standing to bring the application. See **1.10** for details of the standing requirements for bringing an application for judicial review.

A decision to commit the Applicant to prison for 50 days as a result of unpaid fines which was taken by Chancery Lane Magistrates on 10 December 1998[1].

RELIEF SOUGHT[2]

(i) An order of certiorari removing the decision into the Queen's Bench Division of the High Court and quashing the decision that is the subject of this application[3];

(ii) Further, a declaration that the Applicant's detention was unlawful between 10 December 1998 and the date when this application is heard or the date when the Applicant was granted bail if the Applicant is granted bail[4];

(iv) Further, an order that this matter be listed in Part D of the Crown Office list as suitable for an expedited hearing and the time for the respondents to serve their evidence be abridged to 14 days[5];

(v) Further, bail pending the determination of this application for judicial review[6];

(vi) Further, an order that the respondent pay the Applicant's costs; and

(vii) Further or other relief[7].

An oral application is requested[8].

---

1   Although the notice of application must set out the detail of the decision, the document evidencing the decision should also be exhibited to the written evidence. Indeed, where an order of certiorari is sought to quash a decision of an inferior court, r 9(2) of CPR 1998, Sch 1, RSC Ord 53 requires a copy of the decision to be filed and verified by the written evidence unless the applicant accounts for its absence to the satisfaction of the court.
2   The application should specify all forms of relief that are sought. If more than one form of relief is sought, the application should state whether they are sought in the alternative. In particular, it should specify all forms of interim relief that are sought and also state that damages are sought if they are sought. See Chapter 11 for details of the orders that the court may make when considering an application for judicial review.
3   Certiorari is always the appropriate order where the applicant seeks to quash a decision of an inferior court. See **11.6** for further details.
4   A request for a declaration should specify the terms of the declaration sought. In practice, one would probably not seek a declaration in these terms when challenging the legality of a decision to commit to prison in the circumstances of this application. That is because a declaration is unlikely to be of value to the applicant as it may be difficult to seek damages for the period of detention (see **11.8**).
5   In cases where the applicant's detention is being challenged expedition should always be sought. See **6.2** and **6.3** for further details of listing arrangements.
6   In cases where bail is sought the application should be accompanied by a notice applying for bail. See precedent 8.
7   Although the application should always include a request for further or other relief, this should not be regarded as a substitute for specific requests for relief sought.
8   The Form 86A should state that an oral application is requested, if an oral application is requested. See **7.6** for a discussion of the circumstances when an oral application should be requested.

Name and address of Applicant's Solicitors: Brown and Partners
350 Chancery Lane
London, EC4

Dated: 11 December 1998

Signed: [*The application should be signed by the solicitors acting for the applicant.*]

GROUNDS UPON WHICH RELIEF IS SOUGHT

1.   The issues that arise in this application[1]

1.0   Whether the justices erred by taking account of an irrelevant factor when deciding not to impose an attachment of earnings order. The irrelevant factor is variations in the Applicant's earnings. Alternatively the justices misdirected themselves by holding that variations in earnings were a bar to the imposition of an attachment of earnings order.[2]

1.1   Whether the justices erred by failing to give reasons for their decision not to impose an attachment of earnings order.

1.2   Whether comments made by one of the justices showed a real risk of bias.

1.3   Whether the decision of the justices was *Wednesbury* unreasonable in all the circumstances of the case.

2.   Factual background

2.1.   The Applicant is a single parent with one child aged 19 months. The Applicant has sole responsibility for this child. The Applicant has worked for thirteen years as a cleaner at her local school. Her earnings vary from about £50 per week to about £150 per week as they depend on overtime. The Applicant's earnings and child benefit are her only sources of income[3].

---

1   It is helpful for the judge or judges to have some basic guide to the reason for the application when they consider the rest of the application if the application is long.

2   For the purposes of this precedent, it is assumed that one ground only became apparent after the respondent served their evidence as a result of matters revealed in that evidence. Where facts arise that give rise to an additional ground, Form 86A should be amended to plead this additional ground. These amendments should include the additional facts relied on as well as the law relied on and the ground. Where the amendments do not result in fundamental change, it is helpful to present the amended Form 86A to the court with the new passages underlined and deletions struck through. Leave will be required to rely on the amended notice of application. See **7.9** for details of how to seek leave to amend Form 86A.

3   In this case, it is important to include significant details of the applicant's background as one of the grounds is that the decision of the justice to impose the maximum period of imprisonment is *Wednesbury* unreasonable given the significant mitigating factors that exist.

2.2. Chancery Lane Magistrates have imposed fines on the Applicant for two non-imprisonable offences. In relation to those fines the following amounts are outstanding:
   (a) In relation to one matter of no insurance on 13 June 1997 £1635 is outstanding. The original fine was for a total of £2000; and
   (b) In relation to one matter of no vehicle excise licence on 20 June 1997 £350 is outstanding. That is the amount of the original fine.

2.3. On 12 March 1998 the original orders for payment of these fines were varied so that the sums could be paid at the rate of £5 per week. The Applicant appeared at court on that date. Since that date the Applicant has made only one payment of £25 on 15 June 1998[1].

2.4 On 18 July 1998 a default summons was issued which was returnable on 4 September 1998. The Applicant failed to attend and a warrant was issued for her arrest.

2.5 On 10 December 1998 the Applicant appeared before Chancery Lane Magistrates' Court in relation to these fines. The Applicant was represented by the Duty Solicitor, Jackie Jones, who put forward a number of matters in mitigation including the matters set out in paragraph 2.1, above. The Applicant gave evidence on oath to the effect that her employer would have no objection to an attachment of earnings order. One of the justices was heard to whisper during the application that the submissions were a waste of time as you could never trust somebody who refused to pay their fines. The Applicant's solicitor objected to that remark and asked the bench of justices to disqualify themselves as one member of the bench had shown apparent bias. That application was refused.

2.6 On 10 December 1998 the justices found that the Applicant had shown culpable neglect and ordered that she serve 36 days imprisonment in default in respect of the larger fine and 14 days in respect of the smaller fine. The periods of imprisonment were to be served consecutively. No reasons were given for the order other than the finding of culpable neglect.

2.7 <u>The justices completed a pro forma that has been used by Chancery Lane justices to ensure that magistrates consider the alternative methods of enforcement. The justices made a number of findings including, inter alia, that an attachment of earnings order could not be made because of 'wage fluctuations'.</u>

---

1   There is a duty of disclosure imposed on applicants for judicial review. See **7.7** for full details. In practice that means that applicants should give details of significant matters that are adverse to their interests. An application that appears one-sided may be held to fail to comply with the duty of disclosure and will lack credibility.

3. Legal Framework

3.1 By section 82(3) of the Magistrates' Courts Act 1980:

> 'Where on the occasion of the offender's conviction a magistrates' court does not issue a warrant of commitment for a default in paying any such sum ... it shall not thereafter issue a warrant of commitment ... unless ... the court has since the conviction inquired into his means in his presence on at least one occasion[1].'

3.2 By section 82(4) of the Magistrates' Courts Act 1980:

> 'Where a magistrates' court is required by subsection (3) above to inquire into a person's means, the court may not on the occasion of the inquiry or at any time thereafter issue a warrant of commitment for a default in paying any such sum unless:
>
> (a) in the case of an offence punishable with imprisonment, the offender appears to the court to have sufficient means to pay the sum forthwith; or
>
> (b) the court:
>
>   (i) is satisfied that the default is due to the offender's wilful refusal or culpable neglect; and
>
>   (ii) it has considered or tried all other methods of enforcing payment of the sum and it appears to the court that they are inappropriate or unsuccessful.'

3.2A By the Attachment of Earnings Act 1971 the magistrates' court may make an attachment of earnings order so that sums are deducted from the earnings of a fine defaulter by an employer. Section 6(5) of the 1971 Act provides that:

> 'The order shall specify:
>
> (a) the normal deduction rate, that is to say, the rate (expressed as a sum of money per week, month or other period) at which the court thinks it reasonable for the debtor's earnings to be applied to meeting his liability under the relevant adjudication; and
>
> (b) the protected earnings rate, that is to say the rate (so expressed) below which, having regard to the debtor's resources and needs, the court thinks it reasonable that the earnings actually paid to him should not be reduced.'

Schedule 3 to the 1971 Act provides a 'Scheme of deductions' which requires the employer to calculate the amount of money to be deducted from the earnings of a fine defaulter on each pay-day.

3.2B In *R v York Magistrates Court ex p Grimes* (1997) *The Times*, 27 June the Divisional Court held that fluctuating earnings were no bar to the making of an attachment of earnings order.

---

1 Although it is normal practice to cite relevant passages of statutory authorities, the citation of relevant passages does not mean that these authorities should not be included in the bundle of statutory authorities. See **7.4**.

3.2C A decision maker is obliged to take account of all relevant factors and ignore all irrelevant factors (eg *Secretary of State for Education and Science v Tameside MDC* [1977] AC 1014).

3.3 In *R v Higher Education Funding Council ex p Institute of Dental Surgery* [1994] 1 WLR 242 DC, Mr Justice Sedley held, inter alia, that:

> '(1) there is no general duty to give reasons for a decision, but there are classes of case where there is such a duty. (2) One such class is where the subject matter is an interest so highly regarded by the law (for example, personal liberty), that fairness requires that reasons, at least for particular decisions, be given as of right. (3)(a) Another such class is where the decision appears aberrant. Here fairness may require reasons so that the recipient may know whether the aberration is in the legal sense real (and so challengeable) or apparent; (b) it follows that this class does not include decisions which are themselves challengeable by reference only to the reasons for them. A pure exercise of academic judgement is such a decision.' [at p 263A–C][1]

3.4 In *Save Britain's Heritage v Number 1 Poultry Limited* [1991] 1 WLR 153, Lord Bridge stated that reasons had to be 'proper, intelligible and adequate'. He continued as follows:

> 'If the reasons given are improper they will reveal some flaw in the decision-making process which will be open to challenge on some ground other than the failure to give reasons. If the reasons given are unintelligible, this will be equivalent to giving no reasons at all. The difficulty arises in determining whether the reasons given are adequate, whether ... they deal with the substantial points that have been raised or ... enable the reader to know what conclusion the decision-maker has reached on the principal controversial issues. What degree of particularity is required? ... I do not think one can safely say more in general terms than that the degree of particularity required will depend entirely on the nature of the issues falling for decision.' [at pp 166H–167C]

3.5 By section 82(6) of the Magistrates' Courts Act 1980:

> 'Where a magistrates' court issues a warrant of commitment on the ground that one of the conditions mentioned in subsection (1) or (4) above is satisfied, it shall state that fact, specifying the ground, in the warrant.'

3.7 In *R v Oldham Justices ex p Cawley* [1996] 1 All ER 464, the Divisional Court considered the effect of section 82(6) of the Magistrates' Courts Act 1980. Simon Brown LJ held that:

> 'It will be seen that s 82(6) of the 1980 Act applies to adults as well as young offenders and requires the justices in all cases to specify on what particular ground they are issuing the warrant – to state, in short, what category of case for commitment it is.' [at p 468J]

---

1   It is normal practice to cite relevant passages of judgments that support the application for judicial review. Many of the passages that practitioners will require are included earlier in this book.

In *R v Stockport Justices ex p Conlon and R v Newark Justices ex p Keenaghan* (1997) *The Times*, 3 January, the Divisional Court held that section 82(6) of the Magistrates' Courts Act 1980 did not require the magistrates to do more than state on the warrant of commitment which of the conditions in section 82(4) applied[1].

3.8 In *R v York Magistrates Court ex p Grimes* (above) the Divisional Court considered a case where there appeared to be no reason why an attachment of earnings order should not be imposed. Although the court did not reverse the earlier decision in *ex p Conlan* (above) Pill LJ did state when passing judgment that:

> 'The justices accept that they did not announce any reason for their decision. Their unannounced reason, as expressed in the document to which Astil J has referred, was that the order would be inappropriate because of fluctuating earnings.
>
> It is not immediately obvious why [fluctuating earnings] is a reason for considering [an attachment of earnings] order inappropriate ...
>
> In my judgement having failed to canvass the question further the justices were not entitled to hold, in this case, that the criteria in subparagraph (b)(ii) [see para 3.2, above] were satisfied. Having failed to explore the question further with the applicant they could not reasonably make the order which they made.' [Transcript of the judgment][2]

3.9 In *Lloyd v McMahon* [1987] AC 625, Lord Bridge held that:

> 'My Lords, the so-called rules of natural justice are not engraved on tablets of stone. To use the phrase which better expresses the underlying concept, what the requirements of fairness demand when any body, domestic, administrative or judicial, has to make a decision which will affect the rights of individuals depends on the character of the decision-making body, the kind of decision it has to make and the statutory or other framework in which it operates.' [at p 702H]

3.10 In *R v Gough* [1993] AC 646, Lord Goff held that the test for whether there was a risk of apparent bias was whether:

> '[H]aving ascertained the relevant circumstances, the court should ask itself whether, having regard to those circumstances, there was a real danger of bias on the part of the relevant member of the tribunal in question, in the sense that he might unfairly regard (or have unfairly regarded) with favour, or disfavour, the case of a party to the issue under consideration.' [at p 670F]

Thus, in proceedings in a magistrates' court, an intervention from the chairman of the bench stating it was not the practice of the court to call

---

1   Although one can cite passages of judgments, it is equally acceptable to state the ratio of the case if there is no obvious passage of the judgment that supports the point being made.
2   Where a transcript is cited, it must be included in the bundle of statutory materials. Indeed, any case report that is not in a series that is commonly available should be included in the bundle of statutory authorities. See **7.4**. Transcripts of a number of cases can be found on the Internet at www.smithbernal.com. See also *Practice Statement (Supreme Court: Judgments)* [1998] 1 WLR 825 for rules on the use of unreported judgments.

police officers liars resulted in a decision being quashed for apparent bias. This was because the intervention indicated a real danger of unconscious bias in favour of the evidence of police officers (*R v Highgate Magistrates' Court ex p Riley* [1996] COD 12).

3.11 In *Associated Provincial Picture Houses Ltd v Wednesbury Corporation* [1948] 1 KB 223, Lord Greene MR held that the court was able to intervene where the decision was:

> '[S]o unreasonable that no reasonable authority could ever have come to it.'

3.12 Schedule 4 to the Magistrates' Courts Act 1980 provides the maximum terms of imprisonment to be imposed in default of imprisonment. The relevant periods in this case are:

An amount not exceeding £200	7 days
An amount exceeding £200 but not exceeding £500	14 days
An amount exceeding £500 but not exceeding £1,000	28 days
An amount exceeding £1,000 but not exceeding £2,500	45 days

Where there has been part payment, the maximum period applicable to the amount shall be reduced by the same proportion as the part paid bears to the whole sum.

4. Submissions

4.0A It is the Applicant's respectful submission that the Magistrates erred by finding that an attachment of earnings order was not appropriate as a result of 'wage fluctuations'. It is the Applicant's submission that the scheme provided by the Attachment of Earnings Act 1971 is designed to allow for fluctuations in earnings and that as a result 'wage fluctuations' are an irrelevant factor when deciding whether to impose an attachment of earnings order[1].

4.0B Further or alternatively, it is the Applicant's respectful submission that the Magistrates erred by misdirecting themselves in law by finding that an attachment of earnings order was not appropriate as a result of 'wage fluctuations'. It is the Applicant's submission that the scheme provided by the Attachment of Earnings Act 1971 is designed to allow for fluctuations in earnings.

4.1 Further or alternatively, it is the Applicant's respectful submission that the justices erred by failing to give reasons in open court for their decision to reject the suggestion of the Applicant that the justices should impose an attachment of earnings order. In support of this submission the Applicant relies on two further submissions:

> 4.1.1 It is accepted that there is no general duty to give reasons in addition to the reasons required by section 82(6) of the Magistrates' Courts Act 1980. Where, however, it would appear that there

---

[1] It is unnecessary to make direct references to the authorities relied on for this submission which are set out in the proceeding section.

is no reason why some other form of enforcement other than imprisonment should not be used, it is the Applicant's submission that a duty to give reasons arises explaining why that form of enforcement has not been used; and

4.1.2 Alternatively it is the Applicant's submission that the failure of the justices to explain why they had not used some other form of enforcement was a breach of natural justice. The failure of the justices to explain why they had not used some other form of enforcement deprived the Applicant of an opportunity to respond to the justices' reasons for failing to impose an attachment of earnings order.

4.2 Further or alternatively it is the Applicant's respectful submission that the comments made by the one of the justices regarding persons who refuse to pay their fines showed a real danger of bias. As a result the bench should have disqualified themselves from hearing this matter.

4.3 Further or alternatively the length of the period of imprisonment is in all the circumstances Wednesbury unreasonable. In support of this submission the Applicant relies on two further submissions:

4.3.1 The imposition of the maximum term of imprisonment was unreasonable as it failed to take account of the mitigation put forward on behalf of the Applicant

4.3.2 The imposition of the maximum term of imprisonment for each of two outstanding fines failed to take account of the aggregate effect of the terms of imprisonment. Had the sum outstanding been one fine, the total period of imprisonment could not have been as long.

ADRIAN FULFORD QC[1]
14 TOOKS COURT

HUGH SOUTHEY
14 TOOKS COURT

---

1 The pleadings should always be signed by the counsel who were responsible for drafting them if they are drafted by counsel.

3. Other useful clauses

(a) *Other descriptions of applicants*

In a case where the applicant is a member of the general public who seeks to challenge a police policy that has not yet had any direct effect on them, their standing might be questioned[1]. As a result it is important to state the interest of the applicant in the description of the applicant. For example, the description might state:

The Applicant is resident in central London and as a result they are policed by the Metropolitan Police who have adopted the policy that is the subject of this application. In addition the Applicant has a particular interest in policing as a result of her membership of the Chancery Lane Police Monitoring Committee.

(b) *Other forms of relief that might be sought*

If prohibition is sought the 'relief sought' should include a clause similar to the following:

An order of prohibition preventing the police from continuing to apply the policy that is the subject of this application.

or

An order of prohibition preventing Chancery Lane Magistrates' Court committing the applicant for trial in the Crown Court in relation to the matter that is the subject of this application.

If mandamus is sought the 'relief sought' should include a clause similar to the following:

An order of mandamus requiring the Chancery Lane Magistrates' Court to try the applicant.

If the judicial review application relates to an interim decision of justices taken during criminal proceedings, a stay of proceedings should normally be sought[2]. If a stay is sought, the 'relief sought' should include a clause similar to the following:

A stay of the proceedings before the Chancery Lane Magistrates' Court that this application relates to.

If damages are sought, this should be included in the relief sought[3]. A clause similar to the following clause should be used:

Damages for unlawful imprisonment.

Where damages are sought, it is important to ensure that the Form 86A includes a concise statement of the facts needed to establish the claim for damages.

---

1 See **1.10**.
2 See **10.5**.
3 See **11.8** for details of the requirements when drafting the Form 86A in a case where there is a claim for damages.

(c) Details of delay in bringing the application

The duty of disclosure means that the application must include details of any delay in bringing the application[1]. If there has been delay, this should be set out in the factual background, relevant law should then be set out in the legal background and submissions should be made. For example, the application might include the following clauses.

Factual background

2.[ ]　The Applicant applied for Legal Aid on 12 December 1998 which was two days after she had been committed to prison. That application was initially refused and so the Applicant appealed to the Legal Aid area committee. The appeal was heard on 15 March 1999 despite numerous requests that the appeal should be heard earlier. The applicant was granted Legal Aid by the area committee. As a result no application for judicial review was made before 15 March 1999.

Legal framework

3.[ ]　By Order 53, rule 4(1) of the Rules of the Supreme Court:

> An application for permission to apply for judicial review shall be made promptly and in any event within three months from the date when grounds for the application first arose unless the Court considers that there is good reason for extending the period within which the application shall be made.'

3.[ ]　By section 31(6) of the Supreme Court Act 1981:

> 'Where the High Court considers that there has been undue delay in making an application for judicial review, the court may refuse to grant – (a) leave for the making of the application, or (b) any relief sought on the application, if it considers that the granting of the relief sought would be likely to cause substantial hardship to, or substantially prejudice the rights of, any person or would be detrimental to good administration.'

3.[ ]　In *R v Stratford-on-Avon District Council ex p Jackson* [1985] 3 All ER 769, the court held a good reason for the delay may include delay in obtaining Legal Aid.

Submissions

4.1　The Applicant has a good reason for failing to apply earlier for permission to apply for judicial review. Before the 15 March 1999 the Applicant had not obtained Legal Aid to apply for judicial review. The Applicant took all reasonable steps to obtain Legal Aid as soon as possible. The Respondent has not been prejudiced by the delay. As a result it is the Applicant's respectful submission that she should be granted permission to apply for judicial review despite any delay.

1　See **5.2.2** and **7.7**.

(d) Details of any alternative remedy

The duty of disclosure means that the application must include details of any alternative remedy. The failure to take account of any alternative remedy should be pleaded in a similar way to delay.

4. Affidavit in support

The CPR 1998, Sch 1, RSC Ord 53, r 3(2)(b) merely requires that the application is supported by written evidence verifying the facts relied on. This appears to mean that there is no need for the evidence to be in the form of an affidavit. Evidence can, however, always be given by affidavit. The format of witness statements is very similar and a precedent is also included as precedent 6[1].

Affidavits should be produced on A4 paper with 3.5cm margins[2]. They must be legible and typed on one side of the paper[3]. They must be bound securely in a manner that will not hamper filing or otherwise each page should be endorsed with the case number and the initials of the deponent and the person before whom it was sworn[4]. They should be page-numbered consecutively[5].

>   Affidavit No 1 of J JONES
>   Exhibits: JJ1 and JJ2
>   Sworn: 1998
>   Filed: 1998
>   On behalf of the Applicant[6]

IN THE HIGH COURT OF JUSTICE   CROWN OFFICE REF:
QUEEN'S BENCH DIVISION
CROWN OFFICE LIST

IN THE MATTER OF AN APPLICATION FOR PERMISSION TO APPLY FOR JUDICIAL REVIEW OF A DECISION OF THE CHANCERY LANE MAGISTRATES' COURT

BETWEEN

REGINA

v

THE CHANCERY LANE MAGISTRATES' COURT

Ex parte: DORIS SMITH

AFFIDAVIT OF JACKIE JONES

---

1 *Practice Direction (CPR 1998, Part 32 – Written Evidence)* para 1.2. See **7.4**.
2 *Practice Direction (CPR 1998, Part 32 – Written Evidence)* para 6.1(1).
3 *Practice Direction (CPR 1998, Part 32 – Written Evidence)* para 6.1(2).
4 *Practice Direction (CPR 1998, Part 32 – Written Evidence)* para 6.1(3).
5 *Practice Direction (CPR 1998, Part 32 – Written Evidence)* para 6.1(4).
6 This heading must be included on the front page of the affidavit as well as on the backsheet and the exhibit sheet (*Practice Direction (CPR 1998, Part 32 – Written Evidence)* paras 3.2 and 11.3).

Appendix 1: Precedents – Judicial Review – 4. Affidavit in support

I, JACKIE JONES, of 350 Chancery Lane, London, EC4, a solicitor of the Supreme Court of England[1] and Wales STATE ON OATH[2] as follows:

1[3]. I am an assistant solicitor in the employ of Brown and Partners[4] and I have conduct of the above matter on behalf of the Applicant[5]. I am instructed to bring an application for judicial review on the grounds set forth in the Notice of Application for permission of the same date as this Affidavit.

2. Save as set out herein, the matters set out in this affidavit are within my knowledge[6].

3. I have read the Notice of Application. The contents of the Notice of Application accord with the instructions of the Applicant and are true to the best of my knowledge and belief[7].

4. There is now shown to me marked 'JJ 1' a draft affidavit[8]. This affidavit is based on the instructions of the Applicant. Unfortunately, as a result of the urgency of this matter it has not been possible to have this sworn by the Applicant. I undertake that if and when an affidavit sworn by the

---

1 The affidavit should always give the deponent's, name, address, occupation or description. It should also state whether they are a party to proceedings (*Practice Direction (CPR 1998, Part 32 – Written Evidence)* para 4.1).

2 Where the evidence is in the form of an affirmation, this should state 'I, JACKIE JONES, of 350 Chancery Lane, London, EC4, a solicitor of the Supreme Court of England and Wales do SOLEMNLY AND SINCERELY AFFIRM as follows' (*Practice Direction (CPR 1998, Part 32 – Written Evidence)* para 16).

3 The affidavit should be broken down into numbered paragraphs with each paragraph confined to a distinct portion of the subject. As far as possible the paragraphs should be in chronological order (*Practice Direction (CPR 1998, Part 32 – Written Evidence)* para 6.2).

4 Where an affidavit is made by a deponent in their professional or business capacity, the affidavit should clearly state what that capacity is and should also give the name of any employer (*Practice Direction (CPR 1998, Part 32 – Written Evidence)* para 4.2).

5 The person who swears the affidavit in support need not be the applicant for judicial review. Indeed, in many cases where it is important that the application is brought as a matter of urgency, it may be impractical to get the applicant to swear an affidavit. This is particularly true if the applicant is imprisoned. It may, however, be sensible for the affidavit from the applicant's solicitor to exhibit a draft affidavit from the applicant. See paragraph 4 of the affidavit.

6 This statement must be included to comply with *Practice Direction (CPR 1998, Part 32 – Written Evidence)* para 4.2. Affidavits must make it clear which statements are made from the deponent's own knowledge.

7 It is important to include a paragraph in similar terms to this so that no point can be taken by the respondent arguing that is no evidence of matters pleaded in the application.

8 Documents should be exhibited using this wording so that they comply with *Practice Direction (CPR 1998, Part 32 – Written Evidence)* para 4.3(1).

Applicant is received by this office it will be lodged with this Honourable Court[1] as soon as reasonably possible[2].

5. There is now shown to me marked 'JJ 2' the following documents[3]:

5.1 A copy of the register of Chancery Lane Magistrates' Court showing the decision to commit the Applicant to prison[4];

5.2 A copy of the warrant of commitment; and

5.3 A copy of the notes that I took during the hearing that resulted in the Applicant being committed to prison[5].

6. On 10[6] December 1998 the Applicant appeared before Chancery Lane Magistrates' Court in relation to outstanding fines. I represented the Applicant as Duty Solicitor. I put forward a number of matters in mitigation on behalf of the Applicant. In particular I argued that the court should take account of the Applicant's limited financial means and her obligations to her child[7].

7. On the same date the Applicant gave evidence on oath to the effect that her employer would have no objection to an attachment of earnings order. She stated that her earnings did vary significantly as they depended on overtime.

8. During my submissions I clearly heard one of the justices whisper during the application that the submissions were a waste of time as you could never trust somebody who refused to pay their fines. I objected to that remark and asked the bench of justices to disqualify themselves as one member of the bench had shown apparent bias. That application was

---

[1] The High Court should normally be described as 'this Honourable Court' in papers drafted in support of an application for judicial review.

[2] In this case, it is important that the applicant gives evidence about her own background as the grounds state that the justices failed to approach the background properly. As a result, there should be an affidavit or a witness statement from the applicant. If it is important that proceedings are brought urgently so that a bail application can be made and it is not practical to obtain an affidavit or a witness statement from the applicant before the application is lodged, the affidavit should include a paragraph in similar terms.

[3] The affidavit should exhibit any letter before action. If there is no letter before action and the decision-maker is not a court, the affidavit should include an explanation for this.

[4] Where possible the written record of the decision that is being challenged should be exhibited. Indeed, where an order of certiorari is sought to quash a decision of an inferior court, r 9(2) of CPR 1998, Sch 1, RSC Ord 53 requires the decision to be exhibited and verified by an affidavit or witness statement. If the decision is not exhibited and verified by an affidavit or witness statement the applicant must account for its absence to the satisfaction of the court in an affidavit or witness statement. In a case where an executive decision is being challenged, the letter setting out the decision should be exhibited.

[5] The notes should be exhibited where there is a ground that challenges something that happened during the hearing as they tend to corroborate the contents of the affidavit. This is important as there may be a dispute about the factual background of the application for judicial review.

[6] Numbers, including those in dates, should be expressed in figures (*Practice Direction (CPR 1998, Part 32 – Written Evidence)* para 6.1(6)).

[7] Although the applicant's solicitor has endorsed the contents of the application as being true, it is still important that they give direct evidence of all relevant matters.

refused. The bench did not deny that the remark had been made. I also immediately made a note of the remark.

9. Following my submissions and the evidence of the Applicant the justices found that the Applicant had shown culpable neglect and ordered that she serve 36 days imprisonment in default in respect of the larger fine and 14 days in respect of the smaller fine. The periods of imprisonment were to be served consecutively. No reasons were given for the order other than a finding of culpable neglect[1].

10. I have been informed by Doris Smith and do verily believe it to be true that she is a single parent with one child aged 19 months[2]. Ms Smith has sole responsibility for this child. Ms Smith has worked for thirteen years as a cleaner at her local school. Ms Smith's earnings vary from about £50 per week to about £150 per week as they depend on overtime. Ms Smith's earnings and child benefit are her only sources of income.

SWORN at   )
in the County of   )
this   day of   1998)

Before me

A Solicitor empowered to administer Oaths

---

1 It is essential that the affidavit details the state of proceedings in a case where the applicant for judicial review seeks to challenge a decision of a court. Where the decision is an interim decision, the affidavit should also state whether there has been an application for an adjournment of the proceedings and explain why the application is being brought before the conclusion of proceedings.
2 This is the form of wording to be used when hearsay is being relied on.

[Backsheet][1]

Affidavit No 1 of J JONES
Exhibits: JJ1 and JJ2
Sworn: 1998
Filed: 1998
On behalf of the Applicant

CROWN OFFICE REF:

IN THE HIGH COURT OF JUSTICE

QUEEN'S BENCH DIVISION

CROWN OFFICE LIST

IN THE MATTER OF AN APPLICATION FOR PERMISSION TO APPLY FOR JUDICIAL REVIEW OF A DECISION OF THE CHANCERY LANE MAGISTRATES' COURT

BETWEEN:

REGINA

v

THE CHANCERY LANE MAGISTRATES' COURT

Ex parte: DORIS SMITH

AFFIDAVIT OF JACKIE JONES

DATE SWORN: 1998

EXHIBITS: 2

Brown and Partners
350 Chancery Lane, London, EC4

Ref:

Solicitors for the Applicant

---

1 The backsheet should only take up half of the width of the page and should be on the right-hand side of the page.

5. Exhibit to affidavit

Affidavit No 1 of J JONES
Exhibits: JJ1 and JJ2
Sworn: 1998
Filed: 1998
On behalf of the Applicant

IN THE HIGH COURT OF JUSTICE   CROWN OFFICE REF:

QUEEN'S BENCH DIVISION

CROWN OFFICE LIST

IN THE MATTER OF AN APPLICATION FOR PERMISSION TO APPLY FOR JUDICIAL REVIEW OF A DECISION OF THE CHANCERY LANE MAGISTRATES' COURT

BETWEEN

REGINA

v

THE CHANCERY LANE MAGISTRATES' COURT

Ex parte: DORIS SMITH

———————

EXHIBIT JJ 1

———————

This is the exhibit marked 'JJ 1[1]' referred to in the Affidavit of JACKIE JONES sworn this
          day of   1998

Before me

A Solicitor empowered to administer Oaths

---

1   Exhibits should be numbered and where a deponent swears more than one affidavit they should be numbered consecutively throughout the proceedings rather than start again with each affidavit (*Practice Direction (CPR 1998, Part 32 – Written Evidence)* para 4.3(2)).

6. Witness statement in support

If a decision is taken to rely on a witness statement rather than an affidavit, the statement should be in the following format. The requirements regarding the format of witness statements are in all respects identical to those regarding affidavits save where set out below.

> Witness Statement No 1 of J JONES
> Exhibits: JJ1 and JJ2
> Sworn: 1998
> Filed: 1998
> On behalf of the Applicant

IN THE HIGH COURT OF JUSTICE   CROWN OFFICE REF:

QUEEN'S BENCH DIVISION

CROWN OFFICE LIST

IN THE MATTER OF AN APPLICATION FOR PERMISSION TO APPLY FOR JUDICIAL REVIEW OF A DECISION OF THE CHANCERY LANE MAGISTRATES' COURT

BETWEEN

REGINA

v

THE CHANCERY LANE MAGISTRATES' COURT

Ex parte: DORIS SMITH

WITNESS STATEMENT OF JACKIE JONES

I, JACKIE JONES, of 350 Chancery Lane, London, EC4, a solicitor of the Supreme Court of England and Wales STATE as follows:

The body of the statement should be the same as for an affidavit, save that exhibits should be referred to by stating 'I refer to the [description of exhibit] marked...'[1]

The Statement should conclude with the following statement:

I believe that the facts stated in this witness statement are true[2].

Signed ....
Jackie Jones

There should then be a backsheet in a similar form to that for the affidavit. Exhibits should be verified using the following exhibit sheet.

---

1   *Practice Direction (CPR 1998, Part 32 – Written Evidence)* para 18.4.
2   *Practice Direction (CPR 1998, Part 32 – Written Evidence)* para 20.2.

7. Exhibit to a witness statement

Witness Statement No 1 of J JONES
Exhibits: JJ1 and JJ2
Sworn: 1998
Filed: 1998
On behalf of the Applicant

IN THE HIGH COURT OF JUSTICE   CROWN OFFICE REF:

QUEEN'S BENCH DIVISION

CROWN OFFICE LIST

IN THE MATTER OF AN APPLICATION FOR PERMISSION TO APPLY FOR JUDICIAL REVIEW OF A DECISION OF THE CHANCERY LANE MAGISTRATES' COURT

BETWEEN

REGINA

v

THE CHANCERY LANE MAGISTRATES' COURT

Ex parte: DORIS SMITH

_____

EXHIBIT JJ 1
_____

This is the exhibit marked 'JJ 1' referred to in my witness statement.

Signed ....
Jackie Jones

8. Bail application

In theory, CPR 1998, Sch 1, RSC Ord 79 governs only criminal causes or matters. It is, however, accepted that the same procedure should be adopted to apply for bail in matters that are not criminal causes or matters. As a result, the same pleading should be used in either type of case.

Order 79 states that a claim form should be submitted in Form 97. This form was used before the introduction of the CPR 1998 and so requires appropriate amendments to the terminology[1]. The claim form should normally be accompanied by a draft order that sets out the bail conditions being suggested to the court. The order is important as it means that the court is likely to be able to seal an order more speedily. That is important as the prison will want a sealed order before the applicant is released. The rules also state that the claim form must be accompanied by written evidence in support. When bail is sought pursuant to an application for judicial review, the written evidence in support of that application can stand as the written evidence in support of bail providing that it deals with all relevant matters.

CLAIM FORM TO GRANT BAIL (Order 53 and Order 79)

IN THE HIGH COURT OF JUSTICE   CROWN OFFICE REF:

QUEEN'S BENCH DIVISION

CROWN OFFICE LIST

IN THE MATTER OF AN APPLICATION FOR PERMISSION TO APPLY FOR JUDICIAL REVIEW OF A DECISION OF THE CHANCERY LANE MAGISTRATES' COURT

BETWEEN

REGINA

v

THE CHANCERY LANE MAGISTRATES' COURT

Ex parte: DORIS SMITH

Let all parties concerned attend the Honourable Mr Justice [*name*] on the [*day*] day of [*month*] [*year*] at [*time*] o'clock on the hearing of an application on behalf of Doris Smith that she be granted bail pending consideration of her application for judicial review of the decision taken by Chancery Lane Magistrates' Court on 10 December 1998 to commit her to prison.

Dated the [*day*] day of [*month*] [*year*]

This claim form was taken out by Brown and Partners, 350 Chancery Lane, London, EC4 solicitors for the said Doris Smith.

---

1   *Practice Direction (CPR 1998, Part 4 – Forms).*

In the High Court of Justice
Queen's Bench Division
The Honourable Mr Justice

Whereas Doris Smith was previously detained pursuant to a warrant of commitment issued by Chancery Lane Magistrates' Court on 10 December 1998

And whereas Doris Smith has applied for judicial review and pursuant to that application has applied for bail.

And upon hearing counsel for the said Doris Smith and upon reading the affidavit sworn by Jackie Jones and dated 11 December 1998.

It is ordered that the said Doris Smith, after complying with the condition(s) specified in Schedule 1 hereto, shall be released on bail, subject to the condition(s) specified in Schedule 2 hereto, and with a duty to surrender to the Chancery Lane Magistrates' Court on a time and a date to be notified.

Schedule 1

Conditions to be complied with before release on bail

The Applicant will provide one surety of £500 before a justice of the peace at Chancery Lane Magistrates' Court to secure the Applicant's surrender to custody at the time and place appointed[1]

Schedule 2

Conditions to be complied with after release on bail

The Applicant will reside at [*insert address*][2]

---

1   Insert here details of any other conditions that are being offered and that should be complied with prior to release.
2   Insert here details of any other conditions that are being offered and that should be complied with after release.

9. Claim form

The Practice Direction (CPR 1998, Part 4 – Forms) provides that the claim form to be used in an application for judicial review is not the standard claim form used in most civil litigation. Instead, it is in essentially the same form as Form 86 that was used before the introduction of the CPR 1998.

IN THE HIGH COURT OF JUSTICE CROWN OFFICE REF:

QUEEN'S BENCH DIVISION

CROWN OFFICE LIST

IN THE MATTER OF AN APPLICATION FOR JUDICIAL REVIEW

BETWEEN

REGINA

v

THE CHANCERY LANE MAGISTRATES' COURT

Ex parte: DORIS SMITH

Take Notice that pursuant to the permission of [a Divisional Court of the Queen's Bench Division] [the Honourable Mr Justice [*insert name*]][1] given on [*insert date*] the Court will be moved as soon as counsel can be heard on the applicant's behalf for an order for relief in the terms, and on the grounds, set out in the application notice in Form 86A, herewith.

And that the costs of and occasioned by this motion be [paid by the Respondent][2].

And take notice that on the hearing of this claim the Applicant will use the written evidence and exhibits, copies of which accompany this notice.

Dated the   day of 1998

Signed
[*Insert name and address of solicitors for the applicant*]
Solicitor for the Applicant

Ref no

Tel no

Fax no

---

1 Delete as appropriate.
2 Insert costs orders that are sought.

Appendix 1: Precedents – Judicial Review – 9. Claim form 245

To Clerk to Chancery Lane Magistrates[1]

Important

1. Any respondent who intends to use a witness statement or affidavit at the hearing should inform the Crown Office of his intention within 10 days of the service of this notice.

2. Any such witness statement or affidavit must be filed in the Crown Office as soon as practicable and in any event within 56 days of service[2].

Where the applicant has sought judicial review of an interim decision and the High Court has ordered a stay of proceedings, the following paragraph will need to be included in the motion directly above the date:

And also take notice that [a Divisional Court of the Queen's Bench Division] [the Honourable Mr Justice [*insert name*]][3] by order dated [*insert date*] directed that all proceedings in the Chancery Lane Magistrates' Court be stayed until after the hearing of this motion or further order.

---

1 The details of all persons served should be included here. See **7.11** for details of all the people who should be served.
2 This period for service must be amended if any orders for expedition include an order that the time for service of the respondent's evidence is abridged.
3 Delete as appropriate.

10. Witness statement as to service

The written evidence showing service of the claim form can be presented to the court in the form of an affidavit or in a witness statement. As it is unlikely that any issue will arise regarding the credibility of this evidence, there would appear to be absolutely no reason why the evidence should not be presented in the form of a witness statement. The general rules regarding the format of witness statement are set out in the precedent for the affidavit in support.

The exhibit should have a sheet on the front of it signed by the person making the witness statement. The form of this is the same as for the written evidence in support.

> Witness statement No 2 of J JONES
> Exhibits: JJ3[1]
> Sworn: 1999
> Filed: 1999
> On behalf of the Applicant

IN THE HIGH COURT OF JUSTICE   CROWN OFFICE REF:

QUEEN'S BENCH DIVISION

CROWN OFFICE LIST

IN THE MATTER OF AN APPLICATION FOR JUDICIAL REVIEW OF A DECISION OF THE CHANCERY LANE MAGISTRATES' COURT

BETWEEN

REGINA

v

THE CHANCERY LANE MAGISTRATES' COURT

Ex parte: DORIS SMITH

WITNESS STATEMENT OF JACKIE JONES

I, JACKIE JONES, of 350 Chancery Lane, London, EC4, a solicitor of the Supreme Court of England and Wales STATE as follows:

1. I am an assistant solicitor in the employ of Brown and Partners and I have conduct of the above matter on behalf of the Applicant.

2. I did serve the Clerk to the Chancery Lane Magistrates' Court, and Mr Smith, Ms Brown and Ms Walker, the justices[2] who considered the decision that is the subject of this application for judicial review, with copies of the claim form, Notice of Issue of Legal Aid Certificate and

---

1   Exhibits should be numbered consecutively with other exhibits to earlier affidavits or witness statements by the same witness.
2   The justices should be personally served where their conduct is being questioned.

Form 86A[1]. I refer to the exhibit marked 'JJ 3'[2] which contains true copies of the said Notice of Motion, Notice of Issue of Legal Aid Certificate and Form 86A that I served. I served these documents by posting on 15 January 1999 at Chancery Lane Post Office, 400 Chancery Lane, London, EC1, one copy of the said documents by first class post in pre-paid sealed envelopes addressed to each of the above mentioned parties at the Chancery Lane Magistrates' Court, 450 Chancery Lane, London, EC1 which is their address for service[3].

I believe that the facts stated in this witness statement are true.

Signed ....
Jackie Jones

---

1   If there is a party affected who has not been served, the witness statement should confirm this and state why they have not been served.
2   Exhibits should be numbered consecutively with those in prior written evidence of by the same person.
3   The methods of service are considered at **6.7**.

[Backsheet]

Witness statement No 2 of J JONES
Exhibits: JJ3
Sworn: 1999
Filed: 1999
On behalf of the Applicant

CROWN OFFICE REF:

IN THE HIGH COURT OF JUSTICE

QUEEN'S BENCH DIVISION

CROWN OFFICE LIST

IN THE MATTER OF AN APPLICATION FOR JUDICIAL REVIEW OF A DECISION OF THE CHANCERY LANE MAGISTRATES' COURT

BETWEEN:

REGINA

v

THE CHANCERY LANE MAGISTRATES' COURT

Ex parte: DORIS SMITH

WITNESS STATEMENT OF JACKIE JONES

DATE SWORN: 1999

EXHIBITS: 1

Brown and Partners
350 Chancery Lane, London, EC4

Ref:

Solicitors for the Applicant

11. Affidavit in response

The CPR 1998, Sch 1, RSC Ord 53, r 6(4) merely requires that respondents rely on written evidence. This can either be an affidavit or a witness statement[1]. If a respondent does wish to rely on a witness statement, a precedent for the format of a witness statement is included at precedent 6. We have also highlighted differences in the footnotes.

There are a number of general rules regarding the format of affidavits and witness statements. These are set out in the precedent of the written evidence in support and are not repeated in this precedent. See precedents 4 and 5.

Affidavit No 1 of J SMITH	
Exhibit: JS1	
Sworn:	1999
Filed:	1999
On behalf of the Respondent	

IN THE HIGH COURT OF JUSTICE   CROWN OFFICE REF:

QUEEN'S BENCH DIVISION

CROWN OFFICE LIST

IN THE MATTER OF AN APPLICATION FOR JUDICIAL REVIEW OF A DECISION OF THE CHANCERY LANE MAGISTRATES' COURT

BETWEEN

REGINA

v

THE CHANCERY LANE MAGISTRATES' COURT

Ex parte: DORIS SMITH

_____

AFFIDAVIT OF JOHN SMITH

_____

I, John Smith, c/o Chancery Lane Magistrates' Court, a Justice of the Peace STATE ON OATH[2] as follows:

1. I am a Justice of the Peace. I was Chairman of the bench that considered the applicant's case on 10 December 1998. The other members of that bench were Ms Brown and Ms Walker.

---

1 See **7.14**.
2 Where the evidence is in the form of an affirmation, this should state 'I, John Smith, c/o Chancery Lane Magistrates' Court, a Justice of the Peace do SOLEMNLY AND SINCERELY AFFIRM as follows' (*Practice Direction (CPR 1998, Part 32 – Written Evidence)* para 16). The format of this statement is also different if a witness statement is used. See precedent 6.

Appendix 1: Precedents – Judicial Review – 11. Affidavit in response

2. Save as set out herein, the matters set out in this affidavit are within my knowledge[1]. Before swearing this affidavit I have refreshed my memory by reviewing the notes that I made on 10 December 1998, together with notes made by the other justices who formed the bench and notes made by the clerk who advised the bench on that date.

3. There is now shown to me marked 'JS1'[2] the following documents[3]:

   3.1 A copy of the register of Chancery Lane Magistrates' Court showing the decision to commit the Applicant to prison;

   3.2 A copy of the warrant of committal;

   3.3 A copy of the notes that I took during the hearing that resulted in the Applicant being committed to prison;

   3.4 A copy of notes that I am informed by Ms Brown and Ms Walker were taken by them during the hearing of this matter. I verily believe this to be true[4];

   3.5 A copy of notes that I am informed by the clerk who advised the bench during the hearing of the Applicant's matter were taken by him. I verily believe this to be true; and

   3.6 A pro forma that is used by this court to ensure that it considers alternative methods of enforcement and that was completed by me during the consideration of the Applicant's case[5].

4. I have considered the first affidavit of Jackie Jones. I can confirm that it accurately reflects the proceedings that resulted in the Applicant being committed to prison save for the following matters:

   4.1 I do remember Ms Jones objecting to an alleged remark made by a member of the bench. I have reviewed all the exhibits set out in paragraph 3 to see whether there is any reference to this incident, but I can see none. However, as far as I can remember, it was never accepted that any remark had been made. The bench found that Ms Jones was mistaken when she heard a remark;

---

1 This statement must be included to comply with *Practice Direction (CPR 1998, Part 32 – Written Evidence)* para 4.2.
2 The front sheet for the exhibit should be in a similar format to that used in the affidavit in support. See precedent 5.
3 Documents should be exhibited using this wording so that they comply with *Practice Direction (CPR 1998, Part 32 – Written Evidence)* para 4.3(1). The wording is different if a witness statement is used. See precedent 6.
4 This is the form of wording to be used when hearsay evidence is relied on.
5 The affidavit should normally exhibit all relevant documents held by the respondent. There is a normally a duty of candour. See **7.14**.

4.2 I do remember that we stated in court that any methods of enforcement that had not been tried were inappropriate in our opinion. I accept that we gave no reasons for this finding.

SWORN at)

in the County of)
this day of 1999)

Before me

A Solicitor empowered to administer Oaths

[Backsheet]

Affidavit No 1 of J SMITH
Exhibit: JS1
Sworn: 1999
Filed: 1999
On behalf of the Respondent

CROWN OFFICE REF:

IN THE HIGH COURT OF JUSTICE

QUEEN'S BENCH DIVISION

CROWN OFFICE LIST

IN THE MATTER OF AN APPLICATION FOR JUDICIAL REVIEW OF A DECISION OF THE CHANCERY LANE MAGISTRATES' COURT

BETWEEN:

REGINA

v

THE CHANCERY LANE MAGISTRATES' COURT

Ex parte: DORIS SMITH

AFFIDAVIT OF JOHN SMITH

DATE SWORN: 1999

EXHIBITS: 1

The Clerk to the Justices

Chancery Lane Magistrates' Court

12. Application for an interim order

The text drafted below should normally be endorsed on an application notice. The correct form is Form N244 which can be obtained from the Court Service and which is included in Appendix 5.

We, Brown and Partners of 350 Chancery Lane, London, EC4, solicitors for the Applicant, intend to apply for an order (a draft of which is attached) pursuant to rule 42.3 of the Civil Procedure Rules that we be allowed to cease to act as solicitors for the Applicant, Doris Smith, because the Applicant has:

1. failed to supply Brown and Partners with any instructions subsequent to being granted bail by this Honourable Court. Letters to her address have been returned marked 'Not Known'.

2. Has failed to make any payments in respect of a bill for fees delivered on 21 January 1999. In addition, she has failed to make any reasonable offer for payment.

The evidence in the support of the application should state the attempts made to contact the applicant and the attempts made to obtain payment. This evidence can either be produced in a witness statement or affidavit. Alternatively, it can be endorsed on the application form. If it is endorsed on the application form, a statement verifying the truth of the evidence must be signed.

13. Draft interim order

The application for an interim order should normally be accompanied by a draft order[1].

IN THE HIGH COURT OF JUSTICE   CROWN OFFICE REF:

QUEEN'S BENCH DIVISION

CROWN OFFICE LIST

IN THE MATTER OF AN APPLICATION FOR JUDICIAL REVIEW OF A DECISION OF THE CHANCERY LANE MAGISTRATES' COURT

BETWEEN

REGINA

v

THE CHANCERY LANE MAGISTRATES' COURT

Ex parte: DORIS SMITH

NOTIFICATION of the decision following an application by Brown and Partners

BEFORE THE HONOURABLE MR JUSTICE

Upon reading the application notice dated [*insert date*]

IT IS ORDERED that pursuant to Part 42.3 of the Civil Procedure Rules Brown and Partners cease to be the solicitors acting for the Applicant upon compliance with the requirements of Part 42.3(3) of the said rules

Dated 23 March 1999

Signed

---

1   *Practice Direction (CPR 1998, Part 23 – Applications)*, para 12.

14. Skeleton argument

IN THE HIGH COURT CO/...[1]

CROWN OFFICE 12 June 1999[1]

REGINA

v

CHANCERY LANE MAGISTRATES' COURT

Ex Parte: DORIS SMITH

SKELETON ARGUMENT

1. Time estimate

At present it is thought that the Respondent will not be represented. If this is the case it is anticipated that the hearing will take 2 hours.

2. The issues

The issues are set out at paragraphs 1.0 to 1.3 of the Grounds (see bundle at page 000[2]).

3. Propositions to be advanced

3.1 The effect of the Attachment of Earnings Act 1971 is that it is anticipated that attachment of earnings orders can be imposed in circumstances where the offender's earnings are variable. As a result variable earnings are no bar to an attachment of earnings order.

> Section 6 of the Attachment of Earnings Act 1971
> Schedule 3 to the 1971 Act
> *R v York Magistrates Court ex p Grimes* (1997) *The Times*, 27 June

3.2 Judicial review is available where the Magistrates have considered an irrelevant factor when deciding not to impose an attachment of earnings order. For the reasons set out in paragraph 3.1 the decision not to impose an attachment of earnings order was based on consideration of an irrelevant factor namely 'wage fluctuations' (see bundle at page 000).

> *Associated Picture Houses Ltd v Wednesbury Corporation* [1948] 1 KB 223 at 228
> *Secretary of State for Education and Science v Tameside MDC* [1977] AC 1014 at 1048B–D
> *R v Secretary of State for the Environment ex p Hammersmith & Fulham LBC* [1991] AC 521 at 597D–E

---

1 The skeleton argument must include the Crown Office reference and the date of the hearing.
2 The skeleton should include references to the hearing bundle. See **6.4.1**.

3.3 Although there is no general duty to give reasons in addition to those imposed by section 82(6) of the Magistrates' Courts Act 1980, a duty arises where it appears that there is no good reason why an alternative method of enforcement should not be used.

> *R v Higher Education Funding Council ex p Institute of Dental Surgery* [1994] 1 WLR 242 at 263A
> Transcript of *R v York Magistrates Court ex p Grimes* (1997) *The Times*, 27 June (see bundle at page 000)[1]

3.4 The remarks made by one of the justices that one could never trust a person who refused to pay their fines (see bundle at page 000 for evidence of these remarks) showed a real danger of bias.

> *R v Gough* [1993] AC 646 at 670F
> *R v Highgate Magistrates Court ex p Riley* [1996] COD 12

3.5 The decision to impose the maximum period of imprisonment for each fine is unreasonable as it failed to take account of mitigating factors (see bundle at page 000 for evidence of mitigating factors) and the maximum period for a single fine of the same amount as the two fines.

> Schedule 4 to the Magistrates' Court Act 1980

4. Chronology of events

13 June 1997	Applicant is fined £2000 for one matter of no insurance (bundle, at page 000).
20 June 1997	Applicant is fined £350 for no vehicle excise licence (bundle, at page 000).
12 March 1998	An order is made that the two fines be paid at £5 per week (bundle, at page 000).
15 June 1998	Applicant paid £25 towards fine (bundle, at page 000).
18 July 1998	A default summons is issued returnable on 4 September 1998 (bundle, at page 000).
10 December 1998	Applicant appears before Chancery Lane justices and is committed to prison for 50 days (bundle, at page 000).

5. List of essential reading

1. The proforma used by the justices (bundle, at page 000).
2. Paragraphs 6, 7, 8 and 9 of the affidavit of Jackie Jones (bundle, at page 000).

ADRIAN FULFORD QC
HUGH SOUTHEY
14 TOOKS COURT

---

[1] Where a transcript is relied on, it should be included in the bundle of statutory material and should also be included in the trial bundle.

15. Consent order

IN THE HIGH COURT OF JUSTICE
QUEEN'S BENCH DIVISION

IN THE MATTER OF AN APPLICATION FOR JUDICIAL REVIEW BY
DORIS SMITH

Whereas Doris Smith was previously detained pursuant to a warrant of committal issued by Chancery Lane Magistrates' Court on 10 December 1998. And whereas Doris Smith has applied for a judicial review of that decision.

The Applicant and the Respondent do hereby consent to an order of certiorari being issued that the warrant of committal issued by the Respondent on 10 December 1998 be brought up to this Honourable Court and quashed for the reasons set out in the statement of reasons below. Further, the matter be remitted for consideration by a bench of magistrates other than the bench that issued the warrant of committal on 10 December 1998[1]. Further, that there be no order for costs save for Legal Aid taxation of the Applicant's costs[2].

Dated this [*day*] of February 1999

Signed on behalf of the applicant ....

Signed on behalf of the respondent ....

Statement of reasons
It is accepted by the justices that they erred by taking account of the respondent's fluctuating earnings when they decided not to make an attachment of earnings order. It is accepted that following *R v York Magistrates' Court ex p Grimes* (1997) *The Times*, 27 June[3] fluctuating earnings are no bar to the making of an attachment of earnings order. It is agreed that this error is sufficient to enable this Honourable Court to quash the decision that is the subject of this application. It is respectfully submitted that there is no need to determine the merits of the other grounds.

---

1   Where an applicant seeks the quashing of a decision of justices, an order should always be sought requiring that the matter is heard by a different bench of magistrates.
2   Where an application is in receipt of legal aid, it is always important to seek an order for legal aid taxation.
3   A copy of this authority should be supplied to the court with this consent order (*Practice Direction (Crown Office List: Consent Orders)* [1997] 1 WLR 825).

16. Application notice for renewal in the Court of Appeal

The format for this application notice is specified in the Practice Direction (CPR 1998 – The Court of Appeal (Civil Division)). The notice in the Practice Direction requires the applicant to specify the track to which the case is allocated. The Crown Office is not presently tracking cases and so we have omitted that section of the notice as it is unnecessary.

IN THE COURT OF APPEAL CROWN OFFICE REF

A RENEWED APPLICATION FROM THE
HIGH COURT OF JUSTICE
QUEEN'S BENCH DIVISION
CROWN OFFICE LIST

BETWEEN

REGINA

v

[*insert the respondent*]

Ex parte [*insert the applicant*]

Section A

TAKE NOTICE that the Applicant will apply without notice to the Court of Appeal for permission to apply for judicial review of a decision of [*insert details of the decision that is the subject of the judicial review*] which permission was refused by the Honourable Mr Justice [*insert name*] following oral submissions by Counsel for the Applicant in open court on [*date on which permission was refused*].

AND FOR AN ORDER that [*set out costs order applied for*][1]

AND FURTHER TAKE NOTICE that the application will be heard at the Royal Courts of Justice, Strand, London WC2A 2LL on a date and at a time to be notified by the Civil Appeals Office

Section B

We wish to rely on the following evidence in support of this application [*here set out the reasons why the application should be granted*]

Not applicable[2]

---

1 See **12.3** as costs are rarely awarded at the permission stage.
2 There will not normally be any need to rely on additional evidence unless there is an application to apply to extend the time for lodging the application notice. Where there is an application to extend time, the evidence should set out the reasons why the application notice was not lodged in time and why time should be extended.

STATEMENT OF TRUTH

The applicant believes that the facts stated above are true

_____

Signed
Applicant's solicitor

Date _____

Appendix 2: Precedent – Claim Form for Writ for Habeas Corpus

1. Form 87

IN THE HIGH COURT OF JUSTICE   CROWN OFFICE REF:

QUEEN'S BENCH DIVISION

CROWN OFFICE LIST

IN THE MATTER OF [*insert the name of the detainee*]

AND

IN THE MATTER OF AN APPLICATION FOR A WRIT OF HABEAS CORPUS AD SUBJICIENDUM

TAKE NOTICE that pursuant to the direction of [the Honourable Mr Justice [*insert name*]] [a Divisional Court][1], the Queen's Bench Division of the High Court of Justice will be moved on the [*insert the date scheduled for the hearing*], or as so soon thereafter as counsel can be heard on behalf of [*insert the name of the detainee*] for an order that a writ of habeas corpus do issue directed to [*insert the position of the person responsible for detainee, eg the Governor of Brixton Prison*] to have the body of the said [*insert the name of the detainee*] before the Queen's Bench Division of the High Court of Justice at such time as the Court or judge may direct upon the grounds set out in the written evidence of [the said][2] [*insert the name of the detainee or other persons swearing or signing written evidence*] and the exhibits therein respectively referred to used on the application to [the Honourable Mr Justice [*insert name*]] [a Divisional Court][3] for such order, copies of which written evidence and exhibits are served herewith.

---

1   Delete as appropriate.
2   Delete as appropriate.
3   Delete as appropriate.

And that the costs of and occasioned by this application be [*insert details of costs orders that are sought*]

AND TAKE NOTICE that on the hearing of this application the said [*insert the name of the detainee*] will use the written evidence of [the said][1] [*insert the name of the detainee or other persons swearing or signing written evidence*] and the exhibits therein referred to.

Dated the   day of 19

(Signed)
of [*insert the name of the detainee's solicitors*]
Solicitor for said [*insert the name of the detainee*]

To [*insert the position of the person responsible for detainee, eg the Governor of Brixton Prison*]

---

1   Delete as appropriate.

Appendix 3: Precedents – Case Stated

1. Application to state a case

Set out below is a specimen application to state a case. The application relates to a case in which the applicant is challenging a conviction under s 2 of the Protection from Harassment Act 1997. Further precedents in this appendix are based on the same set of fictitious facts. At the end of this precedent are included sample clauses that might be included in other applications.

To Mr Smith, Ms Brown and Ms Jones, justices sitting at the Chancery Lane Magistrates' Court and to the Clerk to the Chancery Lane Magistrates' Court[1].

I, the undersigned, was the defendant in proceedings at the Chancery Lane Magistrates' Court brought by the Crown Prosecution Service that resulted in my conviction by the said Magistrates' Court on 13 January 1999 under the provisions of section 2(1) of the Protection from Harassment Act 1997[2]. I am aggrieved by the said conviction as it is wrong in law or in excess of jurisdiction[3]. As a consequence I apply to you to state a case on the following questions:

1. The complaint about my conduct on 21 October 1998[4]

1.1 By reason of section 2(1) of the Protection from Harassment Act 1997 ('the 1997 Act') it is an offence to pursue a course of conduct that is in breach of section 1(1) of the 1997 Act. Section 1(1) of the 1997 Act provides that:

> 'A person must not pursue a course of conduct:
>
> (a) which amounts to harassment of another; and
> (b) which he knows or ought to know amounts to harassment of the other'

Section 7(3) of the 1997 Act provides that:

> 'A "course of conduct" must involve conduct on at least two occasions.'

1.2 The information that resulted in my conviction was received by the Chancery Lane Magistrates' Court on 16 October 1998. The information was subsequently amended to state that it related to conduct between 10 October 1998 and 21 October 1998.

---

[1] The application should be addressed to both the decision-makers and to the clerk to the magistrates in the magistrates' court and to the officer designated to receive the application in the Crown Court.

[2] The notice should identify the proceedings that are the subject of the appeal and the appellant's interest in those proceedings.

[3] The notice should repeat the terms of s 111 of the Magistrates' Courts Act 1980.

[4] The grounds for making the request should be detailed so that the justice cannot reject the application as 'frivolous' pursuant to s 111(5) of the Magistrates' Courts Act 1980.

1.3 An alleged victim, Ms Green, gave evidence that I had stood looking through her window on 14 October 1998 and 21 October 1998.

1.4 As a consequence the question that I wish to be considered by the High Court in relation to the evidence of Ms Green is:

> Whether the justices were entitled to allow the prosecution to amend the information so that it included allegations of conduct after the date when the information was lodged.

2. The evidence of Ms Blue

2.1 The prosecution called Ms Blue to give evidence. She lived in the same student halls of residence as Ms Green. She gave evidence that she had seen me looking through her window on 10 October 1998. Ms Green was not involved in this incident and Ms Blue was not involved in subsequent incidents. The information alleged that the course of conduct included the incident involving Ms Blue on 10 October 1998 as well as the incidents involving Ms Green.

2.2 It was submitted on my behalf that section 1 of the 1997 Act requires that a course of conduct must be directed at one person if an offence is to be proven. This is a matter that was left undecided in *DPP v Williams* [1998] 11 CL 44.

2.3 As a consequence the question that I wish to be considered by the High Court in relation to the evidence of Ms Blue is:

> Whether the justices were entitled to take account of the evidence of incidents involving separate persons when they determined that there had been a course of conduct governed by s 1 of the Protection from Harassment Act 1997.

3. The absence of sufficient evidence

3.1 If the evidence of the incident on 10 October 1998 and the evidence of the incident on 21 October 1998 had been excluded from evidence, there would have been only evidence of one incident involving Ms Green on 14 October 1998.

3.2 Section 7(3) of the 1997 Act requires at least two incidents.

3.3 As a consequence the question that I wish to be considered by the High Court in relation to the evidence is:

> Whether there was sufficient evidence to entitle the justices to convict me of an offence under s 2 of the Protection from Harassment Act 1997.

....
Wayne Red[1]

---

1 The application must be signed by or on behalf of the applicant: Magistrates' Courts Rules 1981, SI 1981/552, r 76(1).

2. Other useful clauses

(a) The form of application where the appeal is from a decision of the Crown Court

To the Chief Clerk to the Chancery Lane Crown Court.

I, the undersigned, was the appellant in an appeal against conviction at the Chancery Lane Crown Court following my conviction by the Chancery Lane Magistrates' Court on 13 January 1999 under the provisions of section 2(1) of the Protection from Harassment Act 1997. The appeal was dismissed by the Chancery Lane Crown Court on 20 January 1999. I was a party to the appeal in Chancery Lane Crown Court and I question the determination of the appeal as it is wrong in law or in excess of jurisdiction[1]. As a consequence I apply to Her Honour Judge Brown to state a case on the following questions:

(b) The form of the application where the appellant is a prosecutor

I, the undersigned, am a Branch Crown Prosecutor employed by the Crown Prosecution Service. The Crown Prosecution Service brought proceedings at the Chancery Lane Magistrates' Court against Wayne Red for a single offence under the provisions of section 2(1) of the Protection from Harassment Act 1997. Wayne Red was acquitted of that offence by the said Magistrates' Court on 13 January 1999. The Crown Prosecution Service was a party to the said proceedings and wishes to question that acquittal as it is wrong in law or in excess of jurisdiction[2]. As a consequence the Crown Prosecution Service applies to you to state a case on the following questions:

(c) Delay in the Crown Court

Where there has been delay in the Crown Court[3], the application should address this issue and seek an extension of time.

1. An application for an extension of time

1.1 I applied for Legal Aid on 15 January 1999 which was two days after my conviction under section 2(1) of the Protection from Harassment Act 1997 had been upheld following an appeal to the Chancery Lane Crown Court. That application was initially refused and so I appealed to the Legal Aid area committee. The appeal was heard on 15 March 1999 despite numerous requests that the appeal should be heard earlier. I was granted Legal Aid by the area committee. As a result no application was made to state a case before 15 March 1999.

1.2 In *R v Stratford-on-Avon District Council ex p Jackson* [1985] 3 All ER 769 the court held that a good reason for delay may include delay in obtaining Legal Aid.

---

1 The notice should repeat the terms of the Supreme Court Act 1981, s 28(1).
2 The notice should repeat the terms of the Magistrates' Courts Act 1980, s 111(1).
3 There can be no application for an extension of time in the magistrates' court. See **5.6**.

1.3 In the light of my difficulties obtaining Legal Aid I request that the time for applying to state a case be extended to enable this application to be considered.

3. Case stated

IN THE HIGH COURT OF JUSTICE
QUEEN'S BENCH DIVISION
BETWEEN:

WAYNE RED

Appellant

v

THE DIRECTOR OF PUBLIC PROSECUTIONS

Respondent

Case stated by the Justices for the Petty Sessional Division of Chancery Lane, in respect of their adjudication as a Magistrates' Court sitting at Chancery Lane.

CASE

1. On 16 October 1998, an information was preferred by the respondent against the appellant that between 10 October 1998 and 15 October 1998 the appellant had engaged in a course of conduct that amounted to an offence under section 2(1) of the Protection from Harassment Act 1997. At a hearing on 13 January 1999 that information was amended so that it alleged a course of conduct between 10 October 1998 and 21 October 1998.

2. We heard that said information on 13 January 1999 and we found the following facts:

    2.1 That on 10 October 1998 the appellant had looked through the window of Ms Blue at Chancery Lane Student Halls of Residence;

    2.2 That on 14 October 1998 the appellant had looked through the window of Ms Green at Chancery Lane Student Halls of Residence;

    2.3 That on 21 October 1998 the appellant had looked through the window of Ms Green at Chancery Lane Student Halls of Residence; and

    2.4 That the three incidents set out in paragraphs 2.1 to 2.3, above, amounted to a course of conduct contrary to section 1(1) of the Protection from Harassment Act 1997.

    We heard the following evidence when we reached the above findings of fact[1]:

    2.5 Ms Blue gave evidence that she had seen the appellant looking through her window at Chancery Lane Student Halls of Residence on 10 October 1998; and

---

1 The evidence should be included only if there is a challenge to the sufficiency of the evidence.

2.6 Ms Green gave evidence that she had seen the appellant looking through her window at Chancery Lane Student Halls of Residence on 14 October 1998 and on 21 October 1998.

We heard no other evidence.

3. It was contended by the appellant that:

3.1 We had no power to allow the amendment of an information so that it could allege conduct that could not possibly have been included in the information at the time that it was lodged;

3.2 A course of conduct contrary to section 1(1) of the Protection of Harassment Act 1997 can only be directed against one person so that incidents involving Ms Green and Ms Blue formed parts of separate courses of conduct; and

3.3 As a consequence of the matters set out above, there was only admissible evidence of two incidents. These were not part of the same course of conduct. As a result there was insufficient evidence to convict the appellant.

4. It was contended by the respondent that:

4.1 Justices have a broad discretion to allow the amendment of an information;

4.2 By virtue of section 6(c) of the Interpretation Act 1978, the words 'other' and 'another' in section 1(1) of the Protection from Harassment Act 1997 include the plural. Thus a course of conduct could be directed at more than one person;

4.3 As a consequence of the matters set out above, there was evidence of three incidents involving the appellant which clearly could form a course of conduct.

5. We were referred to the following cases:

None

6. We were of the opinion that:

6.1 Justices have a broad discretion to allow the amendment of an information. As a result we were entitled to allow the amendment sought by the prosecution;

6.2 By virtue of section 6(c) of the Interpretation Act 1978, the words 'other' and 'another' in section 1(1) of the Protection from Harassment Act 1997 include the plural. Thus a course of conduct could be directed at more than one person.

6.3 In reaching this decision we noted that the incidents involving Ms Green and Ms Blue occurred at the same student halls of residence. This was significant as we ruled that incidents involving different people must be linked in some way if they are to form a course of conduct;

6.4 As a consequence of the matters set out above, there was evidence of three incidents involving the appellant which clearly could form a course of conduct; and

6.5 As a consequence of the findings of above, we found that the appellant was guilty of an offence contrary to section 2(1) of the Protection from Harassment Act 1997. We sentenced the appellant to a fine of £250.

7. The questions for the opinion of the High Court are:

7.1 Whether the justices were entitled to allow the prosecution to amend the information so that it included allegations of conduct after the date when the information was lodged;

7.2 Whether the justices were entitled to take account of the evidence of incidents involving separate persons when they determined that there had been a course of conduct governed by section 1 of the Protection from Harassment Act 1997; and

7.3 Whether there was sufficient evidence to entitle the justices to convict the appellant of an offence under section 2 of the Protection from Harassment Act 1997.

Dated 20 February 1999

Signed

Mike Smith

Julia Brown

Justices of the Peace on behalf of all the justices adjudicating

(a) Case stated where the appeal is from a decision of the Crown Court

Case stated by the Crown Court at Chancery Lane, in respect of its adjudication sitting on appeal from the Chancery Lane Magistrates' Court.

CASE

1. On 16 October 1998, an information was preferred by the respondent against the appellant that between 10 October 1998 and 15 October 1998 the appellant had engaged in a course of conduct that amounted to an offence under section 2(1) of the Protection from Harassment Act 1997. At a hearing on 13 January 1999 that information was amended so that it alleged a course of conduct between 10 October 1998 and 21 October 1998.

2. On 13 January 1999 justices acting in and for the Petty Sessional Division of Chancery Lane found that the appellant was guilty of an offence contrary to section 2(1) of the Protection from Harassment Act 1997 and sentenced the appellant to a fine of £250.

3. The Appellant appealed against the decision of the said justices to the Crown Court at Chancery Lane, which appeal was heard on 20 January 1999.

4. Notice of entry of a case stated

IN THE HIGH COURT OF JUSTICE
QUEEN'S BENCH DIVISION
BETWEEN:

WAYNE RED

Appellant

v

THE DIRECTOR OF PUBLIC PROSECUTIONS

Respondent

Take notice that the above named Appellant being the defendant to an information preferred by the Respondent and heard before and determined by three of Her Majesty's justices sitting at the Chancery Lane Magistrates' Court on 13 January 1999, being dissatisfied with the determination of the said justices as being wrong in law or in excess of jurisdiction, applied to said justices pursuant to the Magistrates' Court Act 1980, section 111, to state a case for the opinion of a Divisional Court[1] of the Queen's Bench Division of the High Court of Justice.

And take further notice that in pursuance thereof the said justices[2] have stated and signed a case a copy of which is annexed hereto.

And take further notice that this case has been entered for hearing before the Divisional Court[3] of the Queen's Bench Division of the High Court of Justice at the Royal Courts of Justice, Strand, London, WC2A 2LL [on [*date*] or as soon thereafter as Counsel can be heard on behalf of the Appellants][4].

Dated ....

....
Signed

To: The Crown Prosecution Service
              Chancery Lane Branch

And to: The Clerk to the Chancery Lane Magistrates' Court

(a) Where the appeal relates to a decision taken by the Crown Court, the first paragraph should read as follows:

Take notice that the above named Appellant being the appellant in an appeal to the Chancery Lane Crown Court that was heard and determined on 13 January 1999 following a conviction on an information preferred by the Respondent, being dissatisfied with the determination of the said Crown Court

---

1   Delete if the case is not to be heard by a Divisional Court. See **9.13** for details of cases that will be heard by a Divisional Court.
2   In the case of an appeal from the Crown Court, this should read 'Her Honour Judge ...'
3   See footnote 1.
4   The hearing date should be inserted here if known.

as being wrong in law or in excess of jurisdiction, applied to Her Honour Judge Smith pursuant to the Supreme Court Act 1981, section 28, to state a case for the opinion of a Divisional Court[1] of the Queen's Bench Division of the High Court of Justice.

---

1   Delete if the case is not to be heard by a Divisional Court. See **9.13** for details of cases that will be heard by a Divisional Court.

Appendix 4: Procedural Guides

1. Deciding whether to proceed with a judicial review or an appeal by way of case stated

This is a guide to some of the factors to be considered when deciding whether to proceed with a judicial review or an appeal by way of case stated. It should be read in conjunction with Chapter 4 which considers the appropriateness of proceedings in the High Court in the context of the various stages of criminal proceedings.

Is there an alternative remedy?	This may mean that the High Court will be reluctant to consider a judicial review	See **5.4**
	The availability of an appeal to the Crown Court is not normally a bar to bringing judicial review proceedings but tactically there may be reasons why judicial review is not appropriate	*R v Hereford Magistrates' Court ex p Rowlands and Ingram; R v Harrow Youth Court ex p Prussia* [1998] QB 110; see **1.7.1** and **4.12**
	The availability of an appeal to the Crown Court does not prevent an appeal by way of case stated	MCA 1980, s 111
	The prohibition on appealing to the Crown Court if one has appealed by way of case stated means that an appeal by way of case stated will generally not be appropriate where there is a right of appeal to the Crown Court	MCA 1980, s 111(4); see **4.11**
	Judicial review is not normally available to challenge decisions to refuse bail as a result of the jurisdiction of a High Court judge to consider bail applications	*Re Herbage* (1985) *The Times*, 25 October; see **4.5**

Appendix 4: Procedural Guides – 1. Deciding whether to proceed with a judicial review or an appeal by way of case stated

Is the decision a decision of a court?	If it is not, appeal by way of case stated is not available as a result of the statutory scope of appeals by way of case stated	MCA 1980, s 111, SCA 1981, s 28(1); see **1.9**
Is the nature of the complaint one that can be raised by way of judicial review?	If the complaint about the decision raises issues of public law, judicial review is likely to be the appropriate form of proceedings	See **1.9.1**
	If the complaint about the decision raises issues of private law, judicial review is unlikely to be the appropriate form of proceedings	See **1.9.1**
	Although judicial review is likely to be the appropriate form of proceedings if there is a complaint relating to public law, public law defences may be raised during criminal proceedings as an alternative to judicial review proceedings	*Boddington v British Transport Police* [1998] 2 WLR 639; see **4.4**
Is the decision a decision of the Crown Court?	If it is, judicial review and an appeal by way of case stated are not available if the decision is a matter relating to trial on indictment	SCA 1981, ss 28(2) and 29(3); see **1.6**
	Habeas corpus may be available if the liberty of the subject is at stake	*R v Maidstone Crown Court ex p Clark* [1995] 1 WLR 831; see **1.5**
Is the decision a decision of magistrates sitting as examining magistrates?	If it is, there is probably no appeal by way of case stated	*Atkinson v United States Government* [1971] AC 1971; see **1.7**

Appendix 4: Procedural Guides – 1. Deciding whether to proceed with a judicial review or an appeal by way of case stated   275

	Judicial review is available	See eg **4.7** and **4.24**
	The High Court's jurisdiction when considering decisions to commit is wider than that of magistrates as it has a responsibility to uphold the rule of law	*R v Horseferry Road Magistrates' Court ex p Bennett* [1994] 1 AC 42; see **4.7** and **13.10.2**
Is the decision a sentencing decision?	An appeal by way of case stated is very rarely the correct procedure as a consequence of the difference in the High Court's powers when considering appeals by way of case stated compared with the powers when considering judicial reviews	SCA 1981, s 43; see **4.17**
	Judicial reviews are rarely appropriate unless there is no appeal	See **4.18** and **4.19**
Is the decision an interim decision of the courts?	If it is, appeal by way of case stated is not available	*Streames v Copping* [1985] QB 920; *Loade v DPP* [1990] 1 QB 1052; see **4.9**
	Judicial review is available but it may be necessary to justify the decision to bring the judicial review instead of waiting to the conclusion of the criminal proceedings	*Streames v Copping* [1985] QB 920; see **4.10**
Is the decision a decision that is illegal, irrational or one taken following a procedural impropriety?	If it is not, it is unlikely that the grounds exist to bring proceedings in the High Court	See Chapters 2 and 3 for a more detailed consideration of the grounds

Appendix 4: Procedural Guides – 1. Deciding whether to proceed with a judicial review or an appeal by way of case stated

Are the grounds of challenge such that the procedure for judicial review is more appropriate than the procedure for appealing by way of case stated?	If they are not, the High Court will normally expect a person to appeal by way of case stated	*R v Morpeth JJ ex p Ward* (1992) 95 Cr App R 215; see **4.14**
	Where the High Court requires a full record of the findings of fact and law, an appeal by way of case stated will normally be appropriate	See **4.14**
	Where the High Court requires evidence about the procedure in the court whose decision is subject to challenge, judicial review is likely to be appropriate	See **4.14**
Is any form of interim relief sought?	If interim relief is sought, this may influence the decision about whether to proceed by way of judicial review or by way of appeal by way of case stated	See Chapter 10

2. Judicial review

This is a guide to the procedural steps involved in bringing an application for judicial review. It should be read in conjunction with Chapter 7.

Which court?	The application must be brought in the High Court	SCA 1981
Who may bring an application?	A person with sufficient interest	CPR 1998, Sch 1, RSC Ord 53, r 3(7); see **1.10**
When must the application be brought?	Promptly and in any event within 3 months	CPR 1998, Sch 1, RSC Ord 53, r 4(1); see **5.2**
Steps to be taken before the application is commenced	The proposed respondent should be placed on notice and a letter before action should be written in most cases	*R v Horsham District Council* [1995] 1 WLR 680; see **7.2**
How is the application commenced?	The applicant must obtain permission to bring the application	CPR 1998, Sch 1, RSC Ord 53, r 3(1); see **7.8**
	The application for permission is normally commenced by lodging the papers set out below unless an urgent out of hours application is made	See **7.3** for details of out-of-hours applications
Papers to be lodged when seeking permission to bring the application	Form 86A which will contain the grounds	CPR 1998, Sch 1, RSC Ord 53, r 3(2); see precedents 2 and 3 at Appendix 1; see **7.4** and **7.7**
	Written evidence in support of the application. This can be a witness statement or an affidavit	CPR 1998, Sch 1, RSC Ord 53, r 3(2), *Practice Direction (CPR 1998, Part 32 – Written Evidence)* Paragraphs 1.2 to 1.4; see precedents 4, 5 and 6 at Appendix 1; see **7.4** and **7.7**
	Copies of any statutory materials relied on	*Practice Direction (Crown Office List: Legislation Bundle)* [1997] 1 WLR 52; See **7.4**

	A list of essential reading	*Practice Direction (Crown Office List: Preparation for Hearings)* [1994] 1 WLR 1551, [1994] 4 All ER 671; see **7.4**
	A copy of any legal aid certificate	Civil Legal Aid (General) Regulations, SI 1989/339, reg 50(4)
	The court fee	See **7.4**
Requirements to be considered when drafting the documents	Applicants are subject to a duty of candour	See **7.7**
	The documents should be in a paginated and indexed bundle	*Practice Direction (Crown Office List: Preparation for Hearings)* [1994] 1 WLR 1551, [1994] 4 All ER 671; see **6.4**
	The written evidence must comply with the requirements of the practice directions	*Practice Direction (CPR 1998, Part 32 – Written Evidence)*; see **6.4** and precedents 4, 5 and 6 in Appendix 1
How many copies of these documents?	The original and one copy unless the matter is to be heard by a Divisional Court when two copies are required	See **7.4**
Other issues to consider when applying for permission	Decide whether the application for permission is to be made orally or on the papers	See **7.6**
	Decide whether the applicant should seek interim relief such as bail	See **7.5** and **10.2**; see precedent 8 at Appendix 1
	Decide whether the applicant should seek expedition	See **6.2**
	Decide whether the application for permission is likely to take longer than 20 minutes	See **7.5**
	Decide whether there is a need for an order restricting reporting of the application	Contempt of Court Act 1981, s 11; see **5.7**

Appendix 4: Procedural Guides – 2. Judicial review

Special factors when a party is a juvenile	A litigation friend should be appointed unless an order is obtained allowing proceedings to be conducted without a litigation friend	CPR 1998, r 21.2(2); see **5.9**
	An order should be sought restricting reporting	Children and Young Persons Act 1933, s 39; see **5.8**
Can the grounds be amended?	The High Court has a discretion to allow amendment if it thinks fit	CPR 1998, Sch 1, RSC Ord 53, rr 3(6) and 6(2); see **7.9**
Can additional evidence be submitted?	The High Court has a discretion to allow the service of additional evidence if all parties have been given notice and served with copies	CPR 1998, Sch 1, RSC Ord 53, rr 6(2) and 6(3); see **7.9**
When should the application be made to amend grounds or rely on additional evidence?	At any stage before or after the application for permission. If, however, notice of the application is not given at least 5 clear working days before the substantive hearing, the High Court will be reluctant to grant the application	*Practice Direction (Crown Office List: Preparation for Hearings)* [1994] 1 WLR 1551, [1994] 4 All ER 671; See **7.9**
How is the application for permission to bring a judicial review application determined?	Permission is normally granted if the application is arguable	Eg *R v Secretary of State for the Home Department ex p Begum* [1990] COD 107; see **7.8**
Issues that arise at the conclusion of an oral application for permission	The parties may consider applications for costs. However, in general there will be a reluctance to order costs	CPR 1998, r 44.3(6)(e); *R v Honourable Society of the Middle Temple ex p Bullock* [1996] ELR 349; see **12.3**

	If the applicant is in receipt of legal aid, an order for legal aid taxation should be sought	Civil Legal Aid (General) Regulations 1989, SI 1989/339, reg 107; see **12.13**
Further steps if permission is refused	The application can be renewed following a review of the merits. The procedure for renewal depends on whether the case is a criminal cause and how the initial application was determined	CPR 1998, Sch 1, RSC Ord 53, r 3(4) and Ord 59, r 14(3); see **7.10**
When must proceedings be commenced after the grant of permission?	An application for hearing should be entered no more than 14 days after the grant of permission	CPR 1998, Sch 1, RSC Ord 53, r 5(5)
How is the application for hearing entered?	A claim form must be served on all persons directly affected	CPR 1998, Sch 1, RSC Ord 53, rr 5(3) and 5(6); see **7.11**
	The claim form must be accompanied by the Form 86A and grounds	CPR 1998, Sch 1, RSC Ord 53, r 6(1); See **7.11**
	It is good practice to serve a copy of the written evidence with the claim form	See **7.11**
	If the applicant is in receipt of legal aid, a notice of legal aid must be served with the claim form	Civil Legal Aid (General) Regulations 1989, SI 1989/339, reg 50(1)(a); see **7.11**
	The claim form is then filed at court with written evidence of service and the court fee	CPR 1998, Sch 1, RSC Ord 53, rr 5(5) and 5(6); see **7.11**
What should an interested party do if not served with the claim form?	An application can be made to the High Court requesting an order that they should be heard	CPR 1998, Sch 1, RSC Ord 53, r 9(1); see **7.13**
What steps should a party take if they are served with the claim form?	Decide whether they oppose the application	See **7.14**
	Decide whether to serve evidence	See **7.14**

Appendix 4: Procedural Guides – 2. Judicial review

	Decide whether to attend the hearing	See **7.14**
Procedure if the proceedings are to be settled by consent	The High Court may make the order proposed without the attendance of the parties	*Practice Direction (Crown Office List: Consent Orders)* [1997] 1 WLR 825; see **6.6**
The procedural requirements if evidence is to be served by a party other than the applicant	The evidence can either be in the form of a witness statement or an affidavit	*Practice Direction (CPR 1998, Part 32 –Written Evidence)* paras 1.2 to 1.4; see **7.14**
	The evidence should be served within 56 days of the service of the claim form unless time has been abridged	CPR 1998, Sch 1, RSC Ord 53, r 6(4); see **7.14**
	Respondents are subject to a duty of candour	*R v Secretary of State for the Home Department ex p Fayed* [1997] 1 All ER 228; see **7.14**
	The written evidence must comply with the requirements of the practice directions	*Practice Direction (CPR Part 32 – Written Evidence)*; see **6.4** and precedents 4, 5, 6 and 11 in Appendix 1
Can the respondent seek permission to rely on additional evidence after service of their evidence?	The respondent can seek permission to rely on additional evidence. The High Court may be reluctant to grant permission if time for service of respondent's evidence has passed. The additional evidence should normally be served at least 5 clear working days before the substantive hearing	CPR 1998, Sch 1, RSC Ord 53, r 6(4); *Practice Direction (Crown Office List: Preparation for Hearings)* [1994] 1 WLR 1551, [1994] 4 All ER 671; see **7.9** and **7.14**
Should interlocutory applications be made on behalf of a party?	The High Court may make orders for matters such as disclosure and cross-examination of witnesses	CPR 1998, Sch 1, RSC Ord 53, r 8
	The High Court will be reluctant to make such orders	See **7.12**

Appendix 4: Procedural Guides – 2. Judicial review

	One particular order that might be sought by a party other than an applicant is an order setting aside a grant of permission	CPR 1998, r 23.10; see **7.15**
How is an interlocutory order sought?	By filing an application notice and the correct fee with the Crown Office	CPR 1998, r 23.3; see **6.9**
Steps to be taken prior to the substantive hearing of the matter	The applicant must prepare trial bundles and lodge with the Crown Office at least 5 working days before the fixed or warned date	*Practice Direction (Crown Office List: Preparation for Hearings)* [1994] 1 WLR 1551, [1994] 4 All ER 671; see **6.4.1**
	The applicant must lodge a skeleton argument at least 5 working days before the fixed or warned date	*Practice Direction (Crown Office List: Preparation for Hearings)* [1994] 1 WLR 1551, [1994] 4 All ER 671; see **6.4.1**
	The respondent must lodge a skeleton argument at least 3 working days before the fixed or warned date	*Practice Direction (Crown Office List: Preparation for Hearings)* [1994] 1 WLR 1551, [1994] 4 All ER 671; see **6.4.1**
	By 9.30 am on the morning of the hearing, parties must supply a list of authorities	*Practice Direction (Authorities)* [1961] 1 WLR 400; [1961] 1 All ER 541; see **6.4.1**
How many copies of the trial bundles and skeleton argument must be lodged?	Two copies if a Divisional Court is to consider the matter. Otherwise one copy should be lodged	*Practice Direction (Crown Office List: Preparation for Hearings)* [1994] 1 WLR 1551, [1994] 4 All ER 671
Special considerations if Hansard is to be cited	Two copies of the citation and a summary of the argument must be served on the Crown Office. Copies must also be served on the other parties	*Practice Direction (Hansard Extracts)* [1995] 1 WLR 192; see **6.4.1**
Matters to consider at the conclusion of proceedings	The High Court has a discretion about whether to grant relief	See **11.2**

Appendix 4: Procedural Guides – 2. Judicial review

	The High Court can issue orders of mandamus, prohibition, certiorari, an injunction and a declaration	CPR 1998, Sch 1, RSC Ord 53, r 1; see **11.6**
	In sentencing cases the High Court can vary a sentence	SCA 1981, s 43(1); see **11.7**
	The High Court can award damages	CPR 1998, Sch 1, RSC Ord 53, r 7(1); see **11.8**
	The High Court can issue an order for costs	CPR 1998, Part 44; see Chapter 12
	If the applicant is in receipt of legal aid, obtain an order for legal aid taxation	Civil Legal Aid (General) Regulations 1989, SI 1989/339, reg 107; see **12.13**
	Decide whether leave to appeal should be sought	See **7.16**
What costs orders will the High Court make?	The general rule is that the unsuccessful party should pay the costs of the successful party	CPR 1998, r 44.3(2); see **12.2**
	Special considerations apply when the unsuccessful party is in receipt of legal aid	See **12.4**
	Special considerations apply when magistrates are a party	See **12.5**
	Consider whether to apply for costs from central funds	Prosecution of Offences Act 1985, ss 16 and 17; see **12.7**

3. Appeal by case stated from a decision of the magistrates' court

This is a guide to the procedural steps involved in bringing an appeal by case stated from a decision of the magistrates' court. It should be read in conjunction with Chapter 9.

Proceedings commence in the magistrates' court and so are governed by the Magistrates' Courts Rules 1981

Who may bring the appeal?	A party to the proceedings or a person aggrieved	MCA 1980, s 111(1); see **1.10**
When must he bring the appeal?	Within 21 days of the date of decision. There is no discretion to extend this time period	MCA 1980, s 111(2); see **5.6**
How does he appeal?	An application to state a case must be made to the clerk but should also specify that it is being sent to the justices	MCR 1981, r 76(3); see **9.3**
What is the format of an application to state a case?	It must be in writing and it must be signed by or on behalf of the applicant	MCR 1981, r 76(1); see precedents 1 and 2 at Appendix 3; see **9.3**
	It shall identify the question or questions of law or jurisdiction upon which the opinion of the High Court is sought	MCR 1981, r 76(1); see **9.3**
	If it is claimed that there is no evidence to support a finding of fact, that finding should be specified	MCR 1981, r 76(2)
What happens if the application fails to comply with these requirements?	The application is only valid if there is substantial compliance with the rules	*R v Croydon Justices ex p Lefore Holdings Ltd* [1980] 1 WLR 1465; see **5.6** and **9.3**
What is the effect of a valid application?	The application deprives the applicant of the right of appeal to the Crown Court	MCA 1980, s 111(4); see **4.11**

Appendix 4: Procedural Guides – 3. Appeal by case stated from a decision of the magistrates' court

What must the justices do on receipt of the application?	Decide whether they are willing to state a case in sufficient time to enable the clerk to send a draft case to the applicant within 21 days of the application	MCR 1981, r 77(1); see **9.4**
Grounds for refusing to state a case	The application is frivolous	MCA 1980, s 111(5); see **9.4**
	The application is out of time because it is made in excess of 21 days after the date of sentence	MCA 1980, s 111(2); see **5.6**
	There is no jurisdiction to consider the application as it relates to an interim decision	*Streames v Copping* [1985] QB 920; see **4.9**
	The application is not an effective application as there is not substantial compliance with the procedural rules	*R v Croydon Justices ex p Lefore Holdings Ltd* [1980] 1 WLR 1465; see **5.6** and **9.3**
What should the magistrates do if they decide to refuse to state a case?	They may be required to issue a certificate stating that they have refused to state a case	MCA 1980, s 111(5); see **9.4**
	It is good practice to supply brief reasons	*R v Mildenhall Magistrates' Court ex p Forest Heath District Council* (1997) *The Times*, 16 May; see **9.4**
What can an applicant do if he disagrees with the decision to refuse to state a case?	He can seek an order for mandamus by applying for judicial review	MCA 1980, s 111(6); see **9.5**
Obligations that can imposed on the applicant before agreeing to state a case	A recognizance can be sought and, in a case that is not a criminal matter, a fee may be charged	MCA 1980, s 114; see **9.4**
When must the case be stated?	The draft case must be stated within 21 days of receipt of the application	MCR 1981, r 77(1); see **9.6**
	This time period does not start until any required recognizance has been entered into	*R v Warrington Magistrates ex p Worsley* [1996] COD 346; see **9.6**

	If the time period cannot be complied with, the draft case should be sent as soon as practicable after that time	MCR 1981, r 79(1)
What must the draft case contain?	The facts found and the question or questions of law or jurisdiction on which the opinion of the High Court is sought	MCR 1981, r 81(1); see **9.7**
	There should only be a statement of evidence if the sufficiency of evidence is being questioned. In such a case the finding that it is said cannot be supported by evidence must be specified	MCR 1981, r 81(3) and 81(2)
	Any legal argument heard	*DPP v Kirk* [1993] COD 99
	It should comply with the requirements of Form 155 of the Magistrates' Courts (Forms) Rules 1981, SI 1981/553	See precedent 3 at Appendix 3
	The draft case should include a statement of any delay and the reasons for delay	MCR 1981, r 79(1)
	The case stated should be brief but contain all the material required by the High Court	*Riley v DPP* (1990) 91 Cr App R 14; see **9.7**
What happens after the draft case has been prepared?	It must be sent to the applicant and to the respondent or their solicitors	MCR 1981, r 77(1); see **9.8**
What do the parties do upon receipt?	They may make representations in writing which must be signed by them or on their behalf	MCR 1981, r 77(2); see **9.8**

Appendix 4: Procedural Guides – 3. Appeal by case stated from a decision of the magistrates' court

When must the representations be made?	Within 21 days unless an extension of time is obtained	MCR 1981, r 77(2); see **9.8**
What must the magistrates do if they receive representations?	They have 21 days to adjust the case and then state it and sign it unless they extend time	MCR 1981, r 78(1); see **9.8**
	When the final case has been prepared it must be sent to the applicant	MCR 1981, r 78(3)

At this stage proceedings in the High Court commence and so proceedings start to be governed by the Civil Procedure Rules 1998

What must the applicant do upon receipt of the final case stated?	The final case stated must be filed in the Crown Office of the High Court within 10 days of receipt	CPR 1998, Sch 1, RSC Ord 56, r 6(1)(a); see **9.11**
	Three copies of the case should be supplied together with the court fee	See **9.11**
	A copy of any legal aid certificate should be lodged	Civil Legal Aid (General) Regulations, SI 1889/339, reg 50(4)
Other issues to consider when filing the case stated	Decide whether the applicant should seek interim relief such as bail	See **10.2.3**; see precedent 8 at Appendix 1
	Decide whether the applicant should seek expedition	See **6.2**
	Decide whether there is a need for an order restricting reporting of the application	Contempt of Court Act 1981, s 11; see **5.7**
Special factors when a party is a juvenile	A litigation friend should be appointed unless an order is obtained allowing proceedings to be conducted without a litigation friend	CPR 1998, r 21.2(2); see **5.9**
	An order should be sought restricting reporting	Children and Young Persons Act 1933, s 39; see **5.8**

Appendix 4: Procedural Guides – 3. Appeal by case stated from a decision of the magistrates' court

What should an appellant do after they have filed the case?	A notice of entry of the appeal must be served on the respondent with a copy of the case stated within 4 days of filing the case	CPR 1998, Sch 1, RSC Ord 56, r 6(1)(b); see precedent 4 at Appendix 3
What should a party do if they are unhappy with the case stated?	Attempt to obtain the consent of the parties to an amendment	See **9.9**
	The application for amendment should be made by application notice supported by written evidence	*Practice Note (Case Stated)* [1953] 1 WLR 334; see **9.9**
Procedure if the proceedings are to be settled by consent	The High Court may make the order proposed without the attendance of the parties	*Practice Direction (Crown Office List: Consent Orders)* [1997] 1 WLR 825; see **6.6**
Should interlocutory applications be made on behalf of a party?	The High Court may make orders for matters such as extending time for service of notice of entry of the appeal	CPR 1998, Sch 1, RSC Ord 56, r 13(1); see **9.12**
	The High Court will be particularly reluctant to make orders for matters such as disclosure and cross-examination of witnesses	See **9.12**
How is an interlocutory order sought?	By filing an application notice and the correct fee with the Crown Office	CPR 1998, r 23.3; see **6.9**
Steps to be taken prior to the substantive hearing of the matter	The applicant must prepare trial bundles and lodge with the Crown Office at least 5 working days before the fixed or warned date	*Practice Direction (Crown Office List: Preparation for Hearings)* [1994] 1 WLR 1551, [1994] 4 All ER 671; see **6.4.1**
	The applicant must lodge a skeleton argument at least 5 working days before the fixed or warned date	*Practice Direction (Crown Office List: Preparation for Hearings)* [1994] 1 WLR 1551, [1994] 4 All ER 671; see **6.4.1**

Appendix 4: Procedural Guides – 3. Appeal by case stated from a decision of the magistrates' court

	The respondent must lodge a skeleton argument at least 3 working days before the fixed or warned date	*Practice Direction (Crown Office List: Preparation for Hearings)* [1994] 1 WLR 1551, [1994] 4 All ER 671; see **6.4.1**
	By 9.30am on the morning of the hearing, parties must supply a list of authorities	*Practice Direction (Authorities)* [1961] 1 WLR 400; [1961] 1 All ER 541; see **6.4.1**
How many copies must be lodged?	Three copies	see **6.4.1**
Special considerations if Hansard is to be cited	Two copies of the citation and a summary of the argument must be served on the Crown Office. Copies must also be served on the other parties	*Practice Direction (Hansard Extracts)* [1995] 1 WLR 192; see **6.4.1**
Matters to consider at the conclusion of proceedings	The High Court has a discretion about whether to grant relief	See **11.5**
	The High Court may remit the case to the magistrates for amendment	SCA 1981, s 28A(2); see **11.10**
	The High Court may reverse, affirm or amend the determination in respect of which the case has been stated. Alternatively they may remit with the opinion of the Court	SCA 1981, s 28A(3); see **11.10**
	In sentencing cases in the High Court there is no power to vary a sentence	See **4.17**
	The High Court can issue an order for costs	CPR 1998, Part 44
	If the applicant is in receipt of legal aid, obtain an order for legal aid taxation	Civil Legal Aid (General) Regulations 1989, SI 1989/339, reg 107; see **12.13**
	Decide whether leave to appeal should be sought	See **9.13**

What costs orders will the High Court make?	The general rule is that the unsuccessful party should pay the costs of the successful party	CPR 1998, r 44.3(2); see **12.2**
	Special considerations apply when the unsuccessful party is in receipt of legal aid	See **12.4**
	Consider whether to apply for costs from central funds	Prosecution of Offences Act 1985, ss 16 and 17; see **12.7**

4. Appeal by case stated from a decision of the Crown Court

This is a guide to the procedural steps involved in bringing an appeal by case stated from a decision of the Crown Court. It should be read in conjunction with Chapter 9.

Proceedings commence in the Crown Court and so are governed by the Crown Court Rules 1982

Who may bring the appeal?	A party to the proceedings	SCA 1981, s 28(1); see **1.10**
When must he bring the appeal?	Within 21 days of the date of the decision to which the appeal relates	CCR 1982, r 26(1); see **5.6**
	The Crown Court judge may extend this period	CCR 1982, r 26(14); see **5.6**
How does he appeal?	An application to state a case must be made to the appropriate officer of the Crown Court	CCR 1982, r 26(1); see **9.3**
	The application should then be sent forthwith to other parties	CCR 1982, r 26(3); see **9.3**
What is the format of an application to state a case?	It must be in writing	CCR 1982, r 26(1); see precedents 1 and 2 at Appendix 3; see **9.3**
	It shall state the ground on which the decision of the Crown Court is questioned	CCR 1982, r 26(2); see **9.3**
What happens if the application fails to comply with these requirements?	The application is only valid if there is substantial compliance with the rules	*R v Croydon Justices ex p Lefore Holdings Ltd* [1980] 1 WLR 1465; see **5.6** and **9.3**
What must the judge do on receipt of the application?	Decide on receipt of the application whether they are willing to state a case	CCR 1982, r 26(5); see **9.4**
Grounds for refusing to state a case	The application is frivolous	CCR 1982, r 26(6); see **9.4**
	The application concerns a matter that relates to trial on indictment	SCA 1981, s 28(2); See **1.6**

Appendix 4: Procedural Guides – 4. Appeal by case stated from a decision of the Crown Court

	The application is out of time because it is made in excess of 21 days after the date of the decision to which the appeal relates and the judge refuses to extend time	CCR 1982, rr 26(1) and 26(14); see **5.6**
	There is no jurisdiction to consider the application as it relates to an interim decision	*Loade v DPP* [1990] 1 QB 1052; see **4.9**
	The application is not an effective application as there is not substantial compliance with procedural rules	*R v Croydon Justices ex p Lefore Holdings Ltd* [1980] 1 WLR 1465; see **5.6** and **9.3**
What should the judge do if they decide to refuse to state a case?	They may be required to issue a certificate stating that they have refused to state a case	CCR 1982, r 26(6); see **9.4**
	It is good practice to supply brief reasons	*R v Mildenhall Magistrates' Court ex p Forest Heath District Council* (1997) *The Times*, 16 May; see **9.4**
What can an applicant do if he disagrees with the decision to refuse to state a case?	He can seek an order for mandamus by applying for judicial review	Eg *R v Crown Court at Portsmouth ex p Thomas* [1994] COD 373; see **9.5**
Obligations that can imposed on the applicant before agreeing to state a case	A recognizance can be sought	CCR 1982, r 26(11); see **9.4**
What happens when the Crown Court judge decides that a case should be stated?	The applicant should be given notice in writing by the appropriate officer of the Crown Court	CCR 1982, r 26(5)
What does the applicant do on receipt of the notice from the judge agreeing to state a case?	The applicant must draft a case within 21 days	CCR 1982, r 26(8); see **9.6**
	If the time period cannot be complied with, the applicant should apply to the Crown Court judge for an extension	CCR 1982, r 26(14)

Appendix 4: Procedural Guides – 4. Appeal by case stated from a decision of the Crown Court

What must the draft case contain?	The facts found, the submissions of the parties, the decision of the Crown Court in respect of which the opinion is sought and the question on which the opinion of the High Court is sought	CCR 1982, r 26(13); see **9.7**
	It should comply with the requirements of Form 155 of the Magistrates' Courts (Forms) Rules 1981, SI 1981/553	*Practice Direction (Cases Stated by Crown Courts)* (1979) 68 Cr App R 119; see precedent 3 at Appendix 3
	The case stated should be brief but contain all the material required by the High Court	*Riley v DPP* (1990) 91 Cr App R 14; see **9.7**
What happens after the draft case has been prepared?	It must be sent to the appropriate officer of the Crown Court and to the other parties to the proceedings	CCR 1982, r 26(8); see **9.8**
What do the other parties do upon receipt?	They may serve an alternative draft case within 21 days	CCR 1982, r 29(9)(c); see **9.8**
	They may state in writing that they do not wish to take part in proceedings	CCR 1982, r 26(9)(a)
	They may state in writing on a copy of the draft case that they agree with the draft case	CCR 1982, r 26(9)(b)
	The notices set out above should be served on the appropriate officer of the Crown Court within 21 days	CCR 1982, r 26(9)
	If the time period cannot be complied with, the applicant should apply to the Crown Court judge for an extension	CCR 1982, r 26(14)
What must the judge do after they receive the draft cases?	They have 14 days to consider the cases that have been drafted and then sign a case	CCR 1982, r 26(12)(a); see **9.8**

	If no response is received from a party within the time period set for responses, the judge should sign a case within 14 days of the expiry of that period	CCR 1982, r 26(12)(b); see **9.8**
	When the final case has been prepared it must be sent to the applicant	
What happens if the judge is unhappy with the procedure set out above?	The judge may dispense with the procedure set out above but this rarely happens	CCR 1982, r 26(7); see **9.6**

At this stage proceedings in the High Court commence and so proceedings start to be governed by the Civil Procedure Rules 1998

What must the applicant do upon receipt of the final case stated?	The final case stated must be filed in the Crown Office of the High Court within 10 days of receipt	CPR 1998, Sch 1, RSC Ord 56, r 1(4); see **9.11**
	The case must be accompanied by a copy of the judgment, order or decision that is the subject of the appeal	CPR 1998, Sch 1, RSC Ord 56, r 1(3); see **9.11**
	If the decision followed an appeal to the Crown Court, the case must be accompanied by a copy of the judgment, order or decision that was the subject of the appeal in the Crown Court	CPR 1998, Sch 1, RSC Ord 56, r 1(3); See **9.11**
	Three copies of the above documents should be supplied together with the court fee	See **9.11**
	A copy of any legal aid certificate should be lodged	Civil Legal Aid (General) Regulations, SI 1989/339, reg 50(4)
Other issues to consider when filing the case stated	Decide whether the applicant should seek interim relief such as bail	See **10.2.3**; see precedent 8 at Appendix 1

Appendix 4: Procedural Guides – 4. Appeal by case stated from a decision of the Crown Court

	Decide whether the applicant should seek expedition	See **6.2**
	Decide whether there is a need for an order restricting reporting of the application	Contempt of Court Act 1981, s 11; see **5.7**
Special factors when a party is a juvenile	A litigation friend should be appointed unless an order is obtained allowing proceedings to be conducted without a litigation friend	CPR 1998, r 21.2(2); see **5.9**
	An order should be sought restricting reporting	Children and Young Persons Act 1933, s 39; see **5.8**
What should an appellant do after they have filed the case?	A notice of entry of the appeal must be served on the respondent within 4 days of filing the case	CPR 1998, Sch 1, RSC Ord 56, r 4; see precedent 4 at Appendix 3
What should a party do if they are unhappy with the case stated?	Attempt to obtain the consent of the parties to an amendment	See **9.9**
	The application for amendment should be made by application notice supported by written evidence	*Practice Note (Case Stated)* [1953] 1 WLR 334; see **9.9**
Procedure if the proceedings are to be settled by consent	The High Court may make the order proposed without the attendance of the parties	*Practice Direction (Crown Office List: Consent Orders)* [1997] 1 WLR 825; see **6.6**
Should interlocutory applications be made on behalf of a party?	The High Court may make orders for matters such as extending time for service of notice of entry of the appeal	CPR 1998, Sch 1, RSC Ord 56, r 13(1); see **9.12**

	The High Court will be particularly reluctant to make orders for matters such as disclosure and cross-examination of witnesses	See **9.12**
How is an interlocutory order sought?	By filing an application notice and the correct fee with the Crown Office	CPR 1998, r 23.3; see **6.9**
Steps to be taken prior to the substantive hearing of the matter	The applicant must prepare bundles and lodge with the Crown Office at least 5 working days before the fixed or warned date	*Practice Direction (Crown Office List: Preparation for Hearings)* [1994] 1 WLR 1551, [1994] 4 All ER 671; see **6.4.1**
	The applicant must lodge a skeleton argument at least 5 working days before the fixed or warned date	*Practice Direction (Crown Office List: Preparation for Hearings)* [1994] 1 WLR 1551, [1994] 4 All ER 671; see **6.4.1**
	The respondent must lodge a skeleton argument at least 3 working days before the fixed or warned date	*Practice Direction (Crown Office List: Preparation for Hearings)* [1994] 1 WLR 1551, [1994] 4 All ER 671; see **6.4.1**
	By 9.30am on the morning of the hearing, parties must supply a list of authorities	*Practice Direction (Authorities)* [1961] 1 WLR 400; [1961] 1 All ER 541; see **6.4.1**
How many copies must be lodged?	Three copies	See **6.4.1**
Special considerations if Hansard is to be cited	Two copies of the citation and a summary of the argument must be served on the Crown Office. Copies must also be served on the other parties	*Practice Direction (Hansard Extracts)* [1995] 1 WLR 192; see **6.4.1**
Matters to consider at the conclusion of proceedings	The High Court has a discretion about whether to grant relief	See **11.5**
	The High Court may remit the case to the Crown Court for amendment	Eg *Colfox v Dorset County Council* [1996] COD 275; see **11.10**

Appendix 4: Procedural Guides – 4. Appeal by case stated from a decision of the Crown Court

	The High Court may make any other order that they could make following an appeal by way of case stated from the magistrates' court	See **11.10**
	In sentencing cases the High Court has no power to vary a sentence	See **4.17**
	The High Court can issue an order for costs	CPR 1998, Part 44
	If the applicant is in receipt of legal aid, obtain an order for legal aid taxation	Civil Legal Aid (General) Regulations 1989, SI 1989/339, reg 107; see **12.13**
	Decide whether leave to appeal should be sought	See **9.13**
What costs orders will the High Court make?	The general rule is that the unsuccessful party should pay the costs of the successful party	CPR 1998, r 44.3(2); see **12.2**
	Special considerations apply when the unsuccessful party is in receipt of legal aid	See **12.4**
	Consider whether to apply for costs from central funds	Prosecution of Offences Act 1985, ss 16 and 17; see **12.7**

Appendix 5: Legislation and Forms

Civil Procedure Rules 1998
SI 1998/3132

...

SCHEDULE 1
RSC RULES

...

RSC ORDER 53
APPLICATIONS FOR JUDICIAL REVIEW

1 Cases appropriate for application for judicial review

(1) An application for –
   (a) an order of mandamus, prohibition or certiorari; or
   (b) an injunction under section 30 of the Act restraining a person from acting in any office in which he is not entitled to act,

shall be made by way of an application for judicial review in accordance with the provisions of this Order.

(2) An application for a declaration or an injunction (not being an injunction mentioned in paragraph (1)(b)) may be made by way of an application for judicial review, and on such an application the Court may grant the declaration or injunction claimed if it considers that, having regard to –
   (a) the nature of the matters in respect of which a remedy may be granted by way of an order of mandamus, prohibition or certiorari;
   (b) the nature of the persons and bodies against whom a remedy may be granted by way of such an order; and
   (c) all the circumstances of the case,

it would be just and convenient for the declaration or injunction to be granted on an application for judicial review.

2 Joinder of claims for relief

On an application for judicial review any remedy mentioned in rule 1(1) or (2) may be claimed as an alternative or in addition to any other remedy so mentioned if it arises out of or relates to or is connected with the same matter.

3 Grant of leave to apply for judicial review

(1) No application for judicial review shall be made unless the permission of the Court has been obtained in accordance with this rule.

(2) An application for permission must be made to a Judge by filing in the Crown Office –

(a) an application notice in Form No. 86A containing a statement of –
  (i) the name and description of the applicant;
  (ii) the relief sought and the grounds upon which it is sought;
  (iii) the name and address of the applicant's solicitors (if any); and
  (iv) the applicant's address for service; and
(b) written evidence verifying the facts relied on.

(2A) The documents referred to in paragraphs (2)(a) and (b) need not be served on any other person.

(3) The Judge may determine the application without a hearing, unless a hearing is requested in the notice of application; in any case, the Crown Office shall serve a copy of the Judge's order on the applicant.

(4) Where the application for permission is refused by the Judge, or is granted on terms, the applicant may renew it by applying –

(a) in any criminal cause or matter, to a Divisional Court of the Queen's Bench Division;
(b) in any other case, to a single Judge or, if the Court so directs, to a Divisional Court of the Queen's Bench Division:

Provided that no application for permission may be renewed in any non-criminal cause or matter in which the Judge has refused permission under paragraph (3) after a hearing.

(5) In order to renew his application for permission the applicant must, within 10 days of being served with notice of the Judge's refusal, lodge in the Crown Office notice of his intention in Form No 86B.

(6) The Court hearing an application for permission may allow the applicant's statement to be amended, whether by specifying different or additional grounds or relief or otherwise, on such terms, if any, as it thinks fit.

(7) The Court shall not grant permission unless it considers that the applicant has a sufficient interest in the matter to which the application relates.

(8) Where permission is sought to apply for an order of certiorari to remove for the purpose of its being quashed any judgment, order, conviction or other proceeding which is subject to appeal and a time is limited for the bringing of the appeal, the Court may adjourn the application for permission until the appeal is determined or the time for appealing has expired.

(9) If the Court grants permission, it may impose such terms as to costs and as to giving security as it thinks fit.

(10) Where permission to apply for judicial review is granted, then –

(a) if the relief sought is an order of prohibition or certiorari and the Court so directs, the grant shall operate as a stay of the proceedings to which the application relates until the determination of the application or until the Court otherwise orders;
(b) if any other relief is sought, the Court may at any time grant in the proceedings interim remedies in accordance with CPR Part 25.

Amendments—SI 1999/1008.

4 Delay in applying for relief

(1) An application for permission to apply for judicial review shall be made promptly and in any event within three months from the date when grounds for the application first arose unless the Court considers that there is good reason for extending the period within which the application shall be made.

(2) Where an order of certiorari is sought in respect of any judgment, order, conviction or other proceeding, the date when grounds for the application first arose shall be taken to be the date of that judgment, order, conviction or proceeding.

(3) Paragraph (1) is without prejudice to any statutory provision which has the effect of limiting the time within which an application for judicial review may be made.

5 Mode of applying for judicial review

(1) In any criminal cause or matter, where permission has been granted to make an application for judicial review, the application shall be made to a Divisional Court of the Queen's Bench Division.

(2) In any other such cause or matter, the application shall be made to a judge unless the Court directs that it shall be made to a Divisional Court of the Queen's Bench Division.

(2A) An application for judicial review shall be made by claim form.

(3) The claim form must be served on all persons directly affected and where it relates to any proceedings in or before a Court and the object of the application is either to compel the Court or an officer of the Court to do any act in relation to the proceedings or to quash them or any order made therein, the claim form must also be served on the Clerk or Registrar of the Court and, where any objection to the conduct of the Judge is to be made, on the Judge.

(4) Unless the Court granting permission has otherwise directed, there must be at least 10 days between the service of the claim form and the hearing.

(5) The application must be entered for hearing within 14 days after the grant of permission.

(6) Written evidence giving the names and addresses of, and the places and dates of service on, all persons who have been served with the claim form must be filed before the application is entered for hearing and, if any person who ought to be served under this rule has not been served, the written evidence must state that fact and the reason for it; and shall be before the Court on the hearing of the application.

(7) If on the hearing of the application the Court is of opinion that any person who ought, whether under this rule or otherwise, to have been served has not been served, the Court may adjourn the hearing on such terms (if any) as it may direct in order that the claim form may be served on that person.

Amendments—SI 1999/1008.

6 Statements and evidence

(1) Copies of the statement in support of an application for permission under rule 3 must be served with the claim form and, subject to paragraph (2), no grounds shall be relied upon or any remedy sought at the hearing except the grounds and remedies set out in the statement.

(2) The Court may on hearing of the application for judicial review allow the applicant to amend his statement, whether by specifying different or additional grounds or otherwise, on such terms, if any, as it thinks fit and may allow further written evidence to be relied on by him.

(3) Where the applicant intends to ask to be allowed to amend his statement or to rely on further written evidence he shall give notice of his intention and of any proposed amendment to every other party.

(4) Any respondent who intends to use written evidence at the hearing shall file it in the Crown Office and give notice thereof to the applicant as soon as practicable and in any event, unless the Court otherwise directs, within 56 days after service upon him of the documents required to be served by paragraph (1).

(5) Each party to the application must supply to every other party on demand and on payment of the proper charges copies of any written evidence which he proposes to rely on at the hearing, including, in the case of the applicant, the written evidence in support of the application for permission under rule 3.

7 Claim for damages

(1) On an application for judicial review the Court may, subject to paragraph (2) award damages to the applicant if –

   (a) he has included in the statement in support of his application for permission under rule 3 a claim for damages arising from any matter to which the application relates; and
   (b) the Court is satisfied that, if the claim had been made in proceedings for damages begun by the applicant at the time of making his application for judicial review, he could have been awarded damages.

(2) CPR Part 16 shall apply to a statement relating to a claim for damages as it applies to a statement of case.

8 Application for disclosure, further information, cross-examination, etc

(1) Unless the Court otherwise directs, any interlocutory application in proceedings on an application for judicial review may be made to any judge or a master of the Queen's Bench Division, notwithstanding that the application for judicial review has been made to and is to be heard by a Divisional Court.

In this paragraph 'interlocutory application' includes an application for an order under CPR Part 31 or CPR Part 18 or for an order for permission to cross-examine any person who has given written evidence or for an order dismissing the proceedings by consent of the parties.

(2) In relation to an order made by a Master pursuant to paragraph (1) Order 58, rule 1, shall, where the application for judicial review is to be heard by a Divisional Court, have effect as if a reference to that Court were substituted for the reference to a Judge in Chambers.

(3) This rule is without prejudice to any statutory provision or rule of law restricting the making of an order against the Crown.

9 Hearing of application for judicial review

(1) On the hearing of any application for judicial review under rule 5, any person who desires to be heard in opposition to the application, and appears to the Court to be a proper person to be heard, shall be heard, notwithstanding that he has not been served with the claim form.

(2) Where the remedy sought is or includes an order of certiorari to remove any proceedings for the purpose of quashing them, the applicant may not question the validity of any order, warrant, commitment, conviction, inquisition or record unless before the hearing of the application he has filed in the Crown Office a copy thereof verified by witness statement or affidavit or accounts for his failure to do so to the satisfaction of the Court hearing the application.

(3) Where an order of certiorari is made in any such case as is referred to in paragraph (2) the order shall, subject to paragraph (4) direct that the proceedings shall be quashed forthwith on their removal into the Queen's Bench Division.

(4) Where an order of certiorari is sought and the Court is satisfied that there are grounds for quashing the decision to which the application relates, the Court may, in addition to quashing it, remit the matter to the Court, tribunal or authority concerned with a direction to reconsider it and reach a decision in accordance with the findings of the Court.

(5) Where the remedy sought is a declaration, an injunction or damages and the Court considers that it should not be granted on an application for judicial review but might have been granted if it had been sought in a claim begun by the applicant at the time of making his application for judicial review, the Court may, instead of refusing the application, order the judicial review proceedings to continue as proceedings brought under CPR Part 7 and if it does so may give any directions it considers appropriate.

10 Saving for person acting in obedience to mandamus

No action or proceeding shall be begun or prosecuted against any person in respect of anything done in obedience to an order of mandamus.

11 Proceedings for disqualification of member of local authority

(1) Proceedings under section 92 of the Local Government Act 1972 must be begun by the issue of a claim form and brought before a Divisional Court of the Queen's Bench Division.

(1A) Unless otherwise directed, there must be at least 10 days between the service of the claim form and the hearing.

(2) The claim form must set out the name and description of the applicant, the remedy sought and the grounds on which it is sought, and must be supported by written evidence verifying the facts relied on.

(3) Copies of any written evidence must be filed in the Crown Office before the proceedings are entered for hearing and must be supplied to any other party on demand and on payment of the proper charges.

(4) The provisions of rules 5, 6 and 9(1) as to the persons on whom the claim form is to be served and as to the hearing shall apply, with the necessary modifications, to proceedings under the said section 92 as they apply to an application for judicial review.

12 Consolidation of applications

Where there is more than one application pending under section 30 of the Act, or section 92 of the Local Government Act 1972, against several persons in respect of the same office, and on the same grounds, the Court may order the applications to be consolidated.

13 Appeal from Judge's order

No appeal shall lie from an order made under paragraph (3) of rule 3 on an application for leave which may be renewed under paragraph (4) of that rule.

14 Meaning of 'Court'

In relation to the hearing by a Judge of an application for leave under rule 3 or of an application for judicial review, any reference in this Order to 'the Court' shall, unless the context otherwise requires, be construed as a reference to the Judge.

RSC ORDER 54

APPLICATIONS FOR WRIT OF HABEAS CORPUS

1 Application for writ of habeas corpus ad subjiciendum

(1) Subject to rule 11, an application for a writ of habeas corpus ad subjiciendum shall be made to a judge in Court, except that –

  (a) it shall be made to a Divisional Court of the Queen's Bench Division if the Court so directs;
  (b) it may be made to a judge otherwise than in court at any time when no judge is sitting in court; and

(c) any application on behalf of a child must be made in the first instance to a judge otherwise than in court.

(2) An application for such writ may be made without notice being served on any other party and, subject to paragraph (3) must be supported by a witness statement or affidavit by the person restrained showing that it is made at his instance and setting out the nature of the restraint.

(3) Where the person restrained is unable for any reason to make the witness statement or affidavit required by paragraph (2) the witness statement or affidavit may be made by some other person on his behalf and that witness statement or affidavit must state that the person restrained is unable to make the witness statement or affidavit himself and for what reason.

2 Power of Court to whom application made without notice being served on any other party

(1) The Court or judge to whom an application under rule 1 is made without notice being served on any other party may make an order forthwith for the writ to issue, or may –

(a) where the application is made to a judge otherwise than in court, direct the issue of a claim form seeking the writ, or that an application therefor be made by claim form to a Divisional Court or to a judge in court;
(b) where the application is made to a judge in court, adjourn the application so that notice thereof may be given, or direct that an application be made by claim form to a Divisional Court;
(c) where the application is made to a Divisional Court, adjourn the application so that notice thereof may be given.

(2) The claim form must be served on the person against whom the issue of the writ is sought and on such other persons as the Court or judge may direct, and, unless the Court or judge otherwise directs, there must be at least 8 clear days between the service of the claim form and the date named therein for the hearing of the application.

3 Copies of witness statements or affidavits to be supplied

Every party to an application under rule 1 must supply to every other party on demand and on payment of the proper charges copies of the witness statements or affidavits which he proposes to use at the hearing of the application.

4 Power to order release of person restrained

(1) Without prejudice to rule 2(1), the Court or judge hearing an application for a writ of habeas corpus ad subjiciendum may in its or his discretion order that the person restrained be released, and such order shall be a sufficient warrant to any governor of a prison, constable or other person for the release of the person under restraint.

(2) Where such an application in criminal proceedings is heard by a judge and the judge does not order the release of the person restrained, he shall direct

that the application be made by claim form to a Divisional Court of the Queen's Bench Division.

5 Directions as to return to writ

Where a writ of habeas corpus ad subjiciendum is ordered to issue, the Court or judge by whom the order is made give directions as to the Court or judge before whom, and the date on which, the writ is returnable.

6 Service of writ and notice

(1) Subject to paragraphs (2) and (3), a writ of habeas corpus ad subjiciendum must be served personally on the person to whom it is directed.

(2) If it is not possible to serve such writ personally, or if it is directed to a governor of a prison or other public official, it must be served by leaving it with a servant or agent of the person to whom the writ is directed at the place where the person restrained is confined or restrained.

(3) If the writ is directed to more than one person, the writ must be served in manner provided by this rule on the person first named in the writ, and copies must be served on each of the other persons in the same manner as the writ.

(4) There must be served with the writ a notice (in Form No. 90 in the relevant Practice Direction) stating the Court or judge before whom and the date on which the person restrained is to be brought and that in default of obedience proceedings for committal of the party disobeying will be taken.

7 Return to the writ

(1) The return to a writ of habeas corpus ad subjiciendum must be indorsed on or annexed to the writ and must state all the causes of the detainer of the person restrained.

(2) The return may be amended, or another return substituted therefor, by permission of the Court or judge before whom the writ is returnable.

8 Procedure at hearing of writ

When a return to a writ of habeas corpus ad subjiciendum is made, the return shall first be read, and motion then made for discharging or remanding the person restrained or amending or quashing the return, and where that person is brought up in accordance with the writ, his counsel shall be heard first, then the counsel for the Crown, and then one counsel for the person restrained in reply.

9 Bringing up prisoner to give evidence, etc

(1) An application for a writ of habeas corpus ad testificandum or of habeas corpus ad respondendum must be made on witness statement or affidavit to a Judge.

(2) An application for an order to bring up a prisoner, otherwise than by writ of habeas corpus, to give evidence in any proceedings, civil or criminal, before

any Court, tribunal or justice, must be made on witness statement or affidavit to a Judge.

Amendments——SI 1999/1008.

10 Form of writ

A writ of habeas corpus must be in Form No. 89, 91 or 92 in the relevant Practice Direction, whichever is appropriate.

11 Applications relative to the custody, etc, of child

An application by a parent or guardian of a child for a writ of habeas corpus ad subjiciendum relative to the custody, care or control of the child must be made in the Family Division, and this Order shall accordingly apply to such applications with the appropriate modifications.

...

RSC ORDER 56

APPEALS, ETC, TO HIGH COURT BY CASE STATED: GENERAL

1 Appeals from the Crown Court by case stated

(1) Except where they relate to affiliation proceedings or to care proceedings under the Children and Young Persons Act 1969 all appeals from the Crown Court by case stated shall be heard and determined –

- (a) in any criminal proceedings, by a Divisional Court of the Queen's Bench Division;
- (b) in any other proceedings, by a single judge sitting in public, or if the Court so directs, by a Divisional Court of the Queen's Bench Division.

(3) An appeal from the Crown Court by case stated shall not be entered for hearing unless and until the case and a copy of the judgment, order or decision in respect of which the case has been stated and, if that judgment, order or decision was given or made on an appeal to the Crown Court, a copy of the judgment, order or decision appealed from, have been filed in the Crown Office.

(4) No such appeal shall be entered after the expiration of 10 days from the receipt by the appellant of the case unless the delay is accounted for to the satisfaction of the Divisional Court. Notice of intention to apply for an extension of time for entry of the appeal must be served on the respondent at least 2 clear days before the day named in the notice for the hearing of the application.

(5) Where any such appeal has not been entered by reason of a default in complying with the provisions of this rule, the Crown Court may proceed as if no case has been stated.

Amendments——SI 1999/1008.

4 Notice of entry of appeal

Within 4 days after an appeal from the Crown Court by case stated is entered for hearing, the appellant must serve notice of the entry of the appeal on the respondent.

4A Appeals relating to affiliation proceedings and care proceedings

Appeals from the Crown Court by case stated which relate to affiliation proceedings or to care proceedings under the Children and Young Persons Act 1969 shall be heard and determined by a single Judge, or if the Court so directs, a Divisional Court of the Family Division, and the foregoing provisions of this Order shall accordingly apply to such appeals with the substitution of references to the principal registry of the Family Division for references to the Crown Office and such other modifications as may be appropriate.

5 Appeal from Magistrates' Court by case stated

(1) Except as provided by paragraph (2) all appeals from a Magistrates' Court by case stated shall be heard and determined –

  (a) in any criminal proceedings, by a Divisional Court of the Queen's Bench Division;
  (b) in any other proceedings, by a single Judge sitting in public or, if the Court so directs, by a Divisional Court of the Queen's Bench Division.

(2) An appeal by way of case stated against an order or determination of a Magistrates' Court shall be heard and determined by a single Judge or, if the Court so Directs, a Divisional Court of the Family Division if the order or determination appealed against was made or given in family proceedings.

Amendments——SI 1999/1008.

6 Case stated by Magistrates' Court: filing case, etc

(1) Where a case has been stated by a Magistrates' Court the appellant must –

  (a) within 10 days after receving the case, file it in the Crown Office or, if the appeals falls to be heard by a Divisional Court of the Family Division, the principal registry of the Family Division; and
  (b) within 4 days after filing the case as aforesaid serve on the respondent a notice of the entry of appeal together with a copy of the case.

(2) Unless the Court having jurisdiction to determine the appeal otherwise directs, the appeal shall not be heard sooner than 8 clear days after service of notice of the entry of the appeal.

7 Case stated by Ministers, tribunal, etc

(1) The jurisdiction of the High Court under any enactment to hear and determine a case stated by a Minister of the Crown, government department,

tribunal or other person, or a question of law referred to that Court by such a Minister or department or a tribunal or other person by way of case stated, shall be exercised by a single Judge of the Queen's Bench Division, except where it is otherwise provided by these rules or by or under any enactment.

(2) The jurisdiction of the High Court under any enactment to hear and determine an application for an order directing such a Minister or department or a tribunal or other person to state a case for determination by the High Court, or to refer a question of law to that Court by way of case stated, shall be exercised by the Court or Judge having jurisdiction to hear and determine that case or question except where by some other provision of these rules or by or under any enactment it is otherwise provided.

(3) This rule and rules 8 to 12 of this Order shall apply to proceedings for the determination of such a case, question or application and, in relation to any such proceedings, shall have effect subject to any provision made in relation to those proceedings by any other provision of these rules or by or under any enactment.

(4) In this Order references to a tribunal shall be construed as references to any tribunal constituted by or under any enactment other than any of the ordinary Courts of law.

(5) In the following rules references to a Minister shall be construed as including references to a government department, and in those rules and this rule 'case' includes a special case.

8 Application for order to state a case

(1) An application to the Court for an order directing a Minister, tribunal or other person to state a case for determination by the Court or to refer a question of law to the Court by way of case stated must be made by claim form; and the persons to be served with the claim form are the Minister, secretary of the tribunal or other person, as the case may be, and every party (other than the applicant) to the proceedings to which the application relates.

(2) The claim form must state the grounds of the application, the question of law on which it is sought to have the case stated and any reasons given by the Minister, tribunal or other person for his or its refusal to state a case.

(3) The claim must be entered for hearing, and the claim form served, within 14 days after receipt by the applicant of notice of the refusal of his request to state a case.

9 Signing and service of case

(1) A case stated by a tribunal must be signed by the chairman or president of the tribunal, and a case stated by any other person must be signed by him or by a person authorised in that behalf to do so.

(2) The case must be served on the party at whose request, or as a result of whose application to the Court, the case was stated; and if a Minister, tribunal, arbitrator or other person is entitled by virtue of any enactment to state a case,

or to refer a question of law by way of case stated, for determination by the High Court without request being made by any party to the proceedings before that person, the case must be served on such party to those proceedings as the Minister, tribunal, arbitrator or other person, as the case may be, thinks appropriate.

(3) When a case is served on any party under paragraph (2) notice must be given to every other party to the proceedings in question that the case has been served on the party named, and on the date specified, in the notice.

10 Proceedings for determination of case

(1) Proceedings for the determination by the High Court of a case stated, or a question of law referred by way of case stated, by a Minister, tribunal, arbitrator or other person must be begun by claim form by the person on whom the case was served in accordance with rule 9(2) or, where the case is stated without a request being made, by the Minister, secretary of the tribunal, arbitrator or other person by whom the case is stated.

(2) The applicant shall serve the claim form under paragraph (1), together with a copy of the case, on –

   (a) the Minister, secretary of the tribunal, arbitrator or other person by whom the case was stated, unless that Minister, tribunal, arbitrator or other person is the applicant;
   (b) every party (other than the applicant) to the proceedings in which the question of law to which the case relates arose; and
   (c) any other person (other than the applicant) served with the case under rule 9(2).

(3) The claim form must set out the applicant's contentions on the question of law to which the case stated relates.

(4) The claim must be entered for hearing, and the claim form served, within 14 days after the case stated was served on the applicant.

(5) If the applicant fails to enter the claim within the period specified in paragraph (4) then, after obtaining a copy of the case from the Minister, tribunal, arbitrator or other person by whom the case was stated, any other party to the proceedings in which the question of law to which the case relates arose may, within 14 days after the expiration of the period so specified, begin proceedings for the determination of the case, and paragraphs (1) to (4) shall have effect accordingly with the necessary modifications. The references in this paragraph to the period specified in paragraph (4) shall be construed as including references to that period as extended by any order of the Court.

(6) The documents required to be filed in accordance with Order 57, rule 2, before entry of the claim include a copy of the case stated.

(7) Unless the Court having jurisdiction to determine the case otherwise directs, the claim shall not be heard sooner than 7 days after service of the claim form.

11 Amendment of case

The Court hearing a case stated by a Minister, tribunal, arbitrator or other person may amend the case or order it to be returned to that person for amendment, and may draw inferences of fact from the facts stated in the case.

12 Right of Minister to appear and be heard

In proceedings for the determination of a case stated, or of a question of law referred by way of case stated, the Minister, chairman or president of the tribunal, arbitrator or other person by whom the case was stated shall be entitled to appear and be heard.

12A Extradition

(1) Rules 5 and 6 of this Order shall apply to appeals by case stated under –

(a) section 7 of the Criminal Justice Act 1988; and
(b) section 7A of the Fugitive Offenders Act 1967,

as they apply to appeals by case stated from a Magistrates' Court and references in those rules to appellant and respondent shall be construed as references to the requesting state and the person whose surrender is sought respectively.

(2) An application for an order under either of the sections mentioned in paragraph (1) or under section 2A of the Backing of Warrants (Republic of Ireland) Act 1965 requiring a Court to state a case shall be made in accordance with rule 8 of this Order the references in that rule to a tribunal and the secretary of a tribunal being construed for this purpose as references to the Court and the Clerk of the Court respectively.

13 Interlocutory applications

(1) Unless the Court otherwise directs, any interlocutory application in proceedings to which this Order applies may be made to any Judge or a Master of the Queen's Bench Division or, as the case may be, any Judge or a District Judge of the Family Division, notwithstanding that the appeal has been brought by case stated and is to be heard by a Divisional Court.

In this paragraph 'interlocutory application' includes an application for an order extending the time for entry of the appeal or for service of notice of entry of the appeal.

(2) In relation to an order made by a Master or District Judge pursuant to paragraph (1), Order 58, rule 1 shall, where the application is to be heard by a Divisional Court, have effect as if a reference to that Court were substituted for the reference to a Judge.

(3) This rule is without prejudice to any statutory provision or rule of law restricting the making of an order against the Crown.

...

Amendments——SI 1999/1008.

Form N235: Certificate of Suitability of Litigation Friend

Certificate of Suitability of Litigation Friend

If you are acting
- **for a child**, you must serve a copy of the completed form on a parent or guardian of the child, or if there is no parent or guardian, the carer or the person with whom the child lives
- **for a patient**, you must serve a copy of the completed form on the person authorised under Part VII of the Mental Health Act 1983 or, if no person is authorised, the carer or person with whom the patient lives unless you **are** that person. You must also complete a certificate of service (obtainable from the court office)

You should send the completed form to the court with the claim form (if acting for the claimant) or when you take the first step on the defendant's behalf in the claim together with the certificate of service (if applicable)

In the	
Claim No.	
Claimant (including ref.)	
Defendant (including ref.)	

You do not need to complete this form if you do have an authorisation under Part VII of the Mental Health Act 1983 to conduct legal proceedings on the person's behalf.

I consent to act as litigation friend for (claimant) (defendant)

I believe that the above named person is a

☐ child ☐ patient *(give your reasons overleaf and attach a copy of any medical evidence in support)*

I am able to conduct proceedings on behalf of the above named person competently and fairly and I have no interests adverse to those of the above named person.

*I undertake to pay any costs which the above named claimant may be ordered to pay in these proceedings subject to any right I may have to be repaid from the assets of the claimant.

* delete if you are acting for the defendant

Please write your name in capital letters

☐ Mr ☐ Mrs ☐ Miss Surname
☐ Ms ☐ Other _____ Forenames

Address to which documents in this case are to be sent.

I certify that the information given in this form is correct

Signed   Date

The court office at
is open between 10 am and 4 pm Monday to Friday. When corresponding with the court, please address forms or letters to the Court Manager and quote the claim number.

N235 Certificate of Suitability of Litigation Friend (4.99)   *Printed on behalf of The Court Service*

Appendix 5: Legislation and Forms – Form N235

Claim No.

My reasons for believing that the (claimant)(defendant) is a patient are:-

Form N434: Notice of Change of Solicitor

Notice of Change of Solicitor

In the

Note: You should tick either box A **or** B as appropriate **and** box C. Complete details as necessary.

Claim No.	
Claimant (including ref.)	
Defendant	

I (We) give notice that

A ☐ my solicitor *(insert name and address)*
has ceased to act for me and I shall now be acting in person.

B ☐ we *(insert name of solicitor)*
have been instructed to act on behalf of the claimant (defendant) in this claim
(in place of *(insert name and address of previous solicitors)*

C ☐ I (we) have served notice of this change on every party to claim (and on the former solicitor).

Address to which documents about this claim should be sent (including any reference)

		if applicable
	fax no.	
	DX no.	
Postcode	e-mail	

Signed

Defendant/Defendant's Solicitor/ Litigation friend

Position or office held

If signing on behalf of firm or company

Date

The court office at

is open between 10 am and 4 pm Monday to Friday. When corresponding with the court, please address forms or letters to the Court Manager and quote the claim number.

N434 Notice of Change of Solicitor (4.99)   *Printed on behalf of The Court Service*

Appendix 5: Legislation and Forms – Form N244

Form N244: Application Notice

Application Notice

- You must complete Parts A **and** B, **and** Part C if applicable
- Send any relevant fee and the completed application to the court with any draft order, witness statement or other evidence; and sufficient copies of these for service on each respondent

In the

Claim No.

Claimant (including ref.)

Defendant (including ref.)

Date

You should provide this information for listing the application

1. Do you wish to have your application dealt with at a hearing?
   Yes ☐   No ☐   If Yes, please complete 2
2. Time estimate _____ (hours) _____ (mins)
   Is this agreed by all parties? Yes ☐ No ☐
   Level of judge _____
3. Parties to be served: _____

Part A

1. Enter your full name, or name of solicitor

I (We)[1] _____ (on behalf of) (the claimant) (the defendant)

2. State clearly what order you are seeking and if possible attach a draft

intend to apply for an order (a draft of which is attached) that[2]

because[3]

Part B

3. Briefly set out why you are seeking the order. Include the material facts on which you rely, identifying any rule or statutory provision

I (We) wish to rely on: *tick one box*

the attached (witness statement) (affidavit) ☐   my statement of case ☐

evidence in Part C overleaf in support of my application ☐

4. If you are not already a party to the proceedings, you must provide an address for service of documents

Signed _____
(Applicant) ('s Solicitor) ('s litigation friend)

Position or office held _____
(if signing on behalf of firm or company)

Address to which documents about this claim should be sent (including reference if appropriate)[4]

	if applicable	
	fax no.	
	DX no.	
Tel. no. _____ Postcode _____	e-mail	

The court office at
is open between 10 am and 4 pm Monday to Friday. When corresponding with the court, please address forms or letters to the Court Manager and quote the claim number.

N235 Certificate of Suitability of Litigation Friend (4.99)   *Printed on behalf of The Court Service*

Part C Claim No. ☐

I (We) wish to rely on the following evidence in support of this application:

Statement of Truth

*(I believe) (The applicant believes) that the facts stated in this application are true
*delete as appropriate

Signed ☐

(Applicant) ('s Solicitor) ('s litigation friend)

Position or office held ☐
(if signing on behalf of firm or company)

Date ☐

Magistrates' Courts Act 1980

...

PART V

APPEAL AND CASE STATED

Case stated

111 Statement of case by magistrates' court

(1) Any person who was a party to any proceeding before a magistrates' court or is aggrieved by the conviction, order, determination or other proceeding of the court may question the proceeding on the ground that it is wrong in law or is in excess of jurisdiction by applying to the justices composing the court to state a case for the opinion of the High Court on the question of law or jurisdiction involved; but a person shall not make an application under this section in respect of a decision against which he has a right of appeal to the High Court or which by virtue of any enactment passed after 31st December 1879 is final.

(2) An application under subsection (1) above shall be made within 21 days after the day on which the decision of the magistrates' court was given.

(3) For the purpose of subsection (2) above, the day on which the decision of the magistrates' court is given shall, where the court has adjourned the trial of an information after conviction, be the day on which the court sentences or otherwise deals with the offender.

(4) On the making of an application under this section in respect of a decision any right of the applicant to appeal against the decision to the Crown Court shall cease.

(5) If the justices are of opinion that an application under this section is frivolous, they may refuse to state a case, and, if the applicant so requires, shall give him a certificate stating that the application has been refused; but the justices shall not refuse to state a case if the application is made by or under the direction of the Attorney General.

(6) Where justices refuse to state a case, the High Court may, on the application of the person who applied for the case to be stated, make an order of mandamus requiring the justices to state a case.

112 Effect of decision of High Court on case stated by magistrates' court

Any conviction, order, determination or other proceeding of a magistrates' court varied by the High Court on an appeal by case stated, and any judgment or order of the High Court on such an appeal, may be enforced as if it were a decision of the magistrates' court from which the appeal was brought.

Supplemental provisions as to appeal and case stated

113 Bail on appeal or case stated

(1) Where a person has given notice of appeal to the Crown Court against the decision of a magistrates' court or has applied to a magistrates' court to state a case for the opinion of the High Court, then, if he is in custody, the magistrates' court may, subject to section 25 of the Criminal Justice and Public Order Act 1994, grant him bail.

(2) If a person is granted bail under subsection (1) above, the time and place at which he is to appear (except in the event of the determination in respect of which the case is stated being reversed by the High Court) shall be –

- (a) if he has given notice of appeal, the Crown Court at the time appointed for the hearing of the appeal;
- (b) if he has applied for the statement of a case, the magistrates' court at such time within 10 days after the judgment of the High Court has been given as may be specified by the magistrates' court;

and any recognizance that may be taken from him or from any surety for him shall be conditioned accordingly.

(3) Subsection (1) above shall not apply where the accused has been committed to the Crown Court for sentence under section 37 or 38 above.

(4) Section 37(6) of the Criminal Justice Act 1948 (which relates to the currency of a sentence while a person is released on bail by the High Court) shall apply to a person released on bail by a magistrates' court under this section pending the hearing of a case stated as it applies to a person released on bail by the High Court under section 22 of the Criminal Justice Act 1967.

Amendments—Criminal Justice and Public Order Act 1994, s 168(2), Sch 10, para 44.

114 Recognizance and fees on case stated

Justices to whom application has been made to state a case for the opinion of the High Court on any proceeding of a magistrates' court shall not be required to state the case until the applicant has entered into a recognizance, with or without sureties, before the magistrates' court, conditioned to prosecute the appeal without delay and to submit to the judgment of the High Court and pay such costs as that Court may award; and (except in any criminal matter) the clerk of a magistrates' court shall not be required to deliver the case to the applicant until the applicant has paid him the fees payable for the case and for the recognizances.

. . .

Appendix 5: Legislation and Forms – Magistrates' Courts Rules 1981

Magistrates' Courts Rules 1981
SI 1981/552

...

Case stated

76 Application to state case

(1) An application under section 111(1) of the Act of 1980 shall be made in writing and signed by or on behalf of the applicant and shall identify the question or questions of law or jurisdiction on which the opinion of the High Court is sought.

(2) Where one of the questions on which the opinion of the High Court is sought is whether there was evidence on which the magistrates' court could come to its decision, the particular finding of fact made by the magistrates' court which it is claimed cannot be supported by the evidence before the magistrates' court shall be specified in such application.

(3) Any such application shall be sent to the clerk of the magistrates' court whose decision is questioned.

77 Consideration of draft case

(1) Within 21 days after receipt of an application made in accordance with rule 76, the clerk of the magistrates' court whose decision is questioned shall, unless the justices refuse to state a case under section 111(5) of the Act of 1980, send a draft case in which are stated the matters required under rule 81 to the applicant or his solicitor and shall send a copy thereof to the respondent or his solicitor.

(2) Within 21 days after receipt of the draft case under paragraph (1), each party may make representations thereon. Any such representations shall be in writing and signed by or on behalf of the party making them and shall be sent to the clerk.

(3) Where the justices refuse to state a case under section 111(5) of the Act and they are required by the High Court by order of mandamus under section 111(6) to do so, this rule shall apply as if in paragraph (1) –

- (a) for the words 'receipt of an application made in accordance with rule 76' there were substituted the words 'the date on which an order of mandamus under section 111(6) of the Act of 1980 is made'; and
- (b) the words 'unless the justices refuse to state a case under section 111(5) of the Act of 1980' were omitted.

78 Preparation and submission of final case

(1) Within 21 days after the latest day on which representations may be made under rule 77, the justices whose decision is questioned shall make such adjustments, if any, to the draft case prepared for the purposes of that rule as

they think fit, after considering any such representations, and shall state and sign the case.

(2) A case may be stated on behalf of the justices whose decision is questioned by any 2 or more of them and may, if the justices so direct, be signed on their behalf by their clerk.

(3) Forthwith after the case has been stated and signed the clerk of the court shall send it to the applicant or his solicitor, together with any statement required by rule 79.

79 Extension of time limits

(1) If the clerk of a magistrates' court is unable to send to the applicant a draft case under paragraph (1) of rule 77 within the time required by that paragraph, he shall do so as soon as practicable thereafter and the provisions of that rule shall apply accordingly; but in that event the clerk shall attach to the draft case, and to the final case when it is sent to the applicant or his solicitor under rule 78(3), a statement of the delay and the reasons therefor.

(2) If the clerk of a magistrates' court receives an application in writing from or on behalf of the applicant or the respondent for an extension of the time within which representations on the draft case may be made under paragraph (2) of rule 77, together with reasons in writing therefor, he may by notice in writing sent to the applicant or respondent as the case may be extend the time and the provisions of that paragraph and of rule 78 shall apply accordingly; but in that event the clerk shall attach to the final case, when it is sent to the applicant or his solicitor under rule 78(3), a statement of the extension and the reasons therefor.

(3) If the justices are unable to state a case within the time required by paragraph (1) of rule 78, they shall do so as soon as practicable thereafter and the provisions of that rule shall apply accordingly; but in that event the clerk shall attach to the final case, when it is sent to the applicant or his solicitor under rule 78(3), a statement of the delay and the reasons therefor.

80 Service of documents

Any document required by rules 76 to 79 to be sent to any person shall either be delivered to him or be sent by post in a registered letter or by recorded delivery service and, if sent by post to an applicant or respondent, shall be addressed to him at his last known or usual place of abode.

81 Content of case

(1) A case stated by the magistrates' court shall state the facts found by the court and the question or questions of law or juridiction on which the opinion of the High Court is sought.

(2) Where one of the questions on which the opinion of the High Court is sought is whether there was evidence on which the magistrates' court could come to its decision, the particular finding of fact which it is claimed cannot be

supported by the evidence before the magistrates' court shall be specified in the case.

(3) Unless one of the questions on which the opinion of the High Court is sought is whether there was evidence on which the magistrates' court could come to its decision, the case shall not contain a statement of evidence.

...

Supreme Court Act 1981

...

PART II

JURISDICTION

Other particular fields of jurisdiction

...

28 Appeals from Crown Court and inferior courts

(1) Subject to subsection (2), any order, judgment or other decision of the Crown Court may be questioned by any party to the proceedings, on the ground that it is wrong in law or is in excess of jurisdiction, by applying to the Crown Court to have a case stated by that court for the opinion of the High Court.

(2) Subsection (1) shall not apply to –

(a) a judgment or other decision of the Crown Court relating to trial on indictment; or

(b) any decision of that court under the Betting, Gaming and Lotteries Act 1963, the Licensing Act 1964, the Gaming Act 1968 or the Local Government (Miscellaneous Provisions) Act 1982 which, by any provision of any of those Acts, is to be final.

(3) Subject to the provisions of this Act and to rules of court, the High Court shall, in accordance with section 19(2), have jurisdiction to hear and determine –

(a) any application, or any appeal (whether by way of case stated or otherwise), which it has power to hear and determine under or by virtue of this or any other Act; and

(b) all such other appeals as it had jurisdiction to hear and determine immediately before the commencement of this Act.

Amendments—Local Government (Miscellaneous Provisions) Act 1982, s 2, Sch 3, para 27(6).

28A Proceedings on case stated by magistrates' court

(1) The following provisions apply where a case is stated for the opinion of the High Court under section 111 of the Magistrates' Courts Act 1980 (case stated on question of law or jurisdiction).

(2) The High Court may, if it thinks fit, cause the case to be sent back for amendment, whereupon it shall be amended accordingly.

(3) The High Court shall hear and determine the question arising on the case (or the case as amended) and shall –

(a) reverse, affirm or amend the determination in respect of which the case has been stated, or
(b) remit the matter to the justice or justices with the opinion of the court,

and may make such other order in relation to the matter (including as to costs) as it thinks fit.

(4) Except as provided by the Administration of Justice Act 1960 (right of appeal to House of Lords in criminal cases), a decision of the High Court under this section is final and conclusive on all parties.

Amendments—Inserted by Statute Law (Repeals) Act 1993, s 1(2), Sch 2, Pt I, para 9.

29 Orders of mandamus, prohibition and certiorari

(1) The High Court shall have jurisdiction to make orders of mandamus, prohibition and certiorari in those classes of cases in which it had power to do so immeditely before the commencement of this Act.

(2) Every such order shall be final, subject to any right of appeal therefrom.

(3) In relation to the jurisdiction of the Crown Court, other than its jurisdiction in matters relating to trial on indictment, the High Court shall have all such jurisdiction to make orders of mandamus, prohibition or certiorari as the High Court possesses in relation to the jurisdiction of an inferior court.

(4) The power of the High Court under any enactment to require justices of the peace or a judge or officer of a county court to do any act relating to the duties of their respective offices, or to require a magistrates' court to state a case for the opinion of the High Court, in any case where the High Court formerly had by virtue of any enactment jurisdiction to make a rule absolute, or an order, for any of those purposes, shall be exercisable by order of mandamus.

(5) In any enactment –
   (a) references to a writ of mandamus, of prohibition or of certiorari shall be read as references to the corresponding order; and
   (b) references to the issue or award of any such writ shall be read as references to the making of the corresponding order.

...

31 Application for judicial review

(1) An application to the High Court for one or more of the following forms of relief, namely –
   (a) an order of mandamus, prohibition or certiorari;
   (b) a declaration or injunction under subsection (2); or
   (c) an injunction under section 30 restraining a person not entitled to do so from acting in an office to which that section applies,

shall be made in acordance with rules of court by a procedure to be known as an application for judicial review.

(2) A declaration may be made or an injunction granted under this subsection in any case where an application for judicial review, seeking that relief, has been made and the High Court considers that, having regard to –

(a) the nature of the matters in respect of which relief may be granted by orders of mandamus, prohibition or certiorari;
(b) the nature of the persons and bodies against whom relief may be granted by such orders; and
(c) all the circumstances of the case,

it would be just and convenient for the declaration to be made or for the injunction to be granted, as the case may be.

(3) No application for judicial review shall be made unless the leave of the High Court has been obtained in accordance with rules of court; and the court shall not grant leave to make such an application unless it considers that the applicant has a sufficient interest in the matter to which the application relates.

(4) On an application for judicial review the High Court may award damages to the applicant if –

(a) he has joined with his application a claim for damages arising from any matter to which the application relates; and
(b) the court is satisfied that, if the claim had been made in an action begun by the applicant at the time of making his application, he would have been awarded damages.

(5) If, on an application for judicial review seeking an order of certiorari, the High Court quashes the decision to which the application relates, the High Court may remit the matter to the court, tribunal or authority concerned, with a direction to reconsider it and reach a decision in accordance with the findings of the High Court.

(6) Where the High Court considers that there has been undue delay in making an application for judicial review, the court may refuse to grant –

(a) leave for the making of the application; or
(b) any relief sought on the application,

if it considers that the granting of the relief sought would be likely to cause substantial hardship to, or substantially prejudice the rights of, any person or would be detrimental to good administration.

(7) Subsection (6) is without prejudice to any enactment or rule of court which has the effect of limiting the time within an application for judicial review may be made.

...

43 Power of High Court to vary sentence on certiorari

(1) Where a person who has been sentenced for an offence –

(a) by a magistrates' court; or

(b) by the Crown Court after being convicted of the offence by a magistrates' court and committed to the Crown Court for sentence; or

(c) by the Crown Court on appeal against conviction or sentence,

applies to the High Court in accordance with section 31 for an order of certiorari to remove the proceedings of the magistrates' court or the Crown Court into the High Court, then, if the High Court determines that the magistrates' court or the Crown Court had no power to pass the sentence, the High Court may, instead of quashing the conviction, amend it by substituting for the sentence passed any sentence which the magistrates' court or, in a case within paragraph (b), the Crown Court had power to impose.

(2) Any sentence passed by the High Court by virtue of this section in substitution for the sentence passed in the proceedings of the magistrates' court or the Crown Court shall, unless the High Court otherwise directs, begin to run from the time when it would have begun to run if passed in those proceedings; but in computing the term of the sentence, any time during which the offender was released on bail in pursuance of section 37(1)(d) of the Criminal Justice Act 1948 shall be disregarded.

(3) Subsections (1) and (2) shall, with the necessary modifications, apply in relation to any order of a magistrates' court or the Crown Court which is made on, but does not form part of, the conviction of an offender as they apply in relation to a conviction and sentence.

...

Crown Court Rules 1982
SI 1982/1109

...

PART V

MISCELLANEOUS

...

26 Application to Crown Court to state case

(1) An application under section 28 of the Supreme Court Act 1981 to the Crown Court to state a case for the opinion of the High Court shall be made in writing to the appropriate officer of the Crown Court within 21 days after the date of the decision in respect of which the application is made.

(2) The application shall state the ground on which the decision of the Crown Court is questioned.

(3) After making the application, the applicant shall forthwith send a copy of it to the parties to the proceedings in the Crown Court.

(4) On receipt of the application, the appropriate officer of the Crown Court shall forthwith send it to the judge who presided at the proceedings in which the decision was made.

(5) On receipt of the application, the judge shall inform the appropriate officer of the Crown Court as to whether or not he has decided to state a case and that officer shall give notice in writing to the applicant of the judge's decision.

(6) If the judge considers that the application is frivolous, he may refuse to state a case and shall in that case, if the applicant so requires, cause a certificate stating the reasons for the refusal to be given to him.

(7) If the judge decides to state a case, the procedure to be followed shall, unless the judge in a particular case otherwise directs, be the procedure set out in paragraphs (8) to (12).

(8) The applicant shall, within 21 days of receiving the notice referred to in paragraph (5), draft a case and send a copy of it to the appropriate officer of the Crown Court and to the parties to the proceedings in the Crown Court.

(9) Each party to the proceedings in the Crown Court shall, within 21 days of receiving a copy of the draft case under paragraph (8), either –

    (a) give notice in writing to the applicant and the appropriate officer of the Crown Court that he does not intend to take part in the proceedings before the High court; or

    (b) indicate in writing on the copy of the draft case that he agrees with it and send the copy to the appropriate officer of the Crown Court; or

(c) draft an alternative case and send it, together with the copy of the applicant's case, to the appropriate officer of the Crown Court.

(10) The judge shall consider the applicant's draft case and any alternative draft case sent to the appropriate officer of the Crown Court under paragraph (9)(c).

(11) If the Crown Court so orders, the applicant shall, before the case is stated and delivered to him, enter before an officer of the Crown Court into a recognizance, with or without sureties and in such sum as the Crown Court considers proper, having regard to the means of the applicant, conditioned to prosecute the appeal without delay.

(12) The judge shall state and sign a case within 14 days after either –

(a) the receipt of all the documents required to be sent to the appropriate officer of the Crown Court under paragraph (9); or
(b) the expiration of the period of 21 days referred to in that paragraph,

whichever is the sooner.

(13) A case stated by the Crown Court shall state the facts found by the Crown Court, the submissions of the parties (including any authorities relied on by the parties during the course of those submissions), the decision of the Crown Court in respect of which the application is made and the question on which the opinion of the High Court is sought.

(14) Any time limit referred to in this Rule may be extended either before or after it expires by the Crown Court.

(15) If the judge decides not to state a case but the stating of a case is subsequently required by the High Court by order of mandamus, paragraphs (7) to (14) shall apply to the stating of the case save that –

(a) in paragraph (7) the words 'If the judge decides to state a case' shall be omitted; and
(b) in paragraph (8) for the words 'receiving the notice referred to in paragraph (5)' there shall be substitued the words 'the day on which the order of mandamus was made'.

...

Human Rights Act 1998
(1998 c 42)

ARRANGEMENT OF SECTIONS (ss 1–9, Sch 1)

Introduction

Section		Page
1.	The Convention Rights	328
2.	Interpretation of Convention rights	329

Legislation

3.	Interpretation of legislation	330
4.	Declaration of incompatibility	330
5.	Right of Crown to intervene	331

Public authorities

6.	Acts of public authorities	331
7.	Proceedings	332
8.	Judicial remedies	333
9.	Judicial acts	334

...

SCHEDULES:

Schedule 1	The Articles		335
Part I	The Convention		335
Part II	The First Protocol		340
Part III	The Sixth Protocol		340

...

An Act to give further effects to rights and freedoms guaranteed under the European Convention on Human Rights; to make provision with respect to holders of certain judicial offices who become judges of the European Court of Human Rights; and for connected purposes.

[9th November 1998]

Introduction

1 The Convention Rights

(1) In this Act, 'the Convention rights' means the rights and fundamental freedoms set out in –

(a) Articles 2 to 12 and 14 of the Convention,
(b) Articles 1 to 3 of the First Protocol, and
(c) Articles 1 and 2 of the Sixth Protocol,

as read with Articles 16 to 18 of the Convention.

(2) Those Articles are to have effect for the purposes of this Act subject to any designated derogation or reservation (as to which see sections 14 and 15).

(3) The Articles are set out in Schedule 1.

(4) The Secretary of State may by order make such amendments to this Act as he considers appropriate to reflect the effect, in relation to the United Kingdom, of a protocol.

(5) In subsection (4) 'protocol' means a protocol to the Convention –

(a) which the United Kingdom has ratified; or
(b) which the United Kingdom has signed with a view to ratification.

(6) No amendment may be made by an order under subsection (4) so as to come into force before the protocol concerned is in force in relation to the United Kingdom.

2 Interpretation of Convention rights

(1) A court or tribunal determining a question which has arisen in connection with a Convention right must take into account any –

(a) judgment, decision, declaration or advisory opinion of the European Court of Human Rights,
(b) opinion of the Commission given in a report adopted under Article 31 of the Convention,
(c) decision of the Commission in connection with Article 26 or 27(2) of the Convention, or
(d) decision of the Committee of Ministers taken under Article 46 of the Convention,

whenever made or given, so far as, in the opinion of the court or tribunal, it is relevant to the proceedings in which that question has arisen.

(2) Evidence of any judgment, decision, declaration or opinion of which account may have to be taken under this section is to be given in proceedings before any court or tribunal in such manner as may be provided by rules.

(3) In this section 'rules' means rules of court or, in the case of proceedings before a tribunal, rules made for the purposes of this section –

(a) by the Lord Chancellor or the Secretary of State, in relation to proceedings outside Scotland;
(b) by the Secretary of State, in relation to proceedings in Scotland; or
(c) by a Northern Ireland department, in relation to proceedings before a tribunal in Northern Ireland –
   (i) which deals with transferred matters; and
   (ii) for which no rules made under paragraph (a) are in force.

Legislation

3 Interpretation of legislation

(1) So far as it is possible to do so, primary legislation and subordinate legislation must be read and given effect in a way which is compatible with the Convention rights.

(2) This section –

- (a) applies to primary legislation and subordinate legislation whenever enacted;
- (b) does not affect the validity, continuing operation or enforcement of any incompatible primary legislation; and
- (c) does not affect the validity, continuing operation or enforcement of any incompatible subordinate legislation if (disregarding any possibility of revocation) primary legislation prevents removal of the incompatibility.

4 Declaration of incompatibility

(1) Subsection (2) applies in any proceedings in which a court determines whether a provision of primary legislation is compatible with a Convention right.

(2) If the court is satisfied that the provision is incompatible with a Convention right, it may make a declaration of that incompatibility.

(3) Subsection (4) applies in any proceedings in which a court determines whether a provision of subordinate legislation, made in the exercise of a power conferred by primary legislation, is compatible with a Convention right.

(4) If the court is satisfied –

- (a) that the provision is incompatible with a Convention right, and
- (b) that (disregarding any possibility of revocation) the primary legislation concerned prevents removal of the incompatibility,

it may make a declaration of that incompatibility.

(5) In this section 'court' means –

- (a) the House of Lords;
- (b) the Judicial Committee of the Privy Council;
- (c) the Courts-Martial Appeal Court;
- (d) in Scotland, the High Court of Justiciary sitting otherwise than as a trial court or the Court of Session;
- (e) in England and Wales or Northern Ireland, the High Court or the Court of Appeal.

(6) A declaration under this section ('a declaration of incompatibility') –

- (a) does not affect the validity, continuing operation or enforcement of the provision in respect of which it is given; and

(b) is not binding on the parties to the proceedings in which it is made.

5 Right of Crown to intervene

(1) Where a court is considering whether to make a declaration of incompatibility, the Crown is entitled to notice in accordance with rules of court.

(2) In any case to which subsection (1) applies –

    (a) a Minister of the Crown (or a person nominated by him),
    (b) a member of the Scottish Executive,
    (c) a Northern Ireland Minister,
    (d) a Northern Ireland department,

is entitled, on giving notice in accordance with rules of court, to be joined as a party to the proceedings.

(3) Notice under subsection (2) may be given at any time during the proceedings.

(4) A person who has been made a party to criminal proceedings (other than in Scotland) as the result of a notice under subsection (2) may, with leave, appeal to the House of Lords against any declaration of incompatibility made in the proceedings.

(5) In subsection (4) –

'criminal proceedings' includes all proceedings before the Courts-Martial Appeal Court; and
'leave' means leave granted by the court making the declaration of incompatibility or by the House of Lords.

Public authorities

6 Acts of public authorities

(1) It is unlawful for a public authority to act in a way which is incompatible with a Convention right.

(2) Subsection (1) does not apply to an act if –

    (a) as the result of one or more provisions of primary legislation, the authority could not have acted differently; or
    (b) in the case of one or more provisions of, or made under, primary legislation which cannot be read or given effect in a way which is compatible with the Convention rights, the authority was acting so as to give effect to or enforce those provisions.

(3) In this section, 'public authority' includes –

    (a) a court or tribunal, and
    (b) any person certain of whose functions are functions of a public nature,

but does not include either House of Parliament or a person exercising functions in connection with proceedings in Parliament.

(4) In subsection (3) 'Parliament' does not include the House of Lords in its judicial capacity.

(5) In relation to a particular act, a person is not a public authority by virtue only of subsection (3)(b) if the nature of the act is private.

(6) 'An act' includes a failure to act but does not include a failure to –

(a) introduce in, or lay before, Parliament a proposal for legislation; or
(b) make any primary legislation or remedial order.

7 Proceedings

(1) A person who claims that a public authority has acted (or proposes to act) in a way which is made unlawful by section 6(1) may –

(a) bring proceedings against the authority under this Act in the appropriate court or tribunal, or
(b) rely on the Convention right or rights concerned in any legal proceedings,

but only if he is (or would be) a victim of the unlawful act.

(2) In subsection (1)(a) 'appropriate court or tribunal' means such court or tribunal as may be determined in accordance with rules; and proceedings against an authority includes a counterclaim or similar proceeding.

(3) If the proceedings are brought on an application for judicial review, the applicant is to be taken to have a sufficient interest in relation to the unlawful act only if he is, or would be, a victim of that act.

(4) If the proceedings are made by way of a petition for judicial review in Scotland, the applicant shall be taken to have title and interest in relation to the unlawful act only if he is, or would be, a victim of that act.

(5) Proceedings under subsection (1)(a) must be brought before the end of –

(a) the period of one year beginning with the date on which the act complained of took place; or
(b) such longer period as the court or tribunal considers equitable having regard to all the circumstances,

but that is subject to any rule imposing a stricter time limit in relation to the procedure in question.

(6) In subsection (1)(b) 'legal proceedings' includes –

(a) proceedings brought by or at the instigation of a public authority; and
(b) an appeal against the decision of a court or tribunal.

(7) For the purposes of this section, a person is a victim of an unlawful act only if he would be a victim for the purposes of Article 34 of the Convention if proceedings were brought in the European Court of Human Rights in respect of that act.

(8) Nothing in this Act creates a criminal offence.

(9) In this section 'rules' means –

(a) in relation to proceedings before a court or tribunal outside Scotland, rules made by the Lord Chancellor or the Secretary of State for the purposes of this section or rules of court,
(b) in relation to proceeedings before a court or tribunal in Scotland, rules made by the Secretary of State for those purposes,
(c) in relation to proceedings before a tribunal in Northern Ireland –
    (i) which deals with transferred matters; and
    (ii) for which no rules made under paragraph (a) are in force,
rules made by a Northern Ireland department for those purposes,

and includes provision made by order under section 1 of the Courts and Legal Services Act 1990.

(10) In making rules regard must be had to section 9.

(11) The Minister who has power to make rules in relation to a particular tribunal may, to the extent he considers it necessary to ensure that the tribunal can provide an appropriate remedy in relation to an act (or proposed act) of a public authority which is (or would be) unlawful as a result of section 6(1), by order add to –

(a) the relief or remedies which the tribunal may grant; or
(b) the grounds on which it may grant any of them.

(12) An order made under subsection (11) may contain such incidental, supplemental, consequential or transitional provision as the Minister making it considers appropriate.

(13) 'The Minister' includes the Northern Ireland department concerned.

8 Judicial remedies

(1) In relation to any act (or proposed act) of a public authority which the court finds is (or would be) unlawful, it may grant such relief or remedy, or make such order, within its powers as it considers just and appropriate.

(2) But damages may be awarded only by a court which has power to award damages, or to order the payment of compensation, in civil proceedings.

(3) No award of damages is to be made unless, taking account of all the circumstances of the case, including –

(a) any other relief or remedy granted, or order made, in relation to the act in question (by that or any other court), and
(b) the consequences of any decision (of that or any other court) in respect of that act,

the court is satisfied that the award is necessary to afford just satisfaction to the person in whose favour it is made.

(4) In determining –

(a) whether to award damages, or

(b) the amount of an award,

the court must take into account the principles applied by the European Court of Human Rights in relation to the award of compensation under Article 41 of the Convention.

(5) a public authority against which damages are awarded is to be treated –

(a) in Scotland, for the purposes of section 3 of the Law Reform (Miscellaneous Provisions) (Scotland) Act 1940 as if the award were made in an action of damages in which the authority has been found liable in respect of loss or damage to the person to whom the award is made;
(b) for the purposes of the Civil Liability (Contribution) Act 1978 as liable in respect of damage suffered by the person to whom the award is made.

(6) In this section –

'court' includes a tribunal;
'damages' means damages for an unlawful act of a public authority; and
'unlawful' means unlawful under section 6(1).

9 Judicial acts

(1) Proceedings under section 7(1)(a) in respect of a judicial act may be brought only –

(a) by exercising a right of appeal;
(b) on an application (in Scotland a petition) for judicial review; or
(c) in such other forum as may be prescribed by rules.

(2) That does not affect any rule of law which prevents a court from being the subject of judicial review.

(3) In proceedings under this Act in respect of a judicial act done in good faith, damages may not be awarded otherwise than to compensate a person to the extent required by Article 5(5) of the Convention.

(4) An award of damages permitted by subsection (3) is to be made against the Crown; but no award may be made unless the appropriate person, if not a party to the proceedings, is joined.

(5) In this section –

'appropriate person' means the Minister responsible for the court concerned, or a person or government department nominated by him;
'court' includes a tribunal;
'judge' incudes a member of a tribunal, a justice of the peace and a clerk or other officer entitled to exercise the jurisdiction of a court;
'judicial act' means a judicial act of a court and includes an act done on the instructions, or on behalf, of a judge; and
'rules' has the same meaning as in section 7(11).

...

SCHEDULES

SCHEDULE 1

THE ARTICLES

PART I

THE CONVENTION

Rights and Freedoms

Article 2

Right to life

1. Everyone's right to life shall be protected by law. No one shall be deprived of his life intentionally save in the execution of a sentence of a court following his conviction of a crime for which this penalty is provided by law.

2. Deprivation of life shall not be regarded as inflicted in contravention of this Article when it results from the use of force which is no more than absolutely necessary:

   (a) in defence of any person from unlawful violence;
   (b) in order to effect a lawful arrest or to prevent the escape of a person lawfully detained;
   (c) in action lawfully taken for the purpose of quelling a riot or insurrection.

Article 3

Prohibition of torture

No one shall be subjected to torture or to inhuman or degrading treatment or punishment.

Article 4

Prohibition of slavery and forced labour

1. No one shall be held in slavery or servitude.

2. No one shall be required to perform forced or compulsory labour.

3. For the purpose of this Article the term 'forced or compulsory labour' shall not include:

   (a) any work required to be done in the ordinary course of detention imposed according to the provisions of Article 5 of this Convention or during conditional release from such detention;

(b) any service of a military character or, in case of conscientious objectors in countries where they are recognised, service exacted instead of compulsory military service;
(c) any service exacted in case of an emergency or calamity threatening the life or well-being of the community;
(d) any work or service which forms part of normal civic obligations.

Article 5

Right to liberty and security

1. Everyone has the right to liberty and security of person. No one shall be deprived of his liberty save in the following cases and in accordance with a procedure prescribed by law:

(a) the lawful detention of a person after conviction by a competent court;
(b) the lawful arrest or detention of a person for non-compliance with the lawful order of a court or in order to secure the fulfilment of any obligation prescribed by law;
(c) the lawful arrest or detention of a person effected for the purpose of bringing him before the competent legal authority on reasonable suspicion of having committed an offence or when it is reasonably considered necessary to prevent his committing an offence or fleeing after having done so;
(d) the detention of a minor by lawful order for the purpose of educational supervision or his lawful detention for the purpose of bringing him before the competent legal authority;
(e) the lawful detention of persons for the prevention of the spreading of infectious diseases, of persons of unsound mind, alcoholics or drug addicts or vagrants;
(f) the lawful arrest or detention of a person to prevent his effecting an unauthorised entry into the country or of a person against whom action is being taken with a view to deportation or extradition.

2. Everyone who is arrested shall be informed promptly, in a language which he understands, of the reasons for his arrest and of any charge against him.

3. Everyone arrested or detained in accordance with the provisions of paragraph 1(c) of this Article shall be brought promptly before a judge or other officer authorised by law to exercise judicial power and shall be entitled to trial within a reasonable time or to release pending trial. Release may be conditional by guarantees to appear for trial.

4. Everyone who is deprived of his liberty by arrest or detention shall be entitled to take proceedings by which the lawfulness of his detention shall be decided speedily by a court and his release ordered if the detention is not lawful.

5. Everyone who has been the victim of arrest or detention in contravention of the provisions of this Article shall have an enforceable right to compensation.

Article 6

Right to a fair trial

1. In the determination of his civil rights and obligations or of any criminal charge against him, everyone is entitled to a fair and public hearing within a reasonable time by an independent and impartial tribunal established by law. Judgment shall be pronounced publicly but the press and public may be excluded from all or part of the trial in the interest of morals, public order or national security in a democratic society, where the interests of juveniles or the protection of the private life of the parties so require, or to the extent strictly necessary in the opinion of the court in special circumstances where publicity would prejudice the interest of justice.

2. Everyone charged with a criminal offence shall be presumed innocent until proved guilty according to law.

3. Everyone charged with a criminal offence has the following minimum rights:
   (a) to be informed promptly, in a language which he understands and in detail, of the nature and cause of the accusation against him;
   (b) to have adequate time and facilities for the preparation of his defence;
   (c) to defend himself in person or through legal assistance of his own choosing or, if he has not sufficient means to pay for legal assistance, to be given it free when the interests of justice so require;
   (d) to examine or have examined witnesses against him and to obtain the attendance and examination of witnesses on his behalf under the same conditions as witnesses against him;
   (e) to have the free assistance of an interpreter if he cannot understand or speak the language used in court.

Article 7

No punishment without law

1. No one shall be held guilty of any criminal offence on account of any act or omission which did not constitute a criminal offence under national or international law at the time when it was committed. Nor shall a heavier penalty be imposed than the one that was applicable at the time the criminal offence was committed.

2. This Article shall not prejudice the trial and punishment of any person for any act or omission which, at the time when it was committed, was criminal according to the general principles of law recognised by civilised nations.

Article 8

Right to respect for private and family life

1. Everyone has the right to respect for his private and family life, his home and his correspondence.

2. There shall be no interference by a public authority with the exercise of this right except such as is in accordance with the law and is necessary in a democratic society in the interests of national security, public safety or the economic well-being of the country, for the prevention of disorder or crime, for the protection of health or morals, or for the protection of the rights and freedoms of others.

Article 9

Freedom of thought, conscience and religion

1. Everyone has the right to freedom of thought, conscience and religion; this right includes freedom to change his religion or belief and freedom, either alone or in community with others and in public or private, to manifest his religion or belief, in worship, teaching, practice and observance.

2. Freedom to manifest one's religion or beliefs shall be subject only to such limitations as are prescribed by law and are necessary in a democratic society in the interests of public safety, for the protection of public order, health or morals, or for the protection of the rights and freedoms of others.

Article 10

Freedom of expression

1. Everyone has the right to freedom of expression. This right shall include freedom to hold opinions and to receive and impart information and ideas without interference by public authority and regardless of frontiers. This Article shall not prevent States from requiring the licensing of broadcasting, television or cinema enterprises.

2. The exercise of these freedoms, since it carries with it duties and responsibilities, may be subject to such formalities, conditions, restrictions or penalties as are prescribed by law and are necessary in a democratic society, in the interests of national security, territorial integrity or public safety, for the prevention of disorder or crime, for the protection of health or morals, for the protection of the reputation or rights of others, for preventing the disclosure of information received in confidence, or for maintaining the authority and impartiality of the judiciary.

Article 11

Freedom of assembly and association

1. Everyone has the right to freedom of peaceful assembly and to freedom of association with others, including the right to form and to join trade unions for the protection of his interests.

2. No restrictions shall be placed on the exercise of these rights other than such as are prescribed by law and are necessary in a democratic society in the interests of national security or public safety, for the prevention of disorder or

crime, for the protection of health or morals or for the protection of the rights and freedoms of others. This Article shall not prevent the imposition of lawful restrictions on the exercise of these rights by members of the armed forces, of the police or of the administration of the State.

Article 12

Right to marry

Men and women of marriageable age have the right to marry and to found a family, according to the national laws governing the exercise of this right.

Article 14

Prohibition of discrimination

The enjoyment of the rights and freedoms set forth in this Convention shall be secured without discrimination on any ground such as sex, race, colour, language, religion, political or other opinion, national or social origin, association with a national minority, property, birth or other status.

Article 16

Restrictions on political activity of aliens

Nothing in Articles 10, 11 and 14 shall be regarded as preventing the High Contracting Parties from imposing restrictions on the political activity of aliens.

Article 17

Prohibition of abuse of rights

Nothing in this Convention may be interpreted as implying for any State, group or person any right to engage in any activity or perform any act aimed at the destruction of any of the rights and freedoms set forth herein or at their limitation to a greater extent than is provided for in the Convention.

Article 18
Limitation on use of restrictions on rights

The restrictions permitted under this Convention to the said rights and freedoms shall not be applied for any purpose other than those for which they have been prescribed.

PART II

THE FIRST PROTOCOL

Article 1

Protection of property

Every natural or legal person is entitled to the peaceful enjoyment of his possessions. No one shall be deprived of his possessions except in the public interest and subject to the conditions provided for by law and by the general principles of international law.

The preceding provisions shall not, however, in any way impair the right of a State to enforce such laws as it deems necessary to control the use of property in accordance with the general interest or to secure the payment of taxes or other contributions or penalties.

Article 2

Right to education

No person shall be denied the right to education. In the exercise of any functions which it assumes in relation to education and to teaching, the State shall respect the right of parents to ensure such education and teaching in conformity with their own religious and philosophical convictions.

Article 3

Right to free elections

The High Contracting Parties undertake to hold free elections at reasonable intervals by secret ballot, under conditions which will ensure the free expression of the opinion of the people in the choice of the legislature.

PART III

THE SIXTH PROTOCOL

Article 1

Abolition of the death penalty

The death penalty shall be abolished. No one shall be condemned to such penalty or executed.

Article 2

Death penalty in time of war

A State may make provisions in its law for the death penalty in respect of acts committed in time of war or of imminent threat of war; such penalty shall be applied only in the instances laid down in the law and in accordance with its provisions. The State shall communicate to the Secretary of the Council of Europe the relevant provisions of that law.

Index

References are to paragraph numbers, and Appendix numbers and Precedent number or Procedural guide.

Absconding 13.14
Access to courts 13.3
Acquittals 1.10, 4.16
Affidavits
  case stated 3.4
  error 3.4
  forms and precedents App 1:4–1:5, App 1:11
  habeas corpus 8.2, 8.4
Amendments
  case stated procedure 9.9
  discretion 7.9
  evidence 7.9
  grounds for judicial review 7.9
  High Court 7.9
  notices 7.9
  time-limits 7.9
Amicus curiae
Appeals, *see also* Case stated
  convictions 4.11–4.13, 4.20
  cost 4.23
  Court of Appeal 1.6.1, 4.19, 7.11, 9.5
  Crown Court 1.7.1, 4.11, 4.19–4.22
  judicial review 4.12–4.13
  leave 7.16
  magistrates 1.7.1
  sentencing 4.18–4.20
Arrest 1.9.1, 2.6, 4.2

Bad faith 2.15
Bail
  absconding 13.14
  case stated 4.21, 10.2.1, 10.2.3
  claim forms 10.2
  conditions 10.2–10.2.1
  Crown Court 1.6.1, 4.5, 10.2, 10.2.3
  custody time-limits 4.6
  decisions, challenging 4.5, 13.14.2
  disclosure 13.15
  European Convention on Human Rights 13.14
  evidence 10.2
  extradition 10.2.2
  fees 10.2
  forms and precedents App 1:8
  habeas corpus 8.3, 10.2.2
  High Court 10.1, 10.2.1
  convictions 4.12
  interim relief 4.5, 10.2
  judicial review 4.5, 10.2.1
    procedure for applications 7.5
  magistrates 4.5, 10.2–10.2.1, 10.2.3
  presumption in favour of 10.2
  reasons 13.14.1
  recognisances 4.5, 5.1.2
  refusal 13.14.1–13.14.2
  service 10.2
  time-limits 10.2.3
Bias
  European Convention on Human Rights 13.22
  fair trials 2.8.4
  grounds for judicial review 2.8
  licensing 2.8
  magistrates 2.8
  prejudice 2.8
Binding over 2.8.4
Bundles 6.4–6.4.1, 7.10, 7.12
By-laws 2.4, 4.4

Case management 7.1
Case stated, *see also* Procedure for appealing by way of case stated
  acquittals 4.16
  affidavits 3.4
  bail 4.21, 10.2.1, 10.2.3
  children and young persons 5.9
  committals 4.7
  contents 9.7
  convictions 4.11, 4.13, 4.22
  costs 4.23, 11.10
  Crown Court 1.6, 3.4, 11.10
  custody time-limits 4.6
  definition 1.4
  discretion 11.5, 11.10
  driving disqualification 10.3

Case stated – *cont*
  error   2.1, 3.1, 3.3, 3.4
    jurisdiction   3.3
    law, of   3.3
  exclusions   1.6.1
  extradition   4.24
  format   3.4
  forms and precedents   App 3
  grounds for   3.2
    restrictions on   3.4
  habeas corpus   5.5
  High Court powers   11.10
  interim decisions   4.9
  interim relief   1.4
  irrationality   3.3
  judicial review and, differences
    between   3.3
  jurisdiction   1.4, 3.3
  listing   6.3
  locus standi   1.10
  magistrates   1.4, 1.7
  notice of entry   App 3:4
  procedural irregularity   3.3
  public bodies   1.4, 1.9
  remedies   1.4
  remittal   11.10
  sentencing   4.17
  service   6.7, 9.2
  time-limits   5.6
Certiorari   10.5, 11.6
Children and young people   5.9
  case stated   5.9
  Civil Procedure Rules 1998   5.9
  habeas corpus   8.3
  High Court   5.9
  interim decisions   4.6
  litigation friends   5.9
  reporting   5.8
  transfer of proceedings   4.8
  UN Convention on the Rights of the
    Child   13.4
Citations   6.4.1
Civil Procedure Rules 1998
  amicus curiae   7.14
  case management   7.1
  children and young persons   5.9
  costs   12.2–12.3, 12.7, 12.9
  Crown Office proceedings   6.1
  damages   11.8
  declarations   10.6
  evidence   7.4, 7.14
  habeas corpus   8.1, 8.2

  interim applications   6.9
  procedure for bringing judicial review
    applications   7.1
  service   6.7
  single High Court judges   7.16
  terminology   7.1
  text   App 5
  time-limits   6.8
Claim forms   7.11, 7.13, 8.3, 10.2,
    11.8, App 1.9, App 2
Commencement of proceedings
  case stated, procedure for starting
    9.3, 9.11
  claim forms   7.11
  Court of Appeal   7.11
  evidence   7.11
  habeas corpus   8.2
  judicial review   7.11
  legal aid   7.11
  service   7.11
  time-limits   7.11
Committals
  case stated   4.7
  decisions, challenging   4.7
  discretion   4.7
  errors   4.7
  evidence   4.7, 13.10.2
  High Court   4.7
  Human Rights Act 1998   13.10.2
  illegality   2.3
  magistrates   1.7.1, 4.7
Consent orders   6.6, 6.9, 7.14, App
    1:15
Contempt of court   5.7
Convictions
  appeals   4.11, 4.20
  bail   4.12
  case stated   4.11, 4.13–4.15, 4.2
    procedure   9.3
  costs   4.13
  Crown Court   4.11–4.15
  decisions   4.25
  driving disqualification   4.15
  errors   4.11, 4.13
  evidence   4.14
  findings of fact   4.11
  High Court   4.11–4.12, 4.14
  Human Rights Act 1998   13.10.1
  interim decisions   4.10
  irrationality   4.11
  judicial review   1.9, 4.13–4.15
  jurisdiction   4.13
  magistrates' court   1.7.1, 4.11–4.15

Convictions – *cont*
  reasons   4.11
  tactical considerations   4.15
Corporal punishment   13.21
Correspondence, interference with
  13.3, 13.13.4, 13.21
Costs
  advance funds   12.8
  appeals   4.23
  assessment of   12.10
  case stated   4.23, 11.10
  central funds   4.23, 12.7
  Civil Procedure Rules 1998   12.2–12.3, 12.7, 12.9
  conduct   12.2
  convictions   4.13
  Crown Court   4.23
  decisions   2.6
    challenging   4.23
  disclosure   7.7
  discontinuance   12.2
  discretion   12.2–12.3
  documents   6.4.1
  habeas corpus   12.3
  High Court   12.2–12.3, 12.5, 12.8–12.10
  indemnity basis   12.10
  interested parties   12.6
  judicial review   12.3
  legal aid   12.4, 12.12
  magistrates   4.23, 12.5
  practice direction   12.10
  rules governing   12.2
  sentencing   4.23
  single High Court judges   12.7
  standard basis   12.10
  third parties   12.6
  wasted   4.23, 12.9
Court of Appeal   1.6.1, 4.19, 7.11, 9.5
Criminal Cases Review Commission
  1.9, 4.25, 5.1.2
Crown Court
  appeals   1.7.1, 4.11–4.13, 4.19–4.22
    limitations on   4.20
  bail   1.6.1, 4.5, 10.2, 10.2.1, 10.2.3
  case stated   1.6, 3.4, 11.10
    procedure   9.1–9.13
  convictions   4.11–4.15
  costs   4.23
  custody time-limits   4.6
  decisions of   1.6
    challenging   4.22

driving disqualification   10.3
  habeas corpus   3.5
  High Court's jurisdiction   1.6.1
  indictable offences   4.19
  judicial review   1.6, 4.12
  legal aid   1.6.1
  legitimate expectations   2.12
  magistrates' courts   1.7.1, 4.20
  reasons   2.14
  sentencing   4.17–4.19, 11.7
  time-limits   5.6
  transfer of proceedings to   4.8
Crown Office proceedings
  Civil Procedure Rules 1998   6.1
  documents   6.4
  jurisdiction   1.11
  listing   6.3
  procedural matters   6.1–6.9
  solicitors ceasing to act   6.5
  uncontested   6.6
  withdrawn   6.6
Custody time-limits
  bail   4.6
  case stated   4.6
  Crown Court   4.6
  damages   11.8
  decisions, challenging   4.6
  documents   6.4
  extension   4.6
  habeas corpus   4.6
  High Court   4.6
  jurisdiction, acting in excess of   2.5
  magistrates   4.6
  natural justice   4.6
  reasons   4.6.1

Damages
  Civil Procedure Rules 1998   11.8
  claim forms   11.8
  custody time-limits   11.8
  High Court   11.8
  interim relief   10.6
  judicial review   11.8
  legal aid   12.10
  practice directions   11.8
  unlawful imprisonment   11.8
Decisions
  bail   4.5, 13.14.2
  committals   4.7
  condition precedent, acting
    without   2.5

Decisions – *cont*
  convictions   4.25
  costs   2.6, 4.23
  Crown Court   4.22
  custody time-limits   4.6
  delegation   2.9
  extradition   4.24
  grounds for judicial review   2.9
  improper motive   2.11
  judicial review   4.25
  magistrates   1.7, 4.24
  mental state   2.6
  procedural impropriety   2.7
  prosecutions   4.3
  public bodies   4.3, 4.25
  reasons   2.14
  relevant factors   2.11
Declarations   10.6, 11.3, 11.6
Delay
  case stated, procedure for starting 9.6, 9.10, 9.11
  disclosure   5.4, 7.15
  discretion   11.2
  effect of   5.3
  habeas corpus   5.5
  judicial review   1.3, 5.2–5.3
  legal aid   12.12
  practice direction   5.2.2
  rehearings   2.11
  time-limits   5.2
Delegation
  decision-making   2.9
  errors   2.9
  grounds for judicial review   2.9
  High Court   2.9
  magistrates   2.9
Detention, *see also* Habeas corpus   13.3
Diplock trials   13.13.1
Disclosure
  bail   13.15
  costs   7.7
  delay   5.4, 7.14
  discretion   7.7
  European Convention on Human Rights   13.15
  fair hearings   2.8.5
  material facts   7.7
  notices   7.7
  procedure for bringing judicial review applications   7.7
  proper enquiries, carrying out   7.7

  public interest immunity   13.15
  urgent applications   7.3
Discontinuance   12.2
Discretion
  amendments   7.9
  case stated   11.5, 11.10
  committals   4.7
  condition precedent prior to excise of   2.6
  costs   12.2–12.3
  delay   11.2
  disclosure   7.7
  errors   2.6
  fair hearings   2.8.
  habeas corpus   11.4
  High Court   11.2, 11.5
  illegality   2.3
  judicial review   1.3, 11.2
    grounds for   2.2.1, 2.6
  procedural impropriety   2.7
  reasons   2.14.1
  sentencing   5.1.2
  statutory interpretation   2.6
  urgent applications   11.2
Disqualification from driving   4.15, 10.3
Documents
  bundles   6.4–6.4.1
  citations   6.4
  costs   6.4.1
  Crown Office proceedings   6.4
  evidence   7.4
  fees   7.4
  filing requirements   7.4
  habeas corpus   8.2
  Hansard   6.4
  High Court   7.4
  legal aid   7.4
  notices   7.4
  practice directions   7.4
  procedure for bringing judicial review applications   7.4
  service of   6.7
  skeleton arguments   6.4.1
  substantive hearings, filing before   6.4.1
  time-limits   7.4
  urgent applications   7.3
  witness statements   7.4
Driving, suspension or disqualification from   4.15, 4.17, 10.3
Duty solicitors   1.1

EC law   2.4, 4.4
Errors
    affidavits   3.4
    case stated   2.1, 3.1, 3.3, 3.4
    categories   2.2
    committals   4.7
    convictions   4.11, 4.13
    delegation   2.9
    discretion   2.6
    grounds for judicial review   2.1, 2.2
    habeas corpus   2.1, 3.1
    illegality   2.3
    inconsistency   2.13
    irrationality   2.10
    judicial review   11.3
    judiciary   2.1
    jurisdiction, acting in excess of   2.5
    procedural impropriety   2.7
    relevant factors   2.11
    sentencing   4.19
    ultra vires   2.4
European Convention on Human Rights   13.1–13.22
    access to courts   13.3
    bail   13.14
    bias   13.22
    Convention rights   13.5
    corporal punishment   13.21
    correspondence, interference with   13.3, 13.13.4, 13.21
    delay   13.16.1
    detention   13.3
    disclosure   13.15
    evidence   13.13
    experts   13.16
    fair trials   13.3, 13.16, 13.16.1
    family life, right to   13.13.5, 13.18
    hearings   13.16
    hearsay   13.13.2
    homosexuals   13.20
    interpretation   13.2, 13.6
    judicial review   13.10.1, 13.22
    legal aid   12.10, 13.17
    offences, specific   13.20
    prisoners   13.3, 13.21
    private life, right to   13.13.5, 13.18
    proportionality   2.16
    prosecution   13.19
    reasoned judgments   13.16
    reporting   13.13.3
    self-incrimination   13.13.1
    sentencing   13.18
    status in UK   13.2
    website   13.5
    witnesses   13.13.3
Evidence, *see also* Affidavits, Witnesses
    additional   7.9
    amendments   7.9
    bail   10.2
    case stated procedure   9.7
    Civil Procedure Rules 1998   7.4, 7.14
    commencement of proceedings   7.11
    committals   4.7, 13.10.2
    convictions   4.14
    documents   7.4
    European Convention on Human Rights   13.13
    experts   13.16
    extradition   5.1
    filing   7.14
    fresh   8.5
    habeas corpus   8.5
    hearsay   13.13.2
    Human Rights Act 1998   13.11, 13.13
    interested parties   7.14
        on behalf of   7.14
    interim decisions   4.10
    interim relief   10.7
    legal aid   7.12
    letters before action   7.2
    procedure for bringing judicial review applications   7.9, 7.14
    self-incrimination   13.13.1
    service   7.11, 7.14
    special procedure material   5.2
    written   7.4, 7.14, 10.2
Expedition   6.2
Experts   13.16
Extradition
    bail   10.2.2
    case stated   4.24
    decisions, challenging   4.24
    evidence   5.1
    habeas corpus   1.5, 3.5, 4.24, 5.1, 10.2.2
    High Court   4.24
    jurisdiction   4.24
    magistrates   1.7, 4.24

Fair hearings
    binding over   2.8.4

Fair hearings – *cont*
  delay   13.16.1
  disclosure   2.8.5
  Diplock trials   13.13.1
  discretion   2.8.6
  European Convention on Human Rights   13.3, 13.16, 13.16.1
  grounds for judicial review   2.8.1–2.8.6
  hearsay   13.13.2
  immigration   2.8.6
  information, right to receive   2.8.5
  natural justice   2.8
  prejudice   2.8.1
  presumption of innocence   13.13.4
  prisoners convicted of murder   2.8.5
  procedural impropriety   2.8.1–2.8.2
  right to be heard   2.8.2–2.8.4
  sentencing   2.8.5
  who is entitled to   2.8.3
False imprisonment   11.8
Family life, right to   13.13.5, 13.18
Fees
  documents   7.4
  renewals   7.10
Forms and precedents
  bail   App 1:8
  case stated   App 3–4
  claim forms   App 1:9, App 2:1
  consent orders   App 1:15
  habeas corpus   App 2
  interim orders   App 1:12–1:13
  judicial review   App 1
    affidavits in response   App 1:11
    affidavits in support   App 1:4–1:5, App 1:11
    notice of applications   App 1:2
    letters before action   App 1:1
    procedural guides   App 4
    renewal notices   App 1:16
    service   App 1:10
    skeleton arguments   App 1:14
    witness statements   App 1:6, App 1:10
Functus officio   7.2

Grounds for case stated   3.2
Grounds for judicial review   2.1–2.16
  amendment   7.9
  Anisminic decision   2.2.1

bad faith   2.15
bias   2.8
decision-making, delegation of   2.9
discretion   2.2.1, 2.6
errors
  categories of   2.1, 2.2
  law, of   2.6
fair hearings   2.8.1–2.8.6
illegality   2.3
factual disputes   2.2.3
illegality   2.2
improper motive   2.11
inconsistency   2.13
irrationality   2.2, 2.10
judiciary   2.1
jurisdiction
  excess of   2.5
  excluding   2.5
legitimate expectations   2.2, 2.12
natural justice   2.2, 2.8
procedural impropriety   2.2, 2.7
proportionality   2.16
public law, excluding jurisdiction on   2.2.2
reasons, duty to give   2.14
relevant factors   2.11
time-limits   5.2.1
ultra vires   2.4

Habeas corpus
  advising respondents   8.4
  affidavits   8.2
  bail   8.3, 10.2.2
  case stated   3.1, 3.5, 5.5
  children and young people   8.3
  Civil Procedure Rules 1998   8.1–8.2
  claim forms   8.3, App 2
  commencement of proceedings   8.2
  costs   12.3
  Crown Court   3.5
  custody time-limits   4.6
  definition   1.5
  delay   5.5
  discretion   11.4
  Divisional Court   1.11
  documents   8.2
  errors   2.1, 3.1
  evidence   8.4, 8.5

Habeas corpus – *cont*
    expedition   6.2
    extradition   1.5, 3.5, 4.24, 5.1, 10.2.2
    hearings
        substantive   8.5
    High Court   1.11, 11.9
        powers   11.9
    judicial review   1.5, 3.5
    legal aid   8.3, 8.5
    listing   6.3, 8.3
    notices   8.3
    procedure   8.1–8.5
    urgent applications   8.2
    single judges   8.5
    witness statements   8.2
    writ forms   8.1
Hansard   6.4.1
Hearings, *see also* Fair hearings
    case stated, procedure for starting   9.13
    European Convention on Human Rights   13.16
    habeas corpus   8.5
    in camera   5.7
    interested parties   7.14
    procedure for bringing judicial review applications   7.8, 7.16
    single High Court judges   7.16
    time-limits   5.2.1
    urgent applications   7.3
Hearsay   13.13.2
High Court
    academic challenges   11.3
    amendments   7.9
    bail   10.2, 10.2.1
    case stated   11.10
        procedure   9.1–9.13
    committals   4.6
    composition   1.11
    convictions   4.11–4.12, 4.14
    costs   12.2–12.3, 12.5, 12.8–12.10
    criminal proceedings   1.11
        definition of   5.1.2
        when cases should be brought in   4.1–4.25
        whether matter is suitable for   5.1
    Crown Court   1.6.1
    custody time-limits   4.6
    damages   11.8
    declarations   10.6, 11.3
    delegation   2.9
    discretion   11.2, 11.5
    Divisional Court   1.11
    documents   7.8
    expedition   6.2
    extradition   4.24
    habeas corpus   11.9, 1.11
    importance of   1.2, 11.9
    interested parties   7.13, 7.14
    interim decisions   4.10
    interim relief   10.7
    jurisdiction   1.11–1.11
    legal aid   12.4, 12.11, 12.12, 12.14–12.15
    locus standi   1.10
    magistrates' court   1.7, 1.7.1
    police investigations   4.2
    procedure for judicial review applications   7.8
    prosecutions   4.3
    sentencing   4.17–4.19, 11.7
    single High Court judges   7.16
    time-limits   5.6
    transfer of proceedings   4.8
HIV   13.13.5
Homosexual conduct   13.20
Human rights, *see also* European Convention on Human Rights, Human Rights Act 1998
    international obligations   13.4
    UK law in   13.3
Human Rights Act 1998
    application of   13.12
    committals   13.10.2
    convictions   13.10.1
    declarations of incompatibility   13.8.1, 13.9
    effect of   13.7–13.8
    enforcement   13.10
    enter into force   13.2
    evidence   13.11, 13.13
    incorporation of Convention   13.7
    interpretation of legislation   13.8
    judicial review   13.10, 13.10.1
    objectives   13.7
    precedence   13.9
    proportionality   2.16
    public bodies   13.9, 13.10
    remedies   13.11
    text   App 5
    'victims'   13.10

Illegality
  committals 2.3
  discretion 2.3
  errors 2.3
  grounds for judicial review 2.2, 2.3
  legislation, misconstruing 2.3
  public bodies 2.3
Immigration 2.8.5, 2.13
Impartiality, see Bias
Imprisonment 4.19, 11.8
Improper motive 2.11
In camera hearings 5.7
Inconsistency
  errors 2.13
  grounds for judicial review 2.13
  immigration 2.13
  irrationality 2.14
Information
  fair hearings 2.8.5
  right to be given 2.8.5
Injunctions 10.5, 10.6, 11.6
Innocence, presumption of 13.13.1
Interested parties
  amicus curiae 7.13
  consent orders 7.14
  costs 12.6
  evidence 7.14
  hearings 7.14
  High Court 7.13, 7.15
  interlocutory orders 7.15
  procedure for bringing judicial review applications 7.13–7.15
  service 7.13
Interim applications 6.9
Interim decisions
  case stated 4.9
  children and young persons 4.10
  convictions 4.10
  evidence 4.10
  forms and precedents App 1:12–1:13
  High Court 4.10
  judicial review 4.9–4.10
  quashing 4.10
  time-limits 5.2
Interim relief 10.1–10.7
  bail 4.5, 10.1
  case stated 1.4
  damages 10.6
  declarations 10.6
  driving, disqualification or suspension from 10.3
  evidence 10.7
  expedition 6.2
  High Court 10.7
  injunctions 10.6
  oral applications 7.6
  procedure 10.7
  sentencing 4.18
  stays
    enforcement of other penalties 10.4
    judicial review, pending 10.5
Interlocutory orders 7.12, 7.14, 9.12
Investigations 4.2
Irrationality
  case stated 3.3
  convictions 4.11
  errors 2.10
  grounds for judicial review 2.2, 2.10
  inconsistency 2.13
  magistrates 2.10
  reasons 2.14.1
  relevant factors 2.11

Judicial review, see also Grounds for judicial review, Procedure for bringing judicial review applications
  academic challenges 11.3
  affidavits App 1:4–1:5, App 1:11
  applications for
    notices App 1:2
    premature 5.3
  bail 4.5, 10.2.1
  case stated and 3.3
  commencement of proceedings 7.11
  convictions 1.9, 4.12–4.13
  costs 12.3
  Criminal Cases Review Commission 1.9, 4.25, 5.1.2
  Crown Court 1.6
  damages 11.8
  decisions 4.25
  definition 1.3
  delay 1.3, 5.2–5.3
  discretion 1.3, 11.2
  errors 11.3
  European Convention on Human Rights 13.10.1, 13.22
  exclusions 1.6.1
  expedition 6.2

Index

Judicial review – *cont*
  forms and precedents   App 1
  habeas corpus   1.5, 3.5
  Human Rights Act 1998   13.10, 13.10.1
  injunctions   10.6
  interim decisions   4.9–4.10
  locus standi   1.10
  magistrates' courts   1.7, 1.7.1, 4.12, 4.21
  orders   11.6
  police   4.2
  prisoners   1.9, 4.25
  public bodies   1.1, 1.3, 1.9
  public law   1.3, 1.9.1
  remedies   1.3, 11.6
    alternative   5.4
  sentencing   1.7.1, 4.17–4.19
    variation   11.7
  stay of proceedings pending   10.5
  transfer of proceedings   4.8
Judiciary
  errors   2.1
  grounds for judicial review   2.1
  habeas corpus   8.5
  single High Court judges   7.16, 8.5, 9.13
Jurisdiction
  case stated   1.4, 3.3
  condition precedent, acting without   3.5
  convictions   4.13
  Crown Office   1.11
  custody time-limits   2.5
  errors   2.5
  excluding   2.2.2
  extradition   4.24
  High Court   1.1–1.11
  grounds for judicial review   2.2.2, 2.5
  ousting   2.2.2
  precedent facts   2.5
  scope of criminal   1.1–1.11
  sentencing   4.19
  ultra vires   2.4, 2.5
Juveniles, *see* Children and Young Persons   5.9

Legal aid   12.4, 12.13
  certificates   12.13
  case stated procedure   9.11
  commencement of proceedings   7.11
  contributions   12.4
  costs   12.4, 12.12
  Crown Court   1.6.1
  damages   12.10, 12.14
  delay   12.12
  documents   7.4
  emergency   12.12
  European Convention on Human Rights   12.10, 13.17
  evidence   7.12
  future developments   12.15
  habeas corpus   8.3, 8.5
  High Court   12.4, 12.11, 12.12, 12.14–12.15
  injunctions   10.6
  means test   12.11, 12.15
  merits test   12.11, 12.13
  oral arguments   7.6
  reasonableness   12.10
  solicitors ceasing to act   6.5
  statutory charge   12.14
  taxation   7.16, 12.13
  urgent applications   12.12
Legitimate expectations
  Crown Court   2.12
  grounds for judicial review   2.2, 2.12
  magistrates   2.12
  sentencing   2.12
Letters before action   7.1, App 1:1
Limitation periods, *see* Time-limits
Listing arrangements   6.3
  case stated   6.3
    procedure   9.12
  Crown Office proceedings   6.3
  expedition   6.2
  habeas corpus   6.3, 8.3
  oral arguments   7.6
  procedure for bringing judicial review applications   7.6
  time estimates   6.2, 6.3
  time-limits   6.3
Litigation friends   5.9, 5.10
Locus standi
  acquittals   1.10
  case stated   1.10
  High Court   1.10
  judicial review   1.10

Magistrates' court
  appeals   1.7.1
  bail   1.7.1, 4.5, 10.2, 10.2.3
  bias   2.8
  case stated   1.4, 1.7
    procedure   9.1–9.9, 9.12–9.13
  committals   1.7, 4.7
  convictions   1.7.1, 4.11–4.15
  costs   4.23, 12.5
  Crown Court   1.7.1, 4.20
  custody time-limits   4.6
  decisions   1.7, 4.24
  delegation   2.9
  driving disqualification   10.3
  duty solicitors   1.1
  extradition   1.7, 4.24
  High Court   1.7, 1.7.1
  irrationality   2.10
  judicial review   1.7, 4.12, 4.21
  legislation, challenging   4.4
  legitimate expectations   2.12
  licensing   2.8
  natural justice   1.7.1
  powers, changing   1.2
  prosecution   4.4
  sentencing   1.7.1, 4.18–4.19
  stay of proceedings   1.7.1
  time-limits   5.6
  Youth Court   1.8
Mandamus   11.6
Mentally disabled persons   5.10
Mistakes, *see* Errors

Natural justice
  bias   2.8
  custody time-limits   4.6
  fair trials   2.8
  grounds for judicial review   2.2, 2.8
  magistrates   1.7.1
  prejudice   11.3
  sentencing   11.7
Next friends   5.10
No case to answer   9.3
Notices
  amendments   7.9
  application for judicial review   App 1:2
  case stated   App 3:4
    procedure   9.9
  disclosure   7.7
  documents   7.4

  habeas corpus   8.3
  interim applications   6.9
  renewal   7.10, App 1:16
  solicitors ceasing to act   6.5
  urgent applications   7.5
  withdrawal of proceedings   6.6

Police
  arrest   1.9.1, 2.6, 4.2
  investigations   4.2
  judicial review   4,2
  misconduct   4.2
  search warrants   4.2
  sex offenders   4.2
Precedent facts   2.5
Precedents, *see* Forms and precedents
Prerogative powers   4.3, 4.25
Presumption of innocence   13.13.1
Prisoners   1.9, 2.8.5, 4.25, 13.3, 13.13.4, 13.22
Private law/public law distinction   1.9.1, 4.25
Private life, right to   13.13.5, 13.18
Private prosecutions   4.3
Procedural impropriety
  case stated   3.3
  decisions   2.7
  discretion   2.7
  errors   2.7
  fair hearings   2.8.1–2.8.2
  grounds for judicial review   2.2, 2.7
Procedure for appealing by way of case stated   9.1–9.13
  agreement, obtaining   9.8
  amendments   9.9
  bundles   9.12
  commencement of proceedings   9.3, 9.11
  contents of case stated   9.7
  convictions   9.3
  Court of Appeal   9.5
  court's obligations   9.4
  Crown Court   9.1–9.13
  Crown Office, procedure after case has been lodged in   9.12
  delay   9.6, 9.10, 9.11
  documents   9.1
  evidence   9.7
  hearings, substantive   9.13
  High Court   9.1–9.13
  interlocutory applications   9.12

Procedure for appealing by way of case
    stated – *cont*
  legal aid   9.11
  listing   9.12
  magistrates   9.1–9.9, 9.12–9.13
  no case to answer   9.3
  notices   9.9
  obtaining first draft of   9.6
  reasons   9.4, 9.5
  recognisances   9.4
  refusal   9.4–9.5
    challenging   9.5
  remitting case back   9.8
  sentencing   9.3
  service   9.2
  single judges
  time-limits   9.4, 9.6, 9.8, 9.11
  urgent applications   9.10
Procedure for bringing judicial review
    applications   7.1–7.16
  additional matters   7.5
  bail   7.5
  bundles   7.12
  Civil Procedure Rules 1998   7.1
  commencement of proceedings
    7.11
  determination of permission   7.8
  disclosure   7.7
  documents to be lodged   7.4
  hearings
    further steps before   7.12
    preventing from appearing   7.8
    substantive   7.16
  High Court   7.8
  interested parties
    acting for   7.13
    evidence on behalf of   7.14
    steps taken on behalf of   7.15
  interim relief   7.8
  letters before action   7.2
  listing for oral argument   7.6
  permission
    granting   7.8
    refusal   7.10
  remedies, availability of alternative
    7.8
  renewal of applications   7.10
  time estimates   7.5
  urgent out of hours applications
    7.3
Prohibition   10.5, 11.6
Proportionality   2.16

Prosecutions
  by laws   4.4
  decisions   4.3
  EC law   4.4
  European Convention on Human
    Rights   13.19
  High Court   4.3
  legislation, challenging   4.4
  magistrates   4.4
  prerogative powers   4.3
  private   4.3
  public bodies   4.3
  public law   4.3, 4.4
  quashing decisions to start   4.3
  remedies, alternative   4.3
  transfer of proceedings   4.8
  ultra vires   4.4
Public bodies
  case stated   1.4, 1.9
  decisions   1.9, 4.3, 4.25
  declarations   11.3
  Human Rights Act 1998   13.9,
    13.10
  illegality   2.3
  judicial review   1.1, 1.3, 1.9
  prerogative powers   4.25
  private law   1.9.1
  prosecutions   4.3
  public law   1.9.1
Public interest immunity   13.15
Public law
  defences   4.3, 4.4
  judicial review   1.3, 1.9.1
  private law   1.9.1, 4.25
  prosecutions   4.3, 4.4
  public bodies   1.9.1

Reasons
  bail   13.14.1
  case stated procedure   9.4, 9.5
  convictions   4.11
  Crown Court   2.14
  custody time-limits   4.6
  decisions   2.14
  discretion   2.14.1
  driving   4.17
  duty to give   2.14
  European Convention on Human
    Rights   13.16
  grounds for judicial review   2.14
  importance of requesting   2.14.1

Reasons – *cont*
  irrationality   2.14.1
  sentencing   4.17
  time-limits, reasons for   5.2.1
Recognizances   4.5, 5.1.2, 9.4
Refusal
  bail   13.14.1–13.14.2
  case stated   9.5
    procedure   9.4, 9.5
  judicial review   7.10
Rehearings   2.11, 4.18
Relevant factors   2.11
Remedies, *see also* Interim relief,
    Particular remedies (eg Injunctions)
  alternative   4.3, 5.4, 7.8
  case stated   1.4
  Human Rights Act 1998   13.11
  judicial review   1.3, 5.4, 11.6
    procedure for applications   7.8
  prosecutions   4.3
Renewal notices   7.10, App 1:16
Reporting
  children and young people   5.8
  European Convention on Human
    Rights   13.13.5
  limiting   5.7–5.8
  urgent applications   7.3, 7.5

Search warrants   4.2
Self-incrimination   13.13.1
Sentencing
  appeals   4.18–4.20
  case stated   4.17–4.18
    procedure   9.3
  costs   4.23
  Court of Appeal   4.19
  Crown Court   4.17–4.19, 11.7
  discretion   5.1.2
  driving cases   4.17
  errors   4.18, 4.19
  European Convention on Human
    Rights   13.18
  fair trials   2.8.5
  High Court   4.17–4.19, 11.7
  imprisonment   4.19
  interim relief   4.18
  judicial review   1.7.1, 4.17–4.19,
    11.7
  jurisdiction   4.19
  legitimate expectation   2.12
  magistrates' courts   1.7.1, 4.17–4.19

natural justice   11.7
rehearings   4.18
tariffs   2.8.5
'special reasons'   4.17
time-limits   5.6
variation   11.7
Service   6.7
  bail   10.2
  case stated, procedure for starting
    6.7, 9.2
  Civil Procedure Rules 1998   6.7
  claim forms   7.11, 7.13, 10.2
  commencement of proceedings
    7.11
  deemed day of   6.7
  evidence   7.11, 7.14
    additional   7.9
  forms and precedents   App 1:10
  interested parties   7.13
  manner of   6.7
  place of   6.7
  time-limits   7.11
  witness statements   App 1:10
Sex offenders   4.2
Single High Court judges   7.16, 8.5,
  9.13
Skeleton arguments   6.4.1, 7.10, 7.15,
  App 1:14
Solicitors
  ceasing to act   6.5
  duty   1.1
Standing, *see* Locus standi
Statutory charge   12.14
Stay of proceedings
  certiorari   10.5
  injunctions   10.5
  interim relief   10.4–10.5
  judicial review, pending   10.5
  letters before action   7.2
  magistrates   1.7.1
  prohibition   10.5
Sureties   4.5, 5.1.2, 9.4
Suspension from driving   10.3

Time-limits, *see also* Custody time-
    limits   6.8
  amendments   7.9
  case stated   5.6
    procedure   9.4, 9.6, 9.8, 9.11
  ceasing to run   5.2
  Civil Procedure Rules 1998   6.8

Time-limits – *cont*
  commencement of   5.2
  Crown Court   5.6
  delay   5.2
  documents   7.4
  extension of   5.2–5.2.1, 5.6, 9.4, 9.6, 9.8
    reasons   5.2.1
  grounds for judicial review   5.2.1
  hearings   5.2.1
  High Court   5.6
  interim decisions   5.2
  knowledge   5.2
  listing   6.3
  magistrates   5.6
  practice direction   5.2.2
  renewals   7.10
  sentencing   5.6
  service   7.11
Transfer of proceedings
  charges, dismissal of   4.8
  children   4.8
  Crown Court   4.8
  High Court   4.8
  judicial review   4.8
  prosecution   4.8
Trials on indictment, *see also* Hearings   1.6.1

Ultra vires
  by laws   2.4
  EC law   2.4, 4.4
  errors   2.4
  grounds for judicial review   2.4
  jurisdiction, excess of   2.4, 2.5
  prosecutions   4.4
  public bodies   2.4
Unlawful imprisonment   11.8
Urgent applications   7.2, 7.3, 7.5, 8.2, 11.2, 12.12

Wasted costs   4–23, 12.9
Witnesses   13.13.3
  anonymity   13.13.3
  documents   7.4
  European Convention on Human Rights   13.13.3
  habeas corpus   8.2
  service   App 1:10
  statements   7.4, 8.2, App 1:6–1:7, App 1:10

Young people, *see* Children and young people
Youth Court   1.8